THE ORIGINS
OF AUTOCRACY

ALEXANDER YANOV

THE ORIGINS
OF AUTOCRACY

IVAN THE TERRIBLE
IN RUSSIAN HISTORY

Translated by Stephen Dunn

UNIVERSITY OF CALIFORNIA PRESS

BERKELEY   LOS ANGELES   LONDON

University of California Press
Berkeley and Los Angeles, California

University of California Press, Ltd.
London, England

© 1981 by
The Regents of the University of California
Printed in the United States of America

1 2 3 4 5 6 7 8 9

Library of Congress Cataloging in Publication Data
Yanov, Alexander, 1930–
The origins of autocracy.
Bibliography: p.
Includes index.
1. Russia—History—Ivan IV, 1533–1584.
2. Ivan IV, the Terrible, Czar of Russia,
1530–1584. I. Title.
DK106.Y36   947'.043   80-39528
ISBN 0-520-04282-4

To my wife, Lidia, to whom I owe this book
as well as everything I have,
and have not, written

No society in modern times has been more subject to conflicting assumptions and interpretations than that of Russia.

CYRIL E. BLACK

The bloody mire of Mongolian slavery, not the rude glory of the Norman epoch, forms the cradle of Muscovy, and modern Russia is but a metamorphosis of Muscovy.

KARL MARX

What was Russia's place in history? Was she properly to be regarded as one of the families of the Asian systems, as one of the European polities and societies, a variety of either, or as entirely *sui generis*, belonging neither to Europe nor to Asia?

DONALD W. TREADGOLD

CONTENTS

FOREWORD

by Sidney Monas

One of the reasons, I suspect, that Americans show little interest in history (except as a diversion or as a picture of alternative glamor) is that they have almost no sense of the past as something compulsive and limiting. For Americans, at least until the last few years, the future has seemed unlimited in its possibilities—all horizons "wide open." For Russians, on the other hand, the past has always held a compelling power over the future, exerting a force so constraining that it might foster the illusion, in an extreme instance, that if one changed the *accounts* in which the past is recorded and interpreted, one might well lay a magical hold upon the future.

Alexander Yanov's attitude to the past is quite different from the one and from the other. A well-known and iconoclastic Soviet journalist before he came to the United States in 1974, a victim of the regime's all-too-limited tolerance for iconoclasm, he also possesses an advanced degree in history. His journalistic assignments took him all over the USSR and into all sectors of Soviet life; his historical training provoked him to place the problems he confronted in a long-term perspective, to approach the problem of the contemporary nationalist revival in the USSR, for instance, by way of telling the long-term story of slavophilism in Russia.

His monumental *History of Political Opposition in Russia*, a multivolume work resulting from many years of experience, thought, and reading, could never be published in the USSR, and it was largely on this account that he left. The present work is a product of that much vaster effort. In it he sees Russia's past as forming not a single, utterly compelling pattern, but a pattern that, while exercising certain limitations on the shape of the future, also offers a range of choices as to that shape—choices not predetermined, but informed and emancipated to the degree that they take cognizance of the shaping of the past. He also writes—and it is the subject of some of his best-written and most ironic pages—of those who, in examining the past, fell victim to it.

His work does not fit well into the tradition of empirical historiography that has dominated the American historical profession in the recent past. He has done no work in the archives, and he is extremely fond of typologies that, while they are arrived at by a method not altogether foreign to contemporary political science and sociology, have different names and are not easily traceable to the main currents of our academic thought. Some of our historians of Russia think his work is old hat, a "rediscovering of America," but I think they are much mistaken. Many emigré writers, on the other hand, are unhappy with Yanov's critical attitude to nationalism, his relative indifference to religion, his gradualist constitutionalism, and (not so much in the present work as in his controversial *Detente after Brezhnev*) on his seeing possibilities within the Soviet establishment for America to influence and advance liberalization.

Yanov has polemics in his bloodstream, and much of what he says needs to be and should be argued about, not simply accepted as pronouncement. He is *essentially* provocative and controversial. But he is serious, erudite, thoughtful, well informed, witty, and intelligent, and he has something of his own to say that we cannot afford not to hear. Not only historians and political scientists will find this book interesting, but all those who have a sense of the importance of the Soviet Union in our lives, a growing number among whom, I hope, are those who have some inkling that the Soviet Union cannot be understood merely by the face with which it immediately presents itself.

ACKNOWLEDGMENTS

As I read over this book, I feel again how hard it was to write at the open and defenseless border between several genres and disciplines—between history and confession, between political science and philosophy, between historiographic investigation and a search for the origin of political evil. I can imagine how difficult it was for those who read this book in manuscript—Richard Lowenthal, Sidney Monas, Stephen and Ethel Dunn, George Breslauer, Robert Crummey—to make a judgment that required not only tolerance but scholarly courage. The University of California Press and my editor, William J. McClung, in risking the publication of such a book, somehow managed to combine businesslike caution and old-fashioned chivalry. Gianna Kirtley, Ellen Sheeks, Marilyn Schwartz, and my daughter Marina nurtured the manuscript into a book. Peter Dreyer performed editorial miracles, large and small, in the hope of somehow Anglicizing (if I may put it that way) this intransigently Russian work. I am grateful to all of them for their efforts.

This book has a strange history. It is the heart of a manuscript entitled *History of the Political Opposition in Russia*, which I began to write ten years ago in Moscow in the insane hope of guiding it across the reefs of censorship. Soviet censorship is sophisticated and merciless, but I was no novice in the art of fooling it. However, after the first chapter I began to doubt my ability to outwit the censors. After the third I realized I was taking a great risk. After the fifth I became afraid to keep the manuscript at home. After the seventh I concluded that the only way I could keep my self-respect as a writer and human being was to become a smuggler—that is, to turn my life upside down by illegally dispatching the manuscript across the border. Such things are not done alone. Many people helped me—brave people willing to take risks of the most elementary physical kind. I cannot name these people here—either the Russians or the non-Russians. But I cannot fail to be grateful to them to the end of my days.

I was also helped to write this book by my opponents who attacked my views in Moscow and continue to attack them in the West. Their attacks do not surprise me. These people refuse to recognize, as I do, that our fatherland has two faces. One of these is open to the world: the Russia of Herzen, Plekhanov, and Sakharov. I am proud of it. But I never forget that there is also another Russia: the country of pogroms, Black Hundreds, and terror, the land of Purishkevich and Stalin. Of that Russia I am ashamed. All the same, may the Lord give my opponents good health. They have given me patience and wrath, a feeling of grief and indignation, without which this book could not have been written.

I have thanked my tolerant referees, my courageous comrades-in-arms, and my merciless accusers. Now I must await the verdict of readers. This book will not be published in Russian, either by a Soviet publishing house or by a Russian publisher in the West. And there is nowhere left to emigrate. There are no more borders across which I can illegally dispatch my manuscript, hoping that it can be published in Russian. Thus, I seem to have irretrievably lost the greatest thing a writer can lose—an audience in his mother tongue. Will I be able to find a replacement—in a strange country, in an alien language?

October 1, 1980

INTRODUCTION

THE HYPOTHESIS

1. From Greatness to Obscurity?

On October 22, 1721, at the celebration of victory in the second Great Northern War, Chancellor Golovkin was merely expressing the general opinion when he declared the chief service rendered by Peter I to be that he "by indefatigable labor and leadership led us out of the darkness of nonexistence into being and joined us to the society of political peoples."[1] Nepliuev, the Russian ambassador to Constantinople, expressed himself still more openly in 1725: "This monarch . . . taught us to know that we are human beings too."[2] Half a century later, N. Panin, who was in charge of foreign policy under Catherine II, confirmed this opinion of the Petrine politicians. "Peter," he wrote, "by leading his people out of ignorance, thought it a great accomplishment to have made it equal to a second-class power."[3]

Over the course of centuries, the conviction that Peter brought Russia out of "nonexistence" and "ignorance" by teaching us to know that we too are human beings has become such a commonplace that it no longer enters anyone's head to ask when, why, and how Russia happened to find itself in a state of "nonexistence" and "ignorance." Why were we not considered human beings before Peter? Why was it a "great accomplishment" for Russia to become even a second-class power?

In his famous panegyric of Peter, Sergei Solov'ev, one of the best Russian historians, wrote confidently of pre-Petrine Russia as a "weak, poor, almost unknown people."[4] And even his constant adversary Mikhail Pogodin agreed with him entirely on this point. All ten centuries of Russian history before Peter lay, it seems, in obscurity— were, so to speak, prehistory—out of which the Father of the Fatherland led the country to light, glory, and greatness.

1. Cited in V. O. Kliuchevskii, *Sochineniia* (2nd ed.), vol. 4, p. 206.
2. Ibid., pp. 206–7.
3. Ibid., vol. 5, p. 340.
4. S. M. Solov'ev, *Istoriia Rossii s drevneishikh vremen*, Bk. 5, p. 560.

1

This is the stereotype. But does it agree with the known facts? The modern British historian, M. S. Anderson, who has made a special study of English perceptions of Russia in Peter's time, writes that in the seventeenth century *less* was known about Russia in England than a hundred years previously.[5] Richard Chancellor, who in 1553 became the first Englishman to visit Russia, for some reason entitled one of the chapters of his memoirs (published in England in 1589), not, let us say, "Of the Weak and Poor King of a People in a State of Nonexistence," but, on the contrary, "Of the Great and Mighty Tsar of Russia."[6] Another Englishman, Anthony Jenkinson, whose book was also published in England at the end of the sixteenth century, wrote: "The king of these parts is very mighty, since he has won a great many victories, both over the Livonians, Poles, Lithuanians, and Swedes on the one hand, and over the Tatars and pagans on the other."[7] In numerous documents which circulated in the 1560s at the court and in the chancellory of the German emperor, it was said that the grand duke of Moscow was the *mightiest sovereign in the world* after the Turkish sultan, and that, "from alliances with the grand duke, the Christian world would receive an honorable profit and advantage; it would also be an excellent counterforce and resistance to that tyrannical and most dangerous enemy, the Turk."[8] The French Protestant, Hubert Langet, prophesied in August 1558 in a letter to Calvin that, "If any power in Europe is destined to grow, this is that power."[9]

Chancellor found mid-sixteenth-century Moscow to be "as a whole, larger than London and its environs." The scale of trade there astonished the Englishman. The entire territory between Yaroslavl' and Moscow, through which he rode,

> abounds with little villages which are so full of people that it is surprising to look at them. The earth is all well-sown with grain, which the inhabitants bring to Moscow in such enormous quantities that it seems surprising. Every morning you can meet between 700 and 800 sleighs going there with grain. . . . Some people carry grain to Moscow; others carry it away from there, and among those there are some who live not less than 1,000 miles away.[10]

A quarter of a century before Chancellor, before the sea trade began, the ambassador of the German emperor, Sigismund Herberstein,

5. M. S. Anderson, "English Views of Russia in the Age of Peter the Great."
6. *Angliiskie puteshestvenniki v Moskovskom gosudarstve v XVI veke*, p. 55.
7. Ibid., p. 78.
8. Cited in R. Iu. Vipper, *Ivan Groznyi*, p. 83.
9. Ibid., p. 60.
10. *Angliiskie puteshestvenniki*, p. 56.

concluded that Russia was making effective use of its central position between West and East, and was successfully trading in both directions:

> Furs and wax are taken from there to Germany . . . and saddles, bridles, clothing, and leather from there to Tataria; weapons and iron are exported only by stealth or with special permission. . . . However, they export broadcloth and linen garments, axes, needles, mirrors, saddlebags, and other such goods.[11]

W. Kirchner, a German historian, notes that after the conquest of Narva in 1558, Russia became practically the main center of Baltic trade, and one of the centers of world trade. Ships from Lübeck, ignoring Riga and Revel, sailed for the port of Narva. Several hundred unloaded there annually, including vessels from Hamburg, Antwerp, London, Stockholm, Copenhagen, and even France.[12]

This is confirmed by extensive data indicating that the Russian economy grew significantly in the first half of the sixteenth century. Expansion was marked by intensive growth of the new peasant and urban proto-bourgeoisie, migration to the cities, rapid urbanization, development of large-scale manufacturing, and considerable capital formation. We know, for example, that at this time there appeared in the Russian North a multitude of new towns (Kargopol', Turchasov, Tot'ma, Ustiuzhnia, Shestakov). An even greater number of major fortresses were built (Tula, Kolomna, Kazan', Zaraisk, Serpukhov, Astrakhan', Smolensk, and Kitai-Gorod in Moscow). I am not even speaking of the scale of construction of less significant fortress-cities (Elets, Voronezh, Kursk, Belgorod, and Borisov in the South; Samara, Ufa, Saratov, and Tsaritsyn in the East; and Arkhangel'sk and Kola in the North). In the sixteenth century, urbanization became a truly national phenomenon. Some observers even got the impression of a mass migration of the rural population to the cities. In 1520 residents of Narva wrote to Revel:

11. S. Gerbershtein, *Zapiski o moskovskikh delakh*, p. 91.

12. W. Kirchner, "The Rise of the Baltic Question." The modern British historian T. S. Willan reports facts which indirectly confirm the extreme importance of the Muscovite trade. It turns out that the attractiveness of the Russian port was so great that it became a constant subject of argument on the part of free merchants—"crafty persons," as the lawyers for the Moscow Company, who were trying to close the Russian trade to outsiders, called them in a complaint to the royal privy council in 1573. The craftiness of these outsiders consisted in the fact that their vessels passed through the sound with an official destination of Danzig or Revel', when in fact they were going to Narva. This means that the magnetic qualities of the Moscow trade were at that time strong enough to justify the high risk of violating the monopoly (T. S. Willan, "The Russia Company and Narva, 1558–81").

Soon there will be no one in Russia to take the plow any longer, for all are running to the cities and becoming merchants. . . . People who two years ago were carrying fish to market, or were butchers, old-clothes dealers, or market gardeners, have become extremely rich merchants and money-lenders and deal in thousands of rubles.[13]

If, however, Russia was indeed undergoing significant economic expansion, and in particular a building boom, the necessary preconditions which existed in every European country—such as a free labor market, significant free capital, and judicial protection of private property—must have been present there too. As listed in surviving documents, for example, the materials used in the construction of the fortress of Smolensk included three hundred and twenty thousand poods of iron in bars, 15,000 poods of iron rods, 1,000,000 nails, and 320,000 wooden pilings. Inasmuch as iron and timber were not imported from abroad, this implies large-scale specialized production. And neither was such production artificially implanted and patronized and regulated by the state, as was the case under Peter. It was private enterprise in the full sense of the term.

Sixteen thousand workers were directly employed on the construction of the Smolensk fortress alone—all, according to the tsar's decree, freely hired. If we consider that dozens of such fortresses and cities were being erected at the same time, this presupposes an enormous free labor market. As far as free capital is concerned, a long list of extremely wealthy contemporary merchants is supplied by the Soviet historians D. Makovskii and N. Nosov.[14] I will cite only a few examples here. The Smolensk merchant Afanasii Yudin extended credit to English merchants to the sum—enormous for that time—of 6,200 rubles (equivalent to more than 450,000 rubles in gold as of the end of the nineteenth century). Tiutin and Anfim Sil'vestrov extended credit to Lithuanian merchants to the amount of 1,210 rubles (more than 100,000 nineteenth-century rubles in gold). A member of the English company, Anthony Marsh, is recorded as owing 1,400 rubles to S. Emel'ianov, 945 to I. Bazhen, and 525 to S. Shorin. In a contemporary letter to the pope we read that,

Muscovy is extremely rich in money, obtained more from the patronage of sovereigns than through mines—of which, incidentally, there is also no lack—since every year there is brought here *from all corners of Europe*

13. Cited in A. A. Zimin, *Reformy Ivana Groznogo*, p. 158.
14. D. P. Makovskii, *Razvitie tovarno-denezhnykh otnoshenii v sel'skom khoziaistve russkogo gosudarstva v XVI veke*; N. E. Nosov, *Stanovlenie soslovno-predstavitel'nykh uchrezhdenii v Rossii.*

an abundance of money in payment for goods which have almost no value for the Muscovites, while they bring an extremely high price in our parts.[15]

Paradoxically, however, Golovkin, Solov'ev, and Pogodin seem to have been both right and wrong in characterizing pre-Petrine Russia as obscure and poverty-stricken. For where Chancellor in 1553 had found wonderfully populated villages, his compatriot Fletcher a quarter of a century later discovered a desert. In the census books of 1573–78, 93 to 96 percent of the villages of the Moscow region are listed as uninhabited.[16] In the Mozhaisk region, up to 86 percent of the villages were empty; in Pereiaslavl'-Zalesskii, 70 percent. Uglich, Dimitrov, and Novgorod had been put to the torch and stood deserted. In Mozhaisk, 89 percent of the houses were vacant; in Kolomna, 92 percent. And this was the case everywhere in the country.

It seems as if before starting its ascent from obscurity to greatness as the stereotype proclaims, the country had made a terrible descent in the opposite direction—from greatness to obscurity.

The economic and social forces developed in the first half of the sixteenth century, which had seemed to promise normal progress of the European type for Russia, suddenly disappeared as if they had never been. The prominent peasant proto-bourgeoisie vanished. The progressive three-field (short-term fallow) system of tillage was abandoned. Large-scale production ceased. The urbanization of the country gave way to deurbanization. And, what was most important, the

15. *Biblioteka inostrannykh pisatelei o Rossii XV–XVI vekov*, vol. 1, pp. 111–12. Emphasis added.

16. Here is a clear example of the dynamics of this abandonment of the land: in the region of Bezhetsk, in Novgorod Province, in 1551, only 6.4 percent of the land was abandoned (grown up to woods); in 1564 this figure was 20.5 percent, and in 1584, 95.3 percent (S. G. Strumilin, "O vnutrennem rynke Rossii XVI–XVIII vekov"). As a whole in Novgorod province at the beginning of the sixteenth century, living plowland made up 92 percent of the whole, and, in the 1580s, not more than 10 percent (Makovskii, *Razvitie . . .*). So much for agriculture. In industry and trade, the differentiation of entrepreneurs and merchants into the "best" (that is, largest-scale), the "middle," and the "younger" had already gone quite far at the beginning of the sixteenth century. According to the data of the Soviet historian E. I. Zaozerskaiia, who studied the *posad* of Ustiuzhnia Zhelezopol'skaia and the population employed there in metal-working and in the trade in metal articles in 1567, 40 shops there belonged to the "best," 40 to the "middle," and 44 to the "younger" people. "After the passage of 30 years," the author writes, "which were no less difficult for Ustiuzhnia than for the rest of the Russian state, in the census of 1597 in Ustiuzhnia there were no 'best' households, the 'middle' ones did not number more than a dozen, and in addition the census-takers registered 17 empty farmsteads and 286 vacant lots. The *posad* had become deserted" (E. I. Zaozerskaiia, *U istokov krupnogo proizvodstva v russkoi promyshlennosti XVI–XVII vekov*, p. 220).

rapid transformation of the *kholops* (slaves) into freemen gave way to an equally swift reverse process.[17] Henceforth, the free laborer gradually disappeared from the face of the Russian earth, and became a serf belonging either to other men or to the state. And this is how it would be for centuries to come. Even today Russia has not fully recovered from this terrible transformation. Serfdom to the state and its enterprises was a fact of life for all Russian workers up to 1956, and for the rural population it has still not ended—at least not as a rule.

And here we approach the basic question of this book: why? Why was it that Russia, which in the sixteenth century could claim a primary role in European politics, was in the eighteenth glad even of the status of a second-class power? Why was a brilliant future predicted for it in the sixteenth century, while in the eighteenth "we were not considered human beings"? What was the political basis for the economic and military catastrophes which plunged the country into the "nonexistence" of which Russian politicians and historians speak so glibly?

17. "In the sixteenth century, until the 1580s, forced labor—that is, either as serfs or as slaves—could not play any appreciable role. Serf peasants (former slaves now settled on the land) until the 1580s were very few, and slave labor in industry, beginning with the first half of the fourteenth century, was rapidly crowded out and replaced with free hired labor. In the seventeenth and eighteenth centuries we see a reverse picture, in which the labor of free hired persons was replaced by compulsory labor—that is, by serf people, who came more and more to resemble slaves. The proportion of free hiring both in industry and in agriculture in the sixteenth century was certainly far, far higher than in the eighteenth century" (Makovskii, p. 192). After this we can hardly be surprised at the author's conclusion that "capitalist relationships came into being in the middle of the sixteenth century in the Russian state both in industry and in agriculture, and the necessary economic conditions for their development were prepared. . . . But in the period from the 1570s, active intervention by the state in economic relationships occurred. . . . This intervention not only hindered the development of capitalist relationships and undermined the condition of productive forces in the country, but also called forth regressive phenomena in the economy" (ibid., p. 212). Thus, the prerequisites for the capitalist relationships usual in Europe originated in Russia in the sixteenth century, according to an authoritative Soviet historian. Originated and . . . disappeared. Furthermore, they disappeared so thoroughly that according to another even more authoritative historian, Academician N. M. Druzhinin, these prerequisites could not be discovered even in the epoch of Peter—that is, a century and a half later. "The state representing nobility," Druzhinin wrote, "was at the zenith of its power and might: the transformations wrought by Peter . . . strengthened the feudal monarchy, and were neither objective nor subjective signs of the decay of the feudal-serf social order. . . . Therefore one cannot agree with B. V. Iakovlev and other historians that the origins of the capitalist economic system date from the *first half of the eighteenth century* [emphasis added]" (N. M. Druzhinin, "O periodizatsii istorii kapitalisticheskikh otnoshenii v Rossii," p. 71).

2. The Alternatives

In the middle of the thirteenth century, an apparently irresistible wave of cavalry from the Mongolian steppes inundated Russia on its way westward. On the Hungarian plain, which is the end of the gigantic wedge of steppe running from Siberia into Europe, this wave halted and turned back. But the entire eastern part of what had once been known as Kievan Rus' remained for centuries to come a remote European province of what was, in effect, the gigantic colonial empire of the Golden Horde. During all this time, the Russian land did not live, merely survived, while its surplus product was almost entirely confiscated—or so it was intended—by the Tatars, its cities stood deserted, its economic development was artificially stopped, and a collaborationist administration held sway. "There can be scarcely any doubt . . . that domination by a foreign power . . . had a very debilitating effect on the political climate of Russia," Richard Pipes observes.[18]

Ten generations were required before Muscovy—in the course of what may, on the analogy of the expulsion of the Moors from Iberia, be termed the Russian Reconquista—coalesced into a state again, and, in the middle of the fifteenth century, attained its independence by force. In 1480 the last khan of the Golden Horde, Akhmat, encountered a Russian army on the Ugra River, at the distant approaches to the capital, and, unwilling to risk open battle, retreated. The retreat turned into a rout. Akhmat lost his head on the Nogai steppe to Tatar swords. The Golden Horde ceased to exist, and on the crest of a movement of national liberation, Russia came into being. The Ugra, site of the battle which did not take place, became a symbol of its independence.

Three generations after this beginning, Muscovy was no longer on the defensive, but constantly on the attack. Moreover, in retrospect one can perhaps discern something reminiscent of a national purpose, toward which the country seemed stubbornly to be working. Formulated most loosely, this was the resurrection of Kievan Rus' after two centuries as a Tatar colony. Externally, it consisted in completing the Reconquista—that is, in recovering all the territory which had once belonged to Kiev. Internally, it consisted in correcting the economic and sociopolitical deformities brought about by generations of feudal disintegration and colonial existence.

Few historians doubt that Kievan Rus' belonged to the European family of nations. In this sense, we can say that if the national pur-

18. Richard Pipes, *Russia under the Old Regime*, p. 57.

pose of Muscovy consisted in the resurrection of the Kievan state, this meant not only the reconstitution of its territorial integrity, but also its *re-Europeanization*.

Under fifteenth-century conditions, the socioeconomic aspect of the process of re-Europeanization was relatively simple: economic expansion (more or less equivalent to that of the neighboring countries to the West) and the concomitant social evolution (differentiation of the peasantry, migration into the cities, and urbanization) logically resulting, as everywhere in Europe, in the formation of a strong middle class. As we have seen, fifteenth- and sixteenth-century Muscovy was capable of this: its cities were growing rapidly and the differentiation of its peasantry into economic strata was underway. This peasant differentiation, leading to the development of a proto-bourgeoisie, which will be discussed in detail in chapter six, was a highly important sign of the capacity of the Russia of that time to *generate* the process of re-Europeanization.

Another aspect of the problem was, however, the need to *stabilize* the processes leading to the formation of a middle class—in other words, the need to create a political mechanism (which I call the absolutist state) capable, as elsewhere in Europe, of protecting these developments from the destructive influences of the hostile feudal environment. This required: (1) a change in the legislator's perception of the relative value of the soldier and the peasant or merchant—the "middle person"; (2) active legislative protection of private (nonfeudal) property; (3) more or less free discussion of the social and economic strategy of the country; and (4), most important of all, minimal interference by the state in the natural socioeconomic process.

This political aspect of the process involved greater difficulties under the conditions of fifteenth-century Muscovy than in most neighboring European states. The positive socioeconomic developments themselves, artificially restrained for so long under the Tatar yoke, were considerably more fragile in Russia than in other countries, and therefore badly needed the political support and nurturing of the state. The Muscovite administration, however, had not exactly had the best possible background for such a delicate job. An ancient autocratic tradition, sharpened and intensified by centuries of colonial corruption, lurked in its depths, ever ready to reassert itself.

But there also existed factors favorable to the re-Europeanization of the country, primarily Russia's geopolitical status in Europe. Parallel to the disintegration of the northern arm of the Asiatic offensive, the Golden Horde, its new southern arm, the Ottoman Empire, was swiftly gathering strength. In the second half of the fourteenth century, the Turks invaded the Balkan peninsula; in the middle of the fifteenth century, they crushed the Eastern Roman Empire; and by the beginning of the sixteenth century, they threatened the most vital centers of Central Europe. Martin Luther, for one, took the Turkish threat so seriously that he even argued the need for the Reformation on grounds that Europe might easily become the prey of the Ottomans if it did not undergo a spiritual rebirth.[19]

Luther's fears were not unjustified. The Turkish sultan was the mightiest sovereign in the contemporary world. In a letter to the king of France, Sultan Suleiman II referred to himself as the king of kings, the prince of princes, the distributor of crowns to the world, the shadow of God in both parts of the world, the ruler of Asia and Europe, the Black and White Seas. The sultan was only partly bragging. Thirty kingdoms then being subject to his rule, he could reasonably call himself "the distributor of crowns."

The rise of Turkey had altered the political geography of Europe, and from this change a new and constructive role for Russia could have evolved. Muscovy was now in the position of a valuable potential ally in any European anti-Turkish coalition. It was not Russia, but Germany, which now had to look to its security. A general rapprochement between Russia and the West might have developed—a cooperation and alliance, perhaps even convergence. In any case, it was clear that unless Muscovy suddenly collapsed or adopted an active anti-Western policy, no serious threat from that direction lay in store for it. This was an unusual relief for a country just emerging from colonial status, preoccupied with internal affairs, and still threatened from the East and South by the heirs of the Golden Horde.

At this fateful crossroads, Muscovy was presented with a truly historic choice. It could return to the family of independent nations as an ally of Europe, and attain its national purpose, the revival of Kievan Rus', in both external (Reconquista) and internal (re-Europeanization) dimensions. Or, by contrasting itself to Europe, it could take the place of the vanished Golden Horde.

As we now know, Russia did eventually complete its Reconquista, and ultimately transformed itself into a modern superpower. The question at issue was never *whether* it would be able to do this, but *at what price*. By Europeanizing or by de-Europeanizing? Here, at the very source of the Russian historical river, we face a gripping spectacle. For an entire century Muscovy wavered before these fateful alternatives. The choice it made led to national catastrophe—the kill-

---

19. D. Egorov, "Ideia turetskoi reformatsii v XVI veke," p. 7.

ing of its Pushkins and Mandel'shams and the exiling of its Kurbskiis and Herzens. In the end, as Herzen put it, "Muscovy saved Russia by suffocating everything that was free in Russian life."[20]

3. On the Path to Re-Europeanization

Over the course of the "century of choice" (which in this book, for reasons which will be explained later, I call the absolutist century of Russian history), a great deal was done to achieve both the Reconquista and re-Europeanization:

1. Reunification of the country was accomplished without civil war, far ahead of Germany and Italy, and with little blood spilt by comparison, for example, with France.
2. Important administrative, social, and judicial reforms put an end to feudal separatism (these will be discussed in chapter five).
3. A start was made at reforming the church earlier than in other European countries (see chapter six).
4. The White Sea became an avenue of international trade, and Muscovy acquired a port on the Baltic (Narva), which came to be used by European merchants in preference to Riga and Revel.
5. Much important western Russian territory in Lithuanian possession was reconquered.
6. Routing of the Kazan' and Astrakhan' Tatar hordes brought the great path of the Volga under Muscovy's control.
7. The crucial process of peasant differentiation was in no way impeded. Rather, the Muscovite administration actively supported the judicial defense of private (nonfeudal) property, little by little bringing into being a Russian proto-bourgeoisie in the course of the economic boom of the first half of the sixteenth century. Thus, gradually, economic limitations of power were formed.
8. The conditions for a broad-based debate over the future of the country were created. This developed over the course of the entire "century of choice," chiefly in connection with the prospective reform of the church. Thus, gradually, the ideological limitations of power were formed.
9. In creating the bureaucratic apparatus appropriate to a centralized state, and gradually limiting the archaic privileges of

20. A. I. Herzen, *Sobranie sochinenii*, vol. 1, p. 132.

the hereditary aristocracy (the boyars), a mortal struggle between these two elites was nevertheless avoided. Both elites
learned the art of interacting in the decision-making process.
The political functioning of the traditional ("patrimonial") aristocracy, which by reason of its hereditary status was independent of the state, thus represented a strong social limitation of
power.

10. Muscovy showed itself capable of instituting local self-government, a system of trial by jury, and even something reminiscent
of a national parliament—the Assembly of the Land (*Zemskii
Sobor*).

For all these reasons, it may confidently be asserted that the Kievan,
or European, side of the Russian tradition was dominant throughout
the "century of choice." At least until 1560 it might have seemed that,
by continuing in the direction of re-Europeanization, Muscovy would
once again join the European family of nations, as in the days of
Kievan Rus'. The sum of gradually accumulating limitations on royal
power, although not touching directly on the political sphere, nevertheless deprived this power of its unlimited character.

4. The Choice

Certainly, there were sinister signs, too, that the autocratic tradition
was preparing to reassert itself.

Reform of the church had apparently reached an impasse by the
1550s. Unlike the states of Sweden, Denmark, or England, the Muscovite state appeared incapable of breaking the resistance of the
powerful church hierarchy. On the contrary, in seeking to preserve
the enormous worldly wealth of the church, the counter-reformist
clergy managed not only to work out all the ideological preconditions
for an autocratic "revolution from above" but also to defeat the proponents of reform politically. Thus, they cleared the way for a new
Tatar conquest of Rus', so to speak—this time not by the Tatars but by
its own Orthodox tsar.

Side by side with peasant differentiation, which promised Russia a
vigorous middle class in the near future, there appeared another process of differentiation, involving the feudal landowners, which may
for convenience be called feudal differentiation. A growing class of
small service gentry (*pomeshchiki*) sprang up, which unlike the hereditary aristocracy depended on the state not only for its prosperity but
for its very existence. This class, the backbone of Muscovite military
power, hungered above all for land. And, in spite of the limited land

resources at the disposal of the state, this hunger had somehow to be
accommodated. Here lay the greatest danger to re-Europeanization,
for if it were satisfied at the expense of the peasantry, this would
mean an end to peasant differentiation and the extinction of the nas-
cent Russian middle class. Thus, two major social processes—two dif-
ferentiations—competed in Muscovy. The outcome of their rivalry
was to decide the fate of Russia.

Finally, the heir of the former imperial power, the Crimean khanate, still held the entire South of the country, with its black earth, the
nation's main breadbasket and chief hope. The Tatars not only deprived the country of the lion's share of national wealth, but constantly threatened its normal functioning. And, even more important, if so inspired by Turkey, they might at any moment renew the
traditional colonial claims of the Golden Horde.

Under these conditions, the political role of the tsar took on huge
significance. I am stressing the political role, the objective position
rather than the personality of the tsar, because what really mattered,
as I see it, was that:

(a) Land to satisfy the service gentry could be obtained from one
of three sources: by confiscation of the enormous holdings of
the church (i.e., reform of the church); by confiscation of peasant holdings; or from the rich South—that is, in essence, by
confiscation of Tatar holdings.

(b) The powerful church hierarchy stood in the way of a reformation. In the way of confiscation of peasant holdings stood the
powerful boyar aristocracy and the fragile, immature Russian
proto-bourgeoisie. The rival elites of the country were heading
for a confrontation, creating an increasingly unstable and delicate balance of forces. Only the tsar and his bureaucracy were
capable of resolving the issue.

(c) Three options lay before the tsarist administration: it could
throw its weight behind the aristocracy and the proto-bourgeoisie, and reform the church (this was the choice of Ivan III,
the creator of the Muscovite state); it could join with the church
in setting the service nobility against the boyars and the proto-
bourgeoisie, in the process crushing the peasantry; or it could
opt for war against the Tatar South, continuing the Reconquista and at the same time bringing about a provisional national reconciliation.

(d) The most likely outcome of the first course would probably
have been much the same as in Denmark or Sweden—a grad-

ual Europeanization of the country, notwithstanding reversals and mutinies; the most likely result of the second was serfdom and universal service; the most likely result of the third was the ultimately irreversible strengthening of the Russian proto-bourgeoisie, which would have made the transition of Muscovy to the status of a European power even more rapid than the first course.

It was precisely this disposition of political forces which created the role of supreme arbiter, and invested the executor of this role with decisive power. One thing is clear, at least for the modern observer: Russia could not continue to live as it had done for centuries. It was becoming an empire. Its administrative and military apparatus clearly demonstrated its backwardness. Tension in the relations of rival elites—the aristocracy, the church, the service nobility, and the central bureaucracy—was becoming unbearable, and had to be discharged, whether by compromise or mortal struggle.

The heart of the choice remained a strategic question: whether Muscovy should continue its attack on the khanate of the Crimea, and on Turkey, which stood behind it—thus becoming a de facto member of the European anti-Turkish coalition, or whether it should strike at Livonia and the Baltic—"turn against the Germans," as Ivan IV had it—thus becoming a de facto member of the anti-European coalition. The entire political future of the country depended on this choice. Only a great national struggle against the Tatars and Turkey—the logical continuation of the struggle against the yoke of past centuries—could ease the tensions in the nation's establishment; could return to Russia her black earth; could secure her southern frontier; could rescue the peasants from serfdom; could save hundreds of thousands of Russian souls from being carried off into slavery by the Tatars; could unite Russians and give them a clear national goal.

On the other hand, the "turn against the Germans" promised only a transformation of the latent tensions within the establishment into an open struggle, left the southern frontier open to the Tatars, and entailed fruitless attempts at an alliance with Turkey against Europe—not to speak of potentially rousing a European coalition against Russia. An anti-European and thus pro-Tatar strategy was likely to bring on national disaster.

Such, indeed, was the case. The origins of Russia's anti-European autocracy, destined to last for centuries to come, can be traced directly to the "turn against the Germans." This is the core of my hypothesis.

5. *The Catastrophe*

It is difficult to deny that Russia underwent a terrible metamorphosis in consequence of the "turn against the Germans." Only recently the insolent Ivan IV of Muscovy had officially refused to call the kings of Sweden and Denmark "brother," asserting that only the greatest sovereigns—the German emperor and the Turkish sultan—would dare address him thus. He had scolded Queen Elizabeth of England as a "common maiden," and treated King Stefan Batory of Poland as a plebeian among kings. Ivan had just refused an honorable peace with Poland, which had given up the conquered Livonian cities to Russia, including the first-class port of Narva. In a contemptuous letter to the first Russian political émigré, Prince Kurbskii, the tsar declared that God was on his side—in the proof of which the victorious banners of Muscovy floated over the Baltic coast—and that had it not been for traitors like Kurbskii he would, with God's help, have conquered all of Germany. In short, Russia was at the peak of its power.

And suddenly all this changed as though by magic. As might have easily been predicted, by "turning against the Germans," Ivan virtually invited the Tatars to attack. In 1571 Russia was unable to prevent the khan of the Crimea from burning Moscow before the eyes of an astonished Europe. Russia's power and prestige declined to such a point that it became itself, for the first time since the Ugra, the target of greedy neighbors. As of old, the khan of the Crimea suddenly once again began to consider Muscovy a tributary of the horde. He had, in fact, already divided up Russia among his lieutenants and granted his merchants the right to trade there without paying tariffs. One would-be conqueror hastened to outdo the other. A letter to the emperor from the oprichnik Heinrich Staden, who fled Moscow, is headed: "Plan of How to Thwart the Desire of the Khan of the Crimea with the Help and Support of the Sultan to Conquer the Russian Land."

Having in the course of his Oprichnina[21] terrorized and laid waste his country, the haughty tsar suddenly began to construct an impreg-

---

21. According to the latest edition of Professor Nicholas Riasanovsky's textbook, "The Oprichnina . . . came to stand . . . for a separate state administration . . . paralleling the one in existence which was retained for the rest of the country, now known as the *zemshchina*. . . . New men under the direct control of Ivan the Terrible ran the Oprichnina, whereas the *zemshchina* stayed within the purview of the boyar duma and old officialdom. . . . The term *Oprichnina* also came to designate especially this new corps of servants to Ivan the Terrible—called *oprichniki*—who are described sometimes today as gendarmes or political police" (Nicholas Riasanovsky, *History of Russia*, pp. 165–66).

nable fortress in the impassable forests of the Vologda region in the hope of hiding in it from his own people, and opened negotiations with the "common maiden" Elizabeth I for the right of political asylum in England.[22] Muscovy lost not only the 101 Livonian cities—everything which it had conquered over a quarter of a century—but five key Russian cities as well. All this had to be surrendered to the Poles. The Baltic shore which had previously belonged to Russia—that same "window on Europe" which Peter I was to reconquer at the price of yet another Livonian slaughter a century and a half later—went to the Swedes. The seventeenth-century French historian de Thou, generally favorably disposed toward Ivan the Terrible, was obliged to end his panegyric of the tsar on an unexpectedly mournful note:

> Thus ended the Muscovite War, in which Tsar Ivan poorly supported the reputation of his ancestors and his own reputation. The whole country from Chernigov on the Dnieper to Staritsa on the Dvina, and the regions of Novgorod and Lake Ladoga, was utterly ruined. The tsar lost more than 300,000 men, and some 40,000 were carried off as prisoners. These losses turned the regions of Velikie Luki, Zavoloch'e, Novgorod, and Pskov into deserts, because all the youth of these regions were killed and the old people left no descendants behind them.[23]

But de Thou was mistaken. He did not know that by the calculations of that time up to 800,000 people perished or were taken away as prisoners by the Tatars after their campaign against Moscow in 1571 alone. Inasmuch as the entire population of Muscovy at the time was about ten million, it turns out that the life of every tenth person, territorial losses which cut it off from access to the sea, and unprecedented national humiliation were the price paid by Russia for its fatal choice.

Its defeat in the Livonian War was no mere military setback. This was the political collapse of Muscovy. As a market for raw materials, and as a convenient path of communication with Persia, it did not, of

22. No one any longer considered him great or mighty. On the contrary, he was laughed at—both in Asia and in Europe. The khan of the Crimea wrote him when leaving burning Moscow: "And you did not come out and did not stand against us and still boast that, forsooth 'I am the sovereign of Muscovy.' Had there been shame or dignity in you, you would have come out and stood against us." And the Polish King Stefan Batory echoed him: "Why did you not come to us with your troops, and defend your subjects? A poor chicken will cover her chicks with her wings against a hawk or an eagle, but you the two-headed eagle (for such is your crest) hide yourself" (Vipper, p. 161).

23. Ibid., p. 175.

course, cease to exist after the war. But it did effectively cease to exist as one of the centers of world trade and European politics, and was transformed into a third-rate power—something like an eastern Hanover. Here, it seems, is the point at which Russia was transformed into a "weak, poor, almost unknown" nation, as Solov'ev put it, and fell into the void of political nonexistence referred to by Golovkin.

And here we approach the most interesting and mysterious problem of this book. For this is not what Russian historians have traditionally thought, or think today, of the Livonian War. One of them tells us, in fact, that it was precisely in his decision to turn against Europe that Ivan the Terrible "emerges as a great politician" (I. I. Smirnov). Another asserts that precisely because of this decision, the tsar attains "his full stature as a ruler of the peoples and a great patriot" (R. Iu. Vipper). From a third we hear that Ivan "anticipated Peter, and manifested . . . statesman-like perspicacity" (S. V. Bakhrushin). From a fourth, that "Ivan the Terrible understood the interests of the state better than his opponents" (Ia. S. Lur'e). All these are contemporary Soviet historians. But their prerevolutionary colleagues (with the solitary exception of N. I. Kostomarov) held analogous views. In any case, none of them ever interpreted the Livonian War as a historical catastrophe, which laid the basis for the de-Europeanization of Russia. No one has ever seriously tried to analyze the alternative to this war—as though it were natural, fated, inevitable, the sole possible strategy available to Muscovy. No one has ever connected it with the origin of Russian autocracy.

Why?

6. "A Riddle for the Mind"

It is no exaggeration to say that over the past 400 years, a whole library has been written about Ivan IV, his character, his reforms, his wars, his terror, and the Oprichnina: articles, monographs, pamphlets, dissertations, poems, odes, and novels—volumes upon volumes. Everything that these historians, novelists, dissertation writers, and poets have thought about the present of their country, they have sought to justify by reference to the gigantic figure of Ivan the Terrible. In this sense, what I call Ivaniana—the theme of Ivan the Terrible in Russian literature—is a model for the development of Russian public consciousness, and as such deserves special study in itself.

The most honest scholars have often declared in desperation that the riddle of Ivan the Terrible appears to have no solution, and that there can therefore be no end to Ivaniana—at least not until the history of Russia comes to an end. In the eighteenth century, Mikhail Shcherbatov pronounced the unfortunate verdict, which later became classic, that Tsar Ivan "is presented in such varying forms that he does not appear to be one person."[24] At the beginning of the nineteenth century, Nikolai Karamzin cried out in pique that "the character of Ioann [Ivan], a hero of virtue in his youth and the pitiless drinker of blood in his adult years and old age, is a riddle for the mind."[25] At the end of the nineteenth century, Nikolai Mikhailovskii, the greatest ideologist of Russian Populism, wrote:

> For some reason, all the hopes for a firmly established, definite judgment about Ivan the Terrible are destroyed one after another. . . . Considering that the best minds of Russian scholarship, people of brilliant talents and erudition, have participated in the effort to work out this definite judgment, we may perhaps reach the conclusion that the task of removing the disagreements in this particular case is something fantastic . . . if so many intelligent, talented, conscientious and learned people cannot agree, does this not mean that it is impossible to agree?[26]

In our own day, one of the most remarkable of Soviet historians, Stepan Veselovskii, has commented:

> Since the time of Karamzin and Solov'ev, a very large quantity of new sources, both native and foreign, has been found and published, but the maturing of the science of history is going so slowly that the power of human reason as a whole, and not only the question of Tsar Ivan and his time, may be shaken.[27]

There has been a great deal in Ivaniana, as there has been a great deal in Russian history; there have been discoveries and there have been disappointments, there have been hopes and there has been despair. But we are interested here not in what has been, but in what has *not* been in it. And there have been in it no hypotheses about Ivan the Terrible as the forefather—I might even say the inventor—of a political monstrosity which neither coups d'etat, nor reforms, nor revolutions have proved capable of destroying. There have in Ivaniana been no hypotheses about the Livonian War as a sort of alchemical laboratory in which this monstrous form of power—not susceptible, it seems, to time and corrosion—was worked out. There have been

24. Cited in N. K. Mikhailovskii, *Ivan Groznyi v russkoi literature*, vol. 6, p. 131.
25. *Russkoe proshloe. Istoricheskii sbornik*, p. 6.
26. Mikhailovskii, p. 135.
27. S. V. Veselovskii, *Issledovaniia po istorii oprichniny*, p. 35.

no hypotheses about Russian autocracy originating in the "revolution from above" carried out by Ivan the Terrible in January 1565.

The necessary documents, archival discoveries, and textual analyses have not been wanting. "It may be held," wrote Aleksandr Zimin in a book published in Moscow in 1964, "that the main surviving material on the history of the Oprichnina at the present time has already been published."[28] Anthony Grobosky expressed himself still more decisively in a book published in 1969 in New York:

> The debate over Ivan IV's reign is not over miniscule details—there is no agreement on the meaning of the whole period. Lack of source material is hardly to be blamed for this. Even a cursory examination of Karamzin's, Solov'ev's and, for example, A. A. Zimin's and I. I. Smirnov's writing on Ivan will reveal that the most essential sources were already available and known to Karamzin, and that Zimin and Smirnov have but a slight edge over Solov'ev.[29]

But if all the documents necessary for a rational formulation of the "meaning of the whole period" are to hand, why has this question not been formulated rationally? It seems to me that the Oprichnina of Ivan the Terrible was not only a *political revolution* which doomed Russia to a strange cyclical reproduction of its history, and an *economic revolution* which condemned it to the alternation of periods of feverish modernization with long periods of stagnation (repeated attempts to "overtake and pass Europe" always ending in dependence on Europe), it was also a *cultural revolution* which imposed the stereotype of autocracy, and an inability to escape from its limits, on many of the best minds of Russia, including those of her historians.

"Inherited ideas are a curious thing, and interesting to observe and examine," wrote Mark Twain. "*Any* kind of royalty, howsoever modified, *any* kind of aristocracy, howsoever pruned, is rightly an insult; but if you are born and brought up under that sort of arrangement you probably never find it out for yourself, and don't believe it when somebody else tells you."[30] You will not believe it precisely because the angle from which you observe your own political status, and the criteria by which you evaluate it, are firmly introjected into your consciousness by the social milieu in which you were born and brought up, because it is programmed into you by the political culture of your nation, which you took in with your mother's milk.

28. A. A. Zimin, *Oprichnina Ivana Groznogo*, p. 55.
29. A. Grobovsky, *The Chosen Council of Ivan IV; A Reinterpretation*, p. 25.
30. Mark Twain, *A Connecticut Yankee in King Arthur's Court*, pp. 111, 110.

Ivaniana is not only a sad story from the distant past, but bears on modern Russia too, and, most important of all, on the future of my country. That is the major hypothesis of this book, and what makes my task such a personal, complex, and dramatic one.

7. *Scholarship and Expertise*

We know what a miserable place hypotheses occupy in history, but we do not see any reason to discard without consideration everything that seems probable to us. . . . We by no means acknowledge a fatalism which sees in events their absolute inevitability: this is an abstract idea, a cloudy theory, introduced from speculative philosophy into history and natural science. What has occurred, of course, had reason to occur, but this by no means signifies that all other combinations were impossible: they became so only thanks to the realization of the most probable of them—that is all we can assume. The course of history is by no means so predetermined as is usually thought.

ALEKSANDR HERZEN[31]

Why are historians so afraid of naive questions, of diachronic speculation, of historical generalizations, and fundamentally new approaches? Longing, evidently, for the days when "dreams of historical generalizations were followed, but not replaced by the assiduous collection of historical sources," Erwin Chargoff of Columbia University remarked not long ago on the fact that the rise and institutionalization of the expert have driven out what was once called scholarship. "In other words, where expertise prevails wisdom vanishes," he concludes.[32]

Conventional history avoids diachronic enquiry that overleaps the bounds of established specialization—comparing sixteenth-century situations with modern ones, for example. But to me such speculation seems not only necessary, but natural, for my aim is to analyze not artificially separated events *in* Russian history, but Russian history as a whole—a totality in which *all* events are not only interconnected, but also influence each other in the most fundamental way—whether they happened in the sixteenth or in the twentieth century.

This book makes no claims to be the result of the "assiduous collection of historical sources," fashionable cliometrics, or fresh archival discoveries. Rather, it is a new interpretation of well-known facts, re-

31. A. Herzen, *Sobranie sochinenii*, vol. 3, p. 403.
32. Erwin Chargoff, "Knowledge Without Wisdom," p. 41.

plete with hypotheses and speculation. As such, it is an open acknowl-
edgment that the past has something to teach us. It is impossible to
write history once and for all—to canonize theory like a medieval
saint, or tie it to the land like a medieval peasant—and to rethink old
facts can be equivalent to rediscovering them. In any case, I am concerned here primarily with what *might* have happened; not so much
with results as with possibilities.

"Of all sad words of tongue or pen, / The saddest are these: 'It
might have been!'" John Greenleaf Whittier proclaimed sententiously,
and I am all too aware of how open I leave myself to such dismissal.
But though the question "And what if . . . ?" may sound childish
to the academic ear, it nonetheless transforms the historian from a
mere clerk of the court of history, dispassionately registering verdicts
handed down by higher judges, whose decisions are forever beyond
appeal, into a participant in the historical process. History, too, becomes a living school of human experience rather than a compen-
dium of diverse information, useful, if at all, for training the memories of students.

If an anti-Tatar strategy had been implemented in the 1550s, Russian history would undoubtedly have taken on an entirely different
guise. More than this, however, recognition of an alternative, European source of Russian political culture enables us to explain many
things which are otherwise inexplicable: the constant rebirth, in a
somber "garrison state," of drafts for constitutions and plans for reform and the indestructibility of the political opposition.

This is no mere scholastic exercise. For the Russian opposition it is
a matter of life and death. The conundrum of Russia's absolutist century is bound up with the problems of its present: do the current oppositionists have national roots, for example, or are their ideas imported into this garrison state from the West along with Coca Cola
and modern technology? Is it possible for this country to have a decent European future?

"The Muscovite high nobility or service elite occupied the highest
positions in a society and an administrative system that shared characteristics with many contemporary polities and societies but was, in
the final analysis, unique," writes Robert Crummey, a modern American historian. On the one hand, this was a patrimonial, aristocratic
elite, whose representatives, "like their counterparts to the West . . .
derived the core of their income from ownership of land and power
over the peasants who lived on it." On the other hand, they were "imprisoned in a system of universal service to an absolute ruler like the

Ottoman. It was precisely this combination of land ownership, family solidarity, and compulsory state service that made the Muscovite high nobility unique."[33]

I am in full agreement with this perceptive conclusion. It is exactly because of this uniqueness that I call the Russian political structure an autocracy, differing both from absolutism (where there was no obligatory service) and from despotism (where the elite was never in a position to transform itself into an aristocracy). The only thing which disturbs me in Crummey's schema is the chronology. In fact, up to the middle of the sixteenth century, refusal to perform service was not regarded as a crime in Russia (at least according to law), and two centuries later it again ceased to be regarded as such. If we employ Crummey's criteria, it transpires that the Russian elite (and the Russian political structure) was "unique" only during these two centuries. And before this? And afterwards? Was it then perhaps similar to its Western counterparts? Or to the elite of the Ottoman Empire? Why was it that the Ottoman elite appears to have been incapable of overcoming the bondage of universal service, while the Russian elite succeeded?

We see still more clearly the results of the conventional approach (without any "what ifs" at all) in the attempt of another American historian to divide the history of the Muscovite elite (1450–1700) into three periods. "The first period," Richard Hellie writes,

> lasted about a century, with 1556 serving as a suitable terminus. The first service class revolution in Russian history, initiated by mobilizing land (the *pomest'e* system) to support cavalrymen, gathered momentum in those years. . . . The second period also lasted about a century, from 1556 until the Thirteen Years' War (1654–1667), when the old middle service class cavalry was deemed technologically obsolete and replaced by "new formation regiments" of commoners commanded by foreign mercenaries. . . . The third period followed the Thirteen Years' War . . . and lasted until Peter the Great initiated the "second service class revolution" by again requiring service from everyone.[34]

Let us not go too deeply into Hellie's periodization (which, incidentally, leaves us completely ignorant of why a *second* "service class revolution" was needed at all, and of what happened to the Russian ser-

33. Robert Crummey, "The Seventeenth-Century Moscow Service Elite in Comparative Perspective," p. 1.
34. Richard Hellie, "The Muscovite Provincial Service Elite in Comparative Perspective," p. 1.

vice elite after this revolution suffered defeat). Let us merely note that Hellie here imprudently does what Crummey avoids—that is, he extends the uniqueness of the Russian elite (or what is, from his point of view, the same thing, its service-based character) to the period before 1556.

To be sure, the free movement of Russian peasants was indeed restricted in the fifteenth century, and the Russian nobles usually served. What is more, the traditional system of dividing inheritances among male heirs made service especially attractive to the latter as a means of maintaining and increasing their wealth. But, after all, the system of dividing inheritances still existed in Russia in the eighteenth and nineteenth centuries, after universal service was abolished, and the Russian elite managed to cope with it without so much as giving a thought to returning to obligatory service. Why, then, would it have been impossible for it to have coped with the same problem in the sixteenth century *if* things had turned out differently? Does this not at least call for explanation?

It does, and the "if" also sheds unexpected light on other phenomena and processes currently regarded as fully understood. For example, it is possible to show (and I will try to do so in chapter six) that what historians have conventionally perceived as a *restriction* on the free movement of peasants was in actuality a step taken in *defense* of their right of free movement—indeed, a legal guarantee of such movement in the face of growing feudal encroachments. Further, it is possible to show (as will be attempted in chapters two and ten) that along with the tendencies facilitating the introduction of universal service, another ancient and powerful tendency operated in Muscovite society which promoted the aristocratization of the Russian elite; and that it is the *competition* between these two tendencies which has in fact determined the course of Russian history for centuries. While the aristocratizing tendency was destined to lose the struggle in the mid-1500s, it again raised its head at the end of the seventeenth century and, though initially defeated, overcame its competitor in the middle of the eighteenth.

On what basis, then, do historians discount the tendencies opposed to serfdom and universality of service? Because they were defeated? In precisely this way the verdict of the historians is transformed into a slavish copy of the verdict of history—an abdication no less sad than "might have been." Conventional history does not judge the victors, and thereby condemns the vanquished for a second time, without so much as having heard their case. Its interest in the past exclusively as something which has forever disappeared from life, and plunged without a trace into Lethe, gives it a perceptible flavor of fatalism and predetermination.

What interests me in history is its bearing on the present—and, above all, on the future. And for this reason I see my task not so much as one of describing the past, which has been done innumerable times, as of reconstructing it in its possible alternative combinations.

PART I

THE ADVERSITIES
OF THEORY

CHAPTER I

THE LANGUAGE
IN WHICH WE ARGUE

1. Justification of the Chapter

The enigma of Russian history, which I have tried to describe in chapter one, struck me a long time ago, during my school years. When I was a university student, Ivan the Terrible was the idol of Russian historians. Eizenshtein's famous film provoked fierce debates, in which no agreement could be reached. The nucleus and the symbolic axis of these traditional arguments was (just as a century ago) the fateful question: what is Russia—Asia or Europe? The leader of the "East" or the outsider of the "West"? Where do we belong? And consequently, who are we—"Scythians" or "Europeans"? And in a more abstract form: to what class of political structures does the country in which we happen to have been born belong—to "Asiatic despotism" or to "European absolutism"?

Certainly, "Asiatic despotism" was not mentioned in our textbooks. But, on the other hand, in the published works and letters of Marx and Engels, which the student historian was supposed to know backwards and forwards, it was encountered literally at every step. And it had a somber and sinister sound. What did we, ardent and naive debaters of those years, know about this strange topic? That an Asiatic despotism was an Eastern state, which built huge irrigation facilities and governed a society the vast majority of whose members lived in isolated and self-sufficient rural communes? That it was the embodiment of so-called "Asiatic stagnation"? Yes, this was perhaps all that we knew. By European absolutism we understood, correspondingly, a state which did not built irrigation networks and whose inhabitants were not isolated in rural communes. As a consequence of this, they went off to the cities, and in the cities the bourgeoisie grew, entering into competition with the feudal nobility. At the moment when the bourgeoisie became sufficiently strong and the nobility sufficiently weak, absolute monarchy appeared, whose power was based on medi-

ation between the bourgeoisie and the nobility, while at the same time
it remained a dictatorship of the feudal class.

It is not hard to see how many holes there were in the language in
which we argued. The states which were usually considered despotic,
such as Byzantium or Turkey, developed no irrigation facilities whatever. The power of the Chinese emperors, which was certainly despotic, was for some reason not based on the rural commune at all.
The obviously Oriental country of Japan for some reason turned out
to be by no means a despotism. But the main thing was, how was all
this to be related to Russia, where, although there were rural communes, there was no irrigation? And where, on the other hand, until
the very end of the nineteenth century there was no bourgeoisie capable of competing with the nobility? It seemed that the Russian autocracy (*samoderzhavie*), ignorantly repudiating the authoritative conclusions of Marx and Engels, deliberately refused to belong to either
Asiatic despotism or European absolutism. And no third alternative
was offered us.

True, following Lenin, one could still call it "semi-Asiatic," but
what was the concrete meaning of this supposed to be? Which half of
it was Asiatic and which European? Which features separated it from
despotism, which from absolutism? What part of our past was determined by Asia and what part by Europe? And what was still more important—how did they determine our future? There was no answer
to these questions.

On the other hand, a person who a quarter of a century ago se-
cretly read Leonard Schapiro's book *The Origins of the Communist Autocracy* in the USSR had a completely confused feeling. For "autocracy"—so we had been taught—was primarily tsarist power, and this
power had been overthrown in our country in 1917. Since then, Russia had been a republic, with universal, equal, and secret suffrage.
How then could Schapiro—and many, many others in his wake—call
it an autocracy? Did they perhaps mean that the political *nature* of autocracy was by no means exhausted by the power of the tsars, which
was only one of its transitory *forms*? But in this case, why did no one,
not even our secret teachers, to say nothing of our official ones, bring
up this question? Could there perhaps be something wrong with the
very language in which we argued?

Is it really conceivable that modern physiologists would argue
about the functions of the kidneys, for example, or chemists about an
element, without having determined beforehand just what they were
discussing? And that, as a result, it would turn out that by "kidney"
some people actually meant the liver, while others, in referring to an

element, meant the entire periodic table? But isn't this exactly what happens to us when we placidly list "autocracy," "authoritarianism," "absolutism," "unlimited power," "despotism," and "totalitarianism" simply as synonyms, separated from each other only by commas? And is this not why our arguments, instead of generating the truth, as they were supposed to do, are transformed into a babel—a definitional chaos, a dialogue among the deaf?

Faced with the tormenting riddles of Russian history, which over time took on the increasingly urgent and practical outlines of the fateful question of where we are going and what will become of us, I decided on a step as extraordinary as it was presumptuous. What else remained to one who had abandoned Marxist scholasticism as powerless to answer his questions, and was at the same time cut off from any systematic acquaintance with contemporary Western literature, but to suggest his own conceptual language—his own instrumental apparatus, capable, at least, of adequately describing the prerequisites of the task?

I started by asking why, inasmuch as not all non-European states answered the description of Asiatic despotism, all European states must necessarily be absolutist. Had not even Aristotle in his *Politics* posed the question: "Is there in fact only one form of royal power or are there several varieties within it?" And did he not answer it in categorical terms: "It is not hard to see that there exist several forms of royal power and that the very means by which it is manifested are not one and the same"?[1] And, to say nothing of Aristotle, if we are to believe Xenophon, even Socrates recognized this! Is it not strange that the ancient Greeks knew several forms of monarchy, while we—2,500 years later—are shut up like communities of peasants within the bounds of an impoverished bipolar geographical model of political classification?

Having now come to the West, I was glad to discover that many prominent scholars here also think that it is difficult, if not impossible, to analyze the history of a particular country outside of the conceptual context of world history, and that, as Cyril Black, for example, has observed: "One cannot interpret Russian developments without some general conception of what is universal and what is particular in the evolution of societies."[2] Though proceeding from an analogous assumption, my thought in Russia followed a different path, however. It seemed to me necessary first of all to build up as carefully as possi-

1. Aristotle, *Politika*, p. 136; quoted from the Russian edition.
2. Cited in Donald W. Treadgold, ed., *The Develoment of the USSR*, p. 202.

ble a set of, as it were, "ideal constructions" (or paradigms) of both
poles of the bipolar model, and literally to count out their parameters
on one's fingers. Of course, one might as a result obtain something
very schematic, and for this reason debatable—something which in
its pure form has not existed anywhere on earth. This would be something which would show various political structures, as the mathematicians say, "in their extremes," rather than their actual outlines in
this or that country. But I consciously took the risk of this schematiza-
tion: in the final analysis, does one ever get anything without losing
something in exchange? And what I wanted was a great deal. First of
all, I wanted the categories and terms with which we operate to become clear to the point of transparency, so that in the future when we
argued we would at least know what we were talking about. My intention may to the Western reader seem like naive intellectual extremism. So it probably was. But for me, in any case, it cleared up the picture somewhat. The result at which I finally arrived turned out to be
paradoxical. In the first place, as the reader will see in what follows,
none of my ideal constructions described the Russian political structure adequately. It turned out that, beginning at a definite historical
point, this structure behaved very strangely—that it was subject to its
own laws, which coincided with neither the parameters of despotism
nor those of absolutism. And it turned out, moreover, to be considerably more flexible and adaptable than the ideal constructions were.
While what is usually called "modernization" destroys despotism and
has in most cases transformed absolutism into democracy, the Russian
political structure has, as it were, digested this "modernization," while
retaining its basic medieval parameters to this day.

But the paradoxical nature of my findings did not by any means
consist in this. Russian nationalists in all ages have proudly pronounced Russia to be a special civilization, following its own thorny
path between the Charybdis of the West and the Scylla of the East.
This was declared before the emergence of the nineteenth-century
Slavophiles, and it is declared after them. Suffice it to recall the preaching of the fiery Ioakim, patriarch of Moscow in the late seventeenth
century, contrasting Russian piety both to Islam and to Latin heresy,
or the analogous preaching of Aleksander Solzhenitsyn in the late
twentieth century. Assertions of the uniqueness of the historical fate
of a nation constitute the great temptation for nationalists. My results
revealed something much more complex and much more distressing,
however: the Russian political structure not only could not be described with the help of the bipolar model, but it was also not sui generis in its sources. It had been violently *transformed* into what it is

now—that is, an autocracy. Starting like the rest of Europe within the limits of a single absolutist paradigm, at a certain moment—in complete conformity with Aristotle's political conception—Russia "deviated" from the ordinary absolutist axis. But by virtue of a number of historical circumstances, its "deviation" (in contrast to the "deviation" of monarchy toward tyranny, which is usual according to Aristotle) gave rise to a strange new political species, which led to national tragedy for a great people over the course of many centuries. From the ordinary absolutist root there grew a wild, ugly, wayward branch. If there was anything to be proud of, it was only that somewhere in the depths of the national subconscious Russia proved unable entirely to rid herself of her European beginnings, and again and again stubbornly returned to them.

This new political structure, unheard of in European history, was called forth by Ivan the Terrible's Oprichnina revolution. Ivan the Terrible and the origins of the modern Russian political structure were thus indissolubly connected. Such was my result, and there is apparently no other way of familiarizing the reader with it than through the elementary comparison and correction of definitions, and speculations and interpretations at first glance not even related to Ivan the Terrible.

I understand how strange such an abstract theoretical wringing process, full of allusions and terms unfamiliar to the Western ear, must seem. Moreover, it may turn out that in proposing a system of categories for judging political structures, I have, as they say, reinvented the wheel. I understand all this. But I can do nothing about it: otherwise my encounter with the reader is in danger of becoming yet another dialogue of the deaf.

The first part of this book is of necessity theoretical, since it is designed to acquaint the reader with my conception of the origin and nature of the Russian political structure. In this part I seek:

1. To give as precise as possible a description of "despotism" and "absolutism";
2. To give a description of "Russian autocracy";
3. To demonstrate that prior historiography known to me proceeds almost entirely from the bipolar model of political classification;
4. To show that, precisely for this reason, it is incapable of adequately describing the origin and nature of the Russian political structure.

It goes without saying that most Soviet authors reject with an offended air the very possibility that Russia might belong in the category of Asiatic despotism, and decidedly count it in the family of European absolutism, while most Western authors who are sensitive to theoretical issues are convinced of the opposite. For this reason, I will call the first, for brevity's sake, "absolutists," and the latter "despotists."

This chapter will be devoted to definitions. In chapter two, I will try to show how it comes about that the "absolutists" are unable to explain the origin and nature of the Russian political process. The third chapter will be devoted to the "despotists."

2. *The Science of Despotology*

Aristotle knew that in addition to the three regular and three irregular ("deviant") forms of political organization characteristic of the civilized *oikumene*, there existed beyond its boundaries, in the darkness of barbarism, yet a seventh—despotism. Outwardly, it resembles the tyranny well-known to the civilized world, which "is in essence the same as monarchy but implies only the interests of the ruler alone."[3] But this resemblance is only outward, because in the civilized world, tyranny is but one of the transitory forms in an ever-changing sea of political transformations, while despotism in the barbarian world is *permanent*.

The human mind is not capable of understanding how a people can tolerate tyranny on a permanent basis. For this reason Aristotle saw in despotism something inhuman. And this is not surprising if we remember that "barbarism" was, for him, only the external political dimension of the internal political condition of "slavery." Neither the slave nor the barbarian (the potential slave) could be considered a human being, since the first mark of a human being was, for Aristotle, participation in courts and councils—that is, in the administration of society. Man, for him, was a political animal. This, properly speaking, makes it understandable why he could not consider despotism as a political structure at all.

But Aristotle nevertheless does introduce a certain original element into what I would call the science of despotology. In fact, if we try to look at his theory of "deviations" from a modern point of view, we see immediately that he has in mind the problem of divergence between the goals of the social *system* and those of its *administration*. The regular forms, for him, are those in which the common goals of the system prevail over the goals of the administration. The irregular forms are those in which the administration subjects the system to the goals of the social elements it represents (or, what is of decisive impor-

3. Aristotle, p. 112.

tance for us, to its own autonomous goals). This, in Aristotle's terms, is the meaning of "deviation." Oligarchy, for example, subjects the system to the goals of the social "upper crust," and democracy, on the contrary, to those of the "lower depths." Tyranny subjects the system to the goals of the administration as such, which, in modern parlance, becomes an interest group in its own right. Thus, in Aristotle's opinion, social systems may exist which live *not for their own interests, but exclusively for the interests of the "ruler alone,"* who personifies the administration of the system.

The remarkable variety of political forms characteristic of the Greek *polis* was historically short-lived. And it was by no means replaced by the ideal utopian polity of which Aristotle dreamed, nor even by the republic of Plato, but by monarchy, which became the dominant form of political organization for centuries to come and, as Aristotle had predicted, constantly strove to "deviate" in the direction of tyranny, or even—as it seemed to its contemporaries—in the direction of barbarian despotism; that is, permanent tyranny.

Proceeding from the same Aristotelian tradition, European political thought has for centuries made extraordinary efforts to restrain monarchy—at least in theory—from this fateful "deviation." We can find the traces of this dramatic effort as early as the work of the English jurist of the first parliamentary period, Bracton, in the thirteenth century; in the *Praise of English Laws* of John Fortescue in the fifteenth century; in Jean Bodin, Andrei Kurbskii, and Du Plessy Mornay in the sixteenth century; Iurii Krizhanich in the seventeenth century; and Mikhail Shcherbatov and Mercier de la Riviere in the eighteenth. And finally, when tyranny had apparently become an irreversible fact in France, the lessons of this theoretical struggle were summarized by Charles de Montesquieu in his *Spirit of the Laws.*

Montesquieu was a pessimist and a conservative. He was convinced that the days of "moderate government" (as he called European absolute monarchy) were numbered, that the age-old struggle was approaching its political finale—its catastrophe. "As the rivers run to lose themselves in the sea, monarchies strive to dissolve themselves in despotism," he wrote.[4] The only one of all the wealth of "regular" political forms listed by Aristotle, the last heir of civilization—European absolute monarchy—was receding into the external darkness of political nonexistence, never to return.

If we do not forget that Montesquieu was the founder, so to speak, of the geographical approach in history, and that for him "moderate

---

4. C. de Montesquieu, *O dukhe zakonov,* p. 27; quoted from the Russian edition.

government" (as the result of a temperate climate) was identified with Europe, and despotism with Asia, we can see that we stand here at the sources of the bipolar model of political classification which has dominated the minds of modern historians.

Montesquieu was reproached by his contemporaries with not having been able to give an adequate political description of despotism, limiting himself to a brief aphorism: "When the savages of Louisiana wish to obtain fruit, they cut down the tree at the root and obtain it— here is the whole of despotic government."[5] But this reproach is only partially justified. In fact, Montesquieu drew an important theoretical conclusion—second only to that of Aristotle—concerning the nature of despotism: its total inefficiency, the *incapacity for political dynamism* which conditioned its permanent stagnation.

Despite Montesquieu's pessimism, Europe, as we know, survived the eighteenth century. Moreover, it countered the threat of "deviation" toward despotism with the invention of modern democracy, which made possible the continued existence of civilization. And only in the middle of the twentieth century, when the total onslaught of despotism seemed fated to recur, was the third and decisive theoretical step in the description of this political phenomenon taken.

I do not at all mean to say by this that the phenomenon of despotism disappeared from the field of vision of European thinkers in the interim between Montesquieu and Wittfogel. John Stuart Mill introduced the term "Eastern society" to describe it, and Richard Jones that of "Asiatic society," not to mention the well-known comments by Hegel in his *Lectures on the Philosophy of History*, from which we shall have occasion to quote. Unfortunately, the ideas of the remarkable seventeenth century Russian thinker Iurii Krizhanich have for various reasons (we shall speak of them later) not entered into universal despotology, though his conception of "moderate aristocracy" as the main bastion against despotism preceded the analogous observations of David Hume and Alexis de Tocqueville.

It should be noted that there have been times in the history of Europe when despotology has ceased to be mere academic theorizing, and become a weapon in an immediate and urgent political and ideological struggle. We can count at least four such occasions. The first was the attempt by despotic Persia to conquer Athens in the fifth century B.C. (giving rise, in particular, to Aristotle's speculations concerning the existence of "hereditary and *despotic* royal power among the barbarians"). The second, in the fifteenth and sixteenth centuries,

5. Ibid.

was marked by the seemingly irresistible onslaught of the Turks on Europe and the creation of absolutism (giving rise, in particular, to the conceptions of "seignorial monarchy" in France and "autocracy" in Russia). The third such occasion came in the second half of the eighteenth century, when European absolutism appeared to have slid finally into despotism (bringing with it, in particular, Montesquieu's *The Spirit of the Laws*). The fourth came in the middle of our century, when the onslaught of what is now called totalitarianism once again seemed to be irresistible. People who died in 1940 could actually have thought that the hour of the Last Judgment had come. This brought with it, in particular, Karl A. Wittfogel's *Oriental Despotism* as a reaction to the extreme danger to which civilization was exposed.

Wittfogel's book—despite the author's political extremism, and the highly debatable but unconditionally expressed thesis of "hydraulic civilization" as the historic source of despotism—nevertheless gave the first detailed description of this political category. In this sense, it could have marked the transformation of despotology into a science.[6]

6. Wittfogel's book *Oriental Despotism* was received with drawn swords by most specialists, including the historian Arnold Toynbee; the sociologist S. N. Eisenstadt; the sinologist Wolfram Eberhard; Berthold Spuhler, specialist on the Golden Horde; and S. Andreski, a specialist in comparative sociology. It was also attacked in the Soviet press—and, incidentally, from a very interesting point of view. The only review from Moscow known to me berated Wittfogel for not having understood "the real role of despotic society in the East *as inevitable at a certain stage* of political development of society." And furthermore, as a "political form [which] was in some respects *necessary and progressive* (*Sovetskoe kitaevedenie*, no. 3 [1958], p. 195; my emphasis).

In chapter 4, devoted especially to the "despotists," we will consider this unanimous rejection in more detail. Now let us say only that in casting doubt on Wittfogel's concept of "hydraulic civilization" as a determining condition for "agromanagerial despotism," they also reject the notion of despotism as a distinct political structure, declaring it, for example, as Toynbee did, to be a myth invented by the Greeks in the fifth century B.C. and revived by Wittfogel out of purely political considerations.

In fact, nothing in these arguments against the conception of "hydraulic civilization" operates against the phenomenon of despotism as such. In Igor' D'akonov's study of the social structure of ancient Mesopotamia (*Obshchestvennyi i gosudarstbennyi stroi drevnego Dvurech'ia. Shumer*) the existence in predespotic Sumer of city-states headed by rulers (*ensi*) whose power was limited by an aristrocratic senate and an assembly of the people is shown. It follows that large-scale irrigation facilities in ancient Mesopotamia, just as in ancient predespotic China (see L. S. Perelomov, *Imperiia Tsin'—pervoe tsentralizovannoe gosudarstvo Kitaia*), could be supported and regulated not only by a centralized bureaucracy, but by city-states of the ancient type. D'akonov notes, however, that despotism nevertheless did arise in Mesopotamia in the Third Dynasty of Ur (2132–24 B.C.), while Perelomov concedes that it appeared in China under the Ch'in Dynasty, though rejecting it for the Yin and Chou Dynasties.

Neither is the existence of despotism refuted by the constant and fierce struggle

When I constructed my "ideal model" of despotism, I was not familiar with Wittfogel's work; I had never had occasion to encounter it in Moscow, and I am not sure that more than a couple of scholars had read it there. I am glad, however, that, at least in certain essential points, the "construction" which I now intend to offer the reader echoes Wittfogel's description.

3. Despotism

This is how it looks. Despotism is based on the total disposition by the administration of the results of the society's economic activity. The despotic state, possessing supreme sovereignty over the entire national product (that is, being able to extract it without hindrance from the producers), *does not recognize economic limitations on its power.* The absence of economic limitations, by paralyzing the initiative of the producers, naturally leads—in historical perspective—to more or less permanent stagnation. In other words, despotism is incapable of radical economic modernization.

The lack of what we call economic progress is combined with an absence of political dynamism—with what can be called *the simple political reproduction* of despotism. This confirms Montesquieu's assertion that despotism excludes the historical movement of society. In order to exist for millennia under conditions of economic and political immobility, despotism had to work out a special kind of social structure. It is characterized by extreme simplification and polariza-

---

within despotic elites—a struggle which at times made despots dependent on their own bureaucratic power base, as Balazs asserts with regard to China (E. Balazs, *Chinese Civilisation and Bureaucracy*), or on bureaucrats who had succeeded temporarily in turning themselves into semifeudal landlords, as Christensen asserts for Sassanid Persia (see A. Christensen, *L'Iran sous les Sassanides*), or on a priestly oligarchy, as Andreski asserts relative to Egypt during the so-called New Kingdom (S. Andreski, *Elements of Comparative Sociology*, p. 167). Quite the contrary: even Iurii Krizhanich knew that the intraelite struggle, and the dependence of the despot on it, is a *generic trait* of despotism and the cause of its always having been *a structure with an unstable leadership.*

And, in any case, none of these objections alters the fact that there is a class of political structures known to history which over the course of millennia experienced *no political development*, and as a consequence proved incapable of changing their fundamental parameters—if you like, their paradigms—from within. It seems to me that this is what Krizhanich, Montesquieu, Hegel, Jones, and Tocqueville had in mind when they wrote about despotism. Until this is refuted, the phenomenon of despotism requires study, regardless of what attitude we take toward Wittfogel's conception; for he was the first—after Montesquieu—to place what I call the science of despotology in the focus of our attention with such force and clarity.

tion of society—by its reduction into two polar classes: "the governors" and "the governed."[7]

To the economic immobility of this system there corresponds the immobility of the class of the governed (the reduction to a minimum of what is called in modern sociology the horizontal mobility of the population, and its lack of political differentiation, so that the administration confronts not politically discrete society, but a uniform mass of subjects, hypothetically equal before the person of the despot.[8]

The reverse side of this political uniformity of the class of the governed is the equally absolute atomization and instability of the class of the governors—that is, a completely chaotic process of vertical mobility. The selection of top administrative personnel is carried out without regard to corporate membership, to privileges of estate, to wealth, or to ability. Despotism does not know what might be called the category of "political death." Members of the governing class, regardless of rank, pay for mistakes, as a rule, not only with the loss of the privileges connected with rank and the wealth they have accumulated, but with their heads as well. A mistake is equivalent to death. Thus the atomized, unstable elite of despotism, wandering their whole lives in the minefield of the despot's caprices, can never be transformed into an aristocracy—that is, into an elite which is hereditary and therefore independent of the regime, able to compel the system to take into consideration its goals and even to subject the system to these goals. In the absence of stable privileges, the possibility of even the primary form of *social limitations on power* disappears.[9] In

7. Cf. Wittfogel: "The men of the apparatus state are a ruling class in the most unequivocal sense of the term; and the rest of the population constitutes the second major class, the ruled" (p. 303).

8. Cf. Hegel: "In China we have the realm of absolute equality, and all the differences that exist are possible only in connection with the administration, and by virtue of the worth which a person may acquire, enabling him to fill a high post in the government. Since equality prevails in China, but without any freedom, despotism is necessarily the mode of government. . . . The emperor is the center, around which everything turns; consequently, the well-being of the country and people depends on him. . . . There is no other legal power or institution extant, but the superintendance and oversight of the emperor. . . . In China the distinction between slavery and freedom is necessarily not great, since all are equal before the emperor—that is, all alike degraded. . . . And though there is no distinction conferred by birth, and everyone can attain the highest dignity, this very equality testifies to no triumphant assertion of the worth of the inner man, but a servile consciousness" (*Lectures on the Philosophy of History*, pp. 130, 133–4, 137, 145).

9. To the best of my knowledge, this subject was first discussed on a theoretical level by Iurii Krizhanich in the seventeenth century. A Croatian by nationality and a gradu-

other words, the independence of the despot, not only from the class
of the governed but also from that of the governors, is absolute. This
confirms Aristotle's view of despotism as a permanent tyranny, under
which the system is subordinated to "the interests of the ruler alone."

It was Montesquieu who pointed to the role of a different category
of latent limitations on power—*the ideological ones.* He directly connected the degree of stability—or, as he put it, the "susceptibility to
corruption"—of political systems, with their observance of the domi-
nating "principle" of each. Whereas he considered the principle of
monarchy to be the "feeling of honor," he assumed that the principle
of despotism was exclusively that of fear. "Moderate government,"
Montesquieu wrote, generalizing from the political experience of his
time, "can relax the reins as much as it likes, and without danger to
itself. . . . But if, under a despotic government, the sovereign drops
his hands even for a moment, so that he cannot immediately destroy

---

ate of the Catholic college in Rome, Krizhanich had dreamed of Moscow all through his
youth. Finally getting there in the 1660s, he lived in Moscow for only sixteen months
and paid for his liberty of thought with sixteen years of Siberian exile. In the second
half of the 1670s, during the brief "thaw" following the death of Aleksei Mikhailovich,
he in desperation obtained permission to go abroad, where he immediately died in
Vienna. To this day his works await complete translation into Russian (they were written in Old Slavonic). We know that, in the period of the "thaw" just mentioned, his book
Politika was extremely popular in the "upper reaches" of the Muscovite government of
that time.

Like Montesquieu, Krizhanich was concerned primarily with the problem of guar-
anties against despotism. Whereas Persia under the rule of the *shahanshah* served as the
starting-point for Montesquieu's reflections, for Krizhanich this starting point was Turkey under the sultan. "The Turks," he reasoned,

> pay no attention to pedigree (since there is no boyardom among them), but say
> that they look for skill, intelligence, and valor. However, this is not really so, and
> frequently their prominent men are people of no merit, though skillful at flat-
> tery. Thus with one wave of the hand, the lowest become the highest, and the
> highest the lowest. This deprives people of any courage and begets a sense of
> worthlessness and despair. For no one can be sure of his position, wealth, or the
> safety of his life, and no one has reason to work hard for the sake of high honor
> or glory (*Politika,* p. 348).

"The European kings act better, in that along with other good qualities they also look
for noble birth," he notes in contrast.

> After all, men of noble birth, who from ancient times have possessed a
> glorious name and broad estates, take more care to preserve the kingdom and
> their estate in an honourable condition, and more care of the ancient name of
> their clan. . . . Furthermore, the boyars in their youth have more time to learn
> the sciences than do plain people (ibid.).

But along with Turkey, Krizhanich had in mind another sad example: Poland,
where it was precisely the privilege of the aristocracy which had led to chaos and anar-

the people occupying the highest places in the state, then all is lost."[10] And fear as the principle of a system requires, according to Montesquieu, the extreme limitation of the number of political ideas in circulation at any given moment. "Everything must turn on two or three ideas, and no new ones at all are needed. When training an animal, one must be very careful of changing the trainer or the method of instruction: one must hit its brain with two or three movements, no more."[11]

Thus, according to Montesquieu, the negation of *ideological limitations on power* through the minimization and standardization of ideas is an attribute of despotism, which deprives the administration of feedback from the system, excludes any mechanism for correcting mistakes, and consequently makes the personal power of the despot extremely unstable. Of course, Montesquieu describes this in other terms. He says that the despotic principle does not permit either judgment, objections, or independent opinions on the part of executives, and is therefore more subject than other systems to "corruption." Furthermore, it is "corrupted constantly, since it is corrupt by its nature."

What Montesquieu did not articulate with sufficient clarity is the connection between the negation of economic and ideological limitations. But, after all, despotism needs the minimization of ideas precisely for this, so that the thought of the possibility of challenging the constant plundering of the economy cannot even arise. This is why it

---

chy. In the face of this dilemma, insoluble at first glance (at least, as we shall see below, for Soviet historians), Krizhanich does what a scholar must do: he *differentiates among privileges*. There are three kinds of political structures, he reflects. In some, "immoderate privileges" lead to anarchy (Poland); in others, the absence of privileges leads to "tormenting of people," which is what Krizhanich calls despotism (Turkey). The optimum, from his point of view, is a state which permits "moderate privileges" to the aristocracy, which serve as a guarantee against despotism, defending the people against arbitrary action by the authorities, and the king himself against arbitrary action by his own servants. "Among the French and the Spanish," he says,

> the rulers have decent hereditary advantages and privileges, and for this reason neither the plain people nor the military cause the kings any dishonor. And among the Turks, where there are no privileges for people of noble birth, the kings are dependent on the brazen impudence of their simple soldiers. For what the janissaries want, that the king must do (ibid., p. 599).

In other words, what we now call social limitations on power were, in Krizhanich's eyes, "the only method of maintaining justice in the kingdom," and "the only means by which subjects can be defended against the abuse of the king's servants" (ibid., p. 593).

10. Montesquieu, pp. 31–32.
11. Ibid., p. 64.

is compelled to take under its control not only the material, but also the intellectual product of the country. Administering not only people but ideas as well, it must rob the heads of its subjects with as much care as it robs their coffers. Thus, intellectual robbery turns out to be only the reverse side of material robbery. *A regime which denies economic limitations cannot help denying ideological ones.*

This also explains the monstrous stability of despotic systems, since it excludes the possibility of the emergence of a political opposition (or reformist potential) which sets itself the goal not simply of replacing the current occupant of the throne, but of bringing about a qualitative change in the system based on an alternative model of political organization. Victorious mass uprisings in medieval China, for example, which immediately and slavishly copied the despotic structure just destroyed, but with new personnel, confirm Wittfogel's conclusion as to the absence in despotic structures of a political opposition.[12] This inability of despotism to transcend itself even in thought indicates not only its incapacity for institutional modernization, which is already known to us, but also—what is even more important—its tragic incapacity for self-demolition. It can be destroyed only from without.

The absence of these latent limitations—social, economic, and ideological—leads to the inability of despotic systems to resist being subjected to the private goals of the despot. This naturally may lead to mistakes, for the correction of which, as we already know, no mechanism other than murder is envisaged in despotic systems. As paradoxical as this may seem, the death of the despot proves to be the sole means of correcting mistakes of administration. It is precisely the immense degree of divergence of goals, deriving in the last analysis from the complete autonomy of the administration from the system, which makes the unlimited personal power of the despot just as absolutely unstable as despotism itself, considered as a political structure, is absolutely stable.

12. "In contrast to the independent writers who, under Western absolutism, challenged not only the excesses but the foundation of the despotic order, the critics of hydraulic society have in almost every case complained only of the misdeeds of individual officials or of the evils of specific governmental acts. Apart from mystics who teach total withdrawal from the world, these critics aim ultimately at regenerating a system of total power, whose fundamental desirability they do not doubt . . . the embittered subject . . . may defeat the government's men in arms. They may even overthrow a tottering dynasty. But eventually they will only revive—and rejuvenate—the agromanagerial despotism whose incompetent representatives they eliminated. The heroes of China's famous bandit novel, the *Shui-hu-Ch'uan*, could think of nothing better to do than to set up on their rebel island a miniature version of the very bureaucratic hierarchy which they were so fiercely combatting" (K. Wittfogel, pp. 134–35).

For this reason, it is not so much the safety of the system as his personal safety which is the point of the despot's political activity. The sole means of securing this safety proves to be permanent, universal, and fruitless terror[13]—fruitless because, being a terrorist structure par excellence, despotism nevertheless begins and ends as *a structure with an unstable leadership*. During the thousand years of Byzantium's existence, for example, some fifty of its emperors were drowned, blinded, or strangled—an average of one every twenty years.

Naturally, some despots give more attention to the economic functions of the state (manifesting, as Wittfogel has it, "the maximum rationality of the ruler"), and others to wars and conquests. Some succeed, and others suffer defeat. As a result of this, the state experiences fluctuations, periods of expansion and decline. However, no predictability is observed in the alternation of these periods. They are as chaotic as the selection of leadership personnel, as the "purges of the elite," as the rise and fall of the wazirs, ministers, and favorites of the despots, or of the despots themselves. In despotic systems, only unpredictability is predictable.[14]

Considering that permanent economic stagnation placed the system in complete dependence on natural catastrophes and hostile invasions, and that the absence of any limitations on power created a situation of political unpredictability and chaos, in which everyone from the despot himself to his least servant was constantly balancing between life and death, we may say that despotism was subject to the play of elemental forces to such a degree that it is more reminiscent of a phenomenon of nature than of a political commonwealth. And in this sense, by refusing it the status of a political phenomenon, Aristotle would seem to have been right once again. If something which is the polar opposite of civilization can exist, that something is despotism.[15]

13. Wittfogel speaks of it as "routine terror in managerial, fiscal, and judicial procedures that caused certain observers to designate the government of hydraulic despotism as 'government by flogging'" (ibid., p. 143). In another place he speaks of "the standard methods of terror" (ibid., p. 149). Nevertheless, it may be in order to note here that both Montesquieu, with his "principle of fear," and Wittfogel, with his "routine terror," are somewhat simplifying the picture. They never make the distinction between the elites of the despotic states, the "governors," for whom the terror was indeed routine, and the population, "the governed," for whom the terror was at least to a degree tempered by ancient tradition.

14. "Unpredictability is an essential weapon of absolute terror," Wittfogel notes (ibid., p. 141).

15. Of course, the world which seemed to Aristotle an impenetrable darkness may seem to people of another culture a world of eternal equilibrium and harmony—if not entirely just, then at least a tolerable alternative to the restless, dynamic world of "progress." For example, Senator Raul Manglapus, a well-known Filipino politician, and at

Thus, despite the many great empires in which it prevailed—the Egyptian, Assyrian, Chinese, Persian, Mongol, Byzantine, Turkish, and more—despotism has proved to be a political dead end. For all the variety of palace coups, mutinies, putsches, Praetorian conspiracies, and janissary rebellions, it reproduced itself without interruption over the course of centuries in all of its lifeless integrity. This was a closed system, the parameters of which were rigidly laid down in pre-Christian millennia. Its world was an isolated one, like a planetary orbit, exempt from the laws of probability, deprived of choice and real movement. It knew no political alternative. In this sense, it was a spectre. It existed outside history. Of course, like everything else in the cosmos, it moved. But after all, the planets also move: only their orbits are fixed.

4. Absolutism

As the reader may now guess, what I intend to suggest for the classification of authoritarian political structures (and, concretely, for distinguishing absolutism from despotism) will be the conception of latent limitations on power which we have just constructed, summarizing the observations of Aristotle, Krizhanich, Montesquieu, Hegel, and Wittfogel.

In juridical terms, all medieval authoritarian structures are indistinguishable from one another. That is, the source of sovereignty in them is the person of the ruler, to whom God has directly delegated

---

one time (in 1965) even a candidate for the presidency of that country, described the despotic mode of existence in the following terms only a decade ago: "Once all of Asia was in a state of equilibrium, with its agrarian societies relying for survival on a delicate balance between land and population. Land suitable for rice-growing was limited and rice-eating populations struggled for subsistence; they had neither the time, ability nor energy to think of governing themselves or even of participating in government. The task of governing was left to the few, a small, specialized class of scholar-officials. To labor and obey was left to the many. Thus the centralized state came into being, strong enough to protect these precarious balances from ever-threatening natural or artificial forces, skilled enough to undertake the control of the flow of water, the life-blood of the staple production. . . . Confucius gave this stability a philosophic base which sanctified harmony and reverence for authority. . . . This kind of equilibrium was to last four thousand years, until one day Western man arrived with ideas more explosive than the powder the Chinese had invented for firecrackers at the harvest festival (and which the Westerner would later push into the mouths of cannon)" ("Asian Revolution and American Ideology," pp. 344–45).

Sigmund Freud asserted that there are no accidental slips of the tongue, and the fact that Senator Manglapus uses the word "survival" instead of "life" serves, it seems to me, as an exhaustive commentary on the passage quoted here.

the functions of administration, thus freeing the ruler from any control whatever by the system. All of them openly declared their freedom from any limitations, and all of them claimed this freedom to an equal degree.

Nevertheless, John Fortescue distinguished "royal government" from "political." For Jean Bodin, the distinction between monarchy and "seignorial government" was of prime importance. Mercier de la Riviere made a profound distinction between "arbitrary" and "legal" despotism. And Montesquieu, as we have seen, predicted that political catastrophe would ensue from the transformation of absolute monarchy into despotism. In other words, despite the formal identity of all monarchical structures, their contemporaries felt and saw, and furthermore considered vitally important, *not their similarity but the differences between them.* If we summarize all of their attempts, we can say that they stubbornly tried to create some kind of typology of authoritarian structures capable of serving as a kind of basis for political recommendations and prognoses. This was a typology which, if it were to remain within the limits of reality, had to be based on something other than juridical definitions (which no self-respecting absolute monarch would have agreed to recognize). But in that case, what would have been its basis?[16]

16. I understand that the argument about the differences between European political structures and despotism is customarily conducted within the limits of the concept of feudalism. But there is a problem here, inasmuch as there is as yet no agreement as to one small detail: namely, what feudalism is. In one authoritative source, it is defined as follows: "Feudalism is primarily a method of government . . . in which the essential relation is not that between ruler and subject, nor state and citizen, but between lord and vassal" (*Feudalism in History*, pp. 4–5). The forefather of the Russian "absolutists," N. P. Pavlov-Sil'vanskii, in attempting to demonstrate the membership of Russia in the European family, thought it sufficient to assert (in his monograph *Feodalism v drevnei Rusi*), that a feudal hierarchy—that is, relations between lord and vassal—also existed in Russia. Correspondingly, the "despotists" try to show that in Russia—as distinct from Europe—such relations did not exist (see, for example, Tibor Szamuely, *The Russian Tradition*).

However, the authoritative definition of feudalism quoted above is criticized both in the West and in the East. On the one hand, we encounter the following conclusion: "The existence of a hierarchy is no longer thought to be a prerequisite to feudalism in the West, largely because the neat hierarchy assumed to have existed in the West is found to have been virtually a phantom" (Oswald P. Backus III, "The Problem of Unity in the Polish-Lithuanian State," p. 650). On the other hand, Soviet historians have attempted to make the concept of feudalism universal, by declaring it to be one of the stages in the development of mankind and thereby extending it not only to Russia but to the entire *oikumene*: "the Marxist-Leninist conception of the fundamental features of feudalism . . . as a special socioeconomic order . . . is formulated with extreme clarity in *Capital* by Karl Marx and in *The Development of Capitalism in Russia* by V. I. Lenin.

Absolutism, as distinct from despotism, did not possess supreme sovereignty over the entire national product, because it was compelled to tolerate economic limitations on power. Although the most extreme of its apologists proclaimed the right of kings to the property of their subjects, this was never taken as an axiom and was always disputed, both in theory and in practice.[17]

In practice, the attempts to implement this right ran up against the resistance of the system, often ending tragically for the absolute monarchs. In theory, it was precisely on economic limitations to power that the distinction between monarchy and its potential "deviations" was based. Jean Bodin—a contemporary of Ivan the Terrible's and the author of a classic apologia for absolutism which exercised colossal influence on the entire ideological tradition of this structure— appeared in his *The Commonwealth* to be no less radical, at first glance, than Ivan the Terrible in his letters to Kurbskii. He, too, assumed that "on earth there is nothing higher after God than sovereign princes, established by Him as His lieutenants for the governing of people," and that he who "withholds his respect from a sovereign prince, also withholds respect from God, whose image on earth the prince is."[18] Furthermore, Bodin, as distinct from the Aristotelian tradition, considered the essential mark of the citizen to be, not participation in courts and councils, but just the reverse—unconditional submission to the unlimited power of the monarch. But, for all this, Bodin regarded the property of citizens as their inalienable possession, in the disposition of which they were no less sovereign than was the monarch in ruling his people. To tax citizens of a part of their inalienable

---

. . . Its [the social order's] essence is determined by the character of the socioeconomic relationships. The concentration of the means of production, and primarily landed property, in the hands of a ruling class of feudal lords is decisive" (*Kritika burzhuaznykh kontseptsii istorii Rossii perioda feodalizma*, pp. 30, 31). Unfortunately from this it follows "with extreme clarity" only that both despotism and absolutism are equally based on the concentration of the means of production in the hands of a ruling class of feudal lords. Among "feudal lords," the Soviet historians indiscriminately include English barons, Chinese mandarins, Polish pans, and Turkish effendis. But if the "base" was the same, how their "superstructures" come to differ from each other is mysterious. For all these reasons, I have thought it better not to broach this delicate and painful subject here.

17. It is said that when a French diplomat referred in conversation with a British colleague to the well-known declaration of Louis XIV as to the wealth of kings ("Everything which is within the limits of their state belongs to them . . . both the money in their treasuries . . . and that which they leave in circulation among their subjects"), the Englishman replied haughtily: "Did you study public law in Turkey?"

18. Quoted in N. N. Kareev, *Zapadno-evropeiskaia absolutnaia monarkhiia XVI, XVII i XVIII vekov*, p. 330.

property without their voluntary consent was, from Bodin's point of view, ordinary robbery.

Ivan the Terrible, with his sharply polemical temperament, would undoubtedly have seen a logical contradiction in Bodin's conception. And he would have been right. But the essence of the phenomenon of absolutism was contained in this logical contradiction. Absolutism actually was a paradox, albeit a living paradox which lasted for centuries.

Bodin's "contradiction" points up a significant deformation in the integrity of the supposedly unlimited political body, with its constant assertions of divine sovereignty. King François I of France, a contemporary of Ivan III's, in desperate need of money, did not, for example, plunder Marseilles, as any despot would have done in his place (and as Ivan the Terrible did in an analogous situation by pillaging Novgorod), but instead put judicial offices up for sale, thereby involuntarily creating a new privileged stratum—that of hereditary judges—and a new institution, the parliaments. The very fact that these offices were bought, and, consequently, that the government was trusted, and that even in the deepest tyrannical twilight of France these privileges were never violated, is of primary historical importance—a kind of institutional materialization of the apparently ephemeral political paradox of absolutism. Here is how Professor N. Kareev describes this phenomenon: "The unlimited monarchy was compelled to tolerate around itself autonomous corporations of hereditary judges: each of them and all of them together could perhaps be sent wherever the king liked, but they could not be expelled from their posts, because this would have meant . . . *to violate the right of property.*"[19] Bodin, in formulating his contradiction, was simply summarizing the actual practice of his time. And this practice showed that absolutism was compelled to tolerate economic limitations on power.

The presence of these economic limitations, making possible autonomous economic activity on the part of producers, excluded permanent stagnation, and made absolutism capable of fundamental economic modernization and expanded reproduction of the gross national product. The capacity for economic progress characteristic of absolutist structures was combined with their capacity for political dynamism, and for what could be called *expanded political reproduction.* Their gradual transformation into democratic structures leaves no doubt of this.

In place of the reduction and polarization of social forces charac-

19. Ibid., p. 130.

teristic of despotism, absolutism was marked by a multiplicity of social strata. Variety and inequality were its hallmarks. Not immobility and uniformity, but, on the contrary, social and economic differentiation of the peasantry, its constant migration into the cities, and, consequently, urbanization and the formation of a strong middle class, were the leading processes in absolutist societies.

The rapid horizontal mobility in absolutist structures was logically accompanied by well-ordered vertical mobility, based on social limitations of power. In practical terms, this meant that the elevation of the new bureaucratic elite of absolutism brought with it not the dissolution of the hereditary aristocracy in universal service, but a competitive struggle between old and new elites. This constitutes one of the most dramatic differences between absolutism and despotism. Despite the multiplicity of conflicts and the constant, sometimes bloody and cruel struggle of the elites, absolutism agreed to *coexist* with aristocracy, while despotism *did not allow it to come into existence*.

This not only assured the members of the absolutist elite of the right to "political death" (and thereby deprived their struggle of the character of a brutal fight for physical survival), but also created the very possibility of a political struggle, and therefore the mechanism for correcting mistakes in administration, not to speak of powerful sources of independent thought and behavior.

At this point, we may perhaps express a cautious hypothesis: just as the existence of the middle class, being a function of economic limitations, created the possibility of transforming absolutism into democracy, so the existence of the aristocracy, being a function of social limitations, prevented the transformation of absolutist structures into despotism. In other words, *just as democracy is impossible without a middle class, so absolutism is impossible without an aristocracy.*

For despotism, as we have seen, ideological robbery was the other side of robbery of property. The political practice of absolutism gives us the opportunity to prove this theorem, as the mathematicians say, from the inverse. Namely: the absence of robbery of property should lead to the absence of ideological robbery. And, in fact, not being subject to permanent corruption—in other words, not fearing the destruction of its power at any moment—absolutism did not see a mortal threat in the multiplicity of ideas. It therefore spared not only the material potential of the country, but also its intellectual potential, and made no attempt at an ideological monopoly. That is, along with administrative and political functions, it did not also perform an ideological one.

Recognizing the latent limitations on power, absolutism thereby involuntarily promoted the coming into being of a political opposition—that is, the working out of alternative models of political organization. The existence of reformist potential and of alternative models, in turn, made qualitative change in the system possible. It developed out of its own resources.

This excluded terror as a *universal means of administration*. In Europe, as Herzen once said, there was also terror, but it did not occur to anyone to flog Spinoza or to induct Lessing into the army. Even in Spain, which "deviated" in the direction of tyranny more than other European countries, a place was found for Cervantes and Lope de Vega. England knew the heavy hand of Henry VIII and the horrors of Bloody Mary, but for all that, the *Utopia* of Thomas More and the *Novum Organum* of Bacon were written there. France, which saw the massacre of the Huguenots by the Catholics, also found room for Rabelais and Montaigne.

This, of course, does not mean that in the despotic states, during the times of individual "enlightened despots," there were not court astronomers and poets who sometimes achieved great successes in the politically insensitive areas of art and science. The culture of despotism tolerated good poetry and medicine, preserved the works of Aristotle, and created great religious philosophies—which, however, preached not the transformation of reality but escape from it as from an embodiment of chaos. It was a politically mute culture.

Naturally, a certain degree of divergence between the goals of the administration and those of the system is characteristic of all authoritarian structures without exception. Partly for this reason, absolutist governments always found themselves under financial stress, owed gigantic debts, and were never able to achieve a normal balance of income and expenditures. A financial cul-de-sac occasioned the calling of the Long Parliament which ended by sending King Charles I to the block, and the same is true of the Estates General which ended by guillotining Louis XVI. The Austrian constitutional bodies also owed their origin to a financial collapse combined with a military defeat. At the beginning of the eighteenth century, the interest on the British national debt was equal to the entire expenditures on the army and navy, and the debt of Austria exceeded its annual income three-and-a-half times, while in France the national debt was eighteen times the annual revenues of the state. Such was the disordered financial system of absolutism, which originated for the most part in ruinous wars, unskilled management, and vestiges of medieval organization in the economy, which obviously contradicted the goals of the system.

Despotism did not know any of this. It did not live on credit, since no one would have extended a penny's worth of credit to it. It lived by constant robbery of its own people. And thus, it was not only parasitic on the body of the system, as was absolutism, but systematically *disorganized* the system, not allowing it to stand on its feet.

If the reader gets the impression that I am writing an apologia for absolutism, this is only because it is being compared with despotism. Absolutism was a cruel, often bloody and tyrannical authoritarian structure, striving, insofar as this was possible for it, to trample underfoot not only the political, but also the civil rights of its subjects. Louis XI was not a whit better than Shah Abbas, and Henry VIII was no more pleasant than Suleiman the Magnificent. Any authoritarian structure strives to deviate toward despotism, as a compass needle toward the north. Despotism is its ideal, its dream, its crown. But for absolutism it was an unattainable dream—for even in "deviating" toward tyranny, it could never make this tyranny permanent. And it could not do this because the latent limitations on power which it had had to endure did not permit it to disorganize the system to the degree of chronic stagnation.

5. The Historical Function of Absolutism

I understand that the reader may, for these last few pages, have been haunted by the feeling that I am retailing copybook maxims, some of which were known even to the students of Aristotle. In fact, what have we gotten from all of these elementary comparisons? We have examined two equally authoritarian political structures, between which it is impossible to discover any formal juridical difference, and which—on the level of political organization—resemble each other like twins. In one type of state, the government commits violence against its own people; in the other, they are also hanged and enslaved. In the first type, the kings proclaim the unlimited nature of their power, as they also do in the second. In the first type, wars or conquests are waged, rebels slaughtered, and the oppressed peasantry robbed—and so, too, in the second type.

Does this not give us the right to say that there existed—in ancient times and in the Middle Ages, in the East and in the West—simply a certain continuum of authoritarian structures (or traditional—i.e., "unmodernized"—political bodies), a continuum within which we can calmly call absolutism an unrealized despotism, and despotism a realized absolutism? We have yet to see how many experts, both in the East and in the West, do precisely this. And I would have no objection in principle, if the proclamation of such a continuum were not intended to obscure the most essential result of our comparisons. Namely, that the poles of this "continuum" are not only different, but also the very antithesis of each other. Their opposition consists in the fact that, by virtue of all the reasons set forth above, one of them was destined for self-development, and the other was incapable even of self-destruction. It consists in the fact that absolutism *declared* the unlimited nature of its power, while despotism *practiced* it.

The use of the terms "despotism" and absolutism" as synonyms is what hinders our analysis of these political structures. Citing the cruelty, aggressiveness, and authoritarian methods of both, we confuse the "deviation" of absolute monarchies toward tyranny under Louis XI and Henry VIII with the despotism of Shah Abbas and Suleiman the Magnificent. Failure to perceive their antithetical nature—whether by placing them within the limits of a "continuum" or of a conception of "traditional" society—renders our theorizing sterile. Civilization was able to continue precisely because there existed authoritarian structures which, by virtue of certain historical causes, were compelled to tolerate latent limitations on power. We can now formulate this as follows: *the degree of divergence between the goals of the system and those of the administration in authoritarian structures is inversely proportional to the number of latent limitations which they are compelled to tolerate.*

In addition to the three types of latent limitations which have already been mentioned, and which are more or less obvious, there also exists a fourth, whose stratum lies deepest, and which is hardest to grasp, but on which, as their foundation, all the others rest.

Let us assume that in some country the powers that be perceive a political problem—mutiny and opposition—in the hairstyle of their subjects, in the length of their clothes, and in their habit of smoking tobacco. Let us suppose that they consider it their duty to regulate these intimate details by means of police measures and administrative decrees. It is difficult to imagine that even such obvious tyrants as Henry VIII or Louis XIV would have claimed the sole right to determine the width of the farthingale worn by court ladies, or the length of gentlemen's sleeves. For this purpose there existed more subtle mechanisms, in the shape of public decencies or fashions. But in Russia the powers that be knew best how many fingers people should cross themselves with, and how long their beards should be, and whether they should smoke tobacco, drink vodka, and desire or not desire their neighbors' wives. Tsar Aleksei did furious battle against shaving, while Peter the Great, on the other hand, looked on the beards of his subjects as an offense and an act of rebellion, and agreed to tolerate them only as a special item in the revenue. Tsar Mikhail strictly forbade the use of tobacco, and Peter, in turn, sold to the Marquis de Carmartin the sole right to poison the lungs of the Russians with nicotine. In 1692 a decree was issued forbidding civil servants to dress well, since "it is known that those service people who wear such expensive clothing make their fortunes not from their just earnings but by stealing from the treasury of our great sovereign." In other words, it was obvious to the authorities that one does not earn stone palaces by just labor, that even those who had not been caught before were to be considered thieves and their "earnings" themselves evidence of crime and sufficient grounds for punishment.

These details, however, are not the point, which is that people *recognized* the right of the authorities to interfere in the details of their private lives. Not only was a man's home not his castle, even his beard was not considered his property. People's very thoughts and tastes did not belong to them. The cultural tradition had not worked out defensive mechanisms which would have made such interference by the state impossible. Only the opposition—"the people on the right" (the Old Believers) and "the people on the left" (the intelligentsia)—were able to resist such interference in autocratic Russia.

Here we approach directly the phenomenon of political culture. In the context of our discussion, this can most conveniently be defined as the totality of limitations on power, reflected in automatic, everyday activity, and inherited from previous generations as a tradition.

A Connecticut Yankee in King Arthur's Court is a classic study of the conflict between two types of political culture brought face to face with each other. The Yankee is astonished that he has ended up "in a country where the right to say how the country should be governed was restricted to six persons in each thousand of its population. For the nine hundred and ninety-four to express dissatisfaction with the regnant system and propose to change it, would have made the whole six shudder as one man, it would have been so disloyal, so dishonorable, such putrid black treason. So to speak, I was become a stockholder in a corporation where nine hundred and ninety-four of the members furnished all the money and did all the work, and the other six elected themselves a permanent board of direction and took all the dividends. It seemed to me that what the nine hundred and ninety-four dupes needed was a new deal."[20]

The stock-market terminology applied to the analysis of authoritarian structures only seems comic. In fact, it describes the state of

20. Mark Twain, *A Connecticut Yankee in King Arthur's Court*, p. 160.

affairs with extreme precision. The democratic common sense of our Yankee rebels precisely because he evaluates the situation from the point of view of a political culture inherited from his Puritan forebears, who wrote it into the constitution of the state of Connecticut that "all political power is inherent in the people, and . . . they have *at all times* an undeniable and indefeasible right to *alter their form of government* in such manner as they may think expedient."[21]

Let us assume for a moment, however, that our Yankee had visited not the kingdom of King Arthur, but the land of Pharaoh Rameses or Sultan Bajazet. Far from waxing indignant over what the "irreplaceable six" would reply to a proposal that "the form of government be changed," he would be struck by the fact that the thought would not enter anyone's mind. To drown the sultan is an excellent idea, and to strangle the tax-collector or the wazir is still better. But to change the form of government? Unthinkable!

In order for this to become not only conceivable, but necessary, a cultural tradition, independent means of subsistence, sophisticated political thought, inherited aristocratic privileges, and a political opposition are all needed—in short, everything which gives rise to latent limitations on power. And this is the essence of the political culture generated by absolutism.

Of course, the presence of these limitations is not sufficient in itself immediately to bring about a new deal. The constitution which determines the Connecticut Yankee's weltanschauung did not fall from heaven. It was won in the mud and blood of revolution and reaction, religious revolts, terror and desperation, trade, slavery, and wars. As such, it is a certificate of the maturity of the political culture of its creators—testimony to successful completion of the elementary school of political history and their ability to transform latent limitations on power into open political control of the system over the administration.

Just as an individual becomes a personality only when he is able to choose his own fate autonomously, so a human collectivity becomes a people only when it learns to limit the authority of the administration and thereby to affect the fate of its country. From this moment, the people may begin to realize that not only the sultan or the pharaoh, but the "form of government" itself does not suit them particularly well. And does this not mean, perhaps, that neither pharaohs nor sultans nor chairmen of people's republics nor general secretaries of parties are needed?

21. Ibid., p. 159.

It is precisely in this—the gradual accumulation of limitations on power transformed into a cultural tradition—that political progress consists, in my opinion. And political progress itself, from the viewpoint being offered here, can be interpreted as the history of the birth, maturation, and stabilization of latent limitations on power— of their *transformation* into political limitations. It was the historical function of absolutism to be the cultural school of mankind. Only by passing through this school was humanity capable of producing a Yankee who, although he might completely forget the path traversed by his ancestors, would be able, in case of need, to reshuffle the cards and deal them again.

6. Russian Autocracy

Let us now see whether either of our "ideal constructions" describes Russian political history.[22]

In the first place, was the political organization of Russia based on supreme sovereignty of the state over the entire national product? The Russian state intervened in the economic process and attempted to regulate it. However, it did so in a very uneven way. Whereas in the epoch of Peter I or Stalin this intervention was maximal, and sometimes total, at other times it was reduced as far as the historical context permitted. In any case, it lost its total character. It is sufficient to recall the difference between the Oprichnina of Ivan the Terrible (the outstanding Soviet historian I. I. Polosin called it "the war communism of the Muscovite tsar") and the reign of Mikhail Fedorovich, when decisions on new taxes were not taken without the agreement of the Assemblies of the Land, which sometimes remained in session continuously for months. Recall, too, the differences between the "war communism" of the twentieth century and Lenin's NEP.[23]

This alternation prevented the permanent stagnation of the econ-

22. Here and below, when Russian political history is spoken of, reference will be only to its autocratic period—that is, the time following the Oprichnina revolution of 1564.

23. Under despotism, the state's intervention in the economic process was connected with its primitive condition, with the dispersion of the rural communes, and their subsistence economy, and thus served the goal of integrating the stagnant economic organism. In Russia, on the contrary, the intervention of the state increased and became more active as the economic process became more complex, until, finally, in the twentieth century, in the period of its radical modernization and industrialization, the state took this process under its complete control. But even in the twentieth century, as we know, the intensity of this control continued to vary, now hardening and then relaxing.

omy characteristic of despotism. But it also excluded the more or less consistent development of the economy characteristic of absolutism. In place of this, Russia evolved *a third type of economic development, which combined short phases of feverish modernization with long periods of prostration.*[24]

Similarly, it is impossible to describe Russian political development as the simple political reproduction characteristic of despotism. But, on the other hand, neither did Russia develop consistently in the direction of growth of latent limitations on power into political limitations, as was characteristic of absolutism. Instead it evolved *a third type of political development, combining radical change in the institutional structure with the preservation of the basic parameters of its political construction.*

It is sufficient to compare pre-Petrine Russia with post-Petrine; prereform and postreform; prerevolutionary and postrevolutionary, in order to grasp this unique characteristic of its political process, which may be described as the dominance of political heredity over institutional variability.

The reduction of the social structure to two polar classes—governors and governed—was never a constant phenomenon in Russian political history. Whereas Ivan the Terrible, Peter the Great, and Stalin had some success with this, subsequent epochs destroyed their achievements without trace, and the Russian social structure gave birth anew to variety and inequality. In other words, *the social process in Russia had the same alternating character as its economic and political processes.*

Perhaps the most dramatic difference which distinguishes the Russian political structure from both absolutism and despotism lies, however, in the peculiarities in the formation of the Russian elites. In some periods, the administration in Russia, in order to achieve complete independence from the "upper" classes, strove to undermine the existing elites, sometimes to the point of their destruction. For example, the "revolution from above" carried out by Ivan the Terrible not only liquidated the political significance of the Boyar Duma (the basic institution through which the traditional corporate aristocracy influenced the political decision-making process), but also sought to destroy the very basis of its existence—its hereditary property, the *votchiny.* There began a rapid process of transformation of the *votchiny* into *pomest'ia* (holdings conditional on state service, analogous to

---

24. This peculiarity of the economic development of Russia was first described by Alexander Gershenkron (in *Continuity and Change in Russian and Soviet Thought*; see also his *Economic Backwardness in Historical Perspective*). Gershenkron did not, however, connect it with the specific character of the Russian political structure.

the despotic model). A new phenomenon, previously unheard of, emerged from this attempt to abolish the social limitations on power. No stratum of the existing establishment was politically interested in the system's "deviating" so far toward tyranny, all the more so in that such a "deviation" was fraught with total terror and indiscriminate plundering of the entire country. Hence the tyrant had to create a political base unknown in both European and Asian experience—a special stratum or "new class," as it were. The tsar had to invent this practically out of nothing—"out of stone," as Kurbskii expressed it. It comprised people from all walks of life, the dregs of all strata of society, the lowest as well as the highest, with a significant inclusion of international adventurers.

This first "new class" in Russian history, a savage elite that was both ignorant and servile, is known to historians as the *dvorianstvo* (nobility). Somehow it has escaped notice that this creation of the tyrant was not at all reminiscent of the haughty and refined *dvorianstvo* of the eighteenth and nineteenth centuries, a nobility which educated its children in special schools, spoke only French, and had forgotten how to write its native language. The *dvorianstvo* of the time of Ivan the Terrible, or what passed by that name, could not write Russian either. But for quite a different reason: they could not write at all.

In any case, it may seem that the final hour of the Russian aristocracy had struck, and that from this moment on it was to be irretrievably submerged in compulsory universal service. And here one of the most remarkable paradoxes of Russian history occurred: not only did the "new class" fail to fulfill its task and totally destroy the social limitations on power, it itself immediately began to be transformed into what I call the "new new class," a stratum suspiciously reminiscent of the old aristocracy. The destructive process of transformation of the traditional *votchiny* into *pomest'ia* in fact coincided and intertwined with a reverse process of transformation of the *pomest'ia* into *votchiny*. In the law code of 1649, less than a century after the Oprichnina revolution, it is already practically impossible to distinguish landed estates from *votchiny*. For the first time in Russian history, this episode proved that *the aristocratization of the elite is an organic and natural process in the Russian political system*, one which, like the differentiation of the peasantry, develops immediately and unavoidably whenever the tyrant does not halt it by terror.

For the most part, the terrorization has been carried out by a kind of "new class" comprising the same elements as the Oprichnina elite of Ivan the Terrible: people from the lower strata of the society, "experts" from the old elite, and international adventurers. At least, such was the case with Petrine *shliakhta*, a militant "new class" created by the tyrant in the 1700s. And the same paradox occurred again after the tyrant's demise: in the first half of the eighteenth century, the Petrine "new class" again underwent a transformation into a "new new class" which appeared to be a transitional form on its way to aristocratization. Moreover, this time it eventually triumphed. The siege it laid to the administration was so persistent and fierce that the series of women who succeeded one another on the Russian throne, from Anna to Catherine, proved unable to stabilize the system until they granted the "new class" the status of an aristocracy.

Unfortunately, this born-again Russian aristocracy happened to be a slave-holding stratum, which immeasurably weakened its political potential. Having won social emancipation from the government, it proved unable to achieve political emancipation, at least on a scale comparable with Russian boyardom before the Oprichnina revolution. In other words, while their estates were turned into *votchiny*, the new landowners did not become boyars.

As distinct from Ivan the Terrible and Peter the Great, the two dictatorships of the nineteenth century (Nicholas I's and Alexander III's) did not try to create their own "new classes," leaning instead on the conservative and Russophile segments of the existing elites. This made the two tyrannies in question significantly milder than their predecessors, but did not preserve the entrenched aristocracy from eventual extermination and replacement by the savage "new class" created by Lenin after the revolution of 1917 (again comprising the same three elements: people "from below," "bourgeois experts," and international adventurers).[25]

In any case, it seemed that this time the Russian aristocracy had been dealt a deathblow. But again the paradox of aristocratization occurred. Lenin's "new class" thirsted for privileges and independence,

25. The complex character of the "new class" perhaps helps us to understand the stubbornness of the insistence of the Russian new right in general, and Alexander Solzhenitsyn in particular, that the October revolution was violently imposed on the Russian nation by foreigners and thus is totally alien to Russian culture and tradition (see Alexander Yanov, *The Russian New Right*). While international adventurers indeed played a conspicuous role in the revolution of 1917, they played a no less distinguished part in the Oprichnina revolution, as well as in the Petrine one. Consequently, the role of international adventurers in the October revolution only confirms its national—one might say traditional—character, and Solzhenitsyn's argument falls apart. True, as distinct from all previous instances, Stalin's "new class" had a brutally nationalistic thrust (because of which, incidentally, some modern right-wingers could not help but sympathize with Stalin). It is perhaps explained by the fact that this time the "new class" was intended to destroy and replace an obviously "internationalistic" elite.

just as in the seventeenth century, and sought in turn to transform itself into a "new new class"—always the first step on the ladder of aristocratization. And, again as in the seventeenth century, this aristocratizing elite was crushed by a still newer class of Party apparatchiki. Joseph Stalin, systematically liberating himself from the control of the modern analog of the Assembly of the Land, the Central Committee of the Party, and the modern analog of the Boyar Duma, the Politburo, physically exterminated Lenin's elite.

This new catastrophe for the Russian elite, like the preceding ones, was, however, unable to halt aristocratization. Indeed, after the tyrant's demise, transformation of the Stalinist "new class" into a "new new class" began—a process which is taking place right now, this time before our eyes, in "modern" Brezhnevist Russia.[26]

Thus, in addition to a peculiar alternating pattern of economic, political, and social processes, *Russian autocracy developed a unique alternating pattern in the formation of its elites.* This pattern involves new and challenging phenomena unexplained (and perhaps inexplicable) by current political science: the periodic destruction of the elite, subsequent rearistocratization, and particularly the "new class" whose emergence we have had occasion to observe briefly in such absolutely different historical circumstances.

While the peculiarities of the Russian political structure consist in the fact that it has at times rejected and at others recognized social and economic limitations on power, its attitude toward ideological limitations has always been more or less hostile. But, once again, only "more or less." And here we can again see the connection between economic and ideological limitations. It has usually been the periods when the economic limitations were violated with the greatest intensity which proved catastrophic for the Russian intellect as well, and the periods of "relaxation" (or, in contemporary parlance, liberalization) of the regime, which coincided with tolerance of economic limitations, also relaxed ideological control. The number of depoliticized areas increased. The punishment for ideological heresy became more or less consonant with the degree of the heresy. The category of "political death" was repeatedly revived in Russia—under Tsar Aleksei Mikhailovich in the seventeenth century, under Elizaveta Petrovna in the eighteenth, under Alexander I in the nineteenth, and under Nikita Khrushchev in the twentieth.

The political opposition, like a multitude of other phenomena in

26. The problem of the aristocratization of the elite in the contemporary Soviet Union is the subject of chapter 1 of my monograph *Détente After Brezhnev.*

Russian history (the catastrophic decline of the cities, serfdom, political trials and terror, universal service, the denial of latent limitations on power, and political emigration) has its beginnings in the time of Ivan the Terrible. Russian tyrants destroyed this opposition, sometimes in a literal, physical sense. Each time it was reborn as from the ashes after the death of the tyrant, however, following the same alternating pattern as the Russian political process itself. This fact alone indicates that resistance to tyranny is as organic a component of this process as is tyranny itself.

The function of this opposition (or what I understand by this term) differs just as profoundly from that of the opposition in modern democratic systems as autocracy itself differs from such systems. It does not by any means necessarily oppose the existing government or regime. On the contrary, it has frequently been at the helm of the country, as was the case with Dmitrii Golitsyn after the death of Peter, or with Nikita Khrushchev after the death of Stalin. And, in the eighteenth century as in the twentieth, the function of the Russian opposition has never been to amend the policy of the existing system, but to overturn it. In this sense, Russia's revolutionary potential has proved to be practically inextinguishable (if by revolution we do not necessarily mean a mass uprising).

Nevertheless, although the Russian political opposition has repeatedly demonstrated its ability to *generate* a process of political transformation of the system in the direction of Europeanization, it has never been able to *stabilize* this process. Even its most notable successes, such as the rebirth of the aristocracy in the eighteenth century, the abolition of serfdom in the nineteenth, and the overthrow of the monarchy in the twentieth, have always led to a reverse result—that is, to a new "rigidification" of the system. The only political alternatives to the existing regimes which have really worked so far have been those which have come from the left-wing radicals or from radicals of the Russian right, as I call it. These sections of the opposition thus helped to bring Ivan the Terrible, Peter the Great, Paul I, Nicholas I, Alexander III, Lenin, and Stalin to power.[27]

The periodic alternation of "rigid" and "relaxed" phases in the Russian political process has led to an oscillation in the scale and functions of terror. In the "rigid" phases, the Russian political structure frequently became a terrorist structure par excellence; in the

---

27. While I was still in the Soviet Union, I devoted to this topic a monograph titled "The History of the Russian Political Opposition," which is still in manuscript; some parts of it are used in this book.

"relaxed" phases, it used terror as an exception, and only against those who could be looked upon as a threat to the existing regime.

The first Russian intellectual to note and describe this difference in the functions of terror in the various phases of the Russian political process, as far as I know, was Gavriil Derzhavin, in his famous ode "To Felice," dedicated to Catherine II:

> There one may whisper in conversation
> And, without fear of death, while dining
> Not drink to the health of the tsars.
> There Felice's name can be
> Scratched out by a slip of the pen
> Or her portrait carelessly
> Thrown to earth.
> There mock weddings are not played out,
> People not steamed in ice baths,
> The moustaches of diplomats not tweaked
> Princes do not cluck with brood-hens,
> Favorites do not laugh openly at them
> And black their faces with soot . . .

A decade later, Nikolai Karamzin noted that Catherine had "purged the autocracy from admixtures of tyranny." And finally, in the twentieth century, trying to define the specific character of Catherinian liberalization, Plekhanov wrote: "He who did not stand in the mother-sovereign's way, he . . . who did not interfere in matters which should not concern him, could feel secure."[28] That is, whereas *in the rigid phases the fate of an individual did not, as a rule, depend on his behavior, in the relaxed phases it did.*

It will probably be objected that both despotism and absolutism also experienced their periods of flowering and decline, of hardening and relaxing. This is certainly true. But neither has exhibited the rigorous and terrible *regularity* in the alternation of rigid and relaxed phases which has distinguished Russia. In no other place has it vir-

---

28. G. V. Plekhanov, *Sobranie sochinenii*, vol. 21, pp. 36–37. Two centuries before Karamzin, and three centuries before Plekhanov, the director of the London "company of merchants trading to Muscovy," Jeremiah Horsey, wrote, in characterizing the period which began with the death of Ivan the Terrible: "The state of affairs in the administration and the state changed completely; every person lived in peace and quiet, and knew what he owned and what he could use; everywhere good officials were appointed, and everywhere justice was established. Russia became, even in outward appearance, a different country from what it had been under the previous tsar" (quoted in N. V. Latkin, *Zemskie Sobory drevnei Rusi*, p. 87).

tually become *a pattern of political development*. Historical analogies are, for this reason, much feared by the Soviet censorship, which cannot eliminate them despite the greatest vigilance, not even by attempts to control the "uncontrollable allusions," as the censorship bitterly calls them. For in describing the time of Ivan the Terrible, for example, the historian involuntarily—and this is excellently understood by every publisher, every censor, and every reader—at the same time describes the Stalinist period, just as in describing the time of Vasilii Shuiskii, he cannot help describing the period of Khrushchev. This is why the study of history in Russia has always essentially been a political act, dangerous both to the regime and to the historian.

7. The Political Spiral

Russian political history unfolds before our eyes as a kind of spiral, in which one historical cycle, or coil, is regularly and periodically replaced by the following one, which then returns the system to its point of departure and repeats the basic parameters of the preceding cycle, each time at a new level of complexity. And this pattern extends not only to the cycles themselves but to their internal structure, to the phases from which they are built up.

As an example, let us compare the starting phase (1564–84) and the latest phase (1929–53), which obviously took place before the eyes of at least some of my readers. I will take only these two extremes, precisely because in my view they provide the greatest scope for the model which I have promised.

IVAN THE TERRIBLE	JOSEPH STALIN
1. Oprichnina revolution, halting the process of Europeanization of the country.	1. Stalinist "revolution from above," leading to the rout of the NEP (along with accompanying hopes for the political modernization).
2. Liquidation of the latent limitations on power.	2. Liquidation of latent limitations on power.
3. The establishment of terror as a means of administration: liquidation of political opposition, and abolition of the category of "political death."	3. The establishment of terror as a method of administration: liquidation of the political opposition, and abolition of the category of "political death."
4. Explosive modernization: radical transformation of the economic, political and institutional structure of the country.	4. Explosive modernization: industrialization, and transformation of the economic and political structure of the country.

5. Reduction of the social structure, and formation of a "new class."

6. Abolition of the peasants' right of free movement ("St. George's Day"), resulting in cessation of the horizontal mobility of the governed (with the exception of movement controlled by the state).

7. Chaotic intensification of the vertical mobility of the governing class, connected with the liquidation of the category of "political death" (permanent "purge" of the elite).

8. Suppression of the boyar aristocracy.

9. Extirpation of the intellectual potential of the country, connected with the total ideological monopoly of the state.

10. Divergence of goals, amounting to complete autonomy of the administration from the system.

---

5. Reduction of the social structure, and formation of a "new class."

6. Collectivization of the peasantry; workers and clerical personnel prohibited by law from changing jobs, resulting in cessation of the horizontal mobility of the governed (with the exception of movement controlled by the state).

7. Chaotic intensification of the vertical mobility of the governing class, connected with the liquidation of the category of "political death" (permanent "purge" of the elite).

8. Halting of the aristocratization of the elite.

9. Extirpation of the intellectual potential of the country, connected with the total ideological monopoly of the state.

10. Divergence of goals, amounting to complete autonomy of the administration from the system.

In this first phase of the cycle, the Russian political structure, both of the sixteenth century and of the twentieth, approaches that of despotism (or, in modern parlance, becomes "totalitarian") to a maximum degree. But it still cannot become identical with despotism, for two reasons:

First, the "rigidification" of the regime is connected not with a lack of institutional modernization (and a stagnating economy) but, on the contrary, with explosive modernization. The system is rapidly transformed, attempting in one feverish spurt, by mobilizing all of its resources, to outdistance the nations surrounding it.

Secondly, we encounter here one more regularity of the Russian political structure, paradoxical at first glance: namely the fact that, in contrast to despotism as we see it in ancient Egypt or China, or in Byzantium, not one Russian tyrant has been able to continue the "rigid" phase of the cycle beyond his own lifetime. His death has always meant the end of the phase. After Ivan the Terrible there was no other Ivan the Terrible; after Peter the Great there was no other Peter the Great; after Paul there was no other Paul. Nor after Stalin was there any other Stalin. It is obvious that the Russian political structure cannot sustain permanent tyranny (and, in this sense, does not fit the Aristotelian description of despotism). For this reason, I call the starting phase of the cycle the phase of pseudodespotism.

But why can it not sustain permanent tyranny? It seems to me that the most probable explanation consists in the fact that, as distinct from the stagnating system of despotism, we are faced in Russia with a system which is fundamentally dynamic, and which is being *destabilized* by the rigidity and terror of the starting phase of the cycle.

It is possible that, for this reason, the pseudodespotic phase is followed after the death of each tyrant by a "Time of Troubles" characterized by:

1. The rehabilitation of the victims of the terror;
2. The rebirth of the political opposition;
3. The search for alternative models of political organization;
4. The—at least partial—recognition of latent limitations on power;
5. Attempts to work out guarantees against the restoration of the ancien régime—that is, to change the political structure itself.

In any case, these were precisely the functions of the Time of Troubles which followed the death of Ivan the Terrible (1584–1613) and also of the period after the death of Joseph Stalin (1953–64). They characterized the analogous phases after the deaths of Peter I,[29] Paul I, and Nicholas I as well.

However, the phase of the Time of Troubles, although it in principle opens up the possibility of breaking the spiral, has always until now ended in failure in Russian history. Its basic goal—the transformation of latent limitations on power into political limitations—has proved unattainable. The opposition, having just risen out of nothingness, and having by a miracle survived the total terror, has not been able to reconcile the hopes of the various elites of the country and the expectations of the masses. It suddenly turns out that the society which looked so simple and unified under the iron hand of the tyrant is in fact unbelievably complex. And each of its strata has its own interests, its own expectations, its secret dreams. The administrative-political elite, maddened by permanent "purges," thirsts for the stabilization of its position, and, in the final analysis, for the guaranteeing of its privileges to the point of aristocratic status. The reborn "third estate"—the economic elite, sickened by the irrational economic system of pseudodespotism, longs for independence and

29. I have tried to describe this phase in some detail in my essay "The Drama of the Time of Troubles."

radical reforms. The intellectual elite yearns for liberalization—that is, the introduction of elementary civil rights and the reining-in of the censorship. The masses expect the standard of living to be raised. Sometimes a Russian, too, wants not only to drink but also to have a bite to eat, and even a shirt on his back.

In other words, some people need "order" and stabilization, while others need changes and reform. How is all this to be combined? How is a strategy for reconciling the administration and the system to be worked out, when the system itself has suddenly demonstrated such irreconcilable contradictions? And without a strategy, how is it to be transformed? How are guarantees against the restoration of the ancien régime to be worked out?

But there has never been a strategy.

Whether we take Boris Godunov at the end of the sixteenth century, Vasilii Shuiskii at the beginning of the seventeenth century or Vasilii Golitsyn at the end of it, Dmitrii Golitsyn in the eighteenth century, Dmitrii Miliutin in the nineteenth, or Pavel Miliukov and Aleksandr Kerensky—or even Nikolai Bukharin and Nikita Khrushchev—in the twentieth century, we see the same picture everywhere. An enormous desire to correct the mistakes, to rehabilitate the victims of terror, and to restore justice; activism and energy in the introduction of reforms; a leap toward freedom; and sometimes even tactical inventiveness. But at the same time we see an enormous degree of political incompetence, entirely contradictory actions, and an inability to consider the mistakes of one's predecessors. In a word, we see a lack of preparation for the basic sociopolitical transformation of the country which amounts, one might say, to intellectual bankruptcy. Alas, the Russian reformers never relied on a competent social analysis of the society which they were attempting to transform, and never had any experience in setting up workable political coalitions, or any clear-cut idea of what could actually be accomplished, in what order, with the aid of what social forces and political blocs. Trying to formulate this, I would say that in hoping to reshuffle the cards and deal them again, the Russian reformers had not previously gone through the school of absolutism, which alone could have given them the necessary experience. But is this really so surprising? Can pseudodespotism actually serve as a school of political thinking? Can total censorship further the accumulation of social knowledge? Where was this experience, this knowledge, this thinking to be found in Rus'?

Here is the reason why this phase—the most vivid and dramatic, filled with heretical new ideas and plans, brilliant insights, and bitter mistakes—a phase which has sustained intellectual flights, given Russian literary geniuses, and raised whole generations of oppositionists, is followed by the longest, most colorless, dullest segment of the Russian cycle—what one might dub the "Brezhnevist" phase.

The slogan of this third phase is Order, and its function is stabilization. The system has been balanced too long and too dangerously on the historical precipice. The terror of pseudodespotism has led it to the brink of self-destruction. The unbridled play of reformist and liberal ideas during the Time of Troubles, having on the one hand proved incapable of breaking the historical spiral and reconciling the administration with the system, has on the other transformed the country into something unknown and frightening to the graduates of the academy of tyranny, administering it into what they perceive as total "disorder." In the first Time of Troubles, after Ivan the Terrible, the country found itself on the threshold of national disintegration; during the second, after Peter, more than a dozen draft constitutions competed with each other in the Russian political arena; before the Polish uprising of 1863, the administration was apparently unable to resist liberal tendencies, and the political émigré Herzen, with his journal *Kolokol* [*The Bell*], was perceived in Russia literally as a second government; the NEP threatened the "dictatorship of the proletariat" with the irreversible creation of a strong agrarian bourgeoisie, while Khrushchev's reforms of the Party bylaws threatened the complete transformation of the elite and raised the spectre of the creation of a two-party system within the one Party.

This slide into "disorder" has to be stopped. And the third phase stops it. Being eclectic in nature, it attempts to combine the contradictory parameters of both of its predecessors, to mix incompatible elements, to reconcile the terrorist heritage of pseudodespotism with the reformist heritage of the Time of Troubles.

At first the maneuver seems simple: to separate reformism from liberalism. One is reminded of a chess player playing simultaneously on two boards. On the first board, the regime is fighting the liberal heritage of the Time of Troubles. On the second, it is trying to exploit this reformist heritage in order to stabilize the system. This phase permitted the Assemblies of the Land after the first Time of Troubles in the seventeenth century. It created the "second aristocracy" in the eighteenth. It thought out and executed reforms under Alexander I and Alexander II in the nineteenth. It conceived and began to execute a land reform under Nicholas II. Finally, it tried to extend the NEP after the death of Lenin, and to sustain economic reform after the overthrow of Khrushchev.

Just as in its rigid phases the Russian political structure comes to resemble despotism (thereby seducing the "despotist" historians), so in its relaxed phases it comes to resemble absolutism (thereby seducing the "absolutist" historians). However, its real secret, it seems to me, consists in the fact that, just as it is not fated to become despotism, neither is it fated to become absolutism. The third phase of the cycle can therefore more suitably be called pseudoabsolutism.

I add "pseudo" because, as will be remembered, the social and economic limitations on power are indissolubly connected with ideological ones, and constitute their obverse side. When you suppress one, you cannot retain the others. The attempt to do so expresses the basic contradiction of pseudoabsolutism, and the seed of its destruction. As the intelligentsia of the country comes of age and matures, acquiring the experience lacking during the Time of Troubles, the administration more and more sees in it a mortal danger.

Thus the liberal Iurii Krizhanich was exiled to Siberia in the seventeenth century. For Catherine II, Aleksandr Radishchev, author of *A Journey From Petersburg to Moscow*, was, in her own words, "more dangerous than Pugachev" (the leader of a mass peasant uprising which shook Russia in the eighteenth century). The liberal Aleksandr Herzen seemed in the second half of the nineteenth century more dangerous than a foreign invasion. The liberal Pavel Miliukov was perceived at the beginning of the twentieth century as public enemy No. 1. The contemporary government of Russia struggles with the liberal Andrei Sakharov as with a foreign power. It may even seem that it does not understand its own interests. For in what do the interests of this aristocracy (or aristocratizing elite) which dominates the phase of pseudoabsolutism always consist, if not in the firming up of social limitations on power? And who but the intelligentsia of the country, focused in the opposition (open and latent), are capable of working out a strategy which will guarantee the limitations on power against the restoration of the ancien régime?

This gradual growth of conservatism explains the evolution of pseudoabsolutist regimes in the second half of the reign of Aleksei Mikhailovich in the seventeenth century (accompanied by the seemingly organic dying away of the Assemblies of the Land); in the second half of the reign of Catherine the Great in the eighteenth century (marked by the end of a flirtation with "enlightened absolutism"); in the second half of the reign of Alexander I in the nineteenth (with its abandonment of constitutional plans and its routing of the universities); and, finally, in our own day, in the second half of the Brezhnev administration. This growth of conservatism is reflected also in the gradual abandonment by the administration of internal reforms, focusing instead on foreign adventures. This was the case in the seventeenth, eighteenth, and nineteenth centuries, and it is the case now.

In short, in this late part of the third cycle, the system enters an age of *political stagnation*, accompanied by economic and spiritual decline. And this is a clear signal that a new cataclysm, a new restoration of the ancien régime is at the door. The drama which England experienced only once, at the end of the Middle Ages (in 1660–89), which France experienced for an even briefer time (1815–30), Russia has been experiencing all the way through its tortuous history. One might say that it is developing *through and by historic cataclysms*. And for this reason, perhaps, it is even now, at the end of the twentieth century, still a *medieval political system*—an autocracy, as it was under Ivan the Terrible at the end of the sixteenth.

Let me try to describe the mechanism of these repeated restorations, as I see it. The removal of the liberal wing of the opposition by no means signifies the elimination of the opposition as such. It is precisely the increased conservatism of pseudoabsolutist regimes, precisely their obvious inability to solve the vital problems of the country which catalyzes and brings to the surface the dual nature of the opposition. The annihilation of the left "Europeanist" wing means, in reality, not a victory but a defeat for the "gray consensus" of the ruling center. For, by routing the left, they activate the right, transforming it into a real political force.

The rigid phase of the system has, chameleonlike, variously adopted the coloring of Westernism, as under Peter; of Russification, as under Alexander III; of open tyranny, as under Paul; of ideological isolationism, as under Nicholas I; and of Gulag-style industrialization, as under Stalin; but its essence does not change. What it aims at is the elimination (or the greatest possible reduction given the historical context) of the latent limitations on power, and removal from political circulation (often by the method of simple physical annihilation) of both the gray centrist elite and its liberal opponents. And this is when the cataclysm comes.[30]

8. An Explanation to the Reader

I am aware of the extreme vulnerability of my historical modelling. Some readers may find it an impermissible oversimplification, and others an arbitrary manipulation of entire historical periods, each of

---

30. The reader will find a chronological table of these hypothetical cycles of Russian political history in Appendix 2.

which, as we know, had its own inimitable individual aspect. I understand how difficult it is to believe that a historical process can properly
be described geometrically. It is apparent that neither will I avoid
the charges of having artificially organized my material and of being inclined to the same historical fatalism with which I reproach the
conventional historians. However, instead of going into a complex
philosophical discussion on this score, I will confine myself to a few
comments.

In the first place, I do not in the least wish to imply that the analogous phases in different historical cycles were photographic copies of
one another, not only by reason of the constantly increasing complexity of the autocratic system (to which I am always trying to draw the
reader's attention) but also because of the infinite variety of historical
circumstances and characters involved. Therefore, when I speak of
models and analogies, I have in mind only and exclusively the *identity
of functions* of the analogous phases of the cycle. In fact, the problem
here lies only in *whether* the variety of historical circumstances and
characters *excludes* the identification which I have mentioned. I think
that it is difficult for the historian to avoid it in comparing, say, the
periods of Ivan the Terrible and Joseph Stalin, as we have done. It
would also not be easy to ignore the strange fact that the death of
each successive tyrant, and not only of Ivan the Terrible, was accompanied in Russian history by a kind of reformist and liberal thaw.

Do not the strangely repetitive "eccentricities" of Russian history at
least prompt reflection, even knowing that Nicholas I did not resemble Peter (although he tried to), nor Peter Ivan the Terrible (although
he also tried)? The passion which Stalin felt for Ivan the Terrible is
known to everyone in Russia who is able to read (and it will be discussed in detail below). Let us add to this the penetrating observations of Aleksandr Gershenkron as to the periodicity of economic
cycles in Russian history and the constant alternation of feverish explosions of modernization with long periods of prostration. May we
not assume that these economic cycles are somehow correlated with
the phases of the Russian political cycles which are suggested here?

The other comment which I would like to make is that the cyclical
character of Russian autocracy does not, in my opinion, contain even
a grain of fatalism. Precisely the contrary: in its second and third
phases, each cycle remains *open* to radical transformation and Europeanization. The Russian opposition has brought the country to the
very edge of such a transformation many times. It is sufficient to recall its major reforms and plans for reforms in the 1550s, the 1600s,

the 1660s, the 1720s, the 1760s, the 1810s, the 1860s, the 1920s, and the 1950s. If such a transformation had actually taken place, the Russian political structure would have lost its medieval character—which might have happened in the 1860s as well as in the 1960s, but unfortunately did not.

9. The Oprichnina

Tsar Ivan IV carved Russia into two parts—the Land (the Zemshchina) and the Oprichnina—each with its own government, its own capital, its own treasury and its own army. There is no more lively and vivid description of the sinister phenomenon known as the Oprichnina than that given by the remarkable Russian historian V. O. Kliuchevskii:

> This was a kind of order of hermits, who like monks separated themselves from the world and struggled . . . as monks do with the temptations of the world. The very ceremony of induction into the Oprichnina army was surrounded with solemnity, both monastic and conspiratorial. Prince Kurbskii . . . writes that the tsar gathered in to himself from the whole Russian land "evil men, filled with all vices," and compelled them by frightful oaths to have no commerce, not only with their friends and brothers, but even with their parents, and to serve only him, and in token of this, compelled them to kiss the cross.
>
> Thus there arose among the thick forests . . . the capital of the Oprichnina, with its palace surrounded by a moat and a redoubt, and with checkpoints on the roads. In this lair the tsar set up a weird parody of a monastery . . . clothed these official robbers with monastic skullcaps and black veils, wrote for them a monastic rule, and himself climbed the belltower along with the princes in the morning to ring for matins, read psalms and sang in the choir of the church, and performed so many prostrations that his forehead was always bruised. . . . After dinner he liked to speak of the law, dozed, or went into the dungeon to be present at the torturing of suspects.
>
> Tsar Ivan himself considered the Oprichnina which he had founded as his own private estate, a special farm or appanage which he had separated out of the rest of the state. . . . Ivan seemed to recognize that all the rest of the Russian land was under the jurisdiction of the Council, consisting of the descendants of its former rulers . . . who made up the Muscovite boyardom, sitting in the Duma of the Land.[31]

The non-Oprichnina portion of Russia, which was administered, as before, by the aristocratic Boyar Duma, was, however, completely

---

31. Kliuchevskii, *Sochineniia* (1st ed.), vol. 2, pp. 191, 188, 189–190.

removed from participation in political decisions and occupied, as it were, the position of an absolutist island in the stormy ocean of the Oprichnina surrounding it. I say "absolutist" because the latent limitations on power continued to function on the territory of the Zemshchina (at least until the Oprichniki intruded into it), while they had ceased to exist on the territory of the Oprichnina. At its very beginning, in the short period of the "revolution from above" from 1565 to 1572, the Oprichnina was in practical terms a monstrous form of coexistence of despotism and absolutism in one country.

From this point of view, the revolution of Tsar Ivan was an attempt to transform an absolutist political structure into a despotism copied from Byzantine and Tatar-Turkish models. This attempt both succeeded and failed. It failed because, by virtue of the resistance of the absolutist tradition, the Russian structure did not become a despotism. But it also succeeded, in the sense that the absolutist structure was deformed to the point of unrecognizability, and was transformed into something else, unheard of up to that point. Therefore, we may say that when two powerful cultural traditions, absolutist and autocratic, collided and intertwined with each other in the heart of one country for a brief historical instant, the result of this fateful embrace was the destruction of Russian absolutism and the creation of Russian autocracy. Inasmuch as the Oprichnina proved to be not only the starting-point, but also the nucleus of autocracy which determined, or so it seems to me, the entire subsequent historical process in Russia, it makes sense to consider it more closely.

The Oprichniki were the storm troopers of Ivan the Terrible. As soon as they had done their job, the tsar dealt with them the way Hitler dealt with his own Oprichniki on the Night of the Long Knives 370 years later. But terror alone was insufficient to carry out a radical transformation of the political structure. Something more was needed. And the fact that the Oprichnina was this "something" has been noted by the Soviet historians P. A. Sadikov and I. I. Polosin, both of them ardent apologists for Tsar Ivan. Here is how R. Iu. Vipper summarizes their "happy discovery":

> [The Oprichnina was] a separation from the rest of the state of a very important group of lands in order that here, the head of the state, *without being constrained by traditional methods of administration*, might develop *in extenso* new, more flexible, and broader forms of government, and might apply new methods of organization of the military and fiscal systems; the system worked out [in the Oprichnina] was supposed to serve,

according to the reformer's plan, as a *model and school* for the Zem-shchina, which only by this means could be brought into the new and complex economy of the state.[32]

According to Vipper, the division of the country was justified by the fact that, as a result of it, a kind of laboratory model for the total mobilization of all the resources of the system was created—a model which required the abolition of *all* limitations on power. It required that the ordinary administration of the country (in this case the boyar government of the Zemshchina) be totally deprived of its political mandate and functions. It required, in short, the separation of the political apparatus of government from the administration, and the setting up, above the ordinary administrative structure, of a special institution, concentrating in its hands political control over the system being administered. It required the creation *of a two-tiered structure of administration based on two parallel hierarchies of power*. And for this the tsar needed the Oprichnina. While in the capacity of a proto-political police it was necessary for the establishment of total terror, in the capacity of a proto-political party it was necessary for the *institutionalization of the division of functions* between the political and the administrative powers (in modern parlance, between the Party and the state).

If Charles de Montesquieu invented the separation of powers, then Ivan the Terrible invented the separation of functions between powers. The separation of powers leads, as history has shown, to democracy. The separation of functions leads to autocracy. This was the true political significance of the Oprichnina, as I see it. The fact that it began as a direct territorial division of the country relates only to its historical form, and not to its political essence. This was simply a means for maximization of political control with a minimum of administration, given the medieval social structure.

Peter I, who set up his own Oprichnina 150 years later, no longer had any need to divide the country and split the government into administrative and political segments, since he created a centralized apparatus of political control in the form of his own guard. The embodiment of the Petrine Oprichnina was no longer the pseudochivalric order set up by Ivan the Terrible over the Boyar Duma, which continued to enjoy its "traditional methods of administration," but the autonomy of a guard set up over the senate. The role of Ivan the Terrible's Oprichnina capital—Aleksandrovskaia Sloboda—was played

32. Vipper, p. 125.

under Peter by St. Petersburg, the capital of the guard and the bureaucracy.

There was still less need for dividing the country under Lenin, who placed the Party over the Soviets, providing Russian autocracy with its Communist incarnation. And this was even more true under Stalin, who advanced the dual hierarchy of political control, placing the political police over the Party. Stalin's Moscow united in itself both Aleksandrovskaia Sloboda and St. Petersburg. Tsar Ivan's monstrous invention has thus dominated the entire course of Russian history.

CHAPTER II

THE SERF HISTORIANS:
IN BONDAGE TO "STATEMENTS"

---

1. The Struggle With Elementary Logic

The unprejudiced reader, in familiarizing himself with the work of Soviet historians, must first of all be somewhat indulgent. Even when they have something to say, they do not as a rule have the opportunity to express it, let alone to interpret it, in an adequate way—at least in the field of theory. They are phenomenally strong and have gained worldwide reputations in source study, in the investigation of archives and in the analysis of documents—that is, in everything which is depoliticized and without current ideological meaning. But as soon as it becomes a matter of interpreting such documents—not to speak of making judgments about the historical process—they find themselves tightly encircled by inviolable canons, the infraction of which is equivalent to breaking the law in a modern society. These canons are the so-called "*vyskazyvaniia*" (statements) of the classical Marxist authors—Marx, Engels, and Lenin (until 1953 Generalissimo Stalin also had this rank, but he has now been demoted to private).

Though many of these "*vyskazyvaniia*" contradict each other, time has no power over them. Marx died in 1883, Engels in 1895, Lenin in 1924. None of them were professional historians. But everything the classical authors ever said, even in their tenderest years, is immune from revision—on pain of criminal or administrative punishment (with the exception, of course, of those "*vyskazyvaniia*" which the authorities themselves consider to be dangerous or inconvenient at the given moment). A whole army of semiliterate hunters—who know nothing of history except the "*vyskazyvaniia*" currently in use, but on whom, nevertheless, the welfare of historians, their professional advancement, their status, and their publications depend—vigilantly follow every attempt at revision. Under pseudodespotism, the Gulag awaited heretics; in subsequent phases, only daily restriction and harassment. But for people whose calling consists in studying, thinking, and writing, the loss of these privileges (the autocracy considers them not as individual rights but as privileges bestowed by the regime) is sometimes equivalent to death.

When Soviet historians try to *reinterpret* (not revise, reinterpret) the "*vyskazyvaniia,*" this can, therefore, be considered, if not heroic, then at least a brave act, involving serious risk. For a hunter may always turn up to whom the reinterpretation looks like a revision. In a certain sense, moreover, the situation of Soviet historians of Russia is worse than the situation of the medieval scholastics: the former suffer both from a multitude of "*vyskazyvaniia*" and from a shortage of them. For what was said by the classical Marxist authors for the most part does not fit Russian history.

Ask any Soviet historian what he uses as a guide in analyzing the political development of a particular country, and he will tell you right away that he proceeds from the fundamental positions of Marxism—that is, from the idea that at a given point the productive forces in their development outrun the relationships of production, that this discrepancy gives rise to a class struggle which gradually weakens the existing social structure, and that this struggle, growing sharper, leads to revolution, in the course of which the victorious class breaks up the old state machinery (as occurred in the Netherlands in the sixteenth century, in England in the seventeenth, and in France in the eighteenth) and erects on its ruins a new apparatus of class rule.

This is what the "*vyskazyvaniia*" say. This is the law.

But what is the historian of Russia, let us say of the sixteenth to eighteenth centuries, supposed to make of this law? What is he to do if the productive forces here grew so slowly that over the whole course of these centuries they did not outgrow the relationships of production? If the class struggle, although supposed to shatter the structure of autocracy, nevertheless could not shatter it? If, furthermore, the autocracy rose up after each successive rebellion like a phoenix out of the flames, refreshed, and for some reason grown stronger, and, as if nothing had happened, pursued its barbarous line as before? If the old structure did not collapse and, consequently, the rubble on which the new state was to be built, according to the law, was absent? If, impudently neglecting the law, the old state persisted in all its autocratic ignorance right down to the twentieth century?

Why was it that, precisely at the dawn of modern history, when medieval serfdom was breaking up in Western Europe, this same serfdom was initiated in Russia? That when in Europe the modern mode of production was being born and modern forces of production were taking shape, the forces of production were being totally destroyed in

Russia? That while in Europe positive political experience was being accumulated which led in the end to the transformation of latent limitations on power into open political ones, in Russia a grim autocracy was enthroned which destroyed even the existing limitations? That when Shakespeare and Cervantes, Bruno and Descartes, Galileo, Bacon, and Montaigne were announcing the dawn of modern civilization in Europe, the fires and bells of the Oprichnina were announcing the triumph of barbarism in Russia?

Petr Chaadaev in the nineteenth century and Arnold Toynbee in the twentieth were inclined to explain the paradox by the fatal influence of Byzantine culture on the Russian political tradition. Pushkin explained it by the non-European character of Russian culture. The Slavophile Konstantin Aksakov cited the westernization of the country by force. Boris Chicherin referred to the Asiatic despotism characteristic of Russian institutions.[1] Georgii Plekhanov appealed to the same despotism entrenched in the peculiarities of the agrarian structure of Russia. Leon Trotsky noted that Russia was closer in its economic structure to India than to Europe. The ideologist of émigré Eurasianism, Nikolai Trubetskoi, declared that the Russians had inherited their empire from Genghis Khan.[2] Pavel Miliukov asserted that the constant encirclement of Russia by hostile peoples, and military necessity, gave the Muscovite government the opportunity to establish a centralized state of Eastern type.[3] Nikolai Berdiaev declared Russia to be a Christianized Tatar empire.[4] Karl Wittfogel, while admitting that in institutional terms Kievan Rus' belonged to the proto-feudal world of Europe, nevertheless came to the conclusion that the Tatar yoke was responsible for an "institutional time bomb" in Russian political culture, which exploded when the "yoke" came to its end.[5]

In short, there have been many explanations, and we will return to them again. But all of them primarily discuss cultural influences or institutional borrowings, that is, secondary, "superstructural" factors, and by no means the "base"—the relationships of production, productive forces, class struggle, and other serious matters which are supposed to be interpreted according to the law. Consequently, these

1. "In Russia Eastern despotism served as a model," asserted Chicherin categorically in his fundamental work *O narodnom predstavitel'stve*, p. 531.
2. Cited in G. Vernadsky, *The Mongols in Russia*, p. 389.
3. P. N. Miliukov, *Ocherki po istorii russkoi kul'tury*, p. 147.
4. N. A. Berdiaev, *Istoki i smysl russkogo kommunizma*, p. 7.
5. K. Wittfogel, *Oriental Despotism*, p. 225.

hypotheses cannot bear any relation to "genuine science," as Soviet historiography proudly calls itself. For such "bourgeois" explanations, Soviet historians have nothing but the haughty contempt of specialists for dilettantes. Their mockery of bourgeois idealism has a confident, major-key ring. It is as though they had the real explanation in their pockets. But since they have nothing in their pockets except the sacred "*vyskazyvaniia*," this explanation must, of course, consist in the economic backwardness of Russia, in the underdevelopment of its productive forces.

And this explanation would be perfect if it were not also necessary to explain where this economic backwardness came from. And right here is where there is no escape: you have to appeal to the Tatar yoke, to the terrible slaughter of a people which blocked the path of the Huns to the West with its own breast, and paid for an ungrateful European civilization at the price of its own backwardness. This sounds very patriotic. But unfortunately the class struggle and the relationships of production have somehow dropped out of the argument unnoticed. For Aksakov, the Germans were guilty; for Chaadaev, the Greeks; and for "genuine science"—the Tatars? But this is precisely what was asserted by the bourgeois idealists: Chicherin, Trubetskoi, Berdiaev, and Wittfogel. It thus turns out that all of these explanations are different not in nature but only in name—in the names of the guilty parties. For they all reduce, in the final analysis, to the assertion that what is to blame for Russia's historical misfortune is not Russian autocracy, but someone else—whether the Tatar, the Greek or the German, you will agree, is not the essential point. What *is* essential is that as soon as we come to actual analysis, it is not the "*vyskazyvaniia*" to which genuine science appeals, but to those same poor old Tatars.

Alas, this is one of those sensitive areas, where there are not enough suitable and sufficiently patriotic "*vyskazyvaniia*." Ivan the Terrible's Oprichnina is another. No classical author (other than the demoted Stalin) took the trouble to leave a precise and unambiguous "*vyskazyvanie*" as to whether the Oprichnina was progressive or not. On the one hand, it must have served as the starting point of Russian absolutism, and to establish the presence of absolutism in Russia is not so much a scientific as a patriotic duty for Soviet historiography. Everywhere in Europe the establishment of absolutism meant the end of feudal disintegration and the formation of centralized states of the modern type. Why must things have been different with us? Russian absolutism serves as evidence of national respectability, as a certificate of Russia's affiliation with the European family—proof that (despite all the insulting conjectures of "bourgeois" historians) Russia has nothing in common with Oriental despotism. Inability to demonstrate the presence of absolutism in Russia is equivalent not only to capitulation to bourgeois historiography but, far worse, is an admission of the Asiatic character of the Russian historical heritage. And this is fraught with undesirable political and ideological consequences. Therefore, the Oprichnina simply must be progressive.

But on the other hand, it was precisely the Oprichnina which laid the foundations for the establishment in Rus' of serfdom, the most bestial, unproductive, and reactionary mode of exploitation of the people's labor, which subsequently fatally penetrated into all the pores of the Russian political organism. Who could call serfdom progressive? Especially taking into account the development of productive forces (not to speak of the relationships of production). There is a clear contradiction, and some way out of it has to be found. Soviet historians try with all their might to do so.

Discussing the epoch of Ivan the Terrible, one of the most eminent Soviet scholars, Academician D. S. Likhachev, uncompromisingly asserts, for example, that

> of the two contending factions within the feudal class, the service nobility was undoubtedly progressive. . . . What Marx and Engels said about a progressive class can be applied, in a certain degree, to the service nobility. . . . The boyardom tried to preserve the old ways. . . . Kurbskii's ideal is the division of power between the tsar and the boyardom. This was a clear compromise between the old and the new—a compromise to which the most reactionary circles of the boyardom were compelled to resort under the all-conquering pressure of the progressive movement of history.

Sil'vestr, the ideologist of the "Government of compromise" (preceding the Oprichnina), is charged with treacherous and hypocritical machinations, in that "even when addressing the tsar, Sil'vestr speaks in a veiled form of the need to limit the sovereign's power."[6]

I do not know why a convinced Marxist is so terrified by "limitations on the sovereign's power," or why he treats them as a vice and as treason on the part of the "most reactionary circles of the boyardom." Neither is it part of the task of this section to dispute the depiction of the sixteenth century "new class" which helped Ivan the Terrible to destroy these limitations on power as a "progressive class" and the personification of "the all-conquering pressure of the progressive

---

6. D. S. Likhachev, "Ivan Peresvetov i ego literaturnaia sovremennost'," pp. 30, 36, 37.

movement of history." What interests us at the moment is something else, namely that the "progressive class" was opposed not only by "the most reactionary circles of the boyardom." It was also opposed by the peasantry, which was being driven into slavery. The peasants resisted by raising mighty revolts, paying with their blood for the victory of the "progressive class" which Likhachev exalts. Then why does he not also call this still more terrible and bloody resistance to the "progressive movement of history" reactionary? This is required by elementary logic: if the "new class" indeed represented progress, then the forces resisting it—regardless of whether from above (the boyardom) or from below (the peasantry)—must have represented regression or, what is the same thing, reaction.

But Likhachev does not do this. The law forbids it: peasant wars, according to all the "*vyskazyvaniia*," represent class struggles—that is, precisely the above mentioned "progressive historical development." Thus, the "statements" mercilessly drive the poor historian into a logical trap, and compel him to the absurdity of cursing the struggle of the boyardom against the "progressive class" while at the same time blessing the peasantry's struggle against it. He is compelled to sing hymns to enserfers (the "new class") and enserfed (the peasantry) with identical inspiration.

Such tricks are not the exception, but the rule, and what we may call the routine, of "genuine science." Some years later, a no less distinguished scholar, Academician L. V. Cherepnin, reported to a Soviet-Italian congress that "in the peasant war [of the early seventeenth century] we can see one of the causes of the fact that the transition to absolutism in Russia was delayed by more than half a century."[7] But this is open heresy. It turns out that the class struggle, instead of speeding up the "progressive movement of history," slowed it down. This has to be Cherepnin's conclusion if he is to remain within the limits of elementary logic. However, such a conclusion would be not only heresy but public suicide. Cherepnin, of course, does not opt for this, not only because the "*vyskazyvaniia*" stand guard over class struggle and he has no taste for self-sacrifice, but also, to paraphrase Aristotle, because though the peasantry is his friend, absolutism is dearer. And absolutism, grievously involved in a mortal tangle with the Oprichnina and serfdom, must be rehabilitated at any price.

Once again, before the eyes of an astonished public, the scholar is suddenly replaced on the podium by a clown. Recognizing that "the

7. L. V. Cherepnin, "K voprosu o skladyvanii absoliutnoi monarkhii v Rossii," p. 38.

attempts to establish absolutism, connected with the policy of Ivan the Terrible and expressed in the institution of the Oprichnina, resulted in an open dictatorship of the serfholders, which took on the most monstrous forms of despotism," Cherepnin goes on to assert, without drawing breath, that "by weakening the boyar aristocracy and supporting the centralization of the state, the Oprichnina to a certain degree cleared the path for absolutism."[8] In other words, the bloody enthronement of serfdom, connected with the "most monstrous forms of despotism," having successfully overcome the hindrance of class struggle, once again performed its service to the "progressive movement of history"!

Has Cherepnin really moved very far from the hymns to the slaveholding "progressive class" which we heard a decade earlier from Likhachev? And does not the formula of *Istoriia SSSR* [*The History of the USSR*] (officially adopted in 1966 as a textbook for institutions of higher learning), which simple-mindedly asserts that since the Oprichnina was directed against the aristocracy, "it had a progressive character,"[9] sound natural in this context?

2. The Lost Paradise of "Equilibrium"

From the outset I must make the qualification that I intend to analyze only the philosophical aspect of the Soviet discussion on Russian absolutism (1968–1971), and not by any means the scholastic squabbling concerning the "relationship of the feudal and bourgeois elements in the nature and policy of the absolute monarchy" which has absorbed much of the energy of its participants. This squabbling seems to me the more scholastic in that the essential fact of Russian history during the period under study is unquestionably the routing of the Russian proto-bourgeoisie by the Oprichnina, and the blocking by serfdom of the formation of a middle class. After this, what could be the role of "bourgeois elements" in the Russian political process, and what is there actually to dispute? The uniqueness of the Russian autocracy during the first centuries of its existence consisted precisely in the absence of a middle class. And it is precisely this uniqueness which I would have discussed in the debate, had I been its initiator. But the initiator was the well-known Soviet historian, A. Avrekh, who

8. Ibid., pp. 24–25.

9. *Istoriia SSSR*, p. 212. I am neither an orthodox nor a rebellious Marxist—I simply don't have anything in common with this mode of thought. But even a bitter opponent of Marxism would scarcely parody it as brutally as do these writers who claim to have custody of the pure Marxist flame.

began in a quite different way, with a brave reinterpretation of the famous *"vyskazyvanie"* by Lenin to the effect that the concepts of "absolutism," "autocracy," and "unlimited monarchy" are entirely identical. This statement cuts off completely any possibility of separating a definition of "absolutism" out of the general mass of "unlimited monarchies," and essentially excludes any discussion at all. And for this reason Avrekh tactfully attacks it. "In the second edition of the Large Soviet Encyclopedia," he writes,

> absolutism is treated as an unlimited monarchy with the reference to V. I. Lenin cited above. . . . Is this definition adequate *in the given case?* We think not. Is it possible, for example, to establish on the basis of it the difference between absolute monarchy and Oriental despotism? What is to be done about the rights of the people, let us say, under Ivan the Terrible? . . . To argue that Ivan was a limited monarch would be to expose one's own scholarly reputation. To recognize him as an absolutist monarch, since there were no limitations on his power, is still worse.[10]

Why is it worse? Because to do so would "mean compromising the idea of equilibrium." What equilibrium? The point is that parallel to Lenin's *"vyskazyvanie" denying* the specific character of absolutism, there is also a *"vyskazyvanie"* by Engels, *asserting* this specific character and declaring that although every state

> as a general rule is the state of the strongest, economically dominant class . . . exceptional periods are found in which contending classes reach an *equilibrium of power*, such that the power of the state acquires for the time being a certain autonomy in relation to both classes, as an apparent mediator between them. Such was the absolute monarchy of the seventeenth and eighteenth centuries, which held the nobility and the bourgeoisie in equilibrium with each other.[11]

Faced with the choice between two irreconcilable *"vyskazyvaniia,"* the majority of Soviet historians have preferred Engels. "This idea of Marx and Engels," Avrekh testifies, "serves as the basis of all studies of absolutism, whatever country is being discussed. All facts and phenomena are included under it and explained by it, whatever the order to which they belong."[12]

10. A. Ia. Avrekh, "Russkii absoliutizm i ego rol' v utverzhdenii kapitalizma v Rossii," pp. 83, 85. Emphasis added.

11. Karl Marx and Friedrich Engels, *Sochineniia* (2nd ed.), vol. 21, pp. 171, 172. Engels wrote elsewhere that the equilibrium between the landed nobility and the bourgeoisie is the basic condition for absolute monarchy (ibid., vol. 18, p. 254).

12. Avrekh, p. 83.

As we see, the fearless Avrekh issues a challenge to the second classical writer. For if the trouble with Lenin's *"vyskazyvanie"* is that it does not permit the study of absolutism, then the trouble with the *"vyskazyvanie"* by Engels is that it does not fit Russian history, which two generations of experts have passionately searched for such "equilibrium." But neither in the seventeenth, nor in the eighteenth, nor even in the first half of the nineteenth century, let alone in the period of Ivan the Terrible, have they succeeded in finding it. One has to assume that this is because it is just not there—as Avrekh phrases it, their failure is conditioned by the "complete absence of proof of the existence of equilibrium."[13]

It is true that there are yet other *"vyskazyvaniia"* deep in the reserve—one might say in the subconscious—of Soviet historiography. For example: "It is in the terrible and abject school of Mongolian slavery that Muscovy was nursed and grew up. It gathered strength only by becoming a virtuoso in the craft of serfdom. Even when emancipated, Muscovy continued to perform its traditional part of the slave as master . . . to whom Genghiz Khan had, by will, bequeathed his conquest of the earth."[14] This treacherous stab in the back to genuine science was delivered not by some bourgeois miscreant who can be rejected with contempt, but by classical author No. 1 himself. And who was it who said that Russian autocracy "is supported . . . by means of an Asiatic despotism and a degree of arbitrary rule of which we in the West cannot even have any conception"?[15] Classical author No. 2.

But these are precisely the *"vyskazyvaniia"* which are not only not permitted to be used, but about which Soviet historiography passionately wishes to forget and to pretend that they never existed. Marx's work which I have just quoted has never been translated into Russian in the more than sixty years of the Soviet regime. Humiliatingly and inexplicably for Soviet historiography, it appears that the majority of the officially deified classical writers (two out of three) hated Russia, viewed it as the heir of Tatar barbarism and Asiatic despotism, and called on Europe to mount a crusade against this monster. A person who thought in Freudian terms might even suspect that the tormented rejection of the concept of Asiatic despotism by genuine science is dictated by the unconscious hatred which it harbors—despite its loud avowals of love and loyalty—for the founding fathers.

13. Ibid., p. 85.
14. Karl Marx, *Secret Diplomatic History of the XVIII Century*, p. 121.
15. Karl Marx, *Izbrannye proizvedeniia*, p. 537. (This *"vyskazyvanie"* uttered by Engels appeared for some reason in Marx's book).

Thus, Soviet historians find themselves orphaned in a Kafkaesque world of *"vyskazyvaniia"* which slide away under their feet—one not applicable to Russian history, another unacceptable to historians, and a third simply offensive to their best feelings. It is clear why the journal *Istoriia SSSR* needed four years of debate on the nature of Russian absolutism, and why Avrekh opens it with an admission apparently unthinkable in the mouth of a possessor of absolute truth: "Absolutism is not only an important theme but also a treacherous one . . . the more successful the concrete historical study of it, the more confused and vague its essence becomes."[16]

Certainly, even before this discussion, Soviet historians had noted that "equilibrium" had slipped out from under their feet, and made desperate attempts to find a decent replacement for it. Why, in fact, must there necessarily be equilibrium between the nobility and the bourgeoisie? Why not "balance," say (as Likhachev did), the most reactionary strata of boyardom against the progressive class of the service nobility? However, even if we forget that the service nobility were, in fact, the "new class," the janissaries of serf-holding reaction, will this extraordinary gambit solve the problem? Avrekh thinks not. "In recent times," he writes,

> it has been suggested that we consider . . . the balancing struggle between boyardom and the nobles to be the linchpin of Russian absolutism. . . . It is not hard to see that this is a complete capitulation. It is, strictly speaking, no longer the substance but the word which is saved. After all, the entire essence . . . of the statements of Marx and Engels is reduced to the idea that absolutism is the product of an equilibrium of forces between fundamentally different classes—the bearers of different modes of production—and the result of bourgeois development of the country.[17]

But what if we envision an "equilibrium" between the service nobility and the peasantry? Then we might succeed in preserving both "equilibrium" and the class struggle, the more so since, according to Lenin, "Class struggle—the struggle of the exploited part of the people against the exploiting part—lies at the basis of political transformations, and in the final analysis decides the fate of these transformations."[18] B. F. Porshnev bases his conception of absolutism on this, asserting that precisely "the threat of peasant uprisings made necessary the centralization of the state, and this threat, by increasing,

16. Avrekh, p. 82.
17. Ibid., p. 87.
18. V. I. Lenin, *Polnoe sobranie sochinenii*, vol. 9, pp. 333–34.

compelled centralization constantly to be intensified, and finally to reach the stage of absolutism."[19]

This thesis was defended in the debate we are considering by Andrei Sakharov—a double namesake of the famous dissident, and perhaps for this reason especially fierce in his demonstrations of loyalty—who, it is true, does not cite Porshnev, and thereby gives out this author's views as his own: "The struggle between the peasantry and the class of feudal lords during the period of origin of bourgeois relationships in the country was the basic factor in the formation of Russian absolutism from the second half of the seventeenth century."[20]

In the first place, however, can we seriously speak of an equilibrium between the enserfed and downtrodden peasantry, which precisely in the seventeenth century became "legally dead" and politically nonexistent, and the mighty "new new class," which was really able to influence the regime? Equilibrium by definition presupposes *equality of power* between the contending classes. In the second place, why would this struggle between the governed and the governors (or, what is the same thing, between the exploited and the exploiters) necessarily have led to absolutism, and not to despotism? By reducing the structure of Russian society to two polar classes, Sakharov makes the identification of absolutism with despotism irresistible. The logic of his thought (or more accurately, of Porshnev's thought, which he "borrowed") *erases* any difference between these two political structures. And the task of the debate consists precisely in *establishing* this difference.

We can now understand why, for example, A. Chistozvonov is compelled to note that "a careful analysis of the statements of the founders of Marxism-Leninism about absolutism in various countries and of the concrete historical material shows that these complex phenomena cannot be fitted into the models which are currently in circulation among us."[21] This also explains why Avrekh, in initiating the discussion, hastily crosses out both artificial alternative replacements of the "equilibrium," and embarks on a venture extremely rare even for the era of pseudoabsolutism—that of suggesting his own definition of absolutism.

Of course, Avrekh masks his impudence with a battery of "*vyskazyvaniia*" from Lenin. Of course, after quoting Lenin, he humbly

19. B. F. Porshnev, *Feodalism i narodnye massy*, p. 354.
20. A. N. Sakharov, "Istoricheskie faktory obrazovaniia russkogo absoliutizma," p. 123.
21. A. N. Chistozvonov, "Nekotorye aspekty problemy genezisa absoliutizma," p. 49.

asks: "What does all this lead to?" Innocently attempting to give out his own definition as a logical extension of these "*vyskazyvaniia*," he makes a deep bow to classical authority: "It seems to us that precisely this thought is contained in the words of V. I. Lenin which we have cited, only *it is expressed in an indirect form*." However, he still does not succeed in fooling such experienced witch-hunters as A. Sakharov or S. Pokrovskii, and they will in time demonstrate this to him convincingly. But now, in a moment of desperate boldness, Avrekh offers a definition: "Absolutism is a kind of feudal monarchy which by virtue of its internal nature *is capable of evolving* and being transformed into a bourgeois monarchy."[22] He continues:

> What basic features separate the absolutist state from, let us say, the feudal state of the Muscovite tsars? The major difference consists in the fact that it ceases to be despotism—or more accurately, to be *only* despotism. By the latter we understand a form of unlimited autocratic power, under which the despot's will is the only law—a regime of arbitrary personal rule which does not take account of legal process or of laws, customary or written. Absolutism consciously acts against this order of things.[23]

The weakness of this definition is obvious. Even by defining despotism as a regime of arbitrary personal rule (which corresponds to the Aristotelian definition of tyranny) we come out with a paradox: pre-autocratic Russia, with its hereditary aristocracy, Boyar Duma, and Assemblies of the Land, Russia with its free peasantry, proto-bourgeoisie in process of formation, and growing cities, experiencing an economic boom, is declared a despotism ("incapable of evolving"); and autocratic Russia, which has eliminated the proto-bourgeoisie and the limitations of power, the Boyar Duma, and the Assemblies of the Land, which has enserfed the peasantry and halted the urbanization of the country, and is therefore politically stagnating, is declared an absolutism ("capable of evolving"). Nevertheless, Avrekh's suggestion implies the following conclusions as to the nature of Russian absolutism:

1. It excluded (for unspecified reasons) a regime of arbitrary personal power and tended toward some form of due process;
2. It determined (apparently for the same unspecified reasons) the

22. Avrekh, p. 89. Emphasis added.
23. Ibid., p. 92. This contradiction on Avrekh's part is so glaring that Sakharov, of course, immediately jumped on him, commenting ironically: "It turns out that when serfdom was weaker, 'Asiatic despotism' was stronger; but when serfdom became more severe, 'Asiatic forms of government' were relaxed to such a point that 'external' analogies to Western European absolutism appeared" (A. N. Sakharov, p. 113).

capacity of the Russian political structure for evolution toward bourgeois monarchy;

3. It was the embodiment of the negation of the despotism of the Muscovite tsardom;

4. Contrary to all that is known to us, the tyranny of Peter I, Paul I, and Nicholas I was compatible with due process and embodied political progress;

5. The existence of the category of political progress is confirmed, albeit indirectly.[24]

In other words, for the first time in Russian historiography, an attempt has been made to reconcile the two poles of the traditional bipolar model, at least in a chronological sense: the Russian political process is declared both despotic (in the period of the Muscovite tsardom) and absolutist (in the period of the St. Petersburg empire).

For all the poverty and contradictoriness of Avrekh's definition, for all its involvement in the war of quotations about "the relationship between feudal and bourgeois elements," his attempt differs sharply from the vulgar logical clowning to which, as we have seen, genuine science usually resorts in difficult situations. On the contrary, he essentially rebelled against serflike dependence on the sacred "*vyskazyvaniia*," and attempted to think independently about the history and the fate of his country. The discussion could have developed further in either of two directions: it could continue to move toward freedom, or the attempt at rebellion could be suppressed. In 1968, before the Soviet invasion of Czechoslovakia, it seemed that the discussion might take the first direction; in 1969 it swiftly began to be reminiscent of a punitive expedition.

3. Under the Ice of "Genuine Science"

In a publication which followed directly upon Avrekh's, M. Pavlova-Sil'vanskaia recognizes that "his viewpoint . . . that until the be-

24. It should be noted that, in direct form, the category of political progress is lacking in Soviet historiography (and before Avrekh it was lacking even in indirect form). Therefore the criterion of *political* development is also lacking. And there is no knowing what is good or bad here, what is positive and what is negative, or what is moving from what direction and toward what. I emphasize that what is being spoken of is not the trivial Marxist postulate that the replacement of one socioeconomic order by another is inevitable, but political progress—that is, the fact that different political structures possess different *dynamic potentials*. And, for this reason, Avrekh's attempt to declare "St. Petersburg absolutism" (even if it never existed) capable (unlike "Muscovite despotism") of political dynamism, was for its kind a remarkably partisan action in Soviet historiography, as well as a risky one.

ginning of the eighteenth century, the autocracy was only despotism, shows promise." Moreover, Pavlova-Sil'vanskaia improves upon
Avrekh's position, noting that, "according to Avrekh, despotism constitutes a regime of naked power, about the socioeconomic base of
which we know nothing whatever," while "G. V. Plekhanov . . . who
equated tsarism with Oriental despotism . . . relying partly on Marx
and Engels, supported his viewpoint by arguing for the peculiarities
of the agrarian structure of Russia."[25] Consequently, she concludes
that:

> Unlimited monarchy in Russia developed in the guise of Asiatic forms
> of administration—despotism—and centralized unlimited monarchy,
> formed in the struggle with the Mongol empire and its successors on
> the basis of the subsistence economy and the communal organization of
> the countryside, and later strengthened in the process of creation of the
> system of land tenure, the enserfment of the peasantry, and the transi-
> tion to external expansion. This is the starting point of the evolution.[26]

Pavlova-Sil'vanskaia thus agrees both with Plekhanov and with
Avrekh: with the former, that despotism was based "on the peculiarities of the agrarian structure of Russia," and not on a "regime of
naked power"—that is, on the "base" and not on the "superstructure"; and with the latter, that this despotism evolved, being transformed in the eighteenth century into absolutism, and later in the direction of a bourgeois monarchy.

Such a mechanical joining of Plekhanov with Avrekh appears, on
the one hand, to make Pavlova-Sil'vanskaia's position more orthodox,
but on the other only intensifies the theoretical difficulties which face
Avrekh's thesis. After all, if the despotic superstructure rested on the
peculiarities of the agrarian base, then how and by virtue of what factors did it suddenly begin to evolve, while the base remained un-
changed? I am not speaking of the fact, which Avrekh also accepts,
that despotism is *incapable* of evolving toward bourgeois monarchy by
virtue of the peculiarities of its superstructure, which blocks the evolution of the base. Even Marx equated despotism with stagnation.[27]
In other words, the very fact of the evolution of tsarist autocracy contradicts the idea that it was a despotism.

But on the other hand, was it absolutism? Did it actually evolve in
the direction of a bourgeois monarchy? This question was answered

25. M. P. Pavlova-Sil'vanskaia, "K voprosu ob osobennostiakh absoliutizma v Rossii,"
p. 77.
26. Ibid., p. 85.
27. Karl Marx and Friedrich Engels, *Izbrannye pis'ma*, p. 79.

by history. Sometimes it did. But it could not, for some reason, *become* bourgeois monarchy. On the contrary, it became Russian and then Soviet autocracy. In other words, in evolving, it bore within itself—in spite of all reforms and revolutions—some kind of essential nucleus, which resisted transformation into a bourgeois monarchy.

As we see, Pavlova-Sil'vanskaia's attempt to insert a solid Marxist "base" under Avrekh's "superstructural" conception in fact only revealed its contradictions. Furthermore, she incautiously woke up the sleeping lion by putting into circulation the battery of Asiatic-despotic "*vyskazyvaniia*" which, as we already know, are not talked about in genuine science, as one does not talk about rope in a hanged man's house.

However, the bold attempt to think independently proved to be infectious. Avrekh's next opponent, A. Shapiro, cast doubt on the very premise that Russian despotism existed. In fact, he says, "The Boyar Duma (of the fifteenth and early sixteenth centuries) performed administrative and judicial functions with the prince, not only helping him, but also limiting his power (in fact, not juridically)."[28] More than this, the scope of these "de facto limitations" was not decreased but increased in the first half of the sixteenth century:

> The major peculiarity of the political structure of Russia . . . in the late 1540s and early 1550s . . . consisted in the establishment of a central institution, and the general dissemination of local institutions representing the estates. . . . And it was precisely at this time that the Assemblies of the Land originated in Rus' . . . the form of political structure for this period is more correctly characterized as a division of power between the tsar and the Boyar Duma . . . in Russia there was a nonautocratic monarchy, with a Boyar Duma and institutions representing estates.

Further, Shapiro points to the role of the Oprichnina revolution of Ivan the Terrible in the liquidation of this "nonautocratic monarchy." He speaks of the functions of terror in this revolution, and of how,

> out of the members of the Duma who received Duma titles before . . . 1563, at the end of the Oprichnina only individual persons survived. Both they and new members of the Duma were terrorized to such an extent that they did not dare to criticize the manifestations of the personal rule of Ivan the Terrible . . . neither the Boyar Duma nor the Assemblies of the Land any longer exercised an influence on the Oprichnina policy, which must be considered an autocratic policy.

28. A. L. Shapiro, "Ob absoliutizme v Rossii," p. 71.

Shapiro even speculates that "the Oprichnina was rather *a state above the state* than a state within a state."[29] He understands that subsequent to the phase of pseudodespotism (which he calls "spasmodic autocracy") "there took place a certain weakening of the autocracy"[30]—that is, in my language, a phase of pseudoabsolutism. He also sees the restoration of the Oprichnina in the time of Peter I: "The reign of Peter was marked by the complete liquidation of the Boyar Duma and the Assemblies of the Land and the complete victory of the autocratic-absolutist system." In other words, in his conception, the dynamic of the Russian political structure is no longer a flat, unilinear process of evolution "from barbarism to civilization," in the terms of Solov'ev, or "from despotism to bourgeois monarchy," in Avrekh's terms. It pulsates. It hardens, then relaxes, then again hardens. It lives its own complex and peculiar life, separate from European absolutism. Finally, Shapiro sees at least one of the roots of the difference of Russian autocracy from European absolutism: "Nowhere in Europe were absolutism and bureaucracy able to stamp out the estate institutions completely . . . in Russia both the Assemblies of the Land and the regional elected institutions were destroyed by absolutism."[31]

None of these mysterious eccentricities of the Russian historical process escaped Shapiro's penetrating gaze. But somehow they do not compose an autonomous conception of autocracy. On the contrary, as we see, he uses "autocratic-absolutist" with a hyphen, as synonyms—as though something held him on a leash, not permitting him to go beyond precise but transitory observations. What is it that does this? The "*vyskazyvaniia*"? But Shapiro, although he pays them abundant tribute, does so very much in the way that the Muscovite princes paid tribute to the Tatars, thereby securing their own autonomy. The foundation of his conclusions is not so much the "*vyskazyvaniia*" as the studies of modern historians—A. Zimin, R. Skrynnikov, N. Nosov, L. Cherepnin, S. Shmidt. What, then, compels Shapiro to consider Russian autocracy only a variant of Western absolutism?

It seems to me that here we see plainly how beneath the stratum of the sacred writings, which hinder the development of thought in Soviet historiography, there appears another and more profound hindrance: namely, the logic of the bipolar model. If Avrekh is wrong, and there was no Russian despotism, then consequently there was Russian absolutism: for what else could there be?

Shapiro sees that the category of despotism does not describe Russian political reality. He also sees that the category of absolutism in

29. Ibid., p. 72, 73.   30. Ibid., p. 74.   31. Ibid., p. 82.

some strange way stumbles over it, since "the chief and defining feature is its [absolutism's] attitude toward serfdom." The economies of the classical absolutist monarchies were incompatible with serfdom. The Russian economy was compatible with it. Nevertheless, the thought that it could be some third thing—that is, neither despotism nor absolutism—does not even enter his head.

Nonetheless, the ice was broken. Though this was still a timid, almost subterranean movement of thought, synchronous with the Prague Spring, it showed that deep under the ice of haughty and fruitless "genuine science," reformist potential had been preserved. It might perish again. But it might develop too.

4. The Punitive Expedition

But this was not to be its destiny. The signal for the beginning of the witch-hunt had already been given. The military enforcers were preparing a punitive expedition to Prague. And the literary enforcers— knights of the "class struggle" and mercenaries of the "*vyskazyvaniia*"—had already saddled their horses.

At the very beginning of 1969, A. Davidovich and S. Pokrovskii let loose a devastating salvo against Avrekh, accusing him of "an attempt to counterpose the historical process in the West . . . and in Russia."[32] In point of fact, they asserted, there is no "fundamental difference between Russian absolutism and the classical type."[33] For every sort of absolutism is the product of the struggle of exploited classes against exploiters. "The rebellions in the cities in the mid-seventeenth century and the peasant war of 1670–71 showed the ruling class of feudal lords the need to sacrifice some of their medieval privileges in favor of the unlimited power of the tsar for a successful struggle with a mutinous people."[34]

In the fury of the hunt, the rout of Avrekh seemed inevitable; whole pages of "*vyskazyvaniia*" whistled around his head. But the hunters somehow failed to notice that they had fallen into their own trap. In fact, they say, "Lenin defined Russian absolutism as 'the landlord state' [*Complete Works*, vol. 17, p. 309], 'the serf-owning autocracy' [*ibid.*, p. 310], 'the dictatorship of the serf-owning landlords' [*ibid.*, p. 325], 'the land-owner government of the autocratic tsar' [*ibid.*, vol. 20, p. 329]." "So what?" the unsophisticated reader may ask. So, "in

32. A. I. Davidovich and S. A. Pokrovskii, "O klassovoi sushchnosti i etapakh razvitiia russkogo absoliutizma," p. 65.
33. Ibid., p. 62.   34. Ibid., p. 65.

the light of all these statements by the classical authors of Marxism-Leninism, it is abundantly clear that the conclusions of A. Avrekh concerning absolutism . . . are an obvious distortion of historical reality." (As we see, it is not historical reality which verifies the "*vyska-zyvaniia*," but the "*vyskazyvaniia*" which verify historical reality.) It follows indisputably, the hunters think, that "absolutism [the autocracy] . . . is the personification of the dictatorship of the serf-owning service nobility."[35] Here the trap shuts. For what do we do then with classical French or British absolutism, where there is no trace of a "serf-owning service nobility"? How did a nonexistent class carry out its dictatorship there? And if it did not carry it out, then what becomes of absolutism?

Having barely indicted Avrekh for a terrible heresy and solemnly declared that "it is incorrect to counterpose Russian absolutism to Western European,"[36] the hunters thus immediately fell into a still more terrible heresy, making it ultimately impossible to compare Western absolutism and Russian autocracy in any way.

The next disputant, S. Troitskii, as we might expect, struck at Avrekh from another angle, accusing him of separating the "superstructure" from the "base," and of "trying to explain the origin of absolutism in Russia without connecting it with the genesis of bourgeois relationships."[37] Following this, by all the rules for an accusation of political unreliability, comes a long passage about the suspicious closeness of Avrekh's views (and likewise those of A. Chistozvonov) to the view taken by the bourgeois historian P. N. Miliukov. No, Troitskii personally does not see any particular problem in the fact that "here there is an echo of the views of a bourgeois historian." But still, any normal person will understand that "in the works of the classical authors of Marxism-Leninism [and not in any clouded bourgeois source], there are valuable indications which help us to clear up what historical causes called for the transition to absolute monarchy in Russia."[38]

We see at once what these "valuable indications" help Troitskii to clear up. Here is his line of reasoning. "The Russian bourgeoisie was in fact weak and few in number at the initial stage of its development."[39] But in the fourteenth and fifteenth centuries it was also weak

35. Ibid., pp. 60–61.
36. Ibid., p. 62.
37. S. M. Troitskii, "O nekotorykh spornykh voprosakh istorii absoliutizma v Rossii," p. 135.
38. Ibid., p. 139.
39. Ibid., p. 142.

in France and Holland. "And since this was so, it needed the support of the royal power."[40] And the royal power helped it, just as the royal power did in Russia. Thus, carefully avoiding the "equilibrium" compromised by Avrekh, Troitskii still tries to create the impression that absolutism in Russia was nevertheless formed under the influence of the "demands of the bourgeoisie," and that the bourgeoisie "struggled for their implementation against the ruling class of feudal lords."[41] Having driven the long-suffering "equilibrium" out of the door, he attempts to drag it back through the window. Unfortunately, the "valuable indications" once again work against their adept. For in speaking of an equilibrium, Engels had in mind by no means the weakness of the bourgeoisie and the help given it by the state, but precisely the reverse—the weakness of the nobility, which made possible the *independence* of the state from both of these social groups. And the nobility in Russia, as distinct from the bourgeoisie, did not grow weak, but rather grew strong in the seventeenth and eighteenth centuries. If we are to believe the allies of Troitskii, Davidovich, and Pokrovskii, this nobility was even implementing a serf-holding *dictatorship* in Russia at this time. How, then, does the dictatorship of the serf-owners mesh with the independence of the absolutist state?

In conclusion, Troitskii goes after Pavlova-Sil'vanskaia's concept of despotism as the starting-point of the Russian political process. And, to tell the truth, the destruction of this concept presents no great difficulties, since it is based not so much on concrete analysis, as on those same "*vyskazyvaniia.*" But this is precisely what annoys Troitskii. How are we to drive back this genie, incautiously released from the bottle? How are we to neutralize the unequivocal sound of Lenin's "*vyskazyvaniia*"—for example, about the "Asiatic virginity of Russian despotism"?[42] And here in a desperate attempt to combine reality with "*vyskazyvaniia,*" Troitskii ventures on an extraordinary action: he turns Avrekh's conception upside-down, and proposes his own "reversed" periodization of Russian history.

According to this periodization, the epoch of the estate-representative monarchy lasted in Russia from the fifteenth to the middle of the seventeenth century (would not Troitskii's head be taken off by Ivan the Terrible's Oprichnina for such a heresy!); from the middle of the seventeenth to the eighteenth century there was the epoch of absolutism (here Troitskii would have to answer to the Oprichniki of Peter

40. Ibid., p. 143.
41. Ibid., p. 142.
42. V. I. Lenin, *Polnoe sobranie sochinenii*, vol. 9, p. 381.

and Paul); the nineteenth and twentieth centuries (of course, before 1917) were the epoch of the gradual formation of despotism (!):

> The intensification of the features of despotism and of the "Asiatic style" in the internal and foreign policies of Russian absolutism took place at the end of the eighteenth and in the early nineteenth centuries, when, as a result of the victory of bourgeois revolutions, capitalism, the parliamentary system, and bourgeois freedoms had taken hold in a considerable number of Western European states. In Russia, on the other hand, in the first half of the nineteenth century, the serf order was preserved, reaction was intensified in internal policy, and tsarism became the main force of the "Holy Alliance" and the suppressor of freedom. It is precisely of this period, in our opinion, that we may speak of the growth of features of "despotism" and "Asiatic style" in the policy of Russian absolutism. V. I. Lenin in 1905 wrote about "the Russian autocracy, which lags behind history by a whole century."[13]

This is how Troitskii turns Avrekh's conception upside-down: it was not, in his opinion, despotism which grew into absolutism, but absolutism which grew into despotism. However, what is the category of "despotism" supposed to mean in this context? "The suppression of freedom"—when preliminary censorship was abolished, the peasantry was liberated, urban self-government was introduced, and the rapid economic modernization of the country was begun? That is, despotism is supposed to have increased precisely at the time when the outlines of what Shapiro would call "de facto limitations" on power began to emerge most clearly for the first time after the Oprichnina revolution of Ivan the Terrible?

The "valuable indications" have thus actually helped Troitskii, in complete agreement with Lenin, to erase any difference whatever between "absolutism," "autocracy," and "unlimited power." Avrekh began his attack with the rejection of Lenin's "*vyskazyvanie.*" The punitive expedition of the witch-hunters, attempting to save Russian absolutism at any price, has returned to the starting-point of the discussion without even suspecting that all its efforts have been spent in confirming this offensive and unpatriotic "*vyskazyvanie*" of classical author No. 3.

When the chief "hunter," A. Sakharov, finally appeared on the scene with the job of, as it were, giving marks to the participants in the discussion, all that remained for him was to rubber stamp this result. Avrekh gets a *D* + (the plus is for having, at any rate, noted the "combination of feudal and bourgeois elements in the nature and

43. S. M. Troitskii, p. 148.

policies of absolutism").[44] Pavlova-Sil'vanskaia gets a D − (the minus is for having heretically, "following Avrekh, discovered the fertile ground in which a typical Oriental despotism grew, which had been born somewhere in the period of formation of the Russian centralized state"). Shapiro gets a D for considering "serfdom the major and decisive feature for the evaluation of Russian absolutism."[45] On the other hand, Troitskii, who "unlike the authors just mentioned, sees the basic socioeconomic tendency which brought Russia to absolutism in the birth of bourgeois relationships in the feudal base," gets an A. Davidovich and Pokrovskii, who see "a significant influence on the entire policy of the feudal state" in "the action of the class struggle of the working people,"[46] get an A +.

Sakharov himself goes further than all the other witch-hunters. He is not allowed to maintain a shamefaced silence about the terror of Ivan the Terrible, in speaking of the epoch of "the estate-representative monarchy," as Troitskii does. Nor is he, like Shapiro, going to distract the reader's attention by such insignificant details of the Russian political process as serfdom or the eradication of all representative institutions. He intends not to defend, but to attack—by making a devastating critique of the *Oriental despotism of Western Europe*. For this purpose, of course, one cannot make do with "*vyskazyvaniia*" alone. Here there is required the strong tradition, developed to a virtuoso level by generations of housewives raised in the communal apartments of Moscow, who have fought for their place in the kitchen under the age-old slogan "You damn idiot!"

Do the opponents criticize the Assemblies of the Land? But after all, "such a system is very reminiscent of the alliance of the Tudor regime with Parliament, [which] was assembled only in order to sanction the acts of an unconscionable tyranny." Is this not "Oriental despotism in its English variant?" Sakharov asks triumphantly. Do the opponents see despotism in the actions of Ivan IV? But why do they not also see it in the actions of Elizabeth I of England?

> Between the "Oriental despotism" of Ivan IV and the equally "Oriental despotism" of Elizabeth I of England, the difference is not all that great. . . . Between these two forms of "autocracy" with all their "Eastern" accompaniments, in the form of secret police, brutal suppression of the mutinous nobility in England and Scotland, the colonial plundering of Ireland, the bloody legislation of Henry VII and Edward VI, by which tens of thousands of people were hanged and enslaved, with the approximately identical functions of the estate-representative system,

44. A. N. Sakharov, p. 148.   45. Ibid., p. 111.   46. Ibid., p. 112.

there was no fundamental difference. The centralization of the state in France, particularly under Louis XI, was also marked by features of "Oriental despotism." The merciless executions carried out by Louis XI, the severe persecution of separatists, the destruction of the estate-representative institutions under Charles VIII, Louis XII, and François I, the establishment of an extremely brutal punitive impressment, the plundering of the peasantry, the beginning of a broad expansion in terms of foreign policy—all this fits very well into the framework which our authors have outlined for the "Asiatic form of administration" in its autocratic phase. The centralizing French monarchs, Elizabeth I of England, and Ivan IV solved approximately the same historical tasks in the interests of the feudal class, and the methods of solution of these tasks were approximately identical. The Western European feudal monarchies of the fifteenth and sixteenth centuries had not gone very far in the direction of democracy, relative to the Oprichnina of Ivan the Terrible. . . . The chambers of the Bastille and the Tower of London were just as strong as the cells of the Schlüsselburg and the Alekseevskii fortress, the beheadings on the Place de Grève were no less merciful [*sic*] than those on the battlements of the Petropavlovskii fortress or on the Execution Square in Moscow. . . . The absolutist monarchs of Europe, who were ahead of Russian absolutism in point of time, taught the Russian autocrats impressive lessons as to how to struggle with one's own people. These lessons had everything—police terror, barbaric methods of extracting goods from the people, cruelty, medieval repressions: in a word, all that "Asiatic style," which for some reason is stubbornly attached only to Russian absolutism.[47]

All of the arguments of the Soviet "absolutists" are concentrated in this quotation, as in a lens. But doesn't the reader get the impression that, as Shakespeare has it, "the lady doth protest too much"? Certainly, if all the evil, all the cruelty and injustice visited on humanity by authoritarian regimes is to be attributed to absolutism, as Sakharov does, then Russian "absolutists" are no worse than others; in this

47. A. N. Sakharov, pp. 114, 115, 119. This argument on the part of the most aggressive Russian Marxist is followed without deviation by the most aggressive Russian anti-Marxist. Cf.: "There are two names which are repeated from book to book and article to article with a mindless persistence by all the scholars and essayists of this [anti-Russian] tendency: Ivan the Terrible and Peter the Great, to whom—implicitly or explicitly—they reduce the whole sense of Russian history. But one could just as easily find two or three kings no whit less cruel in the histories of England, France or Spain, or indeed of any country, and yet no one thinks of reducing the complexity of historical meaning to such figures alone" (A. Solzhenitsyn, "Misconceptions about Russia Are Threat to America," p. 802). For both A. N. Sakharov and A. I. Solzhenitsyn, the argument seems to begin and end with the personal cruelty of tyrants, never entering the field of political analysis.

abysmal authoritarian darkness, all cats are gray. Even there, however, we were gray in a somewhat different way. For there is no avoiding it, the countries of classical absolutism did not, in the sixteenth to
eighteenth centuries, know the fundamental facts of serfdom and
universal service, which Sakharov carefully avoids when he so heart-
rendingly describes the horrors of Asiatic despotism in Europe; nor
did they experience recurring restorations of the ancien régime,
again and again bringing terror—sometimes total—directed neither
against those who struggled with the king nor against aliens or heretics, but against everyone who was merely fated to be born in that
time and in that country. There is no more mournful reading than
the description of the devastation wrought by the Oprichnina, in the
official documents of Ivan the Terrible's time, which continue to re-
volve mechanically like millstones, describing what no longer exists.
"In the village of Kiuleksha," we read in one of these documents,

> the farm of Ignatka Luk'ianov was laid waste by the Oprichnina: the
> Oprichniki stole his goods, slaughtered his cattle, and he himself died;
> his children ran off to an unknown place . . . the farm of Eremeika
> Afanasov was laid waste by the Oprichnina: the Oprichniki stole his
> goods, and killed him, and he has no children . . . the farm of Melen-
> teika was laid waste by the Oprichnina: the Oprichniki stole his goods
> and slaughtered his cattle, and he ran off to an unknown place.[18]

They go on and on, endlessly, like Russia herself—miles upon paper miles of this census of human suffering. Once again, a farm is laid
waste; once again, goods are stolen; once again, the man has disappeared. And these are not at all "mutinous nobles," or Huguenots, or
"separatists," but simple, peaceful peasants, who have made no attempt against the sovereign's power, and whose entire fault lay in the
fact that they had goods which could be plundered, wives and daughters who could be raped, land which could be taken away. In England
at that time, peasants were also driven from the land, and the violence practiced against them become proverbial ("The sheep ate the
people"). But whereas in England the violence was committed by individual landlords, in Russia it was practiced on a massive, total *statewide* scale by the government itself and its terrorist police, before
which the nation was entirely defenseless. Whereas in England this
violence was the work of a strong, rising class of new landowners,
which at its next step would stretch out its hands for power and carry

48. I. I. Smirnov, *Ivan Groznyi,* p. 99.

out a political revolution, in Russia it was directed toward the liquidation of the proto-bourgeoisie, and thus toward the establishment of
brutal autocracy. Whereas in England this violence was the instrument by which feudalism was destroyed, opening up the path of progress, in Russia it shut it off like a blank wall. England paid this terrible
price for its historical development, and Russia for its *enserfment*.

Theoretically, Sakharov proposed criteria for the description of
absolutism which come down essentially to the practice of violence by
the government against the people (or, in my terms, to divergence between the goals of the administration and those of the system). According to Sakharov, the regimes of Elizabeth in England, Ivan the
Terrible in Moscow, Shah Abbas in Persia, and Sultan Mekhmet in
Turkey, all equally "do not go very far in the direction of democracy,"
for all of them committed violence against the people. But does this
help us to separate out the category of "absolutism" from the general
mass of "unlimited monarchies"? Does it help to explain why Montesquieu regards the sliding of "moderate government" toward despotism as a historical catastrophe? Does Sakharov's criterion help to
explain the *"vyskazyvaniia"* of his own classical writers? Why, for example, does Engels assert that the Russian autocracy is supported by
an Asiatic despotism of which *we in the West* cannot even have any conception? Why did Lenin call Russian autocracy "Asiatically savage"
(*Complete Works*, vol. 12, p. 10), "Asiatically virgin" (*ibid.*, vol. 9,
p. 381), "saturated with Asiatic barbarism" (*ibid.*, vol. 20, p. 387)?

Thus, the more deeply we penetrate the laboratory of "genuine
science," the more convinced we become that, behind the facade of
haughty pretensions to absolute truth, there lies hidden a heap of
paradoxes, confusion, and helplessness, a chaos of definitions. In it,
absolutism grows out of despotism, as Pavlova-Sil'vanskaia would
have it, and despotism out of absolutism, as Troitskii says. We discover from Likhachev that the "progressive class" brings serfdom
with it, while the "most monstrous form of despotism" turns out to be
progressive according to Cherepnin. And so on and so forth—and
there is no end to it.

Not only is "genuine science" incapable of adequately describing
the nature of the Russian political process; it simply has nothing with
which to do so—neither theoretical prerequisites, nor working hypotheses, nor even accurate definitions. Any attempt to create so
much as a preliminary conceptual base for the study of political structures is suffocated, as we have just seen, at the embryonic stage.

The enserfed peasants of Russia waited three hundred years for the Great Reform of 1861 to liberate them. They rebelled against serfdom, and these rebellions did bring them freedom—at least for a while. The enserfed historians of Russia rebel, too, against their miserable medieval "science." Let us hope that these scholars will not have to wait another two hundred years for their 1861.

CHAPTER III

THE "DESPOTISTS": CAPTIVES OF THE BIPOLAR MODEL

1. The Three Faces of "Russian Despotism"

The nature and origin of the Russian political structure is obviously not the most urgent question in the Western literature on the philosophy of history. At least, it was difficult for me to find as representative a debate among the "despotists" as the one among the "absolutists" which I have just analyzed. For this reason, I prefer to take another route in this chapter. I have chosen three well-known names, which from my point of view symbolize three main tendencies in the interpretation of "Russian despotism"—the "Tatar," the "Byzantine," and the "Patrimonial." They are, respectively, Karl Wittfogel, Arnold Toynbee, and Richard Pipes (I consider Tibor Szamuely's book *The Russian Tradition* here only as a supplementary argument to Wittfogel's "Tatar" interpretation).

I am proceeding from the assumption that these authors represent more or less fully the spectrum of arguments in the Western literature dealing with the nature and origin of the Russian political structure. I respect their hypotheses, although I cannot agree with them. As distinct from the *"vyskazyvaniia"* which we considered in the last chapter, they are interesting to argue with, not to speak of the fact that this permits us to throw some additional light on the problem which concerns us. Nevertheless, I cannot help saying in advance that it was difficult for me to find in these fluently, and sometimes even brilliantly, expressed conceptions, very much of relevance to the actual historical process in Russia. It may be that the reason for this (at least, this feeling never left me) is that the authors mentioned have reached their conclusions not so much as a result of studying its historical development as through an a priori resolve to prove that Russia belongs to the despotic family of nations.

However this may be, in passing from the absolutists to the despotists, the unprejudiced reader will be easily persuaded that only the direction of the emotional thrust—only its sign (plus for minus)—is changed. The despotists are obviously not too friendly to Russia, but the picture remains the same: black-and-white. The spectrum of concepts is limited to the bipolar model, to the fateful contrast between "multicentered" and "single-centered" civilizations (Wittfogel), or "Western" and "totalitarian" (Toynbee), or "monarchy" and "patrimonial state" (Pipes). In short, we are dealing with the same absolutism and despotism, under different pseudonyms. This fact, to say the least, seriously complicates the analysis of the Russian historical process for our authors—to the degree that it proves difficult to explain many aspects of this process, not to speak of its origin and nature, with the aid of their hypotheses. This is precisely what I will now try to show.

2. The "Tatar" Interpretation

It is obviously impossible to understand and evaluate Wittfogel's conception adequately without taking into account its basic quality: it is a model of militant scholarship. It is infinitely far from the coquettish "objectivity," the skeptical feeling that one's recommendations are not necessarily valid, the hint of play, and the sense of humor, which are characteristic of the style of many contemporary scholars in our humanistic field, which is suffering from an inferiority complex in this age of the triumph of natural science. In Wittfogel's work there is something deadly serious, rigorous, almost medieval—something between Puritan severity and the pathos of a crusader. This work breathes polemics and boils with passion. Like its author's native country, Germany, it fights on two fronts—the Eastern and the Western—and develops in four directions at once: on the level of abstract theory; on the historical level (or that of applied theory); on the methodological level; and on the political level. All this is terribly awkward to analyze, because it is tied up in such a tight knot that it is impossible either to reject or to accept it totally. It is this homogeneity or synthesis—I do not know how best to express it—which constitutes the second basic feature of Wittfogel's conception. Therefore, before arguing about it, it would perhaps be best to break it up into its component parts, and then to evaluate each one separately.

Certainly, it would be easiest to say that the conception of "Oriental despotism" was only the historical dimension of the political concept of totalitarianism which was fashionable during the years of the Cold War—that, to paraphrase Mikhail Pokrovskii, it was totalitarianism projected into the past. It is still easier to say, as S. N. Eisenstadt does, that "if one wants to write about communism and Stalin, the best way to do it is not necessarily through writing about Oriental despotism. Neither Oriental despotism nor modern communism get their due in this way."[1]

Such arguments are good for rejecting Wittfogel. For understanding him, they are useless. In the first place, history and politics are synthesized for him in a single and indivisible whole, like the root and branches of a tree: no aspect of politics can be understood without involving history in the analysis, and no part of history can be understood if we leave politics aside. In the second place, the interdisciplinary approach, according to Wittfogel, works only in the context of world history (of what he calls an "inter-area" approach). These are his postulates. One may not agree with them; one may regret that he does not always follow them; but one cannot argue with him constructively without understanding them. A poet, as we know, is judged by the laws of his genre.

At any rate, on this methodological plane, Wittfogel struggled (quite unsuccessfully, to judge by many reviews of his work) on the Western front, so to speak, against his super-specialized colleagues from European and American academia, insisting on his right to synthesize history, politics, and theory. In all other dimensions, his struggle took place on the Eastern front.

The thrust of his conception, on the level of abstract theory, consists in the denial of the Marxist postulate as to the *unilinear nature* of the historical process. This theme is painful for him, as for any defrocked Marxist, and he returns many times to the assertion of what he calls the "multilinear theory of social development." This is a highly respectable point of view. The only trouble is that, having triumphantly declared it, Wittfogel is unfortunately by no means in a position to adhere to it. In fact, his central thesis asserts that despotism has *one* historical starting-point—the need to construct gigantic irrigation facilities in Oriental agrarian societies, leading to the formation of a managerial-bureaucratic class which enslaves society. This is why Wittfogel prefers to call despotism a "hydraulic" or "agromanagerial" civilization. However, at this point he encounters a strange phenomenon: some civilizations, which correspond to his description of despotism, turn out to be located outside the "hydraulic" sphere. A historian who has asserted the "multilinear theory of social

1. S. N. Eisenstadt, "The Study of Oriental Despotisms as Systems of Total Power," p. 446.

development" should not be bothered by this circumstance. On the contrary, it should only serve as the starting-point for the analysis of other parallel "lines." However, for some reason, Wittfogel declines to follow the logic of the theory he is defending. Instead, he suddenly starts to erect a highly complex hierarchy of despotisms, intended to free politics from hydraulics and to permit him to extend his conception to the predominant portion of the "nonhydraulic" world. In addition to the "dense" or "nuclear" despotisms, this hierarchy includes "marginal" or even "semimarginal" despotisms, which no longer have even the remotest relation to artificial irrigation of crops. Thus, the entire world—beyond the confines of Western Europe and Japan—regardless of the amount of precipitation, is drawn into the pit of hydraulic despotism, and gradually marshalled in one uniform "line." At this point, Wittfogel's conception suddenly begins to take on, obviously and with frightening clarity, those same features of universalism which he so hates in Marxism. Only, in place of the *unilinear* gospel according to Karl Marx, we get the bilinear (obviously Manichaean) gospel according to Karl Wittfogel. And by this detour, we again return to the same old bipolar model. This is in turn directly connected to the problem of Russia as a "semimarginal despotism."

In the early articles of the 1950s and in his book, Wittfogel does not seem to harbor the slightest doubts as to Russia's membership in the despotic family. However, in answering his opponents Nicholas Riasanovsky and Berthold Spuler during a 1963 debate in *Slavic Review*, he seems a bit more careful. Here is his final formulation:

> The two Oriental nations that especially affected the history of Russia prior to recent times were Byzantium and the Mongols of the Golden Horde. It is generally agreed that during the Kievan period, when Byzantine influence was very great, Russian society was pluralistic ("multi-centered") . . . whereas, at the end of the Mongol (Tatar) period there emerged in Muscovite Russia a single-centered society dominated by an autocratic state that exerted great power. This historical evidence suggests that this state fulfilled a number of managerial functions which in this form—and/or dimension—were not fulfilled by the states of late feudal and post-feudal Europe. It suggests on the other hand that in the Orient many states fulfilled such functions.[2]

Let us assume for a moment that this is precisely how it was: the Muscovite state fulfilled certain functions not carried out by the absolutist states, which at the same time were carried out by the despotic

---

2. Donald W. Treadgold, ed., *The Development of the USSR: An Exchange of Views*, pp. 352–53.

states. However, as we already know, there were also a large number
of features, functions, and peculiarities in the Russian social, economic and political process—in the very institutional dynamics of
it—which were characteristic not of despotism but of absolutism.
What is the logical consequence of this? That Russia belonged to the
despotic family, or that it belonged completely neither to despotism
nor to absolutism? For a historian who believes in the "multilinearity
of social development," this, it would seem, should serve as a stimulus
for the analysis of a new "line."

Alas, the same theoretical contradiction from which Wittfogel's
conception suffers on the abstract level continues to haunt him on the
historical level. He again neglects the logic of the theory he is defending. It is true that whereas in the 1950s he emphasized *only* the
similarities between Russia and "Oriental despotism," in the 1960s he
noticed the differences. But, having encountered resistance in the
historical material, Wittfogel reacts to it, not as a phenomenon requiring new insight, but merely as an annoying hindrance which must be
overcome, in order that one may, *in spite of it*, prove the thesis set up
in advance. Let us see how he sets about doing this.

Where does Wittfogel see the difficulties in interpreting Russia as a
"nonhydraulic subtype" of hydraulic despotism? In the first place, the
Tatars, who, it is assumed, "infected" Russia with the organizational
and fiscal methods of despotism, by no means occupied it. They did
not live on Russian territory, or mix with the local population, or educate it, so to speak, by personal example and shared experience. Instead, they exercised what Wittfogel calls "remote control" over Russia. This naturally made more difficult so total a degree of "infection"
as his hypothesis requires.

In the second place, when the youthful Muscovite state threw off
the Tatar yoke in the process of its Reconquista, it did not turn out by
any means to be fashioned on the Tatar pattern. A whole century was
needed before it began to take on those features which gave Wittfogel
a basis for considering it a despotism, even though "semimarginal."
This strange disjunction in time, which G. Vernadsky has defined by
a kind of metaphor ("influence through delayed action"), requires
explanation. In fact, if in the first case we have to do with "remote
control" in the spatial dimension, here we get the same oddity in the
temporal dimension.

The third peculiarity of "Russian despotism" was the influence ex-
erted on it by the "European commercial and industrial revolution,"
an influence which gave it an entirely unique character. Answering
the challenge of Europe, it behaved as a "hydraulic structure" should

under no circumstances behave—even one of semimarginal status. It developed; it underwent institutional modernization.

Finally, the fourth peculiarity consists in the fact that, as distinct from despotism, the Muscovite state lacked absolute sovereignty over the persons and property of its subjects. Having tried to assert such sovereignty in the seventeenth century, it mysteriously lost it again in the eighteenth. Half of the arable land again became inalienable private property, as it had been after the overthrow of the Tatar yoke.

These are the peculiarities of the Russian historical process (or the hindrances to the classification of Russia as a despotist state) which are registered by Wittfogel himself. As to the first, Wittfogel has nothing concrete to say, confining himself to remarking that "The Mongol's remote control over Russia poses many problems that require further investigation."[3] Let's give him this one. Regarding the second, he has an explanation (true, again a metaphorical, not to say eccentric, one). Let us cite it in full:

> In Russia the slowness of the transformation [into despotism] was due to . . . the Mongol policy of remote control. . . . Whether the centrifugal political order of Kievan Russia—which at best possessed some quasi-feudal aspects—accelerated or retarded the process is a moot question. There is no doubt, however, that the Mongol conquerors of Russia weakened the forces that until 1237 had limited the power of the princes, that they employed Oriental methods of government to keep Russia prostrated and exploited, and that they did not intend to create a strong—and politically challenging—agrodespotic state. Hence the germs of the system of total power they planted could bear fruit only after the end of the Mongol period. . . . [I]t may be said that an institutional time bomb exploded when the Mongol control collapsed.[1]

What the metaphor of the "institutional time bomb" (no less paradoxical than Vernadsky's formula) is supposed to mean, the reader is left to guess. Reviewers queried this, but as far as I know, Wittfogel never explained it. It is all the more unclear why the "explosion" of this bomb took place so slowly. (Whether there are slow explosions at all is a question which, it seems, should be asked of sappers.) One thing is clear: this whole explosion of metaphors would perhaps sound good in a poem, but even in a fantastic novel it would seem dubious. As a description of an actual historical process, it sounds fantastic, the more so since in historical reality there is no basis for it whatever. For example, the Tatars not only took no action against the

3. Ibid., p. 331.
4. Ibid., p. 332.

seigneurial property of the Russian aristocracy as an institution limiting the power of the princes, or against the policy of grants of immunity, i.e., the removal of seigneurial holdings from the competence of the organs of state power, but precisely the contrary—at least judging by their policy in regard to the Orthodox church, which greatly strengthened it.[5] What then, we wonder, is the meaning of Wittfogel's declaration that "the Mongol conquerors weakened the forces that until 1237 had limited the power of the princes"?

But this is not the main point. The chief question is why, having arisen out of Tatar obscurity with an untouched aristocratic tradition (and more than this, having evolved, as we saw in chapter one, in the direction of re-Europeanization in many aspects of institutional development), Muscovy suddenly after a century turned sharply toward a recrudescence of Tatardom, and began to lay waste its own aristocracy? "[Wittfogel's] explanation in fact only creates a problem," says one of his closest cothinkers, Tibor Szamuely, on this point.

> For a system of government, however, that was so utterly alien from all earlier Russian tradition, to have taken root and flourished with such intensity, the force of example, the mere accessibility of the tools, could not have been sufficient. After all, Hungary and the Balkan countries remained under Turkish rule for periods, in some cases, far exceeding the duration of the Tatar yoke, yet none of them emerged from thraldom as Oriental despotisms. This will not do—as in murder investigations, not only opportunity and method, but motive also has to be established. There had to exist in Russia a particular concatenation of circumstances which required, necessitated or called for the introduction of this socio-political system, and that ensured the rationality and success of its operation—or to use the Toynbeean terms, there had to have existed a "challenge" which evoked an appropriate "response."[6]

As for the third peculiarity of "Russian despotism," here Wittfogel's situation is still more complex. In fact, if his entire explanation of Russia's capacity for modernization consists only in the fact that it is situated closer to Europe than the other "agrodespotisms," then the question immediately arises: what about Turkey, which was still closer? Why did the Ottoman Empire prove immune to the European industrial revolution and incapable of modernization, as an ordinary despotism is supposed to be, in spite of its geographical advantages? Why did it have to be destroyed to the foundations in a

5. See, for example, S. V. Veselovskii, *K voprosy o proiskhozhdenii votchinnogo rezhima*; S. M. Kashtanov, *Sotsial'no-politicheskaia istoriia Rossii kontsa XV—pervoi poloviny XVI v.*; Horace Dewey, "Immunities in Old Russia."
6. Tibor Szamuely, *The Russian Tradition*, p. 87.

world war and transformed into an ordinary national state before it could embark on the path of modernization? Wittfogel, to do him justice, sees this difficulty himself. Unfortunately, the explanation which he suggests is still more unclear than in the case of the "institutional time bomb." "In the eighteenth and nineteenth centuries," he writes, "Ottoman Turkey was faced with just this question [modernization], but internal disintegration and external encroachment prevented a successful industrial and military adjustment. Russia, however, was sufficiently independent to meet the new threat."[7]

What Wittfogel means by this in concrete terms again remains obscure. That at the beginning of the eighteenth century (when Russia, according to Wittfogel, began its march toward modernization) Turkey was "insufficiently independent" for an analogous action? But in that case, on whom did it depend? And whose intrusion prevented it from modernizing itself? In fact, the Ottoman Empire at this time was a great and mighty power. More than this, as the Russo-Turkish War of 1711 demonstrates, it was stronger than Russia—and more independent, if only because Turkey did not require either Dutch sea captains or Scottish generals, of whom Russia stood in such need precisely because she was modernizing. It turns out that the whole situation was exactly the reverse. The Ottoman Empire was more independent than Russia because of its *incapacity for modernization.*

Concerning the fourth peculiarity of "Russian despotism," Wittfogel comments as follows:

> The conversion of service land into privately-owned land in 1762 removed one important managerial task from the government roster. But . . . before this occurred the regime had taken on another—the running or supervising of the new (particularly the heavy) industry. By the end of the eighteenth century, state enterprises employed almost two-thirds of all industrial labor. And although in the nineteenth century the private sector expanded conspicuously, until the Emancipation large numbers of laborers continued to work in state enterprises. . . . By 1900 the government still controlled either directly or by means of licensing about 45% of all large modern enterprises of industrial production and communication.[8]

This reasoning again creates a problem—or even several problems. In the first place, what Wittfogel takes as a starting point itself requires explanation. Why is it that so drastic a "conversion," unheard of in any despotic state, all of a sudden took place in Russia?

7. Treadgold, ed., p. 332.
8. Ibid., p. 336.

Let us remember, for that matter, the fundamental position of Marx, on which Wittfogel himself relies: "The state [in Asia] is the supreme owner of the land. Sovereignty here *is* ownership of land, concentrated on a national scale. . . . In this case *no private ownership of land exists*, although both private and communal tenure and use of land do exist."[9] Again, Russia does not fit into Wittfogel's metaphorical conception. And if she constitutes a unique case, an exception, then oughtn't this to be explained?

In the second place, the total sovereignty of the state over all of the national product, which is characteristic of despotism, is one thing, and state control over a definite portion of the industrial enterprises is quite another. And the difference here is not only one of degree, but primarily one of the quality of control. For that part of the industrial sector which was in private hands was—there is no getting out of it—private property, just like the land belonging to the nobility in the second half of the eighteenth century (or like the boyar lands before the second half of the sixteenth century).

In the third place, even according to Wittfogel, it was not the state, but precisely this private sector which proved capable of expansion, and increasingly displaced state ownership, gradually transforming itself into not only a social, but also a political force. In short, this was by no means the "weak private property" characteristic of despotism, incapable (by Wittfogel's definition) of having any political influence and unable to defend itself from the arbitrary action of the regime. On the contrary, this was "strong private property" and—what was still more important—capable of becoming stronger yet.

I have dealt specially only with those peculiarities of the Russian political structure which are noted by Wittfogel himself, without even touching on the decisive fact—its capacity for institutional and social development, unthinkable for despotism. Moreover, right up to the twentieth century, there has never been the kind of managerial class in Russia which, as Wittfogel was convinced, properly comprises the soul of despotism.

3. Opportunity, Means, and Motive

Wittfogel's follower and cothinker, Tibor Szamuely, also, as we have seen, finds his arguments insufficiently convincing. Szamuely believes that "the opportunity and the means" for despotism, supplied to

---

9. Karl Marx and Friedrich Engels, *Sochineniia*, vol. 25, pt. 1, p. 354. Emphasis added.

Muscovy by the Tatars, cannot sufficiently explain the explosion of Wittfogel's "institutional time bomb." A motive was also needed, and Szamuely finds one—or even two motives. The first consists in the enormous dimensions of the country, which in themselves, merely by virtue of the need for effective administration, required a despotic form of rule. "But the exigency which called forth the Muscovite variety of Oriental despotism was more pressing than the mere demand for effective administration," he adds.

> The socio-political system of the great Asian empires had been created by the paramount need for building and maintaining the waterworks upon which the very lives of their peoples depended. Russia knew nothing of this, yet for centuries she too had been confronted by a task which, though different in nature, was for her just as much a matter of life and death: *national survival* depended upon the permanent mobilization and organization of all her meager resources *for defense*, war and colonization, on a scale beyond the European comprehension. Despotic government with all its implications was the instrument she shaped to cope with the everlasting emergency. The ideas may have been brought in from the outside, but the necessity was terrifyingly real.[10]

Szamuely's first "motive" does not stand up to even the slightest contact with the chronology. Russia became the gigantic power which the world now knows only long after the detonation of the institutional time bomb. Consequently, its current dimensions simply cannot have anything to do with the explosion in question.[11]

The second "motive" is considerably more serious—if only because such prominent scholars as Kliuchevskii, Pavlov-Sil'vanskii, and Plekhanov paid some degree of tribute to it, as a result of which it found its way into the majority of popular surveys of Russian history. The geopolitical position of Muscovy—so runs the stereotype—placed it in essentially the same position in which climatic conditions placed the great Asiatic empires. Finding itself for centuries in the position of a besieged fortress, Muscovy had to defend itself by any and every means. Thus, it was geography (represented in this case by the location of the country) which gave rise to the "Muscovite variety of Asiatic despotism," to use Szamuely's words, just as (in the form of the absence of rain) it had conditioned the ancient Egyptian or Chi-

10. Tibor Szamuely, p. 88.
11. Conversely, the resources of Russia were meager only while it remained a relatively small country. When it became gigantic, Russia simultaneously became one of the richest nations in resources.

nese variants. In both cases, national survival depended on geography, which left the respective governments no other choice than to establish a despotism. In this interpretation, despotism was Russia's predestined fate.

We will speak in detail of this stereotype in the concrete historical analysis of Russia's absolutist century immediately preceding the "explosion." But in general terms we must touch upon it here. Surrounded on the West by Lithuania, Poland, Livonia, and Sweden, and on the South and the East by the Tatars, Moscow really did produce the impression of a besieged fortress. And wars did in fact consume a huge part of its resources and energy. Sigismund Herberstein, ambassador of the German emperor, who visited Moscow twice during the reign of Vasilii III, received the impression that, for Muscovy, peace was an accident. During the course of the sixteenth century, it waged ten wars to the West, which took up about fifty years. But the situation in the Tatar South and East was considerably more difficult: from here, if we can believe Fletcher, Muscovy was attacked every year, and sometimes twice a year. Hundreds of thousands of people, and particularly children, who were especially sought after by the Tatar raiders, were driven off into slavery. They were sold in the bazaars of Asia and Africa in such numbers that, Iurii Krizhanich relates, Russian slaves in the Crimea, seeing their fellow countrymen as new prisoners, asked each other whether there were still people in Muscovy or whether they had already all been sold into slavery. This frightening picture, which so struck many Russian historians, requires a closer look, however.

First of all, the wars which Muscovy waged in the West had nothing to do with defense, let alone national survival. Beginning at least in the 1480s, Muscovy was permanently on the offensive against its western neighbors, obtaining western Rus' from Poland-Lithuania, and Kareliia and the Baltic shore from the Swedes and Livonia. Thus, its political "encirclement" was a myth, and its wars in the West were the result of strategic and political choice, and by no means a geographical inevitability.

As for the Tatars, in this direction as well Moscow was so strong under Ivan III that in the East it placed its own candidates as khans on the throne of Kazan', and was at the same time clever enough to channel the Crimean raids into southern Lithuania. If Sigismund Herberstein had visited Moscow under Vasilii III's father, he would probably have gotten an entirely different impression. For the wars which Russia waged during this period (Ivan III reigned for forty-three years) were none of them defensive. Not only were Ivan III's wars all offensive, they were rare for that time. After him, Muscovy passed over to direct attacks on the Tatars. Conquest of the Volga khanates eliminated the threat from the East, and a war was begun against the Crimea which could have eradicated the nest of slave raiders in the South (or, at least, have made it as uncomfortable for them to raid Muscovy as it had been during Ivan III's reign), *if Ivan the Terrible had not suddenly "turned on the Germans."*

This miscalculation cost Muscovy very dear, and not only in terms of human and material resources: it changed Russia's entire history. As I am trying to show, it actually did face the country with the problem of national survival. But this was a *strategic error*, and not a "frighteningly real necessity" following inevitably from the geopolitical position of Russia, as Szamuely tries to persuade us.

On the contrary, in the middle of the sixteenth century (that is, at the moment of the "explosion") Russia's geopolitical position was unusually favorable. It is not impossible that, if she had left the West, from which no one threatened her, in peace, and had concentrated on the liquidation of the threat from the Crimea, she could have established herself on the shores of the Black Sea within two or three generations, and put an end once and for all to Tatar control over her fertile South, and to the predatory raids of the slavers. These are not my speculations. This was the conviction, reflected in documents, of the leaders of the Muscovite government of that time, who, we must assume, knew at least as well what they were talking about as subsequent historians.

It may be objected that war is war, whether it is aggressive or defensive, and that it strains a nation to the limit, and in any case does not exert a favorable influence on its political structure. And this is true. But if wars in and of themselves can be the cause of the establishment of despotism, then the Hundred Years' War between England and France, which consumed four generations of the young people of those countries, should have given rise in the heart of Europe to despotic rigors of which not even Shah Abbas would have dreamed. At the worst, such wars produced tyranny—as was eventually the case in England and France—but not despotism.

4. The "Byzantine" Interpretation

Wittfogel takes very seriously the argument that it was the Tatars, and not the Byzantines, who were the forefathers of despotism in Russia. "Byzantium's influence on Kievan Russia was great, but it was primarily cultural," he writes.

Like China's influence on Japan, it did not seriously alter the conditions of power, class, and property. Ottoman Turkey's influence on 16th century Russia stimulated a regime that was already Orientally despotic, but it did not bring it into being. Tatar rule alone among the three major Oriental influences affecting Russia was decisive both in destroying the non-Oriental Kievan society and in laying the foundations for the despotic state of Muscovite and post-Muscovite Russia.[12]

Though Wittfogel proved unable to demonstrate this thesis, I see nothing illegitimate, let alone offensive, in it. Nonetheless, it seems to be this which, for some reason, annoys the experts most. In any case, in arguing with him, they emphasize primarily that Russia was certainly formed, for the most part, precisely under Byzantine (that is, non-Tatar) influence. Wittfogel himself felt this annoyance. "Let us for the sake of argument assume that the political institutions of tsarist Russia not only resembled those of Byzantium but were actually derived from them," he responded.

> What follows with regard to the overall interpretation of Russia? If the Byzantine Empire was a variant of a multicentered society of the medieval Western type, then, of course, this would be very basic to our argument—but also very puzzling, since tsarist Russia, in contrast to the West, constituted (as generally agreed) a single-centered society. And if the Byzantine Empire was a variant of an Oriental despotism (as comparative institutional analysis suggests), then the establishment of Byzantium as Muscovy's "high model" only replaces an ugly Tatar picture by a culturally attractive picture of an Orientally despotic ancestor.[13]

Indeed, does our conception of the Russian political process change in essence if we dress up its origins in a Byzantine brocade coat rather than a Tatar *beshmet*? Is it easier for us to explain the riddles of Russian history if we replace Wittfogel's arguments with those of Toynbee? Let us see. In his essay "Russia's Byzantine Heritage," Toynbee writes:

> For nearly a thousand years past, the Russians have . . . been members, not of our Western civilization, but of the Byzantine. . . . In thus assuming the Byzantine heritage deliberately and self-consciously, the Russians were taking over . . . the traditional Byzantine attitude towards the West; and this has had a profound effect on Russia's own attitude towards the West, not only before the Revolution of 1917 but after it. . . . In this long and grim struggle to preserve their independence

12. K. Wittfogel, *Oriental Despotism*, pp. 224–25.
13. Treadgold, ed., p. 355.

[from the West], the Russians have sought salvation in the political institution that was the bane of the medieval Byzantine world. Feeling that their one hope of survival lay in a ruthless concentration of political power, they worked out for themselves a Russian version of the Byzantine totalitarian state. . . . This Muscovite political edifice has twice been given a new facade—first by Peter the Great, and then again by Lenin—but the essence of the structure has remained unaltered, and the Soviet Union of today, like the Grand Duchy of Moscow in the fourteenth century, reproduces the salient features of the medieval East Roman Empire. . . . Under the Hammer and Sickle, as under the Cross, Russia is still "Holy Russia," and Moscow still "The Third Rome."[14]

Toynbee despises such workaday topics as irrigation facilities. You will not find in his work mention of the managerial class as a distinguishing feature of despotism. He does not even mention the term "despotism." He is a historian, not of material, but of spiritual culture. And it is natural that he is chiefly interested in such aspects of this history as the millennial hostility between the Romans and the Greeks, each of whom considered themselves a chosen people; as the fortunate failure of Charlemagne to restore the Western empire, and the fatal success of Leo the Syrian in restoring the empire of the East; as the schism between Western and Eastern Christianity, which was only the material embodiment of the same old Greco-Roman cultural hostility; and other similar topics. Even by the word "totalitarianism," he means essentially only the subordination of the church to the state[15]—that is, in terms of our conception, the denial of ideological limitations on power, of which Montesquieu had written some two centuries before him. In other words, for Toynbee, as for Solzhenitsyn thirty years later, economic peculiarities, social differences, and political structures are by-products of ideology, which—as a cultural tradition—is all-powerful and stands alone in determining the direction of the historical process.

But this quite legitimate attempt (even though it is no more valid than Wittfogel's) to explain the *Russian* political process on the basis of an implacable hatred between *Greeks* and *Romans* has its vulnerable points. Toynbee asserts that "In this Byzantine totalitarian State, the

14. A. Toynbee, "Russia's Byzantine Heritage," pp. 83, 87, 94, 95.
15. "[The struggle between the church and the state in Byzantium] ended in the Church's becoming virtually a department of the medieval East Roman State; and a State that has reduced the Church to this position has thereby made itself 'totalitarian'—if our latter-day term 'totalitarian State' means a state that has established its control over every side of the life of its subjects" (Toynbee, ibid., p. 93).

church may be Christian or Marxian, so long as it submits to being the secular government's tool."[16] But by no means every specialist will agree with him that the "Marxian church" is merely a department of the Soviet state; others might assert the precise opposite—namely that the Soviet state is, as yet, a department of the Marxian church. At any rate, which is subordinate to which is not obvious, as it appears to Toynbee, but on the contrary a difficult and debatable point. For example, the followers of Solzhenitsyn in the Russian dissident movement are struggling, it seems, not so much for the separation of the church from the state, as for the separation of the state from the church.

In the second place, "Why did Byzantine Constantinople go down to ruin? And why, on the other hand, did Byzantine Moscow survive?" Again Toynbee himself asks a question which is fatal to his thesis. "The key to both these historical riddles is the Byzantine institution of the totalitarian State,"[17] he triumphantly declares, but this does not seem any more convincing than "the class struggle" of the Soviet absolutists as a solution. Even from a purely methodological point of view, we can predict that Toynbee is exulting a bit prematurely at the beginning of his essay. He will not be able to keep his promise to open two different locks with the same key. Just as the absolutists, in trying to explain Russia's backwardness, appealed for help to the Tatars, so Toynbee must, like his debunked opponent, Wittfogel, in the end appeal to geography for help. Russia, he writes, "owed her survival in the early middle ages [according to the thesis, this sentence should end 'to the Byzantine institution of the totalitarian state'] to a happy geographical accident."[18] Now we've got it again.

In the third place, and most importantly, how does the cultural hostility of Greeks and Romans help us to explain certain events in Russian history? For example, the enserfment of the peasants? And then their liberation? The Oprichnina revolution of Ivan the Terrible? And the Time of Troubles which followed it? The "new classes" bringing periodic catastrophe on the Russian aristocracy? And its equally periodic rebirth? The Russian political opposition? The Stalinist Gulag? And the attempts to de-Stalinize the country which followed it? The reader will agree that these events, and others like them, are the keys to Russian history. And a hypothesis which tries to derive them from the conflicts between John Chrysostom and the Empress Eudoxia, or between Pope Silverius and the Emperor Justin-

16. Ibid., p. 95.   17. Ibid., p. 91.   18. Ibid., p. 94.

ian, would hardly seem any more convincing than Wittfogel's attempt
to explain them by the influence of the Tatars.

Notwithstanding that Toynbee's essay displays to the full his awe-
some erudition in regard to the conflicts between popes and emperors, it appears considerably less well-founded than Wittfogel's argument, and I frankly do not see any adequate basis for the haughty
criticism to which Toynbee subjects his opponent. Rather, both of
them give the impression of being helpless prisoners of the fatal bipolar model, which has deprived them of the possibility of following the
concrete processes of Russian history, and of answering its concrete
questions. They were simply more interested in global constructions
than in the urgent problems of any particular national history. As a
result, however, this particular national history has proved to be
beyond the limits of the global models which they have constructed.

5. The "Patrimonial" Interpretation

Until recently, the lively competition between the "Tatar" and "Byzantine" interpretations has, for the most part, dominated philosoph-
ical-historical thinking about Russia in the West. However, with the
appearance of Richard Pipes's book, *Russia Under the Old Regime*,
which has apparently proved unusually popular,[19] this thinking has
taken on a new dimension. A fundamentally new conception has
emerged, rejecting from the outset the very thought of Russia as an
"Oriental despotism."[20] Instead, Russia is defined as a "patrimonial
monarchy"—that is, a polity "where the rights of sovereignty and
those of ownership blend to the point of becoming indistinguishable;"[21] or, more precisely, a political structure run by its tsars much as

19. When, at the University of California at Berkeley, I recommended that my students read Pipes's book, it turned out that all 12 (!) copies available in the libraries were
in use. I did not hear anything like this about any other book which I recommended.

20. Pipes writes that while "one might have expected Russia to develop early in its
history something akin to the bureaucratic regime of the 'despotic' or 'Asiatic' kind
. . . for a variety of reasons its political development took a somewhat different route.
. . . [I]t knew nothing of central economic management until the imposition of War
Communism in 1918. But even if such management had been required, the country's
natural conditions would have prevented its introduction. One need only consider the
difficulties of transport and communication in Russia before the advent of railroads
and telegraphs to realize that the kind of control and surveillance essential to an 'Oriental Despotism' was entirely out of the question here" (*Russia under the Old Regime*, p. 20).

21. Ibid., pp. 22–23. Amazingly, Pipes's definition almost literally corresponds with
another one already known to the reader. Only Marx had in mind precisely what Pipes
is rejecting: "Oriental despotism."

112 *The Adversities of Theory*

the primitive family is run by the paterfamilias. More than that, the very definition of despotism is subjected to revision. It is treated not as a distinct political structure, but as a "deviation" from normal monarchy, based not on tradition, but on force. The "patrimonial state," on the other hand, is said to be based on tradition ("the primitive family").

> Here conflicts between sovereignty and property do not and cannot arise because . . . they are one and the same thing. A despot violates his subjects' property rights; a patrimonial ruler does not even acknowledge their existence. By inference, under a patrimonial system there can be no clear distinction between state and society in so far as such a distinction postulates the right of persons other than the sovereign to exercise control over things and (where there is slavery) over persons. . . . Classical examples of patrimonial regimes are to be found among the Hellenistic states which emerged from the dissolution of the empire of Alexander the Great, such as Egypt of the Ptolemies (305–30 BC) and the Attalid state in Pergamum (*c.* 283–133 BC).[22]

Let us leave it to experts to judge the equivalence of the political structures of Ptolemaic Egypt and Attalid Pergamum (I'm afraid that they will hardly agree on this) and return, as Rabelais says, to our rams. First of all, let us state with relief that both Wittfogel's Tatars and Toynbee's Byzantines have, in Pipes's interpretation, ceased to be a "high model" (Wittfogel's term) for the Russian political structure. It is true that the reasons for which Pipes has demoted them are somewhat exotic. Neither the Tatars nor the Byzantines can boast of the patriarchal peace which, according to Pipes, must have reigned in the "primitive family" of the Russian patrimonial state. In neither case could matters have gone as smoothly and as naturally as they must have gone there. There was no one in Russia to throw down the challenge to the supreme property rights of the "father of the Russian family." Everyone was content with his family position. No wonder that "[t]he Muscovite service class, from which, in direct line of succession, descend the dvorianstvo of imperial Russia and the communist apparatus of Soviet Russia, represents a unique phenomenon in the history of social institutions."[23] In a society saturated with the "patrimonial mentality,"[24] the notion that property could belong to anyone other than the sovereign could never even enter anyone's head, it seems. Even the Hellenistic states have ceased, within a matter of some fifty pages, to serve as a "high model" for this unique phenomenon.

22. Ibid., p. 23.   23. Ibid., p. 97.   24. Ibid., p. 71.

The very "idea of state was absent in Russia until the middle of the seventeenth century. . . . And since there was no notion of state, its corollary, society, was also unknown," Pipes asserts.[25] Moreover, according to him, "[b]ecause there was no free market, social classes in the customary sense of the word could not arise."[26] It was all the more impossible that there should be political opposition in that primitive family. After all, what cause was there for opposition to arise, if the basic area of social conflicts—the struggle for property—was excluded in the nature of things?

In this patriarchal picture there is, of course, no room for Oprichnina revolutions and Stalinizations, for "Times of Troubles," de-Stalinizations, and analogous political dramas. Sons, it is true, do not always obey their parents, but they don't try to change the structure of their family. They do not introduce local self-government or trial by jury; they do not call Assemblies of the Land; they do not try to carry out major reforms, and—what is most important—they do not make claims on the property naturally belonging to the head of the family. It is not surprising, therefore, that the entire Oprichnina of Ivan the Terrible is accommodated in Pipes's book in two paragraphs and has the character rather of an epic family chronicle than of a "revolution from above." In any case, it is noted that "[t]he method used [by Ivan the Terrible] was basically not different from that first employed by Ivan III on the territory of conquered Novgorod."[27]

In fact, as soon as we and the author pass from the free flight of abstract theory to earthly reality, we immediately enter a world which is precisely the opposite of what has just been described, a world boiling with ferocious struggle and competition—all of it over property, which, according to Pipes, was indistinguishable from sovereignty. And the author himself knows this. "The transformation of Russia into its ruler's patrimony required two centuries to accomplish. The process began in the middle of the fifteenth century and was completed by the middle of the seventeenth," he writes. (In the middle of the seventeenth century, therefore, "the idea of the state" might be supposed to have disappeared from the face of the Russian earth; instead, for some reason it *arose* precisely at this point, by Pipes's own account.) "Between these dates lies an age of civil turbulence *unprecedented even for Russia*, when state and society engaged in ceaseless conflict, as the former sought to impose its will and the latter made desperate attempts to elude it."[28]

---

25. Ibid., p. 70.   26. Ibid., p. 23.   27. Ibid., p. 95.
28. Ibid., p. 85. Emphasis added.

The meaning of this unending conflict consisted precisely in the fact that "in order to fashion their empire on the model of an appanage domain—to make all Russia their votchina . . . the tsars had to . . . put an end to the traditional right of the free population to circulate: all landowners had to be compelled to serve the ruler of Moscow, which meant converting their votchiny into fiefs." In Pipes's interpretation, "Outright property in land . . . was to give way to tenure conditional on royal favour."[29] Here is indistinguishability of sovereignty from ownership for you, when in practice it took two centuries of "civil tumult" and finally "a social revolution imposed from above" to take the property away from its owners.

The author agrees, thus, that there was no such thing as a "patrimonial state" in Russia before the seventeenth century. On the contrary, it turns out that from the beginning of the existence of Russia as a state, in the centuries which Pipes calls "the time of civil tumult," before "the crown . . . expropriated society,"[30] "ownership of land and rendering of service" were "traditionally separated in Russia." Furthermore, in it there existed a strong and proud aristocracy who "took great pride in their ancestry and consciously separated themselves from upstart service families."[31] And even the state itself "had to honour the system or risk the united opposition of the leading houses of the realm."[32]

Thus, for Pipes the "time bomb" explodes a century later than for Wittfogel. It is not only a matter of chronology, however, but one of the character of the "explosion" and of what stood behind it. For Wittfogel, as we know, the fuse to this bomb was laid by the Tatars, who brought Chinese models of Oriental despotism to Russia, and thus Sinicized the country. According to Pipes, it was a conspiracy of the "patrimonial state," on a national scale, against society. It is true that, as he says, this state did not exist before the middle of the seventeenth century, but this did not prevent it from intriguing and conspiring as long ago as the middle of the fifteenth century. This treacherous state "neither grew out of society, nor was imposed on it from above. Rather it grew up side by side with society and bit by bit swallowed it,"[33] until it brought "the process of expropriation [of society] to its conclusion."[34] Just as Mikhail Katkov, the famous right-wing publicist of the 1860s, saw "Polish intrigue" in Russia's every misfortune, so Pipes seems to detect a sort of "patrimonial intrigue" behind her woes.

---

29. Ibid., p. 86.   30. Ibid., p. 94.   31. Ibid., p. 89.   32. Ibid., p. 90.
33. Ibid., p. 21.   34. Ibid., p. 94.

This intrigue, as we know, consisted in transforming the whole country into a gigantic royal domain, so that no patrimonies, no privileges, and no courts other than the tsar's could exist in it. Everything had to belong to the tsar. Everyone had to serve him directly, as his household servants and serfs did. "They are all slaves and just slaves, and no one is more than a slave," as V. O. Kliuchevskii tersely summed up the contents of Ivan the Terrible's revolutionary manifesto—his first letter to Prince Kurbskii.

There is no doubt that Ivan the Terrible thirsted after this. That in the name of this he made Russia dance with his Oprichnina revolution is undisputed. But the history of the Russian state is not reducible to Ivan the Terrible. There was a time before him and a time after him—a time to gather stones, as the Preacher says, and a time to cast them away.

The fact remains that, during the absolutist century of the Muscovite state, the so-called Government of Compromise suddenly introduced local self-government and trial by jury in Russia, and, in addition, called something like a national parliament—the Assembly of the Land. It not only did not try to destroy the privileges of the boyars, or attempt to stop the process of peasant differentiation leading directly to the formation of a bourgeoisie (such was Lenin's opinion, and in this department, after all, he is undeniably an authority), it in fact furthered this process.

In the 1760s, the Russian government, in the "Manifesto on the Freedom of the Nobility," guaranteed to the latter the privileges of a corporation, one of which was the privilege of *not serving* that government. In the 1780s, the government guaranteed the nobility the inalienability of its property. In the 1860s, it again returned to the old, just forgotten experiment of the Government of Compromise, and again, as in the sixteenth century, introduced local self-government and trial by jury. It is true that the final step was not taken at this time. The Assembly of the Land was not called, and Russia was in a fever for another half-century, until in 1906 it was summoned in the shape of the State Duma. At the beginning of the twentieth century, Russia thus again returned to the position from which Ivan the Terrible's Oprichnina revolution had toppled it in the middle of the sixteenth. Unfortunately, it was not for long. A new Oprichnina revolution, this time under the guidance of Vladimir Lenin, again locked it up in the prison of autocracy. Such were the essential facts of this stormy, contradictory, and tragic history.

But let us forget all of this for the moment. Let us agree with Pipes that "during the fifteenth and sixteenth centuries the Moscow mon-

archy succeeded in eliminating alodial holdings and making secular
land tenure a form of possession conditional on state service."[35] We
then have before us a Russia which no longer knows an aristocracy,
alodial tenure, and private patrimonial property, and is fully transformed into a "patrimonial state" in which sovereignty and ownership
are indistinguishable. "The system we have described was so immune
from pressures from below that, in theory at least, it should have per-
petuated itself *ad infinitum*," Pipes writes. "The great patrimonial
states of the Hellenistic world with which the Muscovite state had
much in common collapsed not from internal causes but as a result of
conquest. The same held true of the related regimes of the 'oriental
despotic' type in Asia and Central America."[36]

With the paterfamilias finally heading his "primitive family," we
might expect that "civil tumult" would come to an end forever in Russia, and that an orderly and sedate family life would begin. But after
its victory, the "patrimonial state" begins to conduct itself in a highly
mysterious manner. "It is only in 1785 under Catherine II when Russian landholders secured clear legal title to their estates that private
property in land came once again into being in Russia," Pipes observes.[37] Let us make an elementary calculation: if alodial tenure, private patrimonial property, and aristocracy, which had just ceased to
exist in the second half of the seventeenth century, arise again in the
second half of the following century, then for how many years—even
fully agreeing with Pipes's conception—do we still have the "patrimonial state"? It turns out all of a sudden that what is being spoken
of is not at all "Russia under the old regime," as the title of Pipes's
book suggests, but only one piece of its history.

This is but the beginning of the confusion, however. For the time
set aside for Pipes's "old regime" in Russian history will inevitably, like
Balzac's *peau de chagrin*, get smaller and smaller, until finally it disappears altogether. "In the second half of the seventeenth century, of
the 888,000 households subject to tiaglo [tax] in Russia, 67 per cent
stood on land held by boyars and dvoriane [nobility] . . . and 13.3 per
cent on that held by the church," Pipes says.

> In other words, 80.3 per cent of the tiaglo households were under pri-
> vate control. The crown owned outright only 9.3 per cent. . . . For all
> practical purposes then, by the end of the seventeenth century four out
> of every five Russians had ceased to be subjects of the state, in the sense
> that the state had relinquished to their landlords nearly all authority
> over them.[38]

35. Ibid., p. 69.   36. Ibid., p. 112.   37. Ibid., p. 69.   38. Ibid., p. 104.

Let us continue with our arithmetic. If by the end of the seventeenth century, four out of five of the children of the paterfamilias had escaped from his control, how many years of the "patrimonial state" are left? Fifty? Alas, its situation is even worse than this. For, contrary to Pipes's assertions, the Muscovite state *never* succeeded completely in eliminating alodial property. It is true that the traditional clan patrimony perished under the assault of the Oprichnina revolution and the autocracy established by it, partly being replaced by fiefs (*pomest'ia*). But, simultaneously with the abolition of the *traditional* patrimonial estate and its replacement by *pomest'e*, evolution of the *pomest'ia* into the *new patrimonial estates* of the service gentry took place. In his last work, the late A. M. Sakharov describes the process as follows:

> The *pomest'e* gradually became more and more adapted to the interests of its holder, and revealed more and more elements of patrimonial tenure. With time, there arose the so-called "earned patrimonies." This concept, it seems, was first used in a ukase of 1572, where the clan patrimony was contrasted to the "patrimony given by the sovereign." The beginning of the sale of vacant *pomest'ia* as patrimonies, with the sole condition that the buyer had no right to transfer them to a monastery, dates from the same period. The practice of selling *pomest'ia* as patrimonies subsequently became widespread in the first half of the seventeenth century, along with the granting of *pomest'ia* as patrimonies as a reward for service. Furthermore, after the "Time of Troubles" [that is, at the beginning of the seventeenth century], a definite norm was established: an "earned" patrimony was one-fifth of the regular size of a *pomest'e*. The treasury's need for money and the effort to gain a firmer base of support in the nobility were the causes of the transformation of *pomest'ia* into patrimonies, which constantly increased over the course of the sixteenth and early seventeenth centuries.[39]

Russian history is left with not *a single decade* for the "patrimonial state." There is simply nowhere left to stick it. And, along with it, the "patrimonial-conspiratorial" model of the Russian historical process falls into oblivion. Out of this fundamental contradiction between theory and reality there apparently flows such a massive series of factual contradictions by the author with himself that, in analyzing Pipes's book, my students asked me whether the author himself had read over his own text before sending it to press. I will cite only a few examples. On page 86 we read: "The extension of the domainial order on the country at large was nothing short of a social revolution

39. A. M. Sakharov, "Ob evoliutsii feodal'noi sobstvennosti na zemliu v Rossiiskom gosudarstve XVI veka," p. 28.

imposed from above. The resistance was commensurate." On page
173: "Sovereignty in Russia had been built on the ruins of private
property, by a ruthless destruction of appanages and other votchiny."
And, between these two passages, on page 172: "The Russian state
grew and took shape *without having to contend with entrenched landed interests*—an absolutely fundamental factor in its historic evolution"
(my emphasis).

On page 85, we read that "state and society engaged in ceaseless
conflict" over the course of two centuries (from the middle of the fifteenth to mid-seventeenth), this conflict being required for the destruction of the boyars' patrimonies, and on page 172 that, "During
the three centuries separating the reign of Ivan III from that of
Catherine II the Russian equivalent of the nobility held its land on
royal sufferance."

How can we reconcile the absence of entrenched landed interests
with the "unending struggle" for their extirpation? Or the strong patrimonial boyardom, of which the author himself says that the Duma
which it created was "in the fourteenth, fifteenth and first half of the
sixteenth century . . . pronouncedly aristocratic,"[40] with tenure of
land on royal sufferance? How, in a country where even the ideas of
state and society could not exist, could the state and society wage a
struggle to the death against each other over the course of centuries?
Why did the "patrimonial state," which had for so many years conspired against private property, suddenly begin to destroy the results
of its entire intrigue? I was not able to answer these legitimate questions for my students.

As the reader may have noticed, my role in criticizing *Russia Under
the Old Regime* has been minimal: the author himself, without outside
help, has destroyed his "conspiratorial-patrimonial" thesis by, to use
his own expression, "swallowing it bit by bit."

Of course, Pipes is not obliged to follow the logic of Wittfogel, or
Toynbee, or A. N. Sakharov, or anybody at all, but his own logic he
must follow. And, as strange as it may seem after so much self-contra-
diction, a logic can be discovered to which he still adheres. Alas, this is
the familiar logic of the bipolar model, which he so decisively debunked in the theoretical introduction to his book. "The distinguish-
able characteristic of *la monarchie seigneuriale* was that 'the prince has
become lord of the goods and persons of his subjects,'" Pipes writes,
quoting Jean Bodin, with whom he agrees that "in Europe there were

40. R. Pipes, p. 106.

only two such regimes, one in Turkey, the other in Muscovy, although they were common in Asia and Africa."[41]

This is, once again, the black-and-white version of the political universe: if Russian autocracy differed from European absolutism, then consequently it was . . . what? Certainly, Oriental despotism (Wittfogel would say, in his harsh language, "of the nonhydraulic semimarginal subtype," while Pipes expresses himself more mildly: "of the patrimonial type"). The designations may differ, but the essence is one and the same; the check list of despotic features is identical. There is the absolute sovereignty of the state over the national product of the country. There is the absence of alternatives, and consequently of political opposition ("one can see no way in which the Muscovite population could have altered the system had it wanted to"). There is, finally, the incapacity of the system for internal change.

And if, nevertheless, the system, as distinct from its Hellenistic and Oriental-despotic relatives, did change from within (and as a professional historian of Russia, Pipes can't deny this), this is explained by . . . what would you think, reader, already being familiar with Wittfogel and Szamuely? Well, of course, by geography: what else? It simply turns out that "of all the regimes of the Hellenistic and Oriental-despotic type, Russia was geographically closest to Western Europe."[42] Paraphrasing a well-known saying, we can say that "the patrimonial state" of Richard Pipes is despotism, moderated by geography.

Thus, just as all roads lead to Rome, all the interpretations of Russian history which we have considered—the "Tatar," the "Byzantine," and the "patrimonial"—lead inexorably and inevitably to despotism, and hence to the bipolar model of political development, effectively making it impossible to explain the Russian historical process.

41. Ibid., p. 65.
42. Ibid., p. 112.

PART II

THE ABSOLUTIST
CENTURY

CHAPTER IV

THE GRANDFATHER
AND THE GRANDSON

---

1. The Stereotype

In the work of the contemporary Western despotists, Muscovy is depicted, at the dawn of its existence as a state, as a narrow horseshoe of land caught between the Lithuanian hammer and the Tatar anvil, locked into a miserable northern territory, without an outlet to the sea, where it is not even possible to grow grain in quantity. Having taken this stereotype as sound coin, Tibor Szamuely was sure, it will be remembered, that for Muscovy national survival played the same role that irrigation facilities played in the Asiatic empires.

Even so prominent a native despotist as Georgii Plekhanov was seduced by this logic. One of Plekhanov's strongest arguments was the fact that Nikolai Pavlov-Sil'vanskii, the forefather of the native absolutists, himself conceded that "the external circumstances of the life of Muscovite Rus', its stubborn struggle against its eastern and western neighbors for existence, demanded an extreme expenditure of effort by the people," as a result of which "there was developed in the society a consciousness that the first obligation of each subject was to serve the state to the limit of his ability and to sacrifice himself for the defense of the Russian land."[1]

The "stubborn struggle for existence," "the defense of the Russian land"—in a word, *self-defense*—is the root of the stereotype, which is already so venerable that it does not enter anyone's head to doubt its truth. But is it, after all, true—at least as applied to the time of Ivan III, which took up almost the entire latter half of the fifteenth century, when, according to Wittfogel, the "institutional time bomb" was getting ready to explode; when, according to Pipes, indescribable "civil tumult" was taking place; and when, according to Szamuely, the "Muscovite variety of Asiatic despotism" was being created? Here is

---

1. N. P. Pavlov-Sil'vanskii, *Gosudarevy sluzhilye liudi, liudi kabal'nye i zakladnye*, p. 223.

how this period is described by one of the most authoritative experts, Sergei Solov'ev:

> In regard to political and physical calamities, it must be noted that for the regions which Ivan inherited from his father, his reign was the calmest and happiest: the Tatar incursions involved only the border-lands; but these incursions were very few and the harm caused by them reasonable and quite insignificant; the uprising of the grand prince's brothers only frightened the people; and the other wars were offensive on the part of Muscovy: the enemy did not show himself within the bor-ders of the triumphant state.[2]

Whom are we to believe?

If, in fact, the Muscovy of this period was a garrison state struggling convulsively for its existence, as the stereotype has it, it is hardly likely that people from more favored and less militarized places would have emigrated there. The position of the Muscovite government in the matter of emigration is also indicative. After all, it is unthinkable that the government of Brezhnevist Russia, for example, would issue loud declarations defending the rights of citizens to emigrate. On the contrary, it declares émigrés to be traitors to their country, and regards any help to them as interference in its internal affairs. And there is nothing surprising in this: in our day, no one flees into Russia; they flee from it.

But there was a time when they fled into it. And this was precisely during the reign of Ivan III.

Ivan's Lithuanian neighbor, the Grand Prince Kazimir, was a great diplomat. By a series of profound and brilliantly thought out intrigues, he managed matters so that after his death his sons, the Kazimirovichi, one after another took possession of the four Central European thrones—the Polish, the Czech, the Hungarian, and the Lithuanian, which was ascended by the future son-in-law of Ivan III and the future king of Poland, Aleksandr. This was the high point of Lithuanian history. Lithuania had its troubles—and who did not?—but in any case, no one would have dared to call it a garrison state, and its life and death did not rest upon the toss of a card.

Nevertheless, the current of migration for some reason ran clearly toward Muscovy. Who demanded the punishment of the émigrés—the "runaways"—and branded them "traitors" or "scoundrels"? Who, by threats and entreaties, sought the conclusion of an agreement which would juridically specify the illegality of boyar "flight"? The

---

2. S. M. Solov'ev, *Istoriia Rossii s drevneishikh vremen*, Bk. 3, pp. 174–75.

Lithuanians. And who defended civil rights, and particularly the individual's right to choose his country? The Muscovites.

The flower of the Russian aristocracy, the princes Vorotynskii, Viazemskii, Odoevskii, Bel'skii, Peremyshl'skii, Novosil'skii, Glinskii, Mezetskii—their names are legion—were all of them successful refugees from Lithuania into Muscovy. There were also those who were not successful. In 1482 the great Lithuanian boyars Ol'shanskii, Olenkovich, and Bel'skii prepared to flee to Muscovy. The king heard of it: "Ol'shanskii and Olenkovich were seized," and Fedor Bel'skii fled alone. In 1496 the Lithuanian ruler bitterly complained to the Muscovite sovereign: "The princes Viazemskii and Mezetskii were our servants, and betrayed their oath to us, and slipped into your land, like evil people, and if they had fled to us, they would have gotten from us what such traitors deserve."[3] But they were not fleeing to him.

The Muscovite government, on the contrary, welcomed the royal "traitors," did not give them up to the Lithuanian king, and evidently saw no treason in their actions. For example, in 1504 Ostafei Dashkovich defected to Muscovy with many nobles. Lithuania demanded their extradition, citing the treaty of 1503, which supposedly required that "both sides not accept turncoats, runaways, and evil people." Muscovy craftily and mockingly replied that the text literally read, "a thief, a runaway, a bondsman, a slave, a debtor should be handed over to justice"—and could a great lord be a thief or a bondsman or an evil person? On the contrary, "Ostafei Dashkovich was a person of note at the court and had been a general, and nothing evil had ever been heard about him, and he had great cities under his control, and he came to serve us voluntarily, without causing any harm."[4]

Provided the runaway had not caused any harm—that is, had not fled from criminal prosecution—he was, for Muscovy, a respectable political émigré, and not a traitor. Muscovy insisted, as a matter of principle, on the right of personal political choice, using the strongest legal argument possible in medieval political disputes—appeal to the "old ways." As Ivan III wrote in his answer to the Lithuanian king, "before this, under us and under our ancestors and under their ancestors, people travelled without hindrance in both directions."[5]

Is Ivan not insisting that the king's subjects (like his own) are by no

3. Cited in M. A. D'akonov, *Vlast' moskovskikh gosudarei*, pp. 187–88.
4. Ibid., p. 189.
5. Ibid., p. 191.

means slaves belonging to their suzerain, but free people? Of course, one can say that his declarations were hypocritical. They definitely were. But even in that case, the "patrimonial mentality," which according to Pipes prevailed in the Muscovite garrison state, looks at least dubious. Is it thinkable that *even hypocritically*, the Brezhnev government, for example, would undertake to defend the tradition of free emigration out of the country? Even hypocrisy, obviously, has its political limits.

Of course, I do not mean to say by this that Moscow was more liberal, or freer, or more concerned about civil rights than was Vil'no. The Middle Ages were the Middle Ages. Both governments were equally cruel and authoritarian. What I am talking about is something entirely different: for some reason, it was *advantageous* for people in Lithuania to flee to Muscovy and for the Muscovite government to defend the right to emigrate. This was pointed out as far back as 1889 by the well-known Russian historian Mikhail D'akonov. "This difference of opinion between the governments," he wrote, "could have had only one basis: at the time in question Lithuania was losing a good many more of its servants than it was gaining, while Muscovy, on the contrary, was significantly increasing its service population at the expense of Lithuania."[6]

And here the crucial and inexplicable question arises, at least for those experts whose works I know: why would so many powerful, proud and, what is in this case most important, free (of course, in the medieval sense) people choose to flee to a repressive garrison state? Well, some explanations downplaying this phenomenon can, of course, be thought up. Perhaps these were simply the Orthodox people who left Catholic Lithuania for Orthodox Muscovy. Or it may be that Ivan III offered them irresistible conditions if they became his courtiers. Or else, Muscovy being the winning side in the struggle for the border regions where these people lived, they preferred to join the victor. Or the Muscovite army forced some border nobles to change allegiance. In fact, this is what some experts in fifteenth- and sixteenth-century Kremlin affairs, thoroughly researching and highlighting personal and family connections and conflicts in the Muscovite aristocratic elite, say. In the absence of new generalizations about Russian history, there has developed a kind of medieval Kremlinology, allowing Muscovy to be considered a "service state" even in the fifteenth century. Gustav Alef, for example, the most prominent representative of this school of thought, in a penetrating recent essay

6. Ibid., p. 192.

goes even further, suggesting that "the service state was a product of need for both the monarch and his servants."[7]

This is quite a respectable theory. The only thing it cannot explain is why it was that from the time of the Oprichnina revolution on, and for an entire century to come, when Muscovy was really turned into a service state, the arrow of migration suddenly swung around 180 degrees, as though by magic. After the Oprichnina, Muscovy was still Orthodox, and Lithuania still Catholic. Moreover, Muscovy was still sometimes the winning side in the struggle for the border regions. And its army might still have forced border nobles to change allegiance. But this time Orthodox lords fled from Orthodox Muscovy to Catholic Lithuania. And in the eyes of Vil'no such refugees all of a sudden became not "turncoats," but respectable political émigrés, while Muscovy boiled with rage against them, and proclaimed that "in the whole universe he who takes in a runaway lives in unrighteousness together with him." The Lithuanian king, suddenly filled with liberalism and humane feelings, condescendingly explained to Ivan the Terrible that "people who leave their fatherland to save their necks from bondage and bloodshed" must be pitied and not be surrendered to a tyrant; it is unworthy of a Christian ruler to hand over "those whom God has saved from death."

And even when, a half century later, Boris Godunov sent eighteen young people to Europe to acquire learning and good sense there, seventeen of them became "nonreturners." As Prince Ivan Golitsyn once explained to Polish envoys: "We cannot permit Russian people to serve along with Poles because of temptation. One summer they serve—and the next we would not have a half of the best Russian people left."[8] In the works of Gregory Kotoshikhin, also a political émigré, who left us the first systematic description of Muscovite life in the mid-1600s, we read:

> They do not send their children to other countries to learn science and good breeding, fearing that, having seen the faith and customs and blessed liberty of those countries, they would begin to change their own faith and then go over to another, and would no longer care or think about returning to their homes and to their relatives. And if a person, a prince or a boyar or anyone else, would go, or would send his son or his brother to another country without telling anyone, and without having taken leave of the sovereign, such a person, for such a deed, would be

7. Gustav Alef, "Aristocratic Politics and Royal Policy in the Late Fifteenth and Early Sixteenth Centuries," p. 1.

8. Cited in G. V. Plekhanov, *Sochineniia*, vol. 20, p. 233.

accused of treason. . . . And if someone went himself and left relatives behind him, they would be interrogated to learn whether they knew what their relatives had intended.[9]

What do we learn then from all this? If the medieval Kremlinologists, along with the despotists, are right in suggesting that, even in the fifteenth century, Muscovy was a terrifying service state totally preoccupied with its "national survival," how are we to explain this monstrous change in the minds of its rulers and in the directions of emigration? I would be happy to tell the reader how these experts try to explain this mysterious fact so stubbornly contradicting their theories. Unfortunately, I cannot: to the best of my knowledge they have not tried.[10]

2. "Patrimonies" Versus "Patrimony"

When, in March 1462, at the age of twenty-two, Ivan III ascended the throne, Muscovy could be called a unified state perhaps only in name. It was still formally a vassal and tributary of the Golden Horde. The princedoms of Tver', Riazan', Rostov, and Iaroslavl', which had been the most dangerous competitors of Muscovy in the past, still led a separate existence, sometimes attempting to maneuver between Moscow and Lithuania. In the free cities of Novgorod, Pskov, and Khlynov (Viatka), the popular assemblies still made a stir, and their decisions

9. G. Kotoshikhin, *O Rossii v tsarstvovanie Alekseia Mikhailovicha, Sochinenie Grigoriia Kotoshikhina*, p. 53. Emphasis added.

10. Of course, extrahistorical and, so to speak, personalistic explanations are possible. In his time, V. O. Kliuchevskii considered the Oprichnina, though monstrous, to be an episode in Russian history which was in a certain sense accidental, and in considerable degree conditioned by the personality of Ivan the Terrible. In developing this line of reasoning, the leading modern historians of the Muscovite period in the United States, Richard Hellie and Edward Keenan, offer medical explanations for the Oprichnina. According to Hellie, Ivan the Terrible's actions are to be explained by paranoia; according to Keenan, by physical disease, arthritis and spondylitis, which made him incapable of fulfilling his duties as tsar. (See Edward Keenan, "Vita: Ivan Vasil'evich, Terrible Tsar 1530–1584," p. 49; Richard Hellie, "In Search of Ivan the Terrible," Preface to S. F. Platonov's *Ivan the Terrible*, and "Ivan the Terrible: Paranoia, 'Evil Advisors,' Institutional Restraints and Social Control"). We will deal with this view in the appropriate place, when analyzing the modern phase of Ivaniana. For the time being, it may be noted that Peter I was an epileptic, and, it is said, suffered from a severe form of syphilis, while Stalin was an indubitable paranoiac. Tyrants usually have their occupational diseases. Yet, it would not be easy to explain Stalinism by paranoia, or the reforms of Peter by epilepsy. It must be admitted, further, that the comparative paucity of information about Ivan the Terrible is more conducive to medical speculation, and to the mixing of despotology with pathology, than the analogous cases of Peter and Stalin.

were frequently anti-Muscovite in character. The northern empire of Novgorod, which occupied the maritime regions, was not subject to Moscow, and consequently the country had no access either to the White Sea or to the Baltic. The brothers of the grand prince, who held appanages, were still able to raise the sword against him, and to unleash civil war in the country. The memory was still alive of how, during the preceding civil war, Vasilii, called the Dark, father of the grand prince, had been blinded and exiled by his nephew Dimitri Shemiaka.

From this variegated and amorphous material, Ivan III had to build a unified state, completing the work of his ancestors, the "gatherers" of Muscovite Rus'. This is what the first part both of his life and his political strategy consisted in (in the case of Ivan III, they were one and the same, for he seems to have been moved by few passions other than political ones). He was of the clan of Ivan Kalita ("Moneybags"), "bloodthirsty from of old," as Kurbskii wrote, and renowned for intrigues, treachery, and familial stubbornness; a clan in which each member knew how to follow the great-grandfather's lucky star without turning aside, as though a political compass were mounted inside him.

Ivan III carried out his centralizing task with great political tact and a minimum of spilt blood—or, at any rate, with greater tact and less blood than his French contemporary, Louis XI. The grand prince rather resembled his English contemporary, Henry VII. Both were parsimonious, dry, unprejudiced, farseeing men. Like Henry VII, Ivan thought that a bad peace was better than a good quarrel, and wherever a matter could be settled without a fight, he took that road with no hesitation, even at the price of significant concessions. He was not a coward like his grandson, but knew how to flatter without qualms when this was necessary. He disliked risking everything, and respected his adversary if the latter was deserving of respect, trying not to drive him to extremes, and leaving him the possibility of an honorable exit from the game. Over all else, he set "the old ways," the strongest argument of medieval political logic.

How—a well-known American historian once asked me indignantly—can we permit ourselves such a description of a man who did not leave behind a single document written in his own hand? But Ivan III did leave a record. And it was not only the great power he created, but also the very process by which it was created—maneuvers, campaigns, intrigues, embassies, marriages, and negotiations. From this chaotic mosaic, there emerges a profound strategy, thought out far into the future, reflecting the character and style of a great political architect.

Ivan III, it seems to me, was distinguished from all subsequent Russian tsars by an astonishing feeling for strategy. There was no single political step, no matter how insignificant in itself, which would not in time, perhaps many years afterwards, prove to be a stage on the way to the goal which he had set for himself.

Who could have said in 1477, for example, that the confiscation of monastery lands in Novgorod, a measure lost in the mass of other confiscations, resettlements, and banishments connected with annexation of the northern "patrimony," would many years later prove to be essential in reforming the church? Who could have said in advance that the destructive raids on the Lithuanian lands beyond the Oka during the "unofficial war" of the 1480s, conducted mainly by the princely defectors from Lithuania, were by no means unsystematic freebooting, as it seemed to contemporaries, but part of a colossal plan for dismembering Lithuania by splitting it along ethnic and religious lines? Who could have said that the sentimental interest of a decidedly unsentimental grand prince in the modest sect of "Trans-Volga Elders"—people not of this world, monks who had left their monasteries and lived in lonely forest hermitages—was, in fact, a detail in a broad plan for the creation of a strong political party of "Non-Acquirers," which was destined to become the brains trust of the future church reformation?

And so on for everything he did. Ivan III was decidedly unpredictable to his contemporaries. A cynical pragmatist, a realist, known for his persistence and practical turn of mind, he seemed at the same time to live in some other dimension, incomprehensible to them. In the second part of his life (or of his strategy), when the gathering in of the "patrimony" was completed and the family star followed by ten generations of Muscovite grand princes had finally set, when Rus' (which is to say what remained of the ancient Kievan state) had been united, Ivan immediately and without interruption undertook to formulate new goals, creating a new mission—in which, he may have thought, his grandsons and great-grandsons would compete with him, as he had competed with his grandfathers and great-grandfathers in the mission to "gather in" Rus'. He was not in a hurry. The entire political experience of Muscovy had taught him that affairs of state are not concluded in one generation, that "Moscow is not built in one day," as they say in Russia. He had only to lay the foundation, and, by completing the work of Ivan Kalita, become a new Ivan Kalita.

Fated to live two lives in two different worlds—first in the petty, quarrelsome world of disputes between princes and appanages, and then in the world of high politics, international intrigues, and national tasks—Ivan felt himself at home in both. During his first "life," he prepared the staging areas and starting points for his second, when he would no longer be a provincial Muscovite grand prince but sovereign of a European power.

In fact, as soon as the process of "gathering in" was completed, the Reconquista could continue only in the arena of European politics. The patrimony of Rus' was naturally transformed into something fundamentally different from a royal estate: a member nation of the European family of peoples. And, correspondingly, the *"votchina"* (patrimony) concept became anachronistic in the new *"otchina"* (which in Russian sounds rather like *"otchizna"* or *"otechestvo"*—fatherland). Both *"otchina"* and *"votchina"* are translated into English by a single word, "patrimony." Even in Russian they have the same root and differ only by one letter. In the political life of the country, however, these terms seem to stand not only for different but for opposite things.

Now, after the completion of the "gathering in," as the ideological basis for the Russian Reconquista, *"otchina"* came to be used mainly in the context of foreign policy. The term *starina* ("old times") underwent analogous transformation into a political slogan signifying the common past of all of the Russian lands, as *"otchina"* did their common future. Both were fused into a powerful ideological construct, symbolic of national unity and cemented together by the foreign-policy strategy of Ivan III.

Votchina seems to have gradually undergone a similar transformation, coming to stand mainly not for royal but for private hereditary property, thus laying a firm foundation for the Russian aristocracy. The private *votchina* was in itself the opposite of the idea of the country as a royal *votchina*. In fact, the private *votchina* served as check and balance on the power of the medieval Russian state, imposing both social and economic limitations on it. More than that, maintenance of the private *votchiny* was an absolute political imperative for Ivan III: how could he, otherwise, in forming his aristocratic elite, have attracted to himself boyars and princes from Lithuania, from Tver', and from Riazan', who deserted to him *along with their votchiny*? Why should powerful aristocrats, who had traditionally been indisputable owners of their *votchiny*, have fled to a state in which their rights would be disputed? Had Ivan III actually considered his country a royal patrimony, aristocrats would have absconded from Muscovy rather than fled there. This is how the tradition of "patrimonies" as private estates worked to corrode and gradually destroy the tradition of royal "patrimony." Gathering about him in Moscow "the flower of

Russian aristocracy," as Gustav Alef has expressed it, Ivan III put the
idea of royal "patrimony" in mortal danger. This explains why his
grandson, Ivan the Terrible, needed to foment a revolution and resort to mass terror in a desperate attempt to save it.

Thus, the opposition between two almost identical terms, which
does not even exist in English, conceals a cruel conflict between two
cultural and political traditions, one which ended with catastrophe
for the new-born Russian absolutism.

3. A Historical Experiment

The complexity of history sometimes makes it easier to argue. I do
not know how I would now convince the reader of the difference between the political behavior of the "*otchinnik*" (the absolutist king) and
the "*votchinnik*" (the autocrator), and the decisive difference in their
attitudes towards the country, were it not for the analogous actions to
subdue Novgorod undertaken by the grandfather and the grandson,
separated from each other by what I call Russia's absolutist century.

In the 1460s, when Ivan III mounted the throne, Novgorod was an
autonomous political unit in the complex and loose conglomerate arbitrarily called Muscovy. It was, properly speaking, a republic—something like a Russian Carthage. In formal terms, the popular assembly
[*veche*] was considered to be the highest power, which annually elected a mayor [*posadnik*] and a general [*tysiatskii*], who in turn supervised
the administration, the military establishment, and the organs of justice. In practice, the power of this elected representative body was
limited by the senate (the council of boyars), which exercised the real
power (in the sense that political decisions were initiated, and the
strategy for the republic determined there). The connection of the
republic with the Russian state (apart from the common language
and cultural traditions) consisted chiefly in the fact that Novgorod
paid tribute to Muscovy in return for noninterference in its internal
affairs, that the princes who were invited to command the army were
supposed by tradition to belong to the clan of Riurik (the semimythi-
cal Norse founder of the Kievan state, and progenitor of its royal
house), and that candidates for the post of archbishop of Novgorod
were nominated by the metropolitan of Moscow.

The Novgorod North was the treasure house of Russia, spared by
the Tatar invasion, and closely connected with the Hanseatic commercial republics, which were related to it by their political structure.
Novgorod controlled the roads to the White Sea, to the Baltic, and to
the vast territories beyond the Urals. Its incorporation was, therefore,

absolutely vital for the development of Muscovy as a state, and hence only a matter of time.

The senate of Novgorod had for decades been deeply split into hostile factions. The sympathies of the *veche*, or popular assembly, were chiefly with the pro-Lithuanian faction (most probably because Lithuania was farther away and posed a lesser danger to the autonomy of the republic). The representatives of the grand prince were publicly humiliated; regions of the republic ceded to Moscow in the past were taken back by force; payment of taxes was refused; the position of head of the army was ostentatiously offered to the son of Dimitri Shemiaka, who had blinded the father of the grand prince; negotiations with Kazimir of Lithuania were the order of the day and, to top it all, the archbishop of Novgorod also entered into negotiations with the Uniate metropolitan of Kiev (an appointee of the pope's and probably also of Kazimir's). "Throughout the sixties tension grew," writes John Fennell:

> The split in Novgorod between the pro-Muscovite faction and the pro-Lithuanian party . . . became more sharply defined and led to disorders within the city. Although few people could have foreseen any other fate for Novgorod than her ultimate annexation by Moscow, the pro-Lithuanian faction grew in strength and boldness. It was as though they were attempting to provoke Ivan into a final act of reprisal. . . . In vain Ivan sent his ambassadors to reason with his insubordinate patrimony; Novgorod refused to listen to his complaints. Mere insolence and minor boundary conflicts could hardly be used as a pretext for a major expedition to crush what was after all a Russian and an Orthodox state.[11]

For one who knows the history of Ivan the Terrible's Novgorod expedition, which turned the same Russian and Orthodox city into a desert without any pretext whatever (except, of course, for the suspicion of "treason" which was the standard fabrication in the Oprichnina period when it was necessary to rob someone), this explanation may seem improbable. But between grandfather and grandson there was a great gulf: even when the treachery of Novgorod, both political and religious, was demonstrated beyond doubt, Ivan III punished it not immediately or hastily, but with caution, in two stages. The Novgoroders played a clumsy political game, and were always falling into the traps laid by the grand prince. The challenge he faced lay rather in the powerful authority of the "old ways" embodied in the liberties of Novgorod. Simply to violate them as his grandson would have done, and did, was something of which Ivan III was, it seems, incapa-

11. J. L. I. Fennel, *Ivan the Great of Moscow*, p. 36.

ble. His mind worked in a fundamentally different way. He had in his
hands a tool which tyrants never have: time. Let the republic be the
first to violate the "old ways." Then he would act, in the role not of a
violator but of a *preserver* of national and religious tradition.

He waited them out. The Novgoroders, in desperation, sought
help from the traditional enemies of Rus'—the Livonian Order. Now
the whole world could see who was defending the "old ways" and who
was violating them. The grand prince marched against Novgorod
and, on July 14, 1471, inflicted a crushing defeat on its army at the
river Shelon'. The republic lay at his feet, disarmed and helpless. It
seemed that the moment for which he had patiently waited for a
whole decade had come. What now? Did he disarm Novgorod, destroy it politically, plunder it, kill its people? Did he at least annex its
northern empire? Nothing of the sort. He entered into negotiations
and agreed to a compromise. What was more, in the treaty, along with
words confirming the fact that Novgorod was "our *otchina*," there was
reference to "the free men [of Novgorod]." Fennell notes with mild
astonishment: "Ivan showed remarkable clemency. . . . Why should
the anomaly of an independent freedom-loving republic within the
confines of what was becoming a centralized totalitarian state be tolerated for another seven years?"[12] In fact Ivan III liquidated the grand
princedom of Tver' in exactly the same way, in two stages, thirteen
years later. Thus, too, he organized his pressure campaign against
Lithuania—methodically, unhurriedly, and not all at once. He acted
similarly in his struggle to secularize the church lands. This appears
to have been the universal strategic method of the grand prince of
compromise—the founding father of the absolutist tradition of Russia. Fennell points out:

> Of course, harsh methods at this stage would not make the task of gov-
> erning the city any easier; his undoubted unpopularity amongst certain
> members of the [Novgorod] community would be increased; leaders of
> the opposition would become martyrs in the eyes of the public; the
> merchants, whose support Ivan was only too anxious to court and
> maintain, might well become antagonistic to the cause of Moscow and
> thus disrupt its economic programme.[13]

Not one of these considerations entered the mind of Ivan the Terrible at the time of *his* Novgorod expedition of 1570; *he* mercilessly
robbed the Novgorod traders without any concern for the economic
program of Muscovy, still less for his reputation "among certain

12. Ibid., p. 46.
13. Ibid., p. 47.

members of the community" (these, and others about whom we are uncertain, were simply executed on a mass scale). Certainly, the thought that "harsh methods" would hardly ease the task of governing the city did not stop Ivan the Terrible. All strata of the population, boyars, clergy, rich merchants, poor townsmen, and even the paupers—who were driven out in the middle of a fierce winter, to be frozen alive beyond the city walls—were exterminated methodically, mercilessly, in whole families.

It is as though for the grandson the vertical (temporal) dimension of politics did not exist. Not even the future, let alone the past ("old ways"), had any meaning for him. He thought, one might say, horizontally, and worked outside of the context of time. And although he traced his descent in a direct line from the Roman emperor Augustus, the sacred "old ways" were for him merely a great abstract congeries, in which Moses and the Prophet Samuel and "our forefathers" all blended together—in no sense a living, vital tradition which created a moral imperative, or an authority to which policy had to be adapted.

Let us, however, return to Novgorod. It goes without saying that the anti-Muscovite party there was unreconciled to its defeat. Once more, it entered into negotiations with Lithuania, carrying the *veche* with it. Seven years later, Ivan III—armed, as always, with solid documentary proofs of treachery—once again launched a campaign against the mutinous *otchina* and brought it to its knees. (Once again surprising Fennell: "One marvels at the patience with which Ivan conducted this [operation].") This time, Ivan settled scores with the opposition radically and cruelly: its leaders were exiled and some of them were executed; the historical autonomy of Novgorod was abolished, the bell of the *veche* removed, whole clans of potential traitors were resettled in the South and loyal people put in their place (for the decisive campaign against Lithuania, planned two decades earlier, Ivan needed the sympathy of the border population).

The grand prince then experimented with a mixture of past and future forms. In 1471 Novgorod was given a chance to try to incorporate its local "old ways" into the national structure which was being created, but the compromise combination of *otchina* with "free men" did not work. Ivan recognized his defeat by getting rid of the "free men," but even then he settled scores with the opposition and not with Novgorod itself. The pro-Lithuanian party was definitely routed, but the city survived and prospered as before. The point is that Ivan III felt himself responsible for Novgorod. This was part of his native land, his heritage, to be attached to Muscovy, but not reduced to ashes.

When Ivan the Terrible marched against Novgorod a century later, it was still Great Novgorod, the richest, most highly developed, most cultivated city in the land, the pearl of the Russian crown. But where the Oprichnina has passed, as the saying went, grass does not grow. Never again would there be Great Novgorod. Yet, in 1570, there had for a long time been no republic, no senate, no *veche*, no historical autonomy to be destroyed, no opposition to be decapitated. But we do not yet know the whole picture. In order to give the reader some idea of the bloody escapades of Ivan the grandson in Novgorod, let me quote a modern Soviet historian, R. G. Skrynnikov:

> The Oprichnina judges conducted their investigations with the aid of the cruelest tortures. . . . The recalcitrant were burned at the stake . . . tied to sleighs by a long rope, dragged through the city to the river Volkhov and pushed under the ice. Not only those suspected of treason were killed, but also the members of their families. . . . The chronicler says that some Oprichniki threw women and children tied hand and foot into the Volkhov, while others went about the river in boats and with axes and spears drowned those who succeeded in floating to the surface.[14]

Immediately after the trials and reprisals described above, "the sovereign with his men-at-arms began to ride around Great Novgorod to the monasteries," the chronicler relates. The results of this royal jaunt are also described by Skrynnikov: "The black clergy [monks] were robbed down to the last thread. The Oprichniki plundered St. Sophia's Cathedral, took the valuable church furniture and icons, and broke the ancient Korsunskii gates out of the altar."[15] That all of this had nothing to do with the "treason" of Novgorod is illustrated by the very fact that having finished with the monasteries of Novgorod, the expedition immediately went after those of Pskov. "The Oprichnina laid hands on the treasure of the Pskov monasteries," Skrynnikov continues. "The local monks were again robbed down to the last thread. Not only money, but also icons and crosses, valuable church furniture, and books were taken from them. The Oprichniki removed the bells of the cathedral and took them away."[16]

But even this did not exhaust the sufferings of once great Novgorod. In the interval between the plundering of the Novgorod clergy and the Pskov pogrom, the Oprichniki, according to Skrynnikov,

---

14. R. G. Skrynnikov, *Ivan Groznyi*, p. 150.
15. R. G. Skrynnikov, *Oprichnyi terror*, p. 54; *Ivan Groznyi*, p. 150.
16. Skrynnikov, *Oprichnyi terror*, p. 59.

conducted full-scale attacks against the city. They sacked the Novgorod market and divided the most valuable goods among themselves. The simple goods, such as lard, wax, and linen, they heaped into great piles and burned (that winter a terrible famine prevailed over the Russian North, and it was precisely for this reason that so many paupers accumulated in Novgorod). During the pogrom, large supplies of goods intended for trade with the West were destroyed. Not only the markets were robbed, but also the houses of the townsmen. The Oprichniki broke down the gates, removed the doors, and smashed windows. Citizens who tried to resist the bandits were killed on the spot.[17]

Here we have the difference between the *"otchina"* and the *"votchina"* mentalities, between absolutism and autocracy. Both reprisals against Novgorod were cruel; both were accompanied by executions, persecution, and confiscations; both were, in the final analysis, a question of foreign policy. But in the first case, the reprisal was dictated by political necessity; in the second, it was an act of mass terror to facilitate the plundering of an already frightened people. Ivan III tried as far as possible to preserve Novgorod, though compelling it to function as a part of the nation; his grandson barbarously destroyed it. Where his grandfather had aimed at the maximum rationalization of the national economy possible under medieval conditions, Ivan the Terrible attempted to secure the continuation of an irrational foreign-policy strategy at the price of expropriation and destruction of the national wealth.[18] How do the experts explain this monstrous difference between two analogous events in Russian history? Again I

17. Skrynnikov, *Ivan Groznyi*, p. 152.
18. There are many studies analyzing the economic results of both Novgorod expeditions, at least indirectly. Kareliia, for example, was subject to Novgorod before its annexation by Ivan III. Its inclusion into the Muscovite state, writes R. B. Miuller,

> had a favorable influence on its entire population . . . the land on which the huge majority of the population lived ceased to be the property of the Novgorod boyars and became royal 'black' land. At the beginning, the state apparatus put only very insignificant pressure on the black peasants; the duties were very low, and the opportunity [for peasants] to control the land almost unlimited. . . . The basis for economic differentiation, and for the concentration of land in the hands of some [peasants] and the deprivation of others, appeared in the Karelliian countryside.

In other words, what we may call a normal European process of intensification and rationalization of the economy was taking place, which the author sees as the origin of bourgeois relationships in the Karelliian countryside. The results of the Novgorod expedition of Ivan the Terrible are described by the same author as "an unheard-of devastation and decline of Kareliia. . . . The village land parcels, commercial buildings, and workshops fell vacant. . . . The population was ruined." (R. B. Miuller, *Ocherki po istorii Karelii XVI–XVII vekov*, pp. 90–91). I don't think that these facts need any commentary.

would be happy to report on their attempts. And again I have failed to find any.

But there is yet another possible interpretation of the reprisal of the Oprichniki against Novgorod, which has not, to my knowledge, been suggested previously. Just before the Novgorod expedition, Ivan the Terrible had inspected the new and impregnable fortress—a marvel of fortification for its time—being erected in the impassable forests of Vologda. English craftsmen built an entire fleet for him, capable of carrying all the treasures of Muscovy to Solovki, and thence to England, where the tsar intended to emigrate in case he should be unable to sit out a siege behind the walls of the Vologda fortress. (Negotiations with Randolph, Queen Elizabeth's ambassador, on the granting of political asylum in England to the tsar in case of need, were complete.) The location of Vologda in the northwestern part of the country was so remote that enemy invasion could not threaten it under any circumstances. There was no one to hide from, unless we count Ivan's own people. In view of these facts, the robbery of Novgorod and Pskov may have been dictated by his desire not to arrive in England empty-handed. To be sure, this is only a hypothesis. But whether it is true or not, it is quite obvious that in building the Vologda fleet and applying for political asylum in England, the tsar was thinking least of all of the fate of Russia. It is difficult to imagine anything remotely similar when speaking of Ivan III.

By no means have I tried to draw a rosy picture of the latter here. There were quite a few bloody murders and cruel persecutions in his time. After all, he was no more than a medieval king. But while the medieval Kremlinologists may perhaps triumphantly point this out, what I am stressing is a totally different matter. Ivan III was not an *autocrator*. That is, however cruel and medieval he may have been, he never dared to violate the latent limitations on power. Indeed, as we shall soon see, he tried to strengthen them. For this reason, I think of him as an essentially European king.

4. The Reversed Stereotype

The stereotype which we encountered in chapter one asserted categorically that Russia began its march from barbarism to civilization only with Peter the Great. Historians of socioeconomic relationships in pre-Petrine Russia are inclined, it seems, to an analogous stereotype, but in reverse. They take it as a postulate that from the twelfth to the seventeenth century, in the process of feudalizing its economy and society and gradually enserfing its peasantry, Russia went from relatively free status (in medieval terms) to serfdom, which after Peter was transformed into literal slavery. Peasant self-government was gradually destroyed as the landlords seized the "black" lands—that is, those belonging formally to the state, but actually to the peasants. The peasants' freedom of movement was just as gradually limited in the course of the fifteenth century. Finally, in terms of Ivan III's law code of 1497, the so-called St. George's Day rule, which gave the peasants the choice of leaving their landlords only during two weeks in the year, became law. From here—so runs the stereotype—it was only one step to the complete "tying down" of the peasants, and to the introduction, at the end of Ivan the Terrible's reign, of the "forbidden years," eliminating any movement whatever on their part.

This picture of the triumphal progress of the "service" or "patrimonial" state well suits the despotists, with their "institutional time bomb." True, by the logic of things, it must annoy the Soviet absolutists, if only because it refutes the fundamental Marxist postulate that the movement of the superstructure is determined by the movement of the base. In the Russian case, superstructure and base turn out to move not only in different, but in diametrically opposite directions. The superstructure, as conceived by Soviet historians, moves constantly towards absolutism—that is, in a progressive direction. And the base moves towards slavery—that is, in a regressive direction.

This scandalous behavior of the base does not, however, reduce the optimistic tone of genuine science, which alertly masks its dismay, as we have seen, either by boldly attacking Oriental despotism in the West or by consoling itself with the unusually active class struggle in Russia. Even an honest, although supercautious, historian like S. O. Shmidt, for example, writes with pride that in Russia there existed "conditions for the beginning of mass scale uprisings of the 'mutinous peasantry' cherishing a dream of a peasant state, which had no precedent in the other parts of Europe."[19] Here is how Jerome Blum describes the regularity of the process of disappearance of peasant self-government, in his classical work *Lord and Peasants in Russia*:

> With the increase in privately held property resulting from royal distribution of black land to seigniors, the "volost" form of organization began to disintegrate. Often the princes paid no heed to "volost" boundaries in making their grants so that the organic unity of the commune was destroyed by its land being distributed among several proprietors. The most debilitating development, however, was the penetration of the landlord into the "volost" organization. First, agents of the seignior

19. S. O. Shmidt, *Stanovlenie Moskovskogo samoderzhavstva*, p. 309.

began to bypass the commune's own officials. Then the lord forbade the selection of these officials by the peasants. Instead he named them himself, often selecting them from among his own unfree servants. The final stage was reached when the lord took away all the remaining powers of self-government from the "volost," and placed its entire administration in the hands of one of his employees or slaves. The gradual destruction of the power of the commune on privately-owned land, and the simultaneous disappearance of the black land in much of the state, ended the existence of the independent "volost" as a form of organization so far as most of the peasantry were concerned.[20]

Here you see how regularly and, one might say, organically the process of disintegration of peasant self-government proceeded, parallel with an equally regular process of enserfment of the peasantry. "By the end of the fifteenth century," Blum maintains on this score, "the right of the peasant to free movement had already been curtailed. The Code of 1497 had fixed the two weeks at St. George's Day in autumn (25 November) as the only legal time at which the peasant renter could leave his landlord, and had fixed heavy fees that he had to pay before he could depart."

On the other hand, Blum realizes that this was "also official recognition of the peasant's time-honored right of departure [from the landlord] protecting him against seignioral attempts to take that privilege from him. If the landlord tried to hold him against his will the peasant could turn to governmental authority to enforce recognition of his freedom to leave at the [legally] appointed time."[21] Blum further sees that "in the light of these guarantees it would seem plausible to assume that the peasant-renter had *complete freedom of movement* providing he met the not unreasonable conditions set by the laws."

St. George's Day was November 26 and not 25, and only two pages earlier what are now described as "not unreasonable conditions," were for some reason called a "heavy fee." But let us let the details go and continue the quotation: "From this juristic point of view B. N. Chicherin, one of the first historians of the Russian peasantry, was right when he wrote in 1858 that 'the free movement of the peasantry was a universal phenomenon of old Russia until the end of the sixteenth century.'"[22]

The contradiction is all too evident: on the one hand, it is recognized that freedom of movement was "complete"; on the other, it is

20. Jerome Blum, *Lord and Peasant in Russia from the Ninth to the Nineteenth Century*, p. 97.

21. Ibid., p. 247.

22. Ibid., p. 249. Emphasis added.

asserted that it was "curtailed." Trying to reconcile this paradox, Blum writes that Chicherin "and others who agreed with him, confused legislative fiat with historical fact."[23] In reality, it turns out that in spite of the laws which protected freedom of movement, "the peasant-renter found it increasingly difficult to leave his landlord when he wanted, for the seignior was able to employ a number of devices, both legal and illegal, to keep him from going."[24] Thus, the all-powerful (according to Pipes) "patrimonial state" was (according to Blum) powerless to compel the Russian landlord to respect its wishes.

But let us leave the two historians to argue between themselves on this point. We are interested in quite another problem: namely that in introducing the St. George's Day legislation under Ivan III, the state, as even Blum recognizes, was trying to *defend* the peasants' right to complete freedom of movement, while by introducing the "forbidden years" under Ivan the Terrible, i.e., abolishing St. George's Day, it was trying to *destroy* this freedom, thereby commencing the somber history of serfdom.

This is not to say, of course, that Ivan III was a passionate defender of freedom as such, simply that, unlike his grandson, he was not interested in transforming his subjects into slaves. We have seen how sharply the attitude of the Muscovite government toward the problem of emigration changed over the course of a century—from principled defense of the right to freedom of movement *across* state borders to "imprisonment [of people] as if in a hellish dungeon." In

23. Ibid. Incidentally, it was not only the lawyer Chicherin who recognized that peasants had freedom of movement in Russia up to the last decade of the sixteenth century. M. A. D'akonov and B. D. Grekov were very prominent, if not the most prominent, specialists in the history of the Russiian peasantry. They disagreed about everything except one point. Both of them (contrary to Blum's assertion) thought that despite all the "traps" set by the landlords, St. George's Day worked in a very real way for almost a century after the issuance of Ivan III's law code. D'akonov says that until the second half of the sixteenth century, the peasants took advantage of the right of movement (see M. A. D'akonov, *Ocherki po istorii sel'skogo naseleniia v Moskovskom gosudarstve XVI–XVII vekov*). Grekov, citing the extant books of the St. Joseph monastery of Volokolamsk, gives concrete figures for peasant movement by years. Incidentally, Blum knew this just as well as I do: at least, he cites figures from Grekov's work on pages 250–51 of his book. We also have the testimony of an eyewitness. Heinrich Staden, an Oprichnik of Ivan the Terrible's who fled abroad before the introduction of the "forbidden years," categorically asserts: "All the peasants in the country had the free right to leave on St. George's Day" (see H. Staden, *O Moskve Ivana Groznogo*, p. 123). Staden can hardly be suspected of idealizing Muscovite ways (he was a fierce enemy of Russia's) or of being insufficiently informed (he was himself a landowner and knew the force of St. George's Day from personal experience).
24. J. Blum, p. 249.

the difference between St. George's Day and the "forbidden years," we see an identical transformation in its policy on movement *within* the borders of the state.

So, is the reversed stereotype accurate? Is it not obvious that the expropriation of peasant farms by Ivan the Terrible's Oprichnina and the abolition of St. George's Day under conditions of terror represented, just as in the case of emigration, not a continuation but a rejection of the policies of Ivan III? Continuing to ignore the difference between absolutism and autocracy, how are we supposed to explain this fateful change in the policies of the Muscovite state?

Let us go further, however. Was there a regular feudalization of the structure of Russian society from the twelfth to the seventeenth century, and was peasant self-government uniformly destroyed during this period? The pre-Oprichnina century of Russia was a time, in fact, of intensive movement in the reverse direction, i.e., not toward liquidation, but toward expansion of local, and particularly peasant, self-government. The legislation of Ivan III prepared the great reform introduced several decades later on a national scale, which, at least in intention, was supposed to represent the transition of power in the localities into the hands of the "best people"—the representatives of the properous peasantry and the rising merchant class. This was, in a sense, the creation of a "third estate" in Russian political life. Article 38 of the law code of 1497 forbids the local rulers to hold court "without the elders and without the best people."[25] We can only guess what the actual role of the "elders" in the courts was. But it is obvious that it could have been the beginning of a form of control by the population over judicial procedure. And, as history shows, it was just that.

Article 38 was certainly not so radical a measure as the one specified by the Pinega Charter of February 10, 1552 (discovered a quarter century ago by A. I. Kopanev), where the tsar agrees to the complete removal of the governors from judicial and administrative functions and gives the local people themselves the right to elect "from the peasants of their own *volost'* the best people" or "favorite chiefs," who are to "administer justice in local matters according to our Code."[26] But al-

25. *Pamiatniki russkogo prava*, vol. 3, p. 366.
26. A. I. Kopanev, "Ustavnaia zemskaia gramota trekh volostei Dvinskogo uezda 25 Fevralia 1552," pp. 287–89. That this was not a purely local but in the full sense a national statewide reform is shown by the tsar's speech before the assembly of the church (known as the "Stoglav") in 1551, where he said among other things that "I have also established in all the regions of my kingdom elders and jurors . . . in all cities and suburbs, in all *volosts* and in all parishes" (*Stoglav*, p. 39).

though the legislation of Ivan III did not yet go as far as this, it nevertheless signaled a new view of society on the legislator's part—a view which, we must assume, reflected social processes which can probably be called defeudalization. Thus, in Article 12 of the code of 1497, "good boyars' children" are equated, as witnesses in court, with "good, black peasant elected jurors."[27] D. P. Makovskii has noted a very important difference between the administrative charter for the Dvina land in the fourteenth century and the Belozerskii administrative charter of Ivan III (1488). This difference consists, among other things, in the fact that "in the Belozerskii Charter boyar privileges are no longer seen. Ivan III now addresses not the boyars as his grandfather did but 'the people of Belozersk—city dwellers, villagers and *volost'* people.'"[28] Makovskii also noted that "the law code of 1497 protects all property, including that of peasants. An end is put in this code to the feudal law of inheritance reflected in the *Russkaia Pravda* [a document dating from the Kievan or pre-Mongol period, setting forth the basic provisions of the Eastern Slavic code of law, according to which the property of a peasant who died without issue passed to the landlord]. . . . The boyars and men-at-arms—i.e., feudal lords—are not separated out in terms of right of inheritance into a privileged position, as is the case in the *Russkaia Pravda*."[29]

These are, once more, only negative merits by comparison with the law code of 1550, in which an essentially different, and one might say antifeudal, principle of recompense for dishonor is established. Whereas, in the *Russkaia Pravda* of the twelfth century, the life and honor of a prince's man-at-arms were protected by an indemnity double that of other free people, in the legislation of the "Government of

27. *Pamiatniki russkogo prava*, vol. 3, p. 359. The same is true of Article 46 (ibid., p. 369).

28. D. P. Makovskii, *Razvitie tovarno-denezhnykh otnoshenii* . . . , p. 96.

29. Ibid., p. 97. In fact, Article 60 of the 1497 law code states: "If any person dies intestate and leaves no sons, then all his movable property and land [will pass] to his daughters, and if he leaves no daughters, then it is his relatives who inherit [movable and immovable property]" (*Pamiatniki russkogo prava*, vol. 3, p. 371). The fact that this law, for the first time in Russian history, protects not only the movable property of the peasant but also his land, seems to me even more significant and innovative than the absence of privileges in terms of inheritance to which Makovskii calls attention. This does not look like attachment of the peasants to the land, but rather like attachment of the land to the peasant. It thus confirms once more the contradiction between the social policy of the grandfather and that of the grandson, whose reign was marked by almost complete expropriation of peasant lands. Before the Oprichnina, the peasants in the central regions of the Muscovite state cultivated seven or eight *chetverti* (three or four hectares) per household. After the Oprichnina, their cultivated lands were catastrophically reduced, approximately to the limits of the modern-day kolkhoz household plot.

Compromise" in the middle of the sixteenth century, the indemnity for dishonor was established "against income." This is already essentially, so to speak, the embryo of the bourgeois sense of justice. And this is the only thing which can explain the strange anomaly, for a medieval code, by which an offense to "trading people and townsmen and all of those in the middle [i.e., with medium incomes]" is indemnified at the same rate (five rubles) as an offense to "a good boyar's man." As for "great guests"—i.e., wealthy merchants—the indemnity for offenses to them reaches fifty rubles, or ten times more than for offenses to boyars' men-at-arms.[30]

How are we to explain this gradation, which was revolutionary in terms of the medieval sense of justice? By the fact that Russia, as Makovskii thinks, was being transformed into a bourgeois country? This would, I am afraid, be too much of an exaggeration for boyar Russia, with its *votchiny* the prevailing form of wealth. But if we abandon the class point of view, which distorts our perspective on the past, it is explained quite simply by an elementary concern for the economic welfare of the country. The legislator is beginning to understand that "trading people and townsmen" and, in general, "all those in the middle" (i.e., the proto-bourgeoisie), have a value to the country equal to that of soldiers. Rich merchants, from the legislator's point of view, not only represent the country in foreign trade, but as it were symbolize the flowering of the nation. The more of them there are, and the richer they are, the richer the country is. In this sense, they are *more important* than soldiers (the legislator has made a calculation and found that they are ten times more important). Thus, Ivan III's legislation untied the hands of his heirs and initiated a positive view on the state's part, not only of peasants' freedom of movement but also of economic limitations on power and, in general, of the processes of defeudalization which took place in the pre-Oprichnina century.

Neither peasant self-government, nor trial by jury, nor the economic limitations on power and rationalization of the economy reflected in the legislation of the absolutist century survived the rabid counterattack of Ivan the Terrible's Oprichnina, however. In the code of Tsar Aleksei (1649) there is no longer any mention of any of this. The peasant is again "legally dead"—if it can be so expressed, even "deader" than in the *Russkaia Pravda* of the twelfth century.

30. *Pamiatniki russkogo prava*, vol. 4, p. 238.

5. The Reformation Against the Reconquista

Though there have been at least a dozen biographies of the grandson (the latest, by R. G. Skrynnikov, was published quite recently in the USSR, and another, by Edward Keenan, is now being written in the United States), a biography of the grandfather does not yet exist.[31] The heads of many generations of school children in Russia are stuffed full of the "exploits" of Ivan the Terrible. But who, other than the specialists, knows anything about Ivan III—a figure whose vague outlines melt into the mists of centuries? Nonetheless, Ivan III was one of the three Russian tsars whom posterity has called great, and the tracks which he left in Russian history are no less deep and significant than those of his grandson.

The war for the restoration of the ancient *otchina* of Kievan Rus' was the first of the two imperatives which governed Ivan III's strategy after Muscovite Rus' had been "gathered in." Recovery of the third of the land in the country seized by the church under Tatar auspices, a kind of Reconquista of internal policy, was the second. Unlike Ivan's external opponents, the church continued to gather strength. It was the most active entrepreneur and the richest usurer in the country. Landowners bequeathed their lands to the church in memory of their souls, so that it might pray for them forevermore. It seized, bought, obtained by lawsuit, and took for debt more land, "whitening" it through its immunities, and effectively removing it from the state. The *votchiny* of the Troitse-Sergievskii monastery, B. D. Grekov writes, "grew up on the bones of the boyars."[32] A. I. Kopanev notes of the Kirillo-Belozerskii monastery: "The *votchiny* of the temporal feudal lords, which in the fifteenth century were extensive, had almost completely disappeared at the end of the sixteenth. The largest feudal lord of the district—the Kirillo-Belozerskii monastery—had taken the bulk of the *votchina* lands into its hands."[33] The power of the church was spreading through the country as swiftly as a forest fire.

Church reformation was, in this sense, a logical continuation of the annexation of Tver' and Riazan' and the expeditions against Novgorod. With its own administration, holding court and dispensing retribution in its territories as an actual sovereign, not paying

31. Both of the large-scale works on the period of Ivan III—Fennel's *Ivan the Great of Moscow* and K. V. Bazilevich's *Vneshniaia politika russkogo tsentralizovannogo gosudarstva*—are devoted almost exclusively to foreign policy.

32. B. D. Grekov, *Krest'ane na Rusi s drevneishikh vremen do XVII veka*, p. 604.

33. A. I. Kopanev, *Istoriia zemlevladeniia Belozerskogo kraia v XV–XVI vekakh*, p. 181.

taxes, and ruining the city dwellers by the competition of its artisans, the church was a true state within a state, and a focus of separatism. Ivan III could scarcely tolerate such a competitor, growing stronger with each year.

But here a strategic dilemma lay in wait for him, for any move against the church weakened his position as the leader of the Reconquista. The Lithuanian empire held the Ukraine and Belorussia, which according to the "old ways" belonged to Kievan Rus'. Without partitioning Lithuania, there could be no thought of reestablishing the *otchina*. The way to Kiev—the road of the Reconquista—lay, figuratively speaking, through Vil'no. For Ivan III, the political strategy of the Reconquista therefore consisted in raising the gigantic Russian Orthodox mass of the Lithuanian empire against its Catholic government. Orthodoxy was the sole banner under which Lithuania could be dismembered, and the church, as the guardian of the faith, had to be promoted, not humiliated. The path of primitive plundering of the church on which Ivan the Terrible embarked was excluded for his grandfather. For him the problem may have seemed insoluble. Nevertheless, he solved it. The solution was simple—to split the church, just as he intended to split Lithuania.

The grand prince did not have time to impose this solution, however: his first reformist campaign did not break the resistance of the powerful church hierarchy, just as the first campaign against Lithuania did not succeed in dismembering it. Ivan was accustomed, as we have seen, to do everything in two stages. But now fate did not leave him time for a second attempt: in the heat of the campaign, he was stricken with paralysis. He had proceeded on the assumption that his descendants would follow his star and complete that which he had not had time to finish, just as he had completed the work of Ivan Kalita and Dimitrii Donskoi. But, in the *otchina* which he had created, matters were more complex than in the Muscovite clan *votchina* of his ancestors. And he could not have foreseen Ivan the Terrible.

CHAPTER V

JOSEPHITES
AND NON-ACQUIRERS

---

1. Money Versus Corvée

Until the end of the fifteenth century, the Russian peasantry lived for the most part in communes, working land belonging either to the state or to the feudal corporation of the church, or to private individuals, and paying for this chiefly in kind, or in the form of various obligations. The economic advance which began after Muscovy attained independence created previously unheard-of opportunities for rapid enrichment through agriculture.[1] However, contrary to what the pro-

1. Academician S. G. Strumilin, a major Soviet authority on economic history, is inclined to agree with D. P. Makovskii's opinion that this economic upturn made the Russian economy of the first half of the sixteenth century comparable in scale to the economies of Western European countries contemporary with it. In his preface to the second edition of Makovskii's book, he says:

> This is indirectly confirmed by the large figures for Russian exports; by the presence of many thousands of merchants within Russia; by the fact that these Russian merchants extended credits of millions of rubles to English merchants, and not vice versa; by the large trade flotilla of vessels, for the serving of which there were required on the Volga alone—figuring 500 vessels with 40 people each—20,000 hired workers; by the presence of a considerable circle of manufacturing plants with work forces of 30 to 200 persons or more; by the presence of such large-scale entrepreneurs as the Stroganov family of salt merchants, who employed 10,000 hired workers; and by many other indicative facts. (D. P. Makovskii [2nd ed.], pp. ii–iii).

The word "manufacture" is used here in a specialized Marxist sense, referring to assembly-line production by large groups of workers without the use of machines, as occurred in the large weaving-shops in Italy and the Low Countries during the fifteenth century. Makovskii himself, incidentally, confirms his contention not only with figures but with a Weberian argument (surprising in the mouth of a Soviet historian) about the rise at this time of a kind of bourgeois ethic in Russia: "The thirst for gain, for enrichment, for accumulation . . . took hold of . . . Russia," he writes.

> Russian merchants and industrialists seek roads to the East, to Siberia, to Central Asia. Afanasii Nikitin set off "beyond the three seas"; dozens and hundreds of Russian merchants penetrate into many Oriental markets—into the Crimea,

ponents of the "service state" believe, these opportunities led not to a single, fatal line of development but to *two opposite* lines, corresponding to two opposite social processes taking place simultaneously in the country. It is true that the new service nobility—who had no concern either for the rational exploitation of the land, which they held for short periods, or for the fate of the peasants living on it—naturally strove to extract the maximum gain from peasant labor. The best method of doing so seemed to them to be to set up their own farming operations and to compel the peasants to work the landlord's land. This corvée labor logically led to expropriation by the landlords of the peasants' farms, reducing them to something like the household plots of modern collective farmers. And, inasmuch as the peasants naturally resisted any form of collective economy over which they had no control, the logical extension was enserfment and the destruction of the independent *volost'*.

But the transfer of peasants from rent to corvée—which was apparently simply the economic dimension of the political tendency toward universal service—was by no means universal over the course of the pre-Oprichnina century. It was no more than a shadowy economic tendency, decidedly secondary both in importance and in scale to the process by which peasant rents became payable in money. This, in turn, gave rise to peasant differentiation, which led inevitably, at least in principle, to the opposite result—that is, not to the enserfment of the peasantry, or to its expropriation as a social group, but to the formation of a peasant proto-bourgeoisie capable of exercising political pressure on the government of the country.

In reality, the process of peasant differentiation in the pre-Oprichnina century of Russian history took on such dimensions (especially in the region of highest economic development, the North)[2] that it

---

Turkey, Iran, Bukhara, and Urgench, expeditions are undertaken to establish trade relations with China. Just as, in the fifteenth century, the Russian merchant was the first . . . European to penetrate into India, so, in the sixteenth century, two cossack hetmans sent by the Russian government arrived in Peking. Stable trade relations are established between Russia and all the European countries. Russia has emerged into the world market and has been transformed into a great world power (ibid., pp. 487–88).

2. The North in the sixteenth century not only represented half of all the territory of Russia, but had also, as S. F. Platonov writes,

from a remote backwater of the state become one of its liveliest regions. The entire country, in its relation with the cultural world, had, so to speak, turned its face northward. The commercial and working population . . . streamed toward the northern ports. . . . Not only the routes along which moved the traffic provoked by trade, but entire regions, which served these routes or were dependent

was even able, in many cases, to bring about the *defeudalization* of
these regions—dissolution of the feudal elements into a new stratum
of farmers, entrepreneurs, and merchants of peasant origin.[3]

The vigor of this process is confirmed by the fact that it stimulated
government policy in directions favorable to the peasant proto-bourgeoisie, in particular, the remaking of the entire administrative structure of the country along the lines of local self-government (the Great
Reform of 1551–56). Although in formal terms the black peasantry
of the North cultivated land belonging to the state, practically speaking it was being transformed into private (allodial) property, while the
peasantry itself became a class of freeholders.[4]

As a result of all this, there appeared peasants who were economically stronger not only than most *pomeshchiki*, but also than many boyars—peasants who possessed plow land, truck gardens, hayfields,

on them, had come to life (S. F. Platonov, "Problema russkogo Severa v noveishei
istoriografii," pp. 112–13).

It is important to note that the North became the most flourishing part of the country
precisely after Ivan III's expedition, when

the Muscovite regime transformed the boyar *votchiny* which it had confiscated
. . . into peasant communities and, having freed their population from depen-
dance on private persons, introduced in them the communal organization and
self-government which prevailed in peasant communities generally. As the final
result of this, the entire North took on the character of a peasant country (ibid.,
p. 107).

3. Ivan III confiscated only the church lands and the lands of the "great" boyars,
while the middling and petty boyar families, the so-called *svoezemtsy* (small landowners),
underwent "peasantization"—that is to say, defeudalization. "The lands of the *svoezemtsy*," Kopanev writes, "were first strictly separated from those of the peasants and of the
grand prince, then apparently merged with them, and then disappeared, and the
svoezemtsy came to be on the same footing with the peasants, [which] basically changed
the social relationships here" (see A. I. Kopanev, "K voprosu o strukture zemlevladeniia na Dvine v XV–XVI vv.," pp. 450–51). In a brilliant genealogical study of one
boyar family, the Amosovs, N. E. Nosov has clearly traced all the details of the "rapid
and intensive adaptation of the Amosovs' economy, and that of the peasantized boyars
like them, to the new economic conditions" (N. E. Nosov, *Stanovlenie soslovno-predstavitel'nykh uchrezhdenii v Rossii*, pp. 270–71, 274).

4. One of Kopanev's most important conclusions is that "the active mobilization of
peasant lands shown in the Dvina documents of the fifteenth and sixteenth centuries
had as a result the concentration of great resources of land in the hands of some peasants, and land shortage for others." It was not just a matter of a few more scraps of land
coming into the hands of rich peasants; they bought entire villages: "The Dvina documents show that villages [and] parts of villages become the objects of purchase and sale,
with no limitations whatever." And "the land passes from one holder to another . . . 'forever'"—that is, as property, *as an allodium*, having lost all traces of feudal tenure (Kopanev, "K voprosu o strukture," pp. 452–53; emphasis added).

traplines, stockbarns, and even entire villages. But, what is even more important, they also owned fishing and fur enterprises, craft work-shops, and huge salt ponds. These were the peasants whose geneal-ogies N. E. Nosov was able to trace over the course of many genera-tions, just as S. B. Veselovskii traced the genealogies of the ancient boyar families.

Of course, the formation of this elite (the "best people") was accom-panied by the ruin of masses of other peasants. Russian documents of this period are strewn with the designations "cotters," "children," "Cossacks," "sharecroppers," "hirelings," which variously represent landless people who earned their bread as hired labor. As D. P. Makov-skii has demonstrated, in the twelve villages of Viaz'ma *uezd* (and bear in mind that this was not the North, but the West—the Smolensk coun-ty), of 3,139 existing peasant households, "1,991 households or 45 per cent of the total were the victims of increasing exploitation, in a form especially severe for the minor peasantry—that of money."[5] In an-other passage, the author notes with appropriate anti-bourgeois indignation:

> This separation of the producer from the means of production drove huge masses of people into the street. It was natural that the "poor peo-ple" became the easy prey of various predatory elements which had de-veloped in the depths of the feudal order. Among these predators the most numerous and bloodthirsty were the stratum of "best" or "good" peasants. These peasants not only owned large tracts of land (some . . . up to forty to fifty *desiatiny* in Viaz'ma *uezd*), but were also en-trepreneurs, owning facilities of various kinds—salt ponds, gristmills, stores. . . . Among the wealthy peasants the entrepreneurial renting of land could frequently be observed, which went by the name of "hiring."[6]

Even if we share Makovskii's indignation over the exploitation of the "producer separated from the means of production," we are nev-ertheless not entitled to forget that (as the author himself shows in other sections of his book) the only alternative to it under the condi-tions of sixteenth-century Russia was corvée, which led to serfdom, under which the producer was attached by force to these very "means of production," and . . . became a slave.

Nosov shows how "as a result of the growing property differentia-tion within Dvina *volost'* . . . it completely loses the features of the old rural commune . . . and is transformed into a territorial unit for pur-

5. Makovskii, p. 160.
6. Ibid., pp. 164–65.

poses of administration and taxation . . . a black *volost' mir*,[7] *which united the peasant freeholders* . . . and, what was most important, *represented their common interests vis-à-vis the state.*" But all this was true only for the "golden age" of the Russian peasantry, i.e., *before* the Oprichnina revolution.

And again, as if by the same magic which determined the fate of emigration, everything suddenly swung around 180 degrees *after* this revolution:

> The disintegration of the *volost'*, as a result of the spoliation and seizure of its lands and also of the fact that certain groups of inhabitants of the *volost'* fell into personal or economic dependence on neighboring feudal lords, undermined the foundations of the *volost'* peasant *mir*, deprived the local peasant magnates of their basic support, and thus closed the pathways leading toward bourgeoisification of the peasantry as a whole. [This "closing of the pathways"] took place in the central regions of northeastern Rus' in the sixteenth century, during and after the time of the Oprichnina of Ivan the Terrible, when the process of swallowing up of the black *volost'* lands by the service landholdings reached its apogee there.[8]

The fate of Russia thus became a question of who, in the final analysis, would get the land belonging to the disintegrating communal *mirs*—the *pomeshchiki* living on corvée—that is, the service gentry—or the "best people" of the peasantry—that is, the proto-bourgeoisie.

2. Two Coalitions

The competing socioeconomic forces involved in the historical dispute between the *pomeshchiki* and the proto-bourgeoisie are hardly visible on the political stage in retrospect. Still less obvious is the ideological struggle between the so-called Josephites and Non-Acquirers (see below). The observer sees, rather, a furious struggle between the boyardom and the church.

But the interweaving of these three dimensions of the struggle—the socioeconomic, the political, and the ideological—constitutes the major complexity of this transitional epoch in my view. Who stood with whom? Who represented whom? What was the immanent con-

---

7. The *mir* is the traditional designation for the Russian peasant commune and its governing body, the assembly of shareholding, and originally arms-bearing, males. It should be noted that the *mir* was not necessarily coextensive with the village; some villages included two *mirs*, the members of which held land on different bases.

8. Nosov, *Stanovlenie*, pp. 283–84. Emphasis added.

nection between the various levels of this fateful drama? In order to untangle this bundle of conflicting interests, let us attempt to group the major actors on the Muscovite historical scene according to whether they were fighting *for* or *against* the latent limitations on power.

The interests of the Russian aristocracy—the boyardom—which by definition defended the social limitations on power (since these were a matter of life and death for it), did not contradict the interests of the peasant proto-bourgeoisie, which by definition defended the economic limitations on power (also a matter of life and death). N. E. Nosov even argues that,

> objectively, by virtue of its economic position as an estate of large land-owners, it [the boyardom] was less interested in the mass scale seizure of state lands and in the enserfment of peasants by the state, than was the petty and middling *dvorianstvo* [the *pomeshchiki*], and consequently had less need of the strengthening of a military-bureaucratic autocratic system. In this respect, its interests could sometimes even coincide with those of the upper stratum of merchants.[9]

The connections between the boyardom and the Non-Acquirers, who defended the ideological limitations on power, have long been conceded in classical historiography. Even Soviet historians, who hate the boyardom, and therefore see the Non-Acquirers as a reactionary force, have never questioned this verdict.

Thus, on one side of the historical barricade, there appears a sort of latent absolutist political coalition—the Non-Acquirers, the boyars, and the proto-bourgeoisie. But what about the other side of this barricade? Can an opposite, autocratic coalition be discerned there? Why, after all, should the service gentry, the *pomeshchiki*, oppose the Non-Acquirers? And why should the bureaucracy take up arms against the bourgeoisie?

If the basic problem which the Russian government faced at this time was actually reducible to deciding at whose expense it should satisfy the land hunger of the *pomeshchiki* who constituted its chief military force, the solution seems relatively clear. This hunger could be satisfied *either* by the lands belonging to the boyars and peasants (that is, the proto-bourgeoisie) *or* those belonging to the church. In the absence of an anti-Tatar strategy, there simply was no other choice. Was this not enough to produce a mortal struggle, given that the church hierarchy, too, considered its landholdings a matter of life and death, and was ready to push every available political force, be it the service

9. Ibid., p. 11.

gentry, the bureaucracy, or even the tsar's personal ambitions, into the battle against its opponents, the great lords?

The lesser gentry and the bureaucracy struggled against the great lords everywhere in Europe. But nowhere else did this struggle reach the point of mortal confrontation which it did in Russia, because nowhere else was there such a powerful coalition of forces opposed to Europeanization, inspired and led by so mighty an institution as the Russian Orthodox Church. And here is why, as I see it, the struggle of the Non-Acquirers for the secularization of the church landholdings assumes such a fateful significance. The Non-Acquirers were the ideological side of the absolutist triangle.

3. The Political Function of Secularization

History, unlike boxing, does not usually decide disputes by a knockout. It awards the victory on points—and then only after a long interval, when the original protagonists have long since left the stage. After the Renaissance, for example, it seemed that the entire fabric of society was being swiftly secularized, and that matters would soon end in total separation of the culture from the church. Instead, there followed a period of religious wars—the epoch of the Reformation and Counter-Reformation. Only many centuries afterward would the culture in fact be separated from the church.

The analogy may similarly be applied to the struggle between monetary rent and corvée. With the great expansion of monetary rent in the first half of the sixteenth century, it seemed as though all Europe was on the threshold of bourgeoisification (so, too, it appeared in retrospect in the case of Russia to historians such as Makovskii and Nosov). Then, however, in many countries there followed a time of reaction, when corvée appeared to be on the winning side. Only after many decades did monetary rent triumph there over its rival.

This, at least, was how analogous conflicts turned out in the other states of the northeastern corner of Europe. Take, for example, Denmark and Sweden—also northerly and rather backward countries, whose fate, like that of Russia, was determined in the dispute between the service gentry and the proto-bourgeoisie. Both of these countries, like Russia, came to know the taste of corvée and feudal reaction (in Denmark's case, even the enserfment of the peasantry), and fell into the power of paranoid tyrants like Ivan the Terrible. They stood at the very edge of the precipice of autocracy. But they stood firm there. Why?

The decisive reason seems to have been precisely the secularization of church landholdings. As distinct from Russia, both of these countries slaked the land hunger of the feudal service gentry not at the expense of land belonging to the great lords and the peasantry, but from the church's land fund; thus, they succeeded both in preserving the power of the aristocracy and sustaining peasant differentiation. When King Christian III of Denmark arrested the bishops and took away their lands and privileges in 1536, as a result of which royal landholdings were increased by a factor of three, it meant, in plain terms, that the land hunger of the Danish service gentry was satisfied at the expense of the church. Corvée and serfdom thus triumphed only in one sector of the national economy, and did not spread over the entire country or become state policy. In the second half of the seventeenth century, a time of reaction all over Europe, when the Russian peasantry was already hopelessly enserfed, not more than 20 percent of the peasantry in Denmark was burdened with corvée, and the sale of peasants without land did not become widespread. The history of Sweden provides still clearer indication of the decisive significance of the secularization of church lands. Though this led to the concentration of more than half of Sweden's land in the hands of the gentry, fears of "Livonian slavery"—that is, the total enserfment of the peasants—remained no more than that.[10] Thus, in both cases, sec-

10. In *Istoriia srednikh vekov*, vol. 2, we read: "The lands of the clergy [in Denmark] passed to the king, and subsequently, by gift and sale, from the king to the feudal nobility . . . the service gentry received complete police power over the holders; [they] seized the commune lands, drove off some of the peasants from the allotment land, and increased the corvée, [as a consequence of which] there was a corresponding increase in serf dependence" (pp. 354–55). "Soon after the Reformation, the Swedish kings, like the Danish, resumed the distribution . . . of land to the nobility . . . the land distributions of the sixteenth and seventeenth centuries had the characteristics of naturally guaranteeing state service by the nobility, which became like the Russian service gentry. . . . Correspondingly, corvée obligations began to grow" (pp. 361–62). Though undoubtedly belonging geographically to the region east of the Elbe, i.e., to Eastern Europe, Denmark and Sweden are for some reason excluded from consideration by historians of the region. This is a pity, since in certain circumstances it dooms the historian to the same kind of bipolar view of European history which did so much harm to Wittfogel's interpretation on a global scale. A good example is Immanuel Wallerstein's model of "world-wide division of labor" designed to explain the emergence of serfdom in sixteenth-century Eastern Europe by the fatal influence of rising Western capitalism. True, there is not much evidence presented for such a model in his book *The Modern World-System*. In fact some experts come to quite opposite conclusions. Perry Anderson, for one, argues that "while the corn trade undoubtedly intensified servile exploitation in Eastern Germany or Poland, it did not inaugurate it in either country, and played no role at all in the parallel development of Bohemia or Russia" (*Lineages of the Absolutist*

ularization served as the basis for an absolutist compromise between the various factions and institutions of feudal society, permitting Denmark and Sweden to retain the "equilibrium" of social forces for which Soviet historians now long in vain. The social limitations on power therefore remained untouched in Denmark and Sweden, as distinct from the case in Russia.

In the second place, secularization prevented the eradication of peasant differentiation on lands belonging to the state and the aristocracy, thereby preserving a sector of the country's land fund on which the proto-bourgeoisie could develop. In my terms, this means that, as distinct from what happened in Russia, the economic limitations on power were not destroyed.

And, last but not least, secularization separated the church, and with it the intellectual potential of the country, from the defense of private economic interests. In so doing, it transformed the now landless church into the custodian of the only treasure which remained to it—the ideological limitations on power.

Secularization could not prevent corvée and the depredations of the service gentry, the tyranny of monarchs, or the enserfment of the peasantry. But it could prevent these depredations, this tyranny, this enserfment from becoming total. By furthering the retention of latent limitations on power, it prevented an Oprichnina "revolution from above," Russian-style.

4. The Preparation for the Assault

How did it happen that this "revolution from above" was not prevented in Russia? Why was it that secularization of church lands did not occur there, too, in the key century in which the fate of the country was decided?

The Muscovite sovereigns did not have to defend their authority against the claims of a universal hierarchy. After the Union of Florence in 1439, when the Patriarchate of Constantinople, seeking a last

---

State, pp. 196–97). But even if Wallerstein is correct in relation to some parts of Eastern Europe, his model still fails to explain why in its other parts (Denmark and Sweden) serfdom did not prevail at all. Indeed, the sixteenth-century boom in the Baltic grain trade intensified not one but two different patterns of sociopolitical development, which we may arbitrarily call Polish and Swedish. This again certifies that the choice between Polish and Swedish patterns was still open for sixteenth-century Muscovy. And, having in mind that its political structure was much closer to Sweden than to Poland, one may say that the chance of avoiding serfdom was rather high for Muscovy before the Oprichnina.

refuge from the Turkish onslaught, agreed in desperation to the pope's suzerainty, Greek Orthodoxy became in the eyes of Muscovites a dubious and almost seditious thing. Thus, from the middle of the fifteenth century onward, the state and the church stood opposite each other in Muscovy on the same national ground. But did this make the task of secularization easier? From the point of view of the current stereotypes, it unquestionably did. But, as we shall see shortly, the church was by no means defenseless in the face of the "totalitarian" (to use Toynbee's word) power of the omnipotent "service" state. The fact that the national ecclesiastical leadership could not be presented in Russia as the agents of a foreign hierarchy, as happened in Denmark, Sweden, or England, greatly complicated the state's dispute with the church. And the authority and ideological power of the state and the church were not equal in Russia. The church, contrary to the Toynbeean theory, was much stronger.

When Moscow was still only dreaming of the unification of Rus' and supremacy over it, the Russian church was already unified and rigidly centralized, and had achieved privileges and immunities more extensive perhaps than were enjoyed by any other church in Europe. It owed all of this not to Constantinople or Moscow, but to the Tatars, who were responsible for both its material might and its spiritual worthlessness. If we seek the roots of Tatar influence on Muscovy, then, paradoxical as it may seem, they should be sought primarily in the Orthodox Church. It was no accident that in defending their feudal perquisites as late as the sixteenth century, many years after the yoke had been thrown off, the Muscovite prelates still shamelessly referred to the Tatar *yarlyks*, or decrees issued by the khans of the Golden Horde. The *yarlyks* were, in fact, unbelievably generous. From the church—runs one document of the khans, which had the force of law—"no tribute, or turnover taxes, or tillage taxes, or land and water transport duties, or war taxes, or maintenance of officials are to be exacted; and no royal tax whatever is to be taken." And not only the church but all those under its protection are to be exempt from such impositions: "and the church's people, craftsmen, falconers . . . or men and women servants and any of their people—whoever are hired either for work or as guards." In addition to the guarantee of church property and exemption from all taxes, duties, obligations, and charges, and in general from all the burdens of the "yoke," the church was also granted the supreme power over its people: "The Metropolitan is to give judgment and administer his people in all matters: in robbery and theft with material evidence the Metropolitan alone, or whoever he orders to do so, is to be the judge in all cases."[11] In a subjugated, plundered, and humiliated country, the church was an inviolate and untouched island, a fortress of prosperity. But the Tatars were by no means philanthropists. They were paying the church for its collaboration—for the spiritual sword which Orthodoxy placed at their feet. There is no need for us to explain here how relations between the Orthodox Church and its Muslim suzerains developed over the course of the centuries, and indeed there came a day when the church betrayed the Tatars. But for a long time they had no reason to regret their generosity to it. In any case, it was not the church which was obliged to Moscow for its power, but Moscow which was obliged to the church. In the fourteenth century, the church had helped the Horde to defeat an anti-Tatar uprising led by Tver'. Moscow was its favorite in the rivalry of the Russian princedoms for leadership.

Ivan III, the first Russian sovereign to be aware of the danger of church landholdings, was nevertheless compelled to reckon with the "sacred old ways" which Orthodoxy embodied. There was also the need to split Lithuania by taking advantage of its Orthodox-Catholic antagonisms. Unlike Gustav Vasa in Sweden, or Henry VIII in England, Ivan could not, therefore, simply confiscate the land of the monasteries. The confrontation with the church required deep strategy—and, moreover, in an area where he, as a pragmatist and professional politician, had the least experience. For this confrontation called not so much for political as for ideological skills.

True, there was an ideological breach in the adversary's armor, the old debate about the limits of intervention by the state in the competence of the church. Metropolitan Kiprian in the fourteenth century, as well as Metropolitan Fotii in the fifteenth, had asserted the complete independence of the church. At the beginning of the fourteenth century, however, the elder Akindin had argued for the right of the prince to sit in judgment on the metropolitan himself, if he proved guilty of violating a canon. Kirill of Belozersk, Metropolitan Iona, Iosif of Volokolamsk, Metropolitans Daniil and Makarii, the elder Filofei, and even the teachers of the schism held the same position. The debate was by no means scholastic but profoundly utilitarian. The Russian church, being occupied basically with earthly, secular, not to say economic matters, was never able to cope with heresy in open ideological battle. The sword of the grand prince was needed. The propagandists of the church called down administrative thunder upon the heretics, thereby revealing their own ideological weakness,

11. M. N. Pokrovskii, *Ocherk* . . . , p. 218.

and at the same time giving the state a legal pretext, recognized by the church itself, for interfering in its internal affairs.

A less perspicacious leader than Ivan III might have sought in heresy a means of reforming the church. Many people at his court did precisely this. Elena Stefanovna, his daughter-in-law and the mother of Crown Prince Dimitrii, headed an influential circle of heretics. Heretics also held powerful positions in government. One of the men closest to Ivan, his most eminent diplomat, the high secretary Kuritsyn, was a heretic.[12] But though the grand prince might be the patron of heretics, he could not himself become one. He needed, rather, a moderate ideological doctrine which would imply that land-ownership by the church was *harmful* to Russian Orthodoxy, and hence itself heresy. Essentially, he needed Protestantism, whose existence he didn't even suspect. He needed a strategy analogous to the one by whose aid he had split Novgorod and was preparing to split Lithuania: two contending factions within the church which he could manipulate. But where was he to get Russian Protestantism?

There existed, independently of the strategy of Ivan III, a modest sect of "Trans-Volga elders"—strict anchorites who had taken refuge in the forests from the temptations of monastic greed, and preached "intelligent action" [*umnoe delanie*]. Teaching that "he who prays only with the mouth, and forgets about the mind, prays to the air: God is listening to the mind," the elders believed that true closeness to God was to be achieved not by fasting, deprivation, and disciplinary measures, but by having "the mind keep watch over the heart" and control sinful passions and thoughts deriving from the world and the flesh.

One can interpret this doctrine as a Russian proto-Protestantism, but in any case it was only a sprout which had not yet had time to put down roots, and so weak that it could easily be smothered (like its analog, the proto-bourgeoisie). All of Ivan III's persistence was needed simply in order to discover the meek elders, let alone to draw them into the political arena—the orbit of the furious human passions which were precisely what they were fleeing from. Yet they had to be

---

12. Ia. S. Lur'e, *Ideologicheskaia bor'ba v russkoi publitsystike kontsa XV-nachala XVI vv.*, pp. 183, 185. Admitting that "Fedor Kuritsyn stood at the head of this 'heretical' circle," Lur'e finds it necessary to add that the Russian heresies at the end of the fifteenth century were, like the urban heresies of the West, one of the forms of 'revolutionary opposition to feudalism.'" Inasmuch as Kuritsyn is spoken of in one document of the chronicles as "a person who is listened to by the sovereign in all things," it seems that it was the sovereign himself who headed the "revolutionary opposition to feudalism."

transformed into something reminiscent of political party (later to become known as the Non-Acquirers).

Of course, Ivan III was not the only factor here. Ecclesiastic upheaval was at that time common to all of Europe, and the Russian church was no exception. In the 1480s and 1490s, the crisis was in full swing: the church was shaken by heresy. But in order to create a serious renovationist movement, personnel were needed who were not available, not to speak of high consciousness of duty, of which the inhabitants of the monasteries of that time—pragmatists and men of affairs like their sovereign—were decidedly incapable. The social and the cultural functions of the church were not carried out. Greed consumed discipline; corruption, its spiritual goals. It was a successful usurer, entrepreneur, and landowner, but had ceased to be a pastor of the people and the intellectual leadership of the nation. Though spiritually stagnant, it grew materially like a cancerous tumor, irresistibly spreading through the body of the country. This was clear to everyone—the heretics and the grand prince, the Non-Acquirers and their opponents alike.

In the well-known questions of the tsar to the assembly of the church of 1551, written for him by the Government of Compromise, the state of things is described as passionately and vividly as though the author were the main propagandist of the Non-Acquirer movement himself—the Russian Luther, the monk-prince Vassian Patrikeev, of whom we shall speak soon.

> People go into monasteries not in order to save their souls, but in order to carouse all the time. Archimandrites and abbots buy their positions without knowing either the divine service or brotherhood . . . they buy villages for themselves and some are always asking me for land. Where are the profits, and who gains any advantage from them? . . . Such is the disorder and complete indifference to God's church and the structure of the monasteries. . . . Who is responsible for all this sin? And how are the souls of laymen to gain advantage and to be turned away from all evil? If there [in the monasteries] everything is done not according to God, what good can our worldly flock expect from us? And who are we, to ask for God's mercy?[13]

This is spoken not out of political calculation but by the troubled medieval conscience itself. Something has to be done about the church; otherwise there will be no forgiveness for us even in this world, let alone in the next.

13. A. S. Pavlov, *Istoricheskii ocherk sekuliarizatsii tserkovnykh zemel' v Rossii*, p. 113.

Such was the challenge to which the Russian church responded
with two opposed solutions, which we may arbitrarily call reformation and counter-reformation. And this was also a response common
to all the developing European nations.

5. *The Arguments of the Counter-Reformation*

To the Non-Acquirers, led by the famous monk and writer Nil Sorskii, the secularization of church lands meant the liberation of the
church to fulfill its natural function as the intellectual and spiritual
staff of the nation. For the first time in centuries, Russian Orthodoxy
was offered a chance to cleanse itself of the mire of the Tatar heritage.
The Non-Acquirers were not, of course, concerned about the political
necessity of secularization which preoccupied their royal patron, and
still less about the economic need to protect the interests of the fragile
Russian proto-bourgeoisie. For them, the reformation began and
ended with the reform of the church. They spoke against the execution of heretics; they were outraged by the exploitation of peasants
on monastery lands; they were, in general, proponents of, shall we
say, "Orthodoxy with a human face," and as such defended all the aggrieved and persecuted. But their ideas, particularly at the beginning, lacked any clear political articulation.[14] Their opponents, on the

14. I am compelled to admit that my point of view about the conflict between the
Non-Acquirers and the Josephites (and about the fundamental role of this conflict in
Russian political history) is not shared either by the "despotists" or by the "absolutists."
The position of the despotists is at least consistent: what serious ideological struggle,
what talk of reformation or counter-reformation can there be in a "totalitarian" or "service" state? The absolutists are in worse shape, since, asserting categorically, as is required by genuine science, that "Soviet scholars first posed the question of the social
role of Nil and his followers," they contradict themselves so desperately that they get
mixed up and lead their readers into complete confusion. "One need only throw open
the monastic robes of any of the Non-Acquirers," wrote Academician B. A. Rybakov,
"in order to see the brocade of a boyar's kaftan. Trying to ward off the looming spectre
of the Oprichnina, the boyar pointed the way to the patrimonial estates of the 'un-
buried dead' [the monks]." (Quoted from Lur'e, p. 293.) Rybakov unfortunately does
not explain what is bad about trying to ward off "the looming spectre of the Oprichnina"—that is, national ruin and humiliation. Nevertheless, the authors of practically
all the general textbooks of Russian literature and history agree with him. In *Istoriia
russkoi literatury*, published by the USSR Academy of Science, we read that "the ideas of
Nil Sorskii were a cover for the reactionary struggle of the great patrimonial boyardom . . . a struggle *against the strong grand prince's regime, which was emerging victorious.*"
We read the same thing in *Ocherki po istorii SSSR*: "Under the religious integument of
the doctrine of Nil Sorskii there was hidden an intraclass struggle, directed particularly
against the power of the grand prince, which was growing stronger" (quoted in ibid., p. 293;

other hand, led by the head of the Volokamansk monastery, Iosif, were openly and clearly politicized from the outset.

As early as 1889, M. D'iakonov called attention to the fact that it was precisely Iosif who put forward the "revolutionary thesis" that it is necessary to resist the will of the sovereign if he deviates from the norms of piety. In the heat of the struggle against the secularizing plans of Ivan III, the Josephites advanced the doctrine of the legitimacy of resistance to state power, as V. Val'denberg noted in 1916. Their arguments, the first such in Russian literature, were substantial and serious.

They by no means disputed that the church was in disarray, and they did not deny the need for reforms. They just claimed the role of genuine reformers for themselves. Yes, Iosif agreed, money grubbing is pernicious for monks as individuals subject to moral corruption—but not for monasteries as religious institutions. "It is true that monks sin, but the church of God and the monasteries commit no sin at all."[15] The monk retreats from the world and returns to it no longer as an individual, but as a part of the holy corporation, a tool of its collective will. Hence the reforms proposed by Iosif—the revival of the true norms of monastic life, the dissolution of individuality in the church, and fundamental purification of the monastic collective thereby. Just as the Non-Acquirer movement bore within itself elements of proto-Protestantism, so the Josephite apologia for collectivism had a pronounced Catholic tinge.

But Iosif not only spoke and wrote; he acted. This Muscovite Loyola was not only a brilliant ideologist, but a talented administrator. He transformed his Volokolamsk monastery into a model monastic establishment, a preserve of ecclesiastical culture, and a political academy from which several generations of high Russian prelates came. Who

---

emphasis added). One small question still remains: how are we to reconcile the struggle of the Non-Acquirers against the grand prince with the fact that the Non-Acquirer movement was itself the handiwork of the grand prince? The authors cited above cannot help knowing this. They have at least read in Kliuchevskii that "behind Nil and his Non-Acquirers there stood Ivan III himself, who needed monastery lands" (V. O. Kliuchevskii, *Sochineniia* (1st ed.), vol. 2, pp. 303–4). Even Lur'e declares that "Nil Sorskii's action was staged by Ivan III; Nil spoke as a sort of theoretician of the policy of the grand prince on this question" (Lur'e, p. 281). So there is no need whatever to offend modesty by parting the monastic robes of the elders in order to establish the real political meaning of their actions. But, after all, in Lur'e's work we have already seen Ivan III in the role of leader of the "revolutionary opposition" directed against himself. Why, then, shouldn't the grand prince at the same time head the "reactionary opposition," also directed against himself?

15. Pavlov, p. 97.

could have known at the time that this monastery would remain an isolated ideal, owing its flourishing condition only to Iosif's charismatic leadership? In any case, the Josephites were a serious and formidable foe, and for this reason the Non-Acquirer movement became, for the grand prince, not merely a justification for secularization, but also a political ideology.

6. Before the Assault

Ivan prowled around the idea of secularization for a long time, and prepared for it slowly, as he did everything. Let us not forget that he did not have at his disposal the historical experience of secularization. The German, Scandinavian, and English reforms belonged to the following generation.[16] In his time they were still only maturing in the minds of Europeans—minds to which Ivan III did not have access. He came to this idea independently; he invented it himself; it was dear to him, and he bequeathed it to his successors as the pearl of his political experience.

In 1476–78, in the course of the great confiscations in Novgorod, Ivan III took away from the Novgorod clergy a part of its lands, "since those lands from time immemorial belonged to the grand prince, and [the archbishop and the monasteries] had themselves seized them." Although the standard reference to the "old ways" is again present, as we see, this measure could be—and was—interpreted as political repression. But twenty years later we suddenly read in the chronicle that again "the grand prince took over the patrimonial estates of the church in Novgorod and gave them out to the boyars' children as service estates . . . with the blessing of Metropolitan Simon."[17] This time the "old ways" were not invoked, and the confiscation could not be interpreted as a political act: there was nothing for which the Novgorodian church should be punished. It was rather an attempted frontal attack, without any ideological provisioning. And although the grand prince made several such attempts (by limiting the expansion of the monastery of Saint Cyril at Beloozero, by suggesting to the bishop of Perm' that he return "to the people, the land and forests and pastures which the prelate had taken

16. The secularization of church land in Switzerland began in 1523. In 1525, the grand master of the Teutonic Order resigned his holy office and converted his holdings into a secular dukedom. In 1527, Gustavus Vasa secularized church lands in Sweden; in 1536, secularization began in Denmark, Norway, England, and Scotland, and in 1539 in Iceland.

17. Pavlov, p. 29.

from them," and by forbidding the thirty families of princes of Suzdal' to bequeath their lands to the monasteries "for masses"), it soon became obvious that matters would not go forward this way. The hierarchy started worrying: attacks on the grand prince became open; the matter went so far that he began to be cursed from the pulpit and pamphlets began to be written against him. In short, the fortress of the church, Toynbee's categorical assertion notwithstanding, appeared not to be vulnerable to a frontal attack. Having found this out, Ivan III, as always, retreated.

But, as always, he did so only in order to try to gain his ends by an indirect route. As early as the 1480s, he had turned his attention to the Non-Acquirers, and now he tried to place "his people" in the highest ranks of the church. Nil Sorskii's teacher, the humble hermit of Beloozero, Paisii Yaroslavov, was suddenly appointed to the post of abbot of the Troitsa Monastery. Elevated to the peak of the Orthodox hierarchy, the elder was inevitably caught up in a political campaign.

One after another, over the course of the pre-Oprichnina century, four generations of Non-Acquirers emerged into the political arena, until they were destroyed or implicated as heretics or fled the country under Ivan the Terrible. We will meet some of them later, and see them grow and mature before our eyes. What Ivan the Terrible did to them constitutes the first act in the drama of the Russian intelligentsia.

The post of abbot of the Troitsa was to be only the first step in the political career of the hermit of Beloozero, according to Ivan III's plan. As soon as Metropolitan Gerontii fell ill, Paisii was at once recommended by the grand prince for the metropolitan's chair—that is, for the very helm of church policy.

The metropolitan recovered, however, and, worse, Paisii refused.[18] Ivan III had called on him to struggle against the entire hierarchy. But the Non-Acquirer generation of 1480 was obviously not prepared for this. It was necessary to turn to the heretics.

In 1480, while in Novgorod, Ivan had received denunciations of two heretical priests, Dionisii and Aleksei. Instead of punishing them, he took these seditious persons with him to Moscow, where both of them were suddenly raised to dizzying heights: they became the archpriests of the Uspenskii and Arkhangel'skii cathedrals respectively. Then, after Gerontii died, the grand prince approved the appointment to the metropolitan's chair of the Archimandrite Zosima, who was suspected—apparently not without reason—of being in sympathy with the heretics.

---

18. S. M. Solov'ev, *Istoriia Rossii s drevneishikh vremen*, Bk. 3, p. 185.

Iosif's comrade-in-arms was the ferocious Gennadii, archbishop of Novgorod, who literally every month discovered new nests of heretics in his archdiocese, and constantly called for an antiheretical campaign throughout Russia. The grand prince now forbade him to come to Moscow for the installation of the new metropolitan, who was himself—Gennadii did not doubt for a minute—a heretic. This was an open scandal. Could Gennadii keep silent, when in his letter to the church assembly of 1490 he had declared that it was criminal even to argue about the faith with heretics? ("One has only to convene the assembly in order to execute them, by burning or hanging," he wrote.)[19] Inspired by the example of Spanish Catholicism, Gennadii had praised the way the Catholics had "cleansed their earth."[20] Could Iosif himself be silent, for that matter, after writing to the bishop of Suzdal' that,

> From the time when the sun of Orthodoxy rose over our land, we have never had so much heresy: in houses, on the streets, in the marketplace, everyone—both monks and laymen—is dubiously discussing the faith, basing themselves not on the doctrine of the prophets, the apostles, and the Holy Fathers, but on the words of heretics, apostates from Christianity; they make friends with them, learn Jewishness from them. And the heretics never leave the metropolitan's house, and even sleep there.[21]

New ideas were advanced, disputed, rejected, and advanced again—and not only within closed circles of scholars or government officials. None of the conflicting factions were officially embraced by

19. N. A. Kazakova and Ia. S. Lur'e, *Antideodal'nye ereticheskie dvizheniia na Rusi XIV−nachala XVI veka*, p. 381.

20. Ibid., p. 378.

21. Solov'ev, *Istoriia Rossii s drevneishikh vremen*, p. 190. The doctrine of the Russian heretics in its organizational aspect can be reduced to the denial of the church establishment with its hierarchy, churches, rituals, and so forth. Its theological aspect consisted in the denial of the canonical Trinity (and, consequently, in denial of the divinity of Christ). There is nothing original in all of this: anyone at all familiar with the history of European heresy will recognize its twin in Russian heresy. It is considerably more interesting to look at how the representatives of the Russian right, as early as the fifteenth century, explained *the origin of heresy*. In Iosif's opinion, heresy was brought to Novgorod in 1470 by Jews coming from Kiev. In the opinion of Gennadii of Novgorod, on the other hand, "this evil came from those places through which Kuritsyn traveled from the Ugrian [i.e., Hungarian] lands" (quoted from I. U. Budovnits, *Russkaia publitsistika XVI veka*, p. 51). These two explanations—the one Jewish (kikeish) and the other European—both propose a foreign, non-Russian provenance for the dissident movement. Over the course of the half millennium which has elapsed since that time, the Russian right has not changed its mind.

the government. An open struggle of ideas permeated the air of Muscovy. To me this picture alone certifies beyond any doubt that the government of Ivan III recognized ideological limitations on power.

Well, one might argue that the state did not persecute the heretics because heresy was to its advantage. This is true. But neither did it persecute their opponents. Just after the first confiscations in Novgorod, Gennadii, on his own initiative, included in the ritual of the church a special anathema on those who "offend against the sacred things of the church."[22] Everyone understood perfectly whom Novgorod's priests were cursing from the pulpits of the churches. And nothing happened: Gennadii was not ousted, and the anathema was not even forbidden. In the 1480s, Gennadii's cothinkers published a tract with a title six lines long, which for some reason is known in the literature as "A Short Word in Defense of Monastery Property." The authors of the "Short Word" by no means briefly, and quite openly, took to task tsars who "allowed violations of the law."[23] And the circulation of the tract was not prohibited. Iosif fearlessly pronounced anathema on the grand prince in numerous letters and pamphlets, stating that "if he who wears the crown begins to follow the same sins . . . may he be cursed in this age and in the future one."[24]

Does this boiling Muscovite Athens sound like the voiceless desert of the "service state"?

With the memories of the Tatar heritage still fresh, and national feelings high, Russia argued, harangued, denounced, and preached. There was no official monologue by the state; there was open, ferocious ideological dialogue. And all this was, moreover, on the threshold of the expected end of the world. In a few years, according to the Orthodox calendar, the seventh millennium since the creation would come to an end, and at its conclusion the Messiah was supposed to appear anew before the eyes of an amazed humanity. Passions were heated to the boiling point; the hierarchy was in open revolt. Ivan III did not let matters come to an explosion, however. Once again, he was the first to retreat, turning over to Gennadii several heretics from Novgorod who had fled under his protection to Moscow.

But an antiheretical campaign throughout the nation did not follow. This gambit of the grand prince's was intended, no doubt, to buy off the hierarchy—to let some steam out of the boiling kettle of Josephite passions, and at this price to preserve Kuritsyn, Elena Stefa-

22. Pavlov, p. 50.

23. *Slovo kratko v zashchitu monastyrskikh imushchestv*, p. 25.

24. V. Malinin, *Starets Eleazarova monastyria Filofei i ego poslanie*, p. 129.

novna, and his grandson and heir Dimitrii. But it seems, too, that under the influence of the events in Novgorod, the grand prince evolved
the treacherous and cynical political scenario which was played out a
few years later at the church assembly of 1504—a plan to *trade* heresy
for the church lands.

7. The First Assault

A letter sent by Iosif to the Archimandrite Mitrofan, the grand
prince's personal chaplain, relates an unexpected scene, in which
Ivan III invited Iosif, who had until quite recently been a disgraced
monk, to visit him, and held a long conversation with him about
church affairs. In the course of this, the sovereign suddenly revealed
"to what heresy the archpriest Aleksei adhered and to what heresy
Fedor Kuritsyn adhered," and even denounced his daughter-in-law,
Elena, admitting that "he knew about their heresies" and asking forgiveness. What could be the meaning of this abandonment of friends
and advisors whom he had supported for many years, this humble
request for pardon on the part of a mighty ruler, addressed to a mo-
rose and implacable nonconformist who pursued goals which were
extremely dubious from the grand prince's point of view? What, if
not an offer of a political deal? Apparently, however, Iosif remained
unmoved. It is true that the grand prince did not hasten to fulfill his
pledge to carry out the national campaign which Gennadii and Iosif
had been seeking for more than a quarter of a century and "hunt out
and uproot the heretics." A year after the meeting, Iosif complained
bitterly in the same letter to Mitrofan of Ivan's failure to dispatch the
promised witch-hunters: "I hoped that the sovereign would send
them immediately, but it is already more than a year since that great
day, and he, the sovereign, has not sent them."[25]

Instead of an antiheretical campaign, in fact, the grand prince prepared an unexpected blow at the hierarchy. It came in 1503, at what
was perhaps the most dramatic church assembly in the history of Russian Orthodoxy. The assembly had been called to consider a purely
practical question—whether widowers were to be permitted to serve
in the priesthood. The prelates assembled, spoke, adopted a decision
to forbid widowed priests. Matters of third-rate importance remained
to be dealt with. Suddenly, in the half-empty hall, the grand prince
himself appeared. His speech was entirely unambiguous. As one of

25. Kazakova and Lur'e, p. 438.

the documents describing this dramatic event has it: "The Grand Prince Ivan Vasil'evich wished to take from the metropolitan and the other church dignitaries, and from the monasteries, their villages, and unite them with his own, and to give all the metropolitan and other dignitaries money from his treasury and grain from his granaries."[26] In other words, he wanted to transfer the ecclesiastical businessmen to the state service and put them on salary. The matter did not end there. The sovereign was followed onto the podium by his sons, Vasilii and Dimitrii, then by the Tver' boyar, Vasilii Borisov, then by the high secretaries, the heads of the Muscovite government departments, and, finally—and this was certainly the nucleus of the plan—by the dissidents, led by the leader of the second generation of Non-Acquirers, Nil Sorskii. This time they were not timid, as Paisii had been. They attacked the hierarchy in heated speeches, denouncing monastery landholding as a deviation from Christ's law, a sin, and an injustice. Note that until now the "accusers" (of the grand prince, the metropolitan, and the heretics) had been exclusively Josephites. To use modern language, this had been a critique from the right: the hierarchy attacked the state for deviating from the norms of piety. Now the attack came from the left. The church was finally split. The state now appeared in the role of guardian of the purity of Orthodoxy—the situation for which Ivan III had waited so long in the matter of Novgorod, in the struggle against Lithuania, and in the war with the hierarchy. According to some sources, the Non-Acquirers demanded the secularization not of all the church lands, but merely of those of the monasteries. If this is true (and the attempt to divide the opposition was certainly in the spirit of Ivan III), then this was precisely the compromise path which the English state took three decades later in its struggle with the church. Along with all the other facts, it indicates a well-prepared and organized assault on the fortress of the church.

For the first time the state acted in direct concert with the intelligentsia. (The second time was long delayed: not until 350 years later, in the 1850s, at the time of the Great Reforms, was this alliance renewed.) Nevertheless, the position of the grand prince had one serious flaw—the immaturity of the second generation of Non-Acquirers, who should have more accurately appraised the resistance of the hierarchy and foreseen its arguments. They were responsible for

26. Iu. K. Begunov, "'Slovo inoe'—novonaidennoe proizvedenie russkoi publitsistiki XVI v. o bor'be Ivana III s zemlevladeniem tserkvi," p. 351.

the intellectual side of the operation, so to speak, and they suffered a defeat.[27]

Attacked from all sides, the metropolitan and the assembly nevertheless did not despair, but took counsel and decided to refuse the grand prince's request. A long epistle, replete with quotations from the Bible and the Levitical Books, from the Holy Fathers and the Tatar *yarlyks*, was written and sent to the grand prince by the secretary Levash. Ivan rejected this: neither the Levitical Books nor the Tatar *yarlyks* sufficed to convince him. The assembly again took counsel, prepared a second reply, adding further quotations from the Bible, and went in a body to read it to the sovereign. The Biblical texts once again left the grand prince cold. A. S. Pavlov, the author of a study of the secularization of church lands published in Odessa in 1881, which is in my opinion still unsurpassed, conjectures as to why it was necessary for the assembly to prepare a third response, and why this third reply worked, compelling Ivan to retreat. "Probably the grand prince requested certain additional clarifications; at any rate, the assembly once again sent the secretary Levash to him with a new report literally confirming the content of the first," Pavlov writes. Contradicting himself, he adds that the third version "only gives a considerably more detailed discussion of the Russian princes who gave the church districts and villages."[28]

This was precisely the gist of the matter: the "old ways." The lamentations and accusations of Nil Sorskii could not compete with the iron canons of tradition. And the second generation of the Non-Acquirers had nothing more to offer the grand prince: warriors and politicians they were not, merely moralists. Here is what was said in that fateful addition to the assembly's reply, by which the hierarchy with great inventiveness—one must admit—turned back the first secularizing assault:

> Thus, in our Russian lands, under thy forefathers, the grand princes—
> under Grand Prince Vladimir and his son Grand Prince Iaroslav, and
> after them, under Grand Prince Vsevolod and Grand Prince Ivan, the

27. The assembly of 1503 is described by at least seven different sources, some Josephite, others Non-Acquirer. Naturally, they contradict one another. In regard to one of them, investigators hold diametrically opposed opinions: A. A. Zimin ("O politicheskoi doktrine Iosifa Volotskogo") assumes that this document is of Non-Acquirer origin, and Lur'e (p. 414), and G. N. Moiseeva (*Valaamskaia beseda—pamiatnik russkoi publitsistiki XVI v.*, pp. 22–3) think that it was written by Josephites. The version set forth here is based essentially on Pavlov's classic work, with minor corrections based on an eighth source found by Iu. K. Begunov in the library at Perm' in the 1960s.

28. Pavlov, p. 46.

grandson of the blessed Aleksandr . . . the prelates and the monasteries held cities, regions, settlements, and villages, and received tribute for the church.[29]

A decade later, a third branch of the Non-Acquirer movement arose, and the caustic, tocsinlike preaching of Nil Sorskii's famous pupil, Vassian Patrikeev, with which not even Iosif himself could cope, thundered out over Muscovy. It contained precisely what was needed for a new assault on the fortress of the church. Vassian was a cothinker of the grand prince and a consistent conservative. "Think and reflect," he preached,

> who, of those who radiated sanctity and built monasteries, took care to acquire villages? Who entreated the tsars and the grand princes for privileges for themselves, and for offense to surrounding peasants? Who brought suit against another person in a dispute over property lines, or tormented human bodies with whips or placed them in chains, or took away estates from their brothers . . . as do those who now give themselves out as wonder-workers? Neither Pakhomii or Evfimii or Gerasim or Afanasii of Athos—not one of them lived by such rules, or taught his disciples anything of the kind.

There followed a detailed enumeration of "our Russian . . . founders of monastic life and wonder-workers, Antonii and Feodosii Pecherskii, Varlaam of Novgorod, Sergius of Radonezh, and Dimitrii Prilutskii," who "lived in extreme need so that they often did not even have their daily bread; but the monasteries did not fall into ruin from poverty but grew and flourished in all things, being filled with monks who worked with their own hands and earned their bread in the sweat of their brows."[30]

As for Iosif's dialectical mysticism relating to the individual and the collective, Maxim the Greek replied to it devastatingly: "What you say is ridiculous—being no different than if many persons were living in sin with one harlot, and being found out in this, each of them would say: 'I have committed no sin whatever, for she belongs to all of us equally.'"[31]

The arguments advanced by Vassian and Maxim depicted the contemporary disorders in the church as divine punishment for betrayal of the ancient traditions and desecration of "our Russian old ways." Yes, Ivan III could have answered the Josephite majority in the assembly, had he had Vassian Patrikeev at his back, our pious ancestors,

29. Cited in ibid., p. 46.
30. Cited in ibid., p. 68.
31. Maksim Grek, *Sochineniia prepodobnogo Maksima Greka v russkom perevode*, p. 72.

the grand princes of Muscovy, did donate "cities, regions, settlements, and villages" to the monasteries. We do not deny this. But

> what use can it be to the pious princes who offered all this to God, if you use the offerings unjustly and extortionately, completely contrary to their pious intention? You live in abounding wealth, and eat more than a monk needs, and your peasant brothers, who work for you in your villages, live in dire poverty. . . . How well you repay the devout princes for their pious gifts! . . . They offered their property to God in order that his devotees . . . should practice prayer and silence, unhindered, and spend the excess from their yearly income with love in supporting the poor and the pilgrims. . . . You either turn it into money to lend out in interest, or else keep it in storehouses, in order later to sell it at a high price during times of famine.[32]

We have quoted above Ivan IV's questions to the assembly of 1551, written for him by the fourth generation of Non-Acquirers—the pupils of Vassian Patrikeev and Maxim the Greek, who had by then come to exercise a direct influence on the government of Russia. The Non-Acquirers had grown from hermits and moralists into political fighters and statesmen (and, incidentally, magnificent pamphleteers, with whom neither Herzen nor Dostoevsky would have been ashamed to associate). From the timid Paisii Iaroslavov, who was frightened by the monks of the Troitsa, to Vassian Patrikeev, to whom even Iosif gave in, to Artemii, the tsar's counsellor during the assembly of 1551, Ivan III had summoned into being an intelligentsia capable of interpreting the history of the country as he himself could not. This could have proved to be the beginning of a European course for Russia. But fate decreed otherwise. On July 28, 1503, Ivan III was almost incapacitated by a stroke which "took from him a leg, a hand, and an eye."

Half-paralyzed, he tried to carry on the struggle. At the assembly of 1504, a large group of heretics was handed over to the Josephites, and many of them were burned. But there immediately followed an unexpected event, not yet understood by historians: Archbishop Gennadii, the Russian grand inquisitor, who had reached the summit of his power and had just returned from the assembly as a triumphant victor, was suddenly deposed. How are we to explain this?

The grand prince seems to have been preparing a counterblow. In the 1490s, when a group of heretics was also turned over to the inquisitors, there followed not the expected antiheretical campaign throughout the nation, but the first secularization campaign of 1503.

32. Cited in Pavlov, p. 71.

Might one not anticipate a second such assault after the second handing over of heretics? In other words, the assemblies of 1503 and 1504 may be seen not as the end of the secularization campaign, as the experts have said and continue to say, but as the beginning of a new phase of it. Hardly anyone will dispute that the military campaign of 1500–1503 was only the first round of the assault on Lithuania in the eyes of the grand prince. But no one has ever viewed the secularization campaign of 1503–4 as a first assault on church landholdings.

The campaign against Lithuania ended in the same year of 1503 not with a peace but with a truce. Despite having routed the Lithuanian armies and received by the terms of the truce nineteen cities, seventy volosts, twenty-two fortresses, and nineteen villages—that is, having achieved the most brilliant military success, after the Ugra and the overthrow of the Tatar yoke, of his reign—the grand prince flatly refused to consider the matter closed. (On the contrary, the Muscovite ambassadors were ordered to tell the khan of the Crimea, Mengli-Girei, that "the grand prince has no firm peace with the Lithuanian [king] . . . the grand prince wishes to have his country back from him, and all the Russian lands; but he has made a truce with him now, so as to let the people rest and to attach to himself the cities which have been taken.")[33] Can the sensational ouster of Gennadii, fresh from his triumph, not be interpreted as a sign that with the church, just as with Lithuania, a truce had been concluded in 1503, not a peace?

"The collapse of the plans for secularization put forward by Ivan III was historically predictable. The economic prerequisites for liquidation of feudal ownership of land by the monasteries and churches had not yet matured in the Russian state of the sixteenth century," writes the well-known Soviet historian S. M. Kashtanov.[34] What economic prerequisites were necessary? And why had they matured even in Iceland, but not in Muscovy? It is unknown. Another Soviet historian, Iu. K. Begunov, tells us that

> the events of 1503 showed the presence of a certain equilibrium of forces between the contending sides—the state and the church. . . . Under such conditions a compromise between the office of the priest and the office of the tsar on mutually advantageous conditions was inevitable: the blood of the heretics and new grants of land to the church in exchange for concrete ideological support—prayers for the tsar and

33. Solov'ev, *Istoriia Rossii s drevneishikh vremen*, Bk. 3, p. 122.
34. S. M. Kashtanov, "Ogranichenie feodal'nogo immuniteta pravitel'stvom russkogo tsentralizovannogo gosudarstva," pp. 270–71.

the proclamation of the status of the Russian sovereign as the sole defender of Orthodoxy.[35]

This argument is rather confusing, since if in his struggle against the
hierarchy, the grand prince needed "concrete ideological support," it
could only be the support of the hierarchy's adversaries, which he already had. And, what is more, he needed this support not for giving
the hierarchy "new grants of land" but, on the contrary, for taking its
lands away, which was, after all, one of the two greatest imperatives of
his entire political life-strategy.

G. V. Plekhanov, writing more than sixty years ago, articulated the
point of view which prevails even today:

> The dispute about monastery landholdings, which pushed the thought
> of the Muscovite writers in the same direction in which the thought of
> the Western clerical king-fighters had proceeded so early and so boldly,
> very soon ended with a negotiated peace. Ivan III abandoned the
> thought of secularizing the monastery lands, even agreed to the cruel
> persecution of the "Judaizers," whom the Orthodox clergy hated, and
> whom he had so recently and so unambiguously supported.[36]

In all of these interpretations—in which, incidentally, it is quite
clear that the absolutists, despite all their righteous indignation in
theory, are fully agreed in practice with their opponents the despotists—the struggle of the state with the church in the pre-Oprichnina
century appears as a transient episode in Russian history, which came,
went, and left no trace behind it. But in fact this struggle was an entirely logical continuation of the internal policy of the developing absolutist state. Everywhere in Europe, this process was connected with
the formation of the proto-bourgeoisie, the rise of Protestantism, and
the breaking up of autonomous feudal corporations competing with
centralized authority. So it was in Russia too. One after another, Rostov, Novgorod, and Tver' had fallen. There remained the church—
the mightiest feudal corporation of medieval Rus'. Ivan's campaign
against the Josephites was fundamentally an extension of the battles
of Kulikovo Pole, of the Ugra, and of the Novgorod expedition.

This epochal struggle of the state and the Non-Acquirer movement
against the Josephite hierarchy left behind it the tradition of the Russian intelligentsia and of the Russian political opposition: the tradition
of sympathy for the oppressed little man (all the so-called "peasant-
ophilism" of Russian literature comes from the Non-Acquirers—Vassian Patrikeev was the first peasantophile); the tradition of tolerance

35. Iu. K. Begunov, "Sekuliarizatsiia v Evrope i Sobor 1503 v Rossii," p. 47.
36. G. V. Plekhanov, *Sochineniia*, vol. 20, p. 144.

for the heterodox minority (no one in Muscovy except the Non-Acquirers struggled against the death sentences passed on the heretics, and no one else dared to polemicize against the bloodthirsty Josephites); the tradition of dissidence (and the courage to speak against a frightening majority); the tradition of European rationality, and the belief in reason as the highest force given to man—reason counterposed to external discipline, to the passions, and to blind obedience. Even in a purely political sense, it was the Non-Acquirer literature which in the sixteenth century advanced the idea of a universal council to which "men of all the people" should be called. In other words they were the first in Russian history to call for a national assembly, which clearly meant turning the dispute between the state and the church (where the state proved the weaker party) *into a dispute between the church and the nation.* Only a few decades later, after Ivan III's death, when the government fell once again for a short time into the hands of the absolutists and was under the influence of the Non-Acquirers, the Assembly of the Land was in fact called. Ivan IV's questions to the church assembly of 1551 (i.e., a decade before his coup d'etat) were saturated with the spirit that the Non-Acquirers had breathed into Russian political life.

However, it may be objected, the second campaign of secularization, even if projected by Ivan III, never took place. The countertradition of the Non-Acquirers never worked, and the calling of the Assembly of the Land did not lead to reform of the church. This is true. The Non-Acquirers were defeated. To Russia's cost and their own, the Josephites suffered a crushing victory. But was this victory of theirs inevitable? This is the question, decisive for Russia's past—and for its future—which my opponents try to avoid with the help of vague reflections about "economic prerequisites" and the absence of "ideological support." I cannot, of course, know what Ivan III's real plans were. But neither can my opponents. With what justification, for example, does Plekhanov assert that "Ivan III abandoned the idea of secularizing the monastery lands"?

The hypothesis suggested here may be debatable, but at least it leaves open the question of why Russia, having gone much further than other European countries along the path of church reform, proved incapable of carrying it out.

8. The Pyrrhic Victory of the Josephites

Ivan III's successor, Vasilii III, should have been born long before his father. He was an assiduous "gatherer," a boring and obedient son of the church, entirely without political imagination. For him the plans and achievements of his father did not differ in the least from the achievements of the long and monotonous line of his Muscovite ancestors. The most that he was capable of was copying his father in details. Thus, he did with Pskov the same thing which his father had done with Novgorod. However, having expelled the families of potential rebels from Pskov, he did not—unlike his father—lay a finger on the monastery villages. Having taken Smolensk from the Lithuanians in 1514, he first of all promised to preserve inviolate the rights of the local church. Just as his father had maintained heretics close to him in order to frighten the hierarchy, Vasilii for some time kept Non-Acquirers for this purpose, bringing Vassian Patrikeev into his entourage and acting as patron to Maxim the Greek. But he did not attack the church, he merely defended himself against it. In 1511, when Varlaam, who sympathized with the Non-Acquirers, became metropolitan, "the government of Vasilii III somehow," Kashtanov writes, "succeeded in interrupting the growth of monastery landholdings."[37] The government carried out a partial review of the immunities on church holdings and abolished some of them. But all this was merely a vague shadow of his father's strategy. Meanwhile, the situation changed swiftly—both in European politics and in the life of the country.

What previously could have been regarded as the secondary level of Muscovite strategy emerged into the foreground. The Crimean king succeeded in placing his brother, Saip-Girei, on the throne of Kazan'. Muscovy was taken by surprise by this union of its two sworn enemies in the South and East, which had been long in maturing. It awoke only when both brothers suddenly appeared below its walls in 1521, forcing Vasilii to take refuge in flight. And although even the united forces of the Crimea and Kazan' were unable to take Moscow, its inhabitants were compelled to give the Tatars a humiliating promise to pay them tribute, as in the old days—as though there had been no Ugra. The Tatars took away with them many thousands of prisoners, according to rumors current at the time. It became clear that, beyond the southern horizon, formidable forces were gathering which could again call into question Muscovy's existence as a state. Ivan III had provided the Russian land with a respite from the Tatars for many decades, but not forever.

Moreover, it was no longer possible to split Lithuania, as Ivan III

37. S. M. Kashtanov, *Sotsial'no-politicheskaia istoria Rossii kontsa XV—pervoi poloviny XVI v.*, p. 257.

had hoped to do, by taking advantage of the antagonisms between its Russian Orthodox and Catholic subjects. The Reformation which was raging in Europe had brought about universal ideological changes, as a result of which the Russian Orthodox magnates of Lithuania were now thinking of an alliance not so much with Muscovy as with their Catholic colleagues—an alliance against their common enemy, Protestantism, which was spreading like an epidemic through urban circles and among the educated young people of Lithuania and Poland. Matters were tending toward the formation of a united commonwealth of the two countries. The moment for a campaign against Lithuania had been irretrievably lost by Vasilii, just as he had lost the moment for a second campaign of secularization. The colossal military, diplomatic, and intellectual efforts consumed in preparing the strategy of Ivan III, decades of labor and struggle, were reduced to nothing. Within a single generation, Muscovy might find itself caught between the united Tatar khanates (behind which loomed Turkey) in the East, and united Lithuania and Poland (behind which loomed the Papacy) in the West. The hour of decision had struck. To avoid isolation (which could lead to irreversible changes in the political structure of the country itself) it was necessary to decide with whom and against whom Muscovy would stand, who its allies were and who its enemies.

Under these conditions, the anti-Turkish entente called for by Western diplomats ceased to be a pious hope and became an urgent necessity. The situation demanded a repetition of the Ugra. The cutting edge of Muscovite strategy had to be turned from the West to the East and South, where the Tatars were forging an alliance capable of putting a hundred thousand men into the saddle.[38] But a new Ugra required a new Ivan III—and he was not available. Even the Tatar attack of 1521 taught Muscovy nothing.

Within the country, church landholding continued to spread. And there was now no question of an entente against the Orthodox establishment between the state and the intelligentsia, such as had been

38. This thought first arose among the Non-Acquirers. Even the most peace-loving of them, Maxim the Greek, who was known for the fact that he taught the sovereign: "Honor not him who, contrary to justice, encourages you to quarrels and wars, but him who counsels you to love peace and quiet with neighboring peoples" (Maksim Grek, p. 102), recommended an attack on the Crimea. "It is difficult and ruinous—not to say impossible—to stand against both tormentors [i.e., the Crimea and Lithuania], the more so since there is a third wolf coming against us. This is the serpent whose nest is in Kazan'," he wrote (V. Rzhiga, "Maksim Grek kak publitsist," p. 113). Hence his recommendation to attack Kazan' immediately and then to attack Crimea (ibid., p. 114).

taking shape at the beginning of the century. Left to itself, the Non-Acquirer movement exhausted itself in struggles against a "right wing" offensive which was taking on an increasingly clear nationalist and isolationist character. The monk Filofei of Pskov proposed the tempting theory of "the Third Rome" to the grand prince Vasilii—that is, of Muscovy as the guardian of the true faith, counterposed to the West and the East and destined to play a unique role in the preservation of Christianity until the Second Coming of Christ ("thou art the only Christian king under Heaven"). Iosif, who had been defeated in an open ideological skirmish with the Non-Acquirers, performed one more political maneuver. He no longer gave himself over to meditations on tsars and tyrants, but proposed the still more tempting idea of the theocratic power of the Orthodox sovereign, declaring him "the ruler of all," and the viceroy of God on earth.[39] (Though in so doing he did not abandon his fundamental thesis that "the church's acquisitions are God's acquisitions.")[40]

Thus, the Josephite hierarchy offered the state peace with the church, agreeing to recognize the Russian tsar as an *autocrator*—the head of a new Byzantine empire and the supreme leader of Orthodox (i.e., true Christian) humanity. For this, Vasilii would have to pay not only with new lands but also with the heads of further heretics and Non-Acquirers. He would have to sacrifice not only the radicals, but also the liberals, liquidating the ideological limitations on power—the most precious heritage left to Russia by his father. Taken together, nationalism, isolationism, messianism, and the liquidation of the ideological struggle foretold the end of Russian absolutism even in the 1520s.

But the tradition of Ivan III was strong. If Vasilii lacked the capacity to continue the policy of his father, he also lacked the capacity to change it radically. He drifted with the current. True, he gave up to the Josephites two of their chief enemies—the two most brilliant figures of the Muscovite intellectual world of that time. The assembly of 1525 condemned Maxim the Greek, and that of 1531 condemned Vassian Patrikeev.[41] They left the scene, and were exiled to Josephite

39. A. A. Zimin, "O politicheskoi doktrine Iosifa Volotskogo," p. 175.

40. Malinin, p. 128.

41. Daniil (a pupil of Iosif's and his successor as abbot of Volokolamsk), who was made a metropolitan by Vasilii in 1522, proved, aside from everything else, to be the inventor of an effective political tactic, used with great success many generations later by another leader (who had also had theological training). While his opponents wrote books, made inspired speeches, and edited the canonical texts, Daniil methodically and stubbornly placed his own men in the key positions in the hierarchy. The majority in

monasteries for life. But this did not mean that an end was put to the Non-Acquirer movement as a current of thought. It was beheaded but not yet destroyed. The aristocracy was still firmly in the saddle, and as long as the social limitations on power had not been done away with, the economic limitations prospered under their protection. The law remained the law, although the political life of the country stagnated. Consequently, the proto-bourgeoisie became more numerous, the cities grew, and the obligations of the peasants were increasingly rendered in money. (Half a century later, the "Government of Compromise" would convert the obligations to the state of whole regions into money terms, modernizing the system of taxation.) It seemed that Russian absolutism was destined to survive the rule of Vasilii.

No one yet knew which of the two tendencies would be victorious—feudal or peasant differentiation, corvée or money, the service landholders or the proto-bourgeoisie.

The fourth generation of the Non-Acquirers was still to come. The elder Artemii, from whom the tsar would respectfully take counsel, was to be elevated to the post of abbot of the Troitsa, like his ideological forebear Paisii. Still other bishops and abbots would emerge, despite the Josephite Metropolitan Daniil's intrigues, from the school of Nil Sorskii and Maxim the Greek. The assembly of 1551, with its famous royal questions, was also still to come.

But this assembly would not be a victory for the Non-Acquirers. It would be turned into their ultimate defeat. True, it would adopt important anti-Josephite decisions to return the land confiscated by churchmen for debt to the original owners, and to take away the service estates and regions given to churchmen during the sovereign's nonage. However, a terrible price would be exacted by the Josephites for these purely tactical concessions. Whereas Ivan III turned over the heretics to the Josephites in order to save the Non-Acquirers, Ivan the Terrible turned the Non-Acquirers over to them in order to destroy both victors and vanquished.

A mere two years after the assembly of 1551, the Josephite Metro-

---

the assembly consisted of men who were personally loyal to him, and when matters came down to a vote, the Non-Acquirer leaders proved to be generals without an army. Only a month after he became a metropolitan, Daniil appointed Iosif's brother Akakii to be bishop of Tver', and then appointed Iosif's nephew Vassian Toporkov as bishop of Kolomna; later, the ordained monk Savva Slepushkin of the Volokolamsk Monastery was appointed bishop of Smolensk, and Makarii (the future metropolitan and comrade-in-arms of Ivan the Terrible) was made archbishop of Novgorod. Thus, exactly as Stalin did later, Daniil smothered the opposition in its cradle, and made it voiceless in the church assemblies.

politan Makarii, a member of the "Government of Compromise," using the heresy of Matvei Bashkin as a pretext, impugned Artemii for cooperating with heretics, and another Non-Acquirer, Abbot Feodorit, for cooperating with Artemii. Their cothinker Bishop Kassian of Riazan' was deprived of his office. All of them were condemned and exiled and the Non-Acquirer movement itself was declared a heresy. This was a catastrophe, and not only for the Non-Acquirers. In the middle of the sixteenth century, the movement already had much more of a political than a religious character. This was perhaps the first time in Russian history that political dissent was condemned as heresy, and the first real political trial in Moscow. The most sinister portent was that the "Government of Compromise," of which Sil'vestr, who was the patron of the Non-Acquirers, and the Josephite Makarii were equally members, was unable to avert it.

The government had just conquered Kazan', thereby destroying forever the plan of uniting the two Tatar khanates and reviving the Golden Horde. It had just called the Assembly of the Land, at which there was an attempt to reconcile all the competing political forces in the country. It had succeeded in creating a broad ruling coalition. On the wings of success, it had conceived a broad program for modernizing the country—administratively, fiscally, and politically. It was carrying out this program effectively, reforming the obsolete institutions, and building an absolutist state. And it apparently did not consider the sacrifice of the intelligentsia too great a price to pay. In any case, the fact that the "right" Josephites were part of the compromise coalition which formed the base of its power and the "left" Non-Acquirers were excluded from it after 1553 did not particularly disturb the government. And this was a fatal mistake. In fact, the elimination of the ideological limitations on power could not help but sooner or later bring with it the elimination of the social and economic limitations. As history shows, it is impossible to extract the component parts of an organic, absolutist complex with impunity. And the collapse of one of these presaged the collapse of the rest. Thus, we can say that it was not the famous coup d'etat of Ivan the Terrible in 1560 and the "revolution from above" in 1565 which were the beginning of the end of Russian absolutism, but rather a small event, almost unnoticed by historians—the condemnation of the Non-Acquirers in 1553. Many successes were still ahead for the "Government of Compromise," but it no longer had a future. And its doom came from within the ruling coalition—from the triumphant Josephites, who thought that having rid themselves at last of their opponents they had secured their own interests permanently.

Did they have a foreboding that their victory was the beginning of their defeat? Quite soon Ivan the Terrible would suppress them, rob them, sack their monasteries to the last thread, without any laws or assemblies whatever and without asking anyone's agreement. He would appoint and depose metropolitans at will, and kill them when he liked. The humble Metropolitan Filipp, pushed to the limit, dared finally to throw in the face of the tsar, who had come to him in the Uspenskii Cathedral in half-joking Oprichnina costume, the bitter words: "I do not recognize the tsar in that costume. I do not recognize him in the affairs of the kingdom either. Fear the judgment of God. We here bring a bloodless sacrifice and behind the altar flows the blood of the innocent."[42] He was deposed, and then strangled. So, too, in their time, had fallen the Archpriest Sil'vestr; the head of the "Government of Compromise," Adashev; Cheliadnin-Fedorov, the head of the Zemshchina; and Viskovatyi, who had directed the foreign policy of Muscovy—as did all, without distinction of rank or title, who dared to raise their voices against the will of the autocrator who had now become the sole law of Muscovy, its sole church, and its sole faith.

The Josephites would pay dearly for their naive Catholic illusions and the senseless extermination of their political opponents, which left them face to face with the fearsome and unpredictable monster of autocracy that they themselves had created. For an opposition is not a luxury, but a necessity for a normally functioning political system. It is a mechanism for correcting mistakes, an institutionalized alternative—no more, but also no less. These are the basic rules of the political game. Ivan III apparently understood them. In any case, he was not the one to break the rules. The Josephites broke them.

Their gross miscalculation probably lay in the fact that they modelled their political behavior on the absolutist Muscovy of Ivan III, where it was possible to contradict the tsar, to be in opposition to him (as they themselves had been for decades), and in general to be mistaken without risking one's head. It apparently seemed to them that, having achieved the predominant influence on the sovereign, and having even declared him autocrator, they would be able to hold him in their hands.

But there was another possibility, not foreseen either by them or by Ivan III: given a choice between West and East, Russia might reject *both* orientations, and respond to the historical challenge facing it with an isolationist tyranny—autocracy. Given a choice between the

42. Solov'ev, *Istoriia Rossii s drevneishikh vremen*, Bk. 3, p. 556.

reformist, secularizing ("Protestant") tendencies of the liberal intelligentsia and the conservative, theocratic ambitions of the church hierarchy, the autocrator might respond with the creation of a "new
class" capable of ruining *both.*

How could this happen—unexpected and undesired, as it seems,
by any significant force in the Russian establishment? One segment of
the establishment, let me anachronistically call it the "Russian right,"
appeared powerful enough not only to end the debate about the future of the country and silence its opponents, but also to exterminate
them. Faced with this challenge, the moderate "centrist" segment of
the establishment, instead of joining forces with the "left" spokesmen
of the reforms, chose to sacrifice them. At this price the moderates
apparently hoped to save what it was still possible to save. They were
mistaken. With the extermination of the "left," the entire reformist
process came to a halt. This resulted in political stagnation, which in
turn led to a "revolution from above."

Thus, this chain of events turned out to be a chain of fateful mistakes, in which every segment of the then Russian establishment was
destined to lose, and eventually to perish. The moderates succeeded
the "left-wingers" as victims of the Oprichnina, and the "right-wingers" succeeded the moderates. Civil society was conquered by the
state and virtually destroyed.

What is even more mysterious about this chain of mistakes is that it
has—in different ways and in different circumstances—been repeated in all of Russia's major crises: in the 1680s, before Peter I; in
the 1780s, before Paul; in the 1820s, before Nicholas I; and so on, to
this very day, when it is repeating itself before our eyes. Once again,
the powerful "right-wingers" have broken the rules of the game and
stopped the process of reform. Once again, the "centrists" have betrayed the spokesmen of this reform. Once again, the nation has entered the zone of political stagnation, setting the stage for a restoration of the ancien régime.

What is the reason for these fatal repetitions? Is the Russian establishment uniquely incapable of learning from history? Or have the
historians of Russia, perhaps, failed to educate this establishment in
the mistakes of the past? Have they, instead of using history to shape
the future, merely justified the past, putting all the blame for Russia's
misfortunes on obsolete stereotypes? "One cannot accuse Russian historiography of lack of hard work; it labored much, but I would not be
sinning against the truth in saying that it does not know itself what to
do with its subject matter," V. O. Kliuchevskii wrote bitterly, and I am

afraid that this seems all too true. It is thus that, even in our own day, a modern American expert once again repeats the stereotype of the "state school":

> Unquestionably, the civil society in Russia (that is, social groups and institutions with their own structure and autonomous functions) appeared comparatively late and was quite weak at the beginning of our century. It is important to note the paradox of Russian history: the civil society was in part a creation of the state (the reforms of Peter I and Alexander II) and therefore its development was partly artificial and slow.[43]

We have already seen, and will see further, that the Russian aristocracy grew hand in hand with the Russian state, that the peasant commune was much older than the state, and that the Orthodox church was stronger than the state (at least in the time of Ivan III, i.e., centuries before Peter I and Alexander II). Thus, the artificial creation of Russian civil society by the state seems more than questionable. Speaking in the crude terms of the stereotype, it would seem that the state rather *destroyed* civil society in the course of Ivan the Terrible's "revolution from above." Moreover, it demolished this society again and again in the course of almost each new autocratic revolution.

But to say only this is still to say very little. The real question is how the state achieved these spectacular results. And here, instead of dolefully masticating obsolete wisdom, we are compelled to note the fateful role of the Russian right of the sixteenth century, the Josephites. They were the ones who succeeded in halting reform. They provided the messianic theory of the Third Rome. They supplied all the ideological ammunition for the autocratic dream of Ivan the Terrible, thus initiating the process leading to his "revolution from above." This is, moreover, what their spiritual descendants have been doing ever since. For centuries the Russian right has been virtually collaborating in the destruction of civil society. This has been the ultimate result of its ideas, its intolerance and hatred, its insistence on the extermination of its opponents. The Josephites deserved their punishment. What was unfair was that along with them the entire nation had to go to its Golgotha.

But if this is where the Pyrrhic victories of the Russian right have invariably brought the nation, should it not be one of the basic lessons which the Russian establishment—again and again faced with the

43. M. Raev, "O knige Allena Bezansona," p. 220.

same choice between West and East, between reform and stagnation—needs to learn from the historians? Is it not here that their part in the historical drama begins—especially inasmuch as the spiritual descendants and intellectual heirs of the Josephites are once again trying to push the nation in the same direction?[44]

44. See, in this respect, Alexander Yanov, *The Russian New Right.*

CHAPTER VI

THE END OF
RUSSIAN ABSOLUTISM

1. The Heritage of the Absolutist Century

The age of Russian absolutism was short, its end tragic. But did it in fact disappear without a trace? Was it simply an accidental episode in Russian history—a liberal intermezzo in the autocratic symphony, a vague dream, dissipated forever?

Let us assume that the Great Reform of the 1550s—the legislative introduction of local self-government on a national scale, accompanied by trial by jury and income tax—was not rescinded "in the stormy years of Ivan the Terrible's long wars . . . by the *voevodal* form of vicegerency."[1] Let us assume that the Assembly of the Land called in 1549 was able to transform itself into a representative body, and the Boyar Duma into the House of Lords (or Senate) of this Russian parliament. Let us assume that Article 98 of the law code of 1550, stating that all new enactments (that is to say, those not provided for in the law code itself) were to be adopted only "on the report of the sovereign and by the verdict of all the boyars," actually played its intended role as a constitutional limitation on power.[2] Let us assume that the church lands were secularized at the assembly in 1551. Let us assume that the replacement of the amateur cavalry made up of landowners by a regular army (the creation of which began in 1550) was not dragged out for a whole century more, and that the military monopoly of service landholders was therefore undermined as early as the sixteenth century. Let us assume, arising out of this, that the total expropriation of peasant lands was avoided. Let us assume that ser-

1. A. A. Zimin, *Reformy Ivana Groznogo*, p. 435.
2. The author of the classical work on the history of Russian law, V. I. Sergeevich, holds precisely this point of view on Article 98. "In order to add new provisions to the law code," he writes, "a verdict by all the boyars is required. This is undoubtedly a limitation of the tsar's power, and a novelty; the tsar is only the chairman of the College of Boyars, and cannot issue new laws without its agreement" (*Russkie iuridicheskie drevnosti*, vol. 2, p. 360).

183

vice did not become universal in the Russian state. (It may perhaps be that the quarter-century Livonian War, which was doomed to end in defeat, and led to a national catastrophe, would not have taken place given such a turn of events.)

What, in fact, is fantastic in these assumptions? Even under the conditions of autocracy, all of this, without exception, *was eventually carried out* (or revived) for a longer or shorter period of time, as a result of reforms or revolutions. A regular army was created (at the beginning of the eighteenth century). Service ceased to be universal in the Russian state (in the second half of the eighteenth century). The church lands were secularized (at the same time). The institution of local self-government, with trial by jury and income tax, was reborn (in the second half of the nineteenth century). The Assemblies of the Land did become a form of national representative body (under the name of the State Duma) beginning in May 1906. The first attempt to realize Article 98 was undertaken as early as half a century after the publication of the code of laws, during the first Russian Time of Troubles, when Vasilii Shuiskii was elevated to the throne on May 17, 1606. As Kliuchevskii says:

> The elevation of Prince Vasilii to the throne marked an epoch in our political history. On ascending the throne, he limited his power, and set forth the conditions of this limitation officially in a document which he sent out to the provinces, and for which he kissed the Cross on ascending the throne.[3]

The next attempt was made four years later, on February 4, 1610, in the so-called constitution of Mikhail Saltykov. Kliuchevskii thinks that "this is a fundamental law for a constitutional monarchy, establishing both the structure of the supreme power and the basic rights of the subjects."[4] And even so venomous a critic of the Russian political heritage as B. N. Chicherin (whom all of the "despotists" put together might have envied) is compelled to admit that this document "contains significant limitations on the power of the tsar; if it had been put into effect, the Russian state would have taken on an entirely different form."[5] One more attempt to realize Article 98 was undertaken by the supreme privy council in the so-called constitution of Dimitrii Golitsyn (January 23, 1730). Finally, this article was once again

---

3. V. O. Kliuchevskii, *Sochineniia* (1st ed.), vol. 3, p. 37. "Kissing the cross" was the customary old Slavic form for taking an oath in any context, whether judicial or political.
4. Ibid., p. 44.
5. B. N. Chicherin, *O narodnom predstavitel'stve*, p. 543.

"put into effect," 356 years after its adoption and 300 years after the first attempt to realize it, on May 6, 1906—only to be once more violated by the tsar the very next year, and finally abolished on October 25, 1917. But even after the 1917 revolution, the Bolshevik autocracy was compelled, although temporarily, to give back to the peasantry the land taken from it by the first Oprichnina revolution in the sixteenth century.

It is true that the autocracy distorted and mystified all of these developments, and deprived them of the *integrated* absolutist character in which they were conceived in the sixteenth century. It dragged out their implementation for hundreds of years, tried to use them in its own interests, and, when this proved impossible, destroyed them again. But does this change the simple fact that even the autocracy proved unable to ignore them, and was sooner or later compelled to return to them in one form or another? This apparently means that we are dealing not with something accidental or ephemeral which has disappeared once and for all from Russia's political heritage, but, on the contrary, with something fundamental and organic, which could not be destroyed even by total terror, and which, when driven out of the door, stubbornly returned through the window. In brief, we are dealing with an absolutist tradition, and with an absolutist alternative to autocracy.

The struggle for this alternative did not end when the founding father of the Russian absolutist tradition, Ivan III, ended his days on earth in 1505. On the contrary, its decisive battles were still ahead. At the beginning of the 1550s, when the so-called "Government of Compromise"[6] took the helm, it may even have seemed that the scales

---

6. Until recently, the Muscovite government of the 1550s has been identified with the "Chosen Rada," a term used by Kurbskii in his *History of Ivan IV*: "And at that time those counselors of his were named the Chosen Rada; in truth according to their deeds they had this name, for by their counsel they produced all that was select and distinguished, that is to say true impartial justice, both for rich and for poor, such as is best in the tsardom" (p. 21). This term has become so firmly established in classical historiography that many historians have even adduced lists of the members of the "Chosen Rada," although Kurbskii mentions no names other than the Archpriest Sil'vestr, *Okol'nichii* (the second rank below that of boyar at the Muscovite court) Aleksei Adashev, and Metropolitan Makarii. For example, V. I. Sergeevich compiled the following list: Sil'vestr, Adashev, Makarii, Prince Andrei Kurbskii (a boyar since 1556), Prince Dmitrii Kurliat'ev (a boyar since 1549), Prince Semen Rostovskii, and the three Morozov brothers—Mikhail (a boyar since 1549), Vladimir (an *okol'nichii* since 1550), and Lev (an *okol'nichii* since 1553). M. V. Dovnar-Zapol'skii also included in the Chosen Rada Maxim the Greek (who lived out his last years in a monastery), Abbot Artemii, and Bishop Kassian—that is, all the major representatives of the fourth generation of Non-Acquirers, as well as others, to a total of sixteen (*Vremia Ivana Groznogo*, p. 173). S. V.

were inclined in favor of the continuers of Ivan III's cause—in favor
of the reformers, the Non-Acquirers, and what may, in general, be
called the coalition of hope.

2. *The Great Reform*

In order for the reader more easily to imagine the scope and tendency of the reforms of the Government of Compromise, it is necessary to remember how the Russian land had been administered
previous to it. It was divided into regions called *uezdy*. Within each
uezd there were two kinds of holdings, administered in completely
different ways. The holdings of great landlords—the church and the
boyars—were administered as everywhere in medieval Europe: by
the holders themselves (they held immunities, called *tarkhany*). The
central regime was essentially powerless to control them, for by tradition its agents "took no part in anything"—that is, did not have the
right to interfere either in the courts or in the administration of the
landlords. What ruled here was not so much the written law as customary law, the "old ways." On the other category of lands—those belonging to peasants and to service gentry—judicial and administrative functions were carried out by the agents of the central power, the
namestniki (vicegerents). Sent out from Moscow, usually for a year or
two, they kept order and collected taxes with the help of the servants
whom they took with them from *uezd* to *uezd*. They were called
kormlenshchiki ("people whom it is necessary to feed") because they
also had to collect their food (*korm*)—that is, maintenance—themselves; the government paid them nothing. It is not surprising that
the most eminent families competed fiercely with each other for these
assignments; in a year or two, if they landed in a rich *uezd*, they could

---

Bakhrushin revised this list in 1954, identifying the "Chosen Rada" with the "Close
Duma" of the tsar ("Izbrannaia Rada Ivana Groznogo"). I. I. Smirnov threw doubt on
the existence of the "Chosen Rada" as an institution and identified this term with the
"political friends" of Kurbskii—that is, with those whom he considered the boyar party
(*Ocherki politicheskoi istorii russkogo gosudarstva 30–50kh gg. XVI veka*). Finally, in 1969,
the American historian A. Grobovsky, in a brilliant and detailed critical analysis,
showed the unfounded nature of all these hypotheses (*The "Chosen Council" of Ivan IV:
A Reinterpretation*). Most Soviet historians continue to employ this debatable term. Nevertheless, the following facts seem indisputable: (1) throughout the 1550s, the country
was ruled by a government at the head of which stood Adashev and Sil'vestr; (2)
Kurbskii was in sympathy with this government and reflected its viewpoint; (3) in addition to Kurbskii's testimony, the existence of this government is confirmed by its acts,
which are considered in this chapter. Following S. V. Bakhrushin and S. O. Shmidt, I
use the term "Government of Compromise."

make a fortune—not so much from "maintenance," which was limited from above, as from malfeasance in judicial and administrative functions. Civil cases in the *uezd* were usually won by those who could offer the largest bribe. The most unscrupulous of the vicegerents behaved even worse—for example, throwing a corpse into the courtyard of a rich peasant and then later ruining him with court costs. A few fabricated cases yielded them more income than their official maintenance allowance. The victims of such extortion, of course, were those who had something which could be taken away, the "best people" of the Russian countryside, its maturing proto-bourgeoisie, particularly since the legal competence of these vicegerents included surveillance of local trade and tariff rules. Naturally, the peasants did not keep silent. Hardly had the vicegerents "left with the maintenance" (that is, returned to home base with what they had collected) than they were followed to Moscow by swarms of complainants. The Moscow courts were crammed with suits against the collectors. Since the time of Ivan III, the government had tried to ensure redress by requiring the participation in court proceedings of elected "jurors," but this was apparently not much help. In any case, as the chronicle tells us: "Many cities and *volosts* were laid waste by the vicegerents . . . who had for many years despised the fear of God and the enactments of the sovereign and performed many evil deeds there; they were not pastors and teachers . . . but persecutors and sowers of ruin."[7]

With the formation of a centralized state in Russia and the emergence of the country into the arena of European politics, expenditures increased: the metropolitan establishment expanded, the formation of a regular army began, and artillery became an inseparable part of it. The country was experiencing swift economic growth, and could pay more taxes, but the government was practically deprived of the opportunity to take advantage of this. One half of the land was "*tarkhanized*," and consequently paid no taxes, while the other was "laid waste" by the vicegerents. Everyone was agreed that the administration required a radical overhaul.

The Government of Compromise, which had just come to power, had two options. The first, on the same level as the conception of the Muscovite "service state," was to replace the amateur and temporary administration of the vicegerents with professional administration by permanent governors (or *voevody*, as they were called in seventeenth-century Russia), who would get their "maintenance" from the state treasury. Such a police-bureaucratic reform could have served as an

7. Cited in N. E. Nosov, *Soslovno-predstavitel'nye* . . ., p. 377.

excellent fuse for exploding the "institutional time bomb" (if such a thing existed).

The second possibility was the diametrical opposite of the first. It consisted in not only continuing but logically developing the absolutist tradition of Ivan III, transforming elected jurors from simple "sworn officers" in the courts of the vicegerents into judges themselves, and, furthermore, into the local "landed" (that is to say, elected) officers of government, and entrusting to them the entire administration in the *uezdy*, including the collection of taxes for the state. Had it gone along these lines, the administrative reform would, I think, have fully deserved the title of Great Reform. In any case (under the conditions of the sixteenth century, when the peasantry was still free), it would have deserved it no less than the reform of the 1860s, which the historians actually do call great. For the essence of the reform of the 1860s consisted, in addition to the emancipation of the peasants and the abolition of preliminary censorship, precisely in the introduction of local self-government and trial by jury. Like its famous analog in the nineteenth, the administrative reform of the sixteenth century was undoubtedly a step in the direction of the defeudalization of the Russian state—a step toward its transformation into a bourgeois monarchy. For the chief social stratum which stood to gain from such reforms would have been the same "best people" of the Russian countryside and cities who chiefly suffered the vicegerents' administration. The reform would have given them the opportunity to rationalize the administration in the interests of capital accumulation and increase their social and political weight.

The "Government of Compromise" followed precisely this path. The Oprichnina government which replaced it returned to the system of unpaid vicegerents, who were gradually turned into *voevody*, first in the outlying regions of the state and then over its entire extent.[8]

And again we face a formidable question: what was reflected by this tortuous change in the administrative policies of the two governments (formally headed by the same person, Ivan IV), which was no less significant than the changes in their emigration and peasant policies? It seems to me that, apart from everything else, it reflected the

8. "The form of [local] government administered by the *voevody* was born in the stormy years of the long wars of Ivan the Terrible. . . . For example, in 1578 the city of Nevel' was given to I. Karamyshev as maintenance. In the same year Karamyshev was named in one decree as vicegerent, and in another as vicegerent and as *voevoda*. In 1570 *voevody* governed in Vasil', in 1571 in Kurmysh, in 1577 in Korel'" (Zimin, *Reformy*, p. 435).

different constituencies on which the two governments rested. Just as the secularization campaign was the first attempt of the government to collaborate with the intelligentsia of the nation in Russian history, the Great Reform was an attempt to collaborate with its proto-bourgeoisie. And both were ruined by the "revolution from above."

In fact, the natural question which arises in connection with the Great Reform of the 1550s (and which, as far as I know, no one has yet asked) is why and under the influence of what forces the Muscovite government showed a preference for local self-government over *voevodal* administration. The single reference to "the stormy years of the long wars of Ivan the Terrible," to which Zimin resorts, is of no help here. The point is that the administrative reform (like the abolition of the *tarkhany*) was proclaimed precisely at the height of a war with Kazan', which lasted at least four years (1547–52). This war, before ending in a brilliant victory, twice led to severe defeats, after which the tsar returned home "with many tears." Nevertheless, the government took a firm course toward local self-rule. Why?

Part of the explanation lies in the fact that the first decrees assigning power in the individual *uezdy* to elected organs were only answers to the numerous requests, complaints, and demands of the "best people." The government was not contemplating a national reform of local administration. It adopted it under the pressure of public opinion, if we may so express ourselves in relation to medieval society. This was the pressure of particular interest groups in that society, but opposed interest groups also existed. This means that there was something more important moving the government along this liberal path. And that something was money. The decree of reform issued in September 1557 to the Dvina *uezd* states that the grand prince

> ordered his Dvina vicegerents . . . not to give judgment and not to take their maintenance or any income, and his tax collectors and judicial officials not to go to those communities; and instead of the taxes and duties taken by the vicegerents, he ordered the people to pay a quitrent which they should bring to the treasury in Moscow, to our secretary Putilo Nechaev in the amount of twenty rubles from each unit of taxable land [*sokha*], and in addition a tariff of six kopeks for each ruble.[9]

There is nothing remarkable in this formula, until one compares it with the dimensions of the "maintenance" which the *uezdy* paid to the vicegerents before the reform, which amounted to only one ruble and thirteen kopeks per Muscovite *sokha* (and to less than two rubles when

9. Nosov, *Soslovno-predstavitel'nye*, p. 344.

taken together with all other duties). In other words, it was not at all a matter of the government *granting* self-government to the Russian land. Self-government was *sold* to it—and at a price ten times higher than it paid before the reform!

One might expect such a monstrous rise in the tax rate to have provoked, if not open resistance, then at least a burst of indignation in the *uezdy*. Nothing of the kind is to be noted. There is no trace of peasant complaints about the reform. On the contrary, it was received with a sigh of relief. This, incidentally, is not surprising if we remember that such peasant families as the Makarovs, Shul'gins, Poplevins, or Rodionovs—and all of these were in only one *uezd*—were sufficiently rich and powerful to pay the taxes for the entire *uezd*. It is hard not to agree with N. E. Nosov's conclusion:

> The peasants of the Dvina region "bought off" the feudal state and its organs, receiving broad judicial and administrative autonomy. The price was high . . . but what did the "buying off of the vicegerents" mean to the rich people of the Dvina, if the Kologrivov family alone could, if it liked, have paid the taxes for the entire Dvina *uezd*? And what an advantage this gave them in developing their commercial and industrial activity, released at last from the mercenary tutelage of the feudal vicegerents—and, more important, in the exploitation not only of the entire wealth of the North, but of the poor people of the Dvina! And was this not a step (and a substantial one) toward the development of new bourgeois relationships for the Dvina?[10]

Thus, the *uezdy* bought themselves the right to have the agents of the central power "not go" to them, and to be able to "do justice among themselves," and to have the peasants divide the rent "among themselves . . . according to their livings and occupations"—that is, according to the incomes of individual families. Thus, the creation of the institution of self-rule was accompanied by the introduction of an entirely bourgeois income tax. (This was the fundamental difference between the new institution and the old peasant commune, oriented toward the equality of its members). Does not this mean that the government thereby recognized legislatively the differentiation of the peasantry (and among city people) and the existence of the proto-bourgeoisie? Doesn't it mean that, for the first time in Russian history, the government recognized that a new stratum of taxpayers had appeared—a kind of "middle class"—whom it was more profitable to exploit in a rational way than to rob by turning them over to the arbitrary action of the vicegerents? This goose could lay golden eggs. And

10. Ibid., pp. 365–66.

the absolutist government naturally was smart enough not to waste them, which just as naturally was not the case with its Oprichnina successor.

The Great Reform of the 1550s was drowned in the blood and dirt of an autocratic revolution. But its doom was by no means the automatic result of some process developing fatally and inexorably in Muscovy since 1450, as Richard Hellie thinks,[11] or any other year. Rather, the facts cited compel us to assume something quite different: namely, that the doom of the Great Reform was the result of a crushing defeat of the Government of Compromise and the absolutist coalition which stood behind it.

3. At the Crossroads

One of the basic failures of the Government of Compromise was that it was not able to implement the testament of Ivan III and organize a victorious secularization campaign. This, of course, neither means that it did not understand the need for such a campaign nor that it did not try to implement one. "There is every reason to consider Sil'vestr the author of the tsar's questions [to the church assembly in 1551]," writes A. A. Zimin. "An analysis of the ideological content . . . of the questions shows the indubitable closeness of their compilers to the Non-Acquirers, whose de facto head in the mid-sixteenth century was Sil'vestr."[12] Sil'vestr was hardly the head of the Non-Acquirers, but no one disputes the fact that, as one of the most influential people in the Government of Compromise, he was a convinced adherent of secularization. In 1551, precisely for this reason, "a confrontation developed between the government of Adashev and Sil'vestr, which strove to use the self-interest of the boyars and service landholders in liquidating the landed wealth of the church, and the Josephite leadership of the church, led by Makarii."[13]

Literally on the eve of the church assembly, Kassian, bishop of Riazan', who proved to be the *only* opponent of the Joesphites among the ten participants, was inducted into the highest ranks of the church hierarchy. This lineup of forces sufficed to ensure the defeat of the Non-Acquirer program of the government, despite all the sharpness of the tsar's questions. The weakness of the organizational preparation of the second secularization campaign is obvious, if only

11. Richard Hellie, "The Muscovite Provincial Service Elite in Comparative Perspective."
12. Zimin, *Reformy*, p. 379.
13. Ibid., p. 378.

from the fact that the restructuring of the hierarchy did not begin until *after* the assembly. Ivan III had deposed the chief Josephite inquisitor, Archbishop Gennadii of Novgorod, after the assembly of 1504; Feodosii, also archbishop of Novgorod, who was just as implacable as Gennadii, was similarly deposed by the government in 1551, three months after the fateful vote, but only in November 1552 was the Non-Acquirer Pimen appointed to replace him. In May 1551 (that is, also after the vote) Trifon, archbishop of Suzdal', was deposed, and the ideologist of the Non-Acquirer movement, Artemii, was simultaneously appointed abbot of the Troitsa monastery, while his comrade-in-arms Feodorit became abbot of the monastery of St. Efim in Suzdal'. This shakeup would have been meaningful if the government had indeed been energetically preparing a third secularization campaign, but it was not doing so. In any case, it was unable to prevent Makarii from organizing the inquisitorial trial of heretics in 1553 in which he skillfully involved both Artemii and Feodorit, as well as Bishop Kassian, and obtained their removal and banishment. (Artemii, incidentally, escaped from the Solovetskii monastery where he had been exiled and fled to Lithuania, where he shared with Prince Kurbskii the mournful fate of the political émigré.)

But the root of the failure of the Government of Compromise lay not so much in this organizational incompetence as in its lack of political skill. It finally had in its hands the tool which Ivan III had not had—a national representative body, the Assembly of the Land. It had at its disposal, too, something even more important, which Ivan III also lacked—the European experience of secularization. Had not the Ricksdag (the Swedish equivalent of the Assembly of the Land) afforded Gustav Vasa support for his secularization campaign in 1527? Had not the Reform Parliament proclaimed the king the head of the church in England in 1534, and were not all the monasteries in England closed by law and their property and lands confiscated by the state? Foreign experience had thus shown that secularization could be carried out only by openly setting the nation against the hierarchy on the strength of Non-Acquirer reformist ideology, and not with the help of appeals to the hierarchy or even by restructuring it, as Ivan III had thought. The Government of Compromise neither officially adopted the Non-Acquirer ideology nor appealed to the nation, so it lost the fateful battle for secularization.

Furthermore, the government had serious difficulties even in implementing the laws adopted by the Assembly of the Land. Nosov's study shows that the administrative reform was in practice introduced in two stages, in 1551–52 and in 1555–56. In the interim, a reverse movement appears to have taken place. Over a period of several years, the fate of the Great Reform hung by a thread. In this case, the government's efforts were crowned by success. In the question of the abolition of the immunities, where the immediate interests of the church were at stake, it appeared unable, however, to force the retreat of the Josephite hierarchy, despite the fact that the hierarchy itself had voted for the new code of laws in the Assembly of the Land. This vote showed with remarkable clarity that only in the context of the Assembly of the Land was it possible to break the resistance of the hierarchy, but the government *did not* go back to the Assembly of the Land on this question, and thus lost its battle for the abolition of the immunities.

The government committed a no less serious error in regard to the pace of modernization of the army. This problem had arisen in connection with the Kazan' war and the administrative reform. The amateur cavalry of the service gentry, which received its "maintenance" in the form of land with the peasants living on it, had by the middle of the sixteenth century, as the first battles of the Kazan' war demonstrated, shown itself to be as antiquated an institution as the "maintenance" administration of the vicegerents. And, like the latter, it should have been replaced—by an army having as its core professional infantry, equipped with firearms and paid in cash. The bottleneck in a military reform of this kind was apparently money. But this was precisely what could be obtained by the government through sale of the institution of self-rule. That the government was not unaware of this problem is shown by the introduction into the Muscovite army of a core of 6,000 infantry in 1550, when the administrative reform was being prepared. One need only read the chapter on the storming of Kazan' in the *History of Ivan IV*, written by Kurbskii in exile, in order to understand the decisive role played by the infantry (along with artillery) in the great victory over the Tatars. Without the infantry and the artillery, victory would never have been achieved. Just as local self-rule was a competitor of the *voevody*, so the infantry could have been a competitor of the service gentry—and an effective one.

But here the problem of military modernization passed over into the problem of political modernization. For the formation of a permanent professional army automatically deprived the service gentry of the military monopoly which was the only thing on which their social and political claims could rest. Certainly, it was not a question of the immediate exclusion of the service nobility from the army (as an officer corps and as a cavalry force they would be retained for a long time). It was a matter only of the pace and direction of modernization, capable of creating a normal European balance between infantry and cavalry.[14]

The sum of 140 rubles, which the Dvina *uezd*, say, had paid into the treasury before the reform, represented the "maintenance" of a single vicegerent. For 1400 rubles, which the treasury now received directly, bypassing the vicegerents, the government could maintain either a cavalry force, staffed by service gentry, for the whole Smolensk county, or a regiment of infantry. The government chose cavalry. The logical result of this mistake was the statute on military service of 1556, which for the first time in Russian history made this service obligatory in a legislative sense. Hardly anyone in the government understood the fateful significance of this act. From that moment, service in the Russian state became universal.

And now, it seems to me, we can already recognize the political pattern which predetermined all the mistakes of the Government of Compromise. Wherever the national interest contradicted the interests of the numerous factions represented in the government, in the army, and in the Assembly of the Land, the government hesitated, and usually compromised, which increasingly weakened its position as arbiter. The church hierarchy did not wish to yield its land, and did not even wish to yield to any significant degree in the question of the immunities; the service nobility was not at all eager for the modernization of the army, but instead wanted land and money; and the government was not prepared for severe pressure, but tried at all costs to maintain the atmosphere of "reconciliation" of all political forces within the country, on which, so it assumed, its power was based.

In order to better understand the nature of its failure, let us briefly

14. According to the prevailing stereotype, the cavalry of the service gentry revealed its technological backwardness only in the seventeenth century. However, this backwardness was obvious even two centuries earlier, in the time of Ivan III. For example, in 1501, when Plettenberg, the master of the Livonian Order, attacked Pskov, a huge army under the best Muscovite *voevoda*, Daniil Shchenia, was sent against him. Though many times superior in numbers to the small Livonian detachment, this army could not defeat it, indicating that the Muscovite military organization suffered from some organic defect which compelled it to yield before the German infantry. The army of Ivan the Terrible, which knew only how to attack in a mass, and was quite lost when its furious assault did not lead immediately to decisive success, was on the Tatar level of military action, and not only was not capable of waging a European war, but needed European modernization even to win victories over the Tatars. All this was apparent even during the Kazan' War at the beginning of the 1550s. Russian historians, without a single exception, admit the technological, tactical, and organizational backwardness of the Muscovite army during the period of the Livonian War. Thus, in terms of technology and military organization, the modernization of the army became an urgent question as early as the middle of the sixteenth century.

review the situation in which the Government of Compromise came to power, or more precisely the "mandate" with which it came to power, following a stormy and fruitless decade of so-called "boyar government." Vasilii had died when his heir, the future Ivan the Terrible, was three years old. When the boy reached the age of seven, his mother also died. The throne became a bone of contention for numerous cliques of the tsar's relatives and prominent clans, who in the course of a permanent quarrel completely lost sight of the national interest. This Muscovite equivalent of the Wars of the Roses did not lead to civil war, but nevertheless sowed chaos and confusion in the land. By the end of the 1540s, the situation had deteriorated into mass riots in the cities. A terrible fire and open mutiny broke out in Moscow itself. It was on this wave of general bitterness and animosity of all against all that the Government of Compromise came to power at the first "assembly of reconciliation."

It began its work excellently, achieving the desired stabilization. But, after a while, it suddenly began to appear that its policy of compromise was simply too broad to be effective. Stabilization was not an end in itself, but merely a condition for the fulfillment of the strategic task of transforming the country. Compromise at all costs made this transformation unthinkable. Within the broad political base to which the government stubbornly clung, there gradually emerged competing and irreconcilable blocs of interests. Representing both of them became a sheer political impossibility. The time came to make a choice between the peasant-Non-Acquirer absolutist coalition, which the boyars could support, since it was directed against their enemies, and the service gentry-Josephite autocratic coalition, supported by the bureaucratic apparatus.[15]

Metropolitan Makarii, the head of the hierarchy, was the tsar's ideological tutor, and he understood quite well that, as long as Sil'vestr played the leading role in the government, there would be no respite for the church landholdings. He impressed on the tsar the ideas of the previous generation of Josephites. These, it will be remembered, included the tempting concept of the Muscovite tsar as the heir of the Byzantine autocrators, before whom all others were slaves. Even more indicative was the wide distribution in Moscow at that time (in what can quite appropriately be called "samizdat" in modern terms) of the pam-

15. By "coalition," I am referring here not so much to actual political alliances as to blocs of interest groups whose goals at the given historical stage were identical. In this sense, it is more a matter of latent, or potential, coalitions. Nevertheless, a cautious hypothesis may be appropriate here as to the correlation between the degree of actualization of the latent coalitions and the intensity of change in the autocratic system.

phlets of Ivan Peresvetov, who proposed to the tsar, among other things, a program of autocratic "revolution from above." Contrary to the official version in the chronicles, which attributed the fall of Byzantium to heresy, Peresvetov boldly preached that it had fallen because the emperor had put too much trust in his high nobles, his "advisors" (read: the Government of Compromise). The conquerer of Byzantium, the Turkish Sultan Mehmed, had not trusted his "advisors," and this was why he had won. Having discovered the malfeasance of his viceroys, for example, Mehmed did not substitute local self-rule, as had the rotten liberal "advisors" of the Russian tsar. He did not even bother to try them.

> He merely skinned them alive and spoke thus: if they grow flesh again their guilt will be forgiven. And he ordered their skins to be taken off and stuffed with paper and ordered iron nails to be driven into them and the following to be written on their skins: "Without such terror [*groza*] it is impossible to introduce justice into the kingdom. . . . As an unbridled horse beneath the tsar, so is a kingdom without terror."[16]

In addition to this apology for terror as the guaranty of the welfare of the state, Peresvetov also proposed copying the tool of this terror from the Turkish janissary corps, in terms so reminiscent of the later Oprichnina that many scholars have even doubted whether Peresvetov's pamphlets were written before the introduction of the Oprichnina or afterwards. "If the Christian faith had been joined with Turkish law, the angels could have talked with him [the Sultan]," Peresvetov declared, handing the Orthodox tsar an interesting brief.[17]

This sharp increase in the activity of the Russian right most probably meant that, despite all of the government's mistakes, the tide was running against the autocratic bloc. The code of laws that repealed the immunities and introduced the norms of bourgeois law was confirmed by the Assembly of the Land. Local self-rule opened up enormous opportunities for the enrichment of the proto-bourgeoisie, and for the increase of its social and, in the final analysis, political weight. Peasant differentiation and the economic boom worked in the same direction. The modernization of the army could not be permanently delayed. Ivan III's strategy had brought the Europeanization of Russia to a decisive point: if it were not stopped now it would perhaps be futile to try to stop it in the future. The advance of "money" was inexorable unless some drastic action were taken to turn back this eco-

16. V. F. Rzhiga, *I. S. Peresvetov—publitsist XVI veka*, p. 72.
17. Ibid., p. 78.

nomic and social process, unless the chief opponents of the autocratic bloc, the proto-bourgeoisie and the Non-Acquirers, along with their patrons, the boyars, who represented the political side of this absolutist triangle, were disarmed and ultimately crushed.[18]

The autocratic reaction required three things for the success of its counterattack—a strong leader, a strategic plan, and a pretext with which to put the tsar at odds with the Government of Compromise. All these three things were combined in the Livonian War.

4. The Anti-Tatar Strategy

As early as the 1520s, after the first Tatar invasion of Muscovy since the time of the Ugra, Maxim the Greek suggested a general reorientation of Muscovite foreign policy. Unfortunately, there was at that time no one to listen to him. Instead, in the course of the general pogrom against the Non-Acquirers, Grand Prince Vasilii accused Maxim of spying on behalf of the Turks. Less than two decades later, Saip-Girei stood before Moscow with his army. With him were soldiers of the Turkish sultan, with their cannons and arquebuses, and the Nogai, Kafa, Astrakhan', Azov, and Belgorod Hordes as well. It seemed that the ancient nightmare of Muscovy had again come to life, and that the whole might of the Tatars was moving against it, as under the leaders of the Golden Horde of evil memory—Tokhtamysh, Edigei, and Akhmat.

---

18. I understand that some of my readers—particularly those who cherish a weakness for Marxism—may now be asking a puzzled question (if they have not asked it already): is it really possible that in the historical conflict between "money" and "corvée," the boyars, which is to say the feudal lords, should suddenly turn up on the side of "money"? How can it be that they would struggle against the immunities which make up the essence of the feudal order? I would like to ask these readers in turn: how did it happen that the intellectual and political elite of the Russian serf-holding aristocracy rebelled in the mid-nineteenth century against serfdom, which was the essence of the feudal order? How could it be that this elite not only supported the Great Reform in the struggle against the mass of service landholders who were interested in retaining serfdom, but also became one of the prime political movers in this reform? Standard Marxist criticism is obviously powerless to explain this paradox. But in the case of the Great Reform of the 1860s, it is nevertheless not prepared to deny the facts. On the other hand, what basis do we have for denying the analogous—that is to say, essentially anti-feudal—position of boyardom, or at least of its intellectual and political elite, in the mid-sixteenth century? Why should what was possible in connection with one great reform not be possible in connection with another? Why should the Decembrists and the Slavophiles (most of whom, after all, were serf-owning landholders) turn up on the side of "money" and against "corvée" in the nineteenth century, and the same not be true of the leaders of boyardom in the sixteenth century?

Saip Girei and his allies were driven back from Moscow, and from the end of the 1540s Muscovite policy turned decisively against the Tatars, resulting in the conquest and annexation of the trans-Volga khanates of Kazan' and Astrakhan' in the 1550s. This could not be regarded by the Government of Compromise as the finale of the anti-Tatar strategy, however. The Crimea, after all, remained; and behind the Crimea stood Turkey.

Moreover, the conquest of Kazan' did not improve the international position of Muscovy, and certainly complicated it. Kazan' was a Tatar kingdom only in name. In fact, it was a multinational state. Five tongues, as Kurbskii expressed it, sat there under the Tatars: the Mordvas, the Cheremises, the Chuvashes, the Votyaks, and the Bashkirs. Muscovy had become an empire, whereas the Reconquista rested on the principle of the national and religious homogeneity of the Russian state. It was on this principle that Ivan III had constructed his strategy of dismembering the heterogeneous Lithuanian state. Now Muscovy had become heterogeneous in its turn.

The Tatars constructed their own strategies along similar lines. As early as 1520, the khan of the Crimea had called Kazan' "our yurt," which in Tatar meant what "*otchina*" meant for Ivan III, that is, fatherland. From here it was only a step to the sultan himself declaring Kazan' his yurt, and claiming a legitimate right to seek the dismemberment of Muscovy. Unless Tatar claims were disposed of once and for all, the Damoclean sword of a new attack would hang over Muscovy for decades, and perhaps centuries. The Ugra, it suddenly turned out, had been merely a symbolic liberation from Tatar rule, complete liquidation of which was a historical prerequisite of the Reconquista. The very status of Muscovy as a great power now depended on this. How could Russia enter the European family of nations as a full member if the shadow of Tatar domination still hung over it?

But, besides all these abstract considerations, the Crimea not only kept under its control extremely rich sections of the Russian land, it constantly threatened to destabilize economic life within Muscovy. Even if it could not conquer the country, it was capable of provoking a national crisis at any time. Thus historians have, for example, attributed the economic catastrophe which shook Muscovy in the 1570s to the attack by Devlet Girei in 1571. To cite M. N. Pokrovskii:

> The Tatars burned the entire *posad* of Moscow to the ground, and . . . seventeen years later it had not yet been entirely rebuilt. A whole series of cities suffered the same fate. According to the stories told at the time,

as many as 800,000 persons perished in Moscow and its environs alone, and another 150,000 were taken away as captives. The total loss of population must have exceeded one million, and the kingdom of Ivan Vasil'evich hardly contained more than ten million inhabitants. In addition, it was the long established and most cultured regions which were laid waste: it was not accident that the people in Moscow for a long period reckoned time from the ruination by the Tatars, just as in the nineteenth century they for a long time reckoned from the year 1812 [that is, Napoleon's invasion]. A good part of the almost instantaneous desolation which scholars note in the central *uezdy*, beginning precisely in the 1570s, must be laid at the door of the Tatar ruination. [This] is *the chronological point of departure for the desolation of most of the uezdy of the central region of Muscovy*. . . . The faint beginnings of a population exodus which were observed in the 1550s and 1560s were now transformed into an intensive and extremely pronounced flight of peasants from the central regions.[19]

If we remember that Soviet historians usually use this "instantaneous desolation of the center of Muscovy" to explain the beginning of the enserfment of the peasantry (although without mentioning the abandonment of the anti-Tatar strategy as a cause of this phenomenon),[20] the consequences of the Tatar attack of 1571 for the whole course of Russian history begin to look truly sinister. The more so since a second attack was scheduled for the following year. In 1572, in the words of Heinrich Staden,

19. M. N. Pokrovskii, *Izbrannye proizvedeniia*, bk. 1, pp. 320–21. *Posad*: the commercial and artisan district of a Russian town, usually situated outside the city walls.

20. Here, for example, is how B. D. Grekov explains the enserfment of the peasants in his classical work *Peasants in Rus'*: "As the economic dislocation of the seventies and eighties increased, the number of peasant migrations grew. . . . The mass of service people could not remain calm. The state serving the interests of these landholders also could not be silent. A radical and immediate solution of the peasant question became inevitable. The abolition of St. George's Day was carried out in the interests of this stratum, and for the purpose of strengthening their material position" (*Krestiane na Rusi s drevneishikh vremen do XVII veka*, vol. 1, p. 297). True, this murky passage raises more questions than it offers answers. The fact that enserfment was neither in the interests of the peasants nor in those of the boyars to whom the peasants went when they left the service landholders is obvious. But how is it that the "progressive service landholders" suddenly turn out to be the bearers of feudal reaction? The logical implication of what Grekov says is, furthermore, that if there had not been the "economic dislocations," neither would there have been serfdom in Russia. But if the fate of Russia, or at least the fate of the peasantry in Rus', depended on these "dislocations," would it not have been fitting for an expert on the Russian peasantry to give some thought to the question of where these determining "dislocations," which changed the entire character of Russian history, originated? He did not, and neither did the Soviet historiography which he headed during the Stalinist period.

The cities and *uezdy* of the Russian land were already divided up and distributed among the lords (*murzas*) who were with the Crimean tsar, as to who should hold what land. The Crimean tsar also had with him a number of noble Turks, who were to supervise this matter: they had been sent by the Turkish emperor. . . . The Crimean tsar bragged before the Turkish emperor that he would take all of the Russian land in the course of the year, and would bring the grand prince as a prisoner to the Crimea and with his *murzas* occupy the Russian land. . . . He gave his merchants and many others papers to the effect that they should go with their wares to Kazan and Astrakhan and trade there without paying duty, since he was the emperor and lord of all Rus'.[21]

Even so passionate an apologist for Ivan the Terrible as R. Iu. Vipper does not dare to ignore this testimony. "Staden," he writes, "teaches us to properly evaluate . . . the epoch of the Crimean danger."[22]

Devlet Girei did not succeed in carrying out his intentions, but their very dimensions and the fact that his troops included not only Tatars, but also all the previous allies of Muscovy—the Nogais, and even the Kabardinian Prince Temriuk, Ivan the Terrible's father-in-law, who had swiftly abandoned the sinking ship of Muscovy—indicate how real this danger was. There can hardly be any serious doubt that if the Turks had been able to help Devlet Girei in 1572, as they had helped him previously, Muscovy would have been brought to the brink of collapse. The country was desolated and demoralized, its best military cadres had been exterminated by the Oprichnina, and its capacity for resistance catastrophically reduced. Fortunately, the complete defeat of the Turkish fleet by Don Juan of Austria at Lepanto in 1571 tied the hands of Turkey, and compelled it for the time being to pass from the offensive to the defensive. Thus, it was Europe which helped Muscovy, albeit involuntarily, in this, its most terrible hour. And how did Ivan the Terrible repay it for this help? Immediately after Lepanto, he suggested to the Turkish Sultan Selim II a plan for an anti-European coalition, a Russo-Turkish alliance "against the Roman emperor and the Polish king and the Czech king and the French king and other kings and against all the Italian princes."[23]

The sultan scorned this proposal, however, thereby confirming that *the abandonment of the anti-Tatar strategy inevitably condemned Russia to complete isolation in European politics*, which led not only to irreversible changes in its internal political structure, but to the necessity of paying tribute to the Tatars for another whole century.

In the first half of the seventeenth century alone, up to a million

21. Cited in R. Iu. Vipper, p. 115.   22. Ibid., p. 116.
23. H. Staden, *Zapiski* . . . , p. 20.

rubles went to the Tatars in "gifts," as they were shamefully called by
the Muscovite ambassadors, or in "tribute," as they were frankly interpreted in the Crimea. This was the very time when the tsar was
humbly begging King James of England for a subsidy of 120,000 rubles. Furthermore, this tribute did not prevent the Tatars from carrying away into captivity and selling as slaves 200,000 Russians. One
cannot read without sadness Iurii Krizhanich's secret memorandum
that,

> On all of the Turkish warships, almost no oarsmen except Russians are
> to be seen, and in the cities and towns in all of Greece, Palestine, Syria,
> Egypt, and Anatolia—that is, in all of the Turkish kingdom—there is
> such a multitude of Russian slaves that they usually ask their fellow
> countrymen, newly arrived, whether anyone is still left in Rus'.[21]

Thus, in the 1560s the "turn against the Tatars" was a strategic imperative for Muscovy. The "turn against the Germans," war on Livonia and consequently on Europe, proposed at that time by the Russian
right as an alternative to the anti-Tatar strategy, inevitably led to isolation and ruin. And indeed it brought both. Russia simply ceased to be
either a European power or a great one. In the words of a modern
historian,

> Until the beginning of the eighteenth century, Russia had remained
> scarcely more than a name to the West, where it was thought to be an
> amorphous geographical area occupied by barbarous schismatics owing
> a vague allegiance to a priest-king. It was thought of little importance to
> Europe save as a source of raw materials and a pasture for impover-
> ished German Baltic barons.[25]

5. Russia Versus Europe

Livonia had regressed so thoroughly since the time of Ivan III that it
must have seemed an overripe fruit which would fall of its own accord
into the hands of the conqueror. In practical terms, it had ceased to be
a unified state, and had been transformed into an amorphous conglomerate of commercial cities and the fiefs of bishops and knights.[26]

24. P. Berezhkov, *Plan zavoevaniia Kryma*, p. 68.
25. Lester Hutchinson, Introduction to Karl Marx's *Secret Diplomatic History of the Eighteenth Century*, p. 19.
26. "The multilayered and divided government was extremely weak: five bishops, a master of the order, eight commanders, and eight governors owned the land; each had his cities, districts, staff, and customary laws," writes N. M. Karamzin (*Istoriia gosudarstva Rossiiskogo*, vol. 8, p. 261).

However, this was the deceptive weakness of a no-man's-land situated between several strong predators, all of whom coveted its ports, its wealthy cities, and its first-class fortresses; all waiting for one of the others—the stupidest—to take the initiative. For the very fragmentation and decentralization of Livonia were, paradoxically, its main strength. It had no one nerve center at which to strike. Each fortress had to be conquered separately, and there were hundreds of fortresses. A war could not be brought to an end either by a swift attack or by a pitched battle; Livonia was a hopeless quagmire, capable of absorbing the bones of a whole generation of would-be conquerors. The one who struck first not only risked losing prestige by openly taking on the aggressor's role, but would also unite against himself a strong coalition of other predators, who would reap the spoils at the expense of the first under the guise of justice. This was why *to act against the Livonians was equivalent to acting against Europe*—Lithuania, Poland, Sweden, Denmark, the Hanseatic cities, and the emperor who stood behind them. Under the conditions of the sixteenth century, this signified a world war.

Ivan III would rather have left to someone else the dubious pleasure of beating his head against the impregnable walls of Riga and Revel', and then taken the choicest morsel from the paws of the exhausted victor. He prepared for his descendants territorial positions suitable for just such a strategy. The only Livonian prize that really interested Muscovy was the first-class port of Narva, situated at the mouth of the Narva River, on the other bank of which Ivan III had providently built a Russian city named for himself (Ivangorod), and the taking of Narva was a question of one good bombardment, of one frontal attack (as happened on May 11, 1558). It was not necessary to challenge all of Europe and involve oneself in a twenty-five-year war—the more so since Muscovy was absolutely unprepared for such a war.

"Among the . . . Lithuanians, not to speak of the Swedes, it was easy to note a greater degree of military skill than among the troops and generals of Muscovy . . . in almost all of the major confrontations with Western opponents on an open field, the Muscovite troops lost. . . . Tsar Ivan understood this excellently, if not better than anyone else," admits S. M. Solov'ev.[27] "The feudal militia of the Muscovite tsar could not hold their own in hand-to-hand combat against the regular armies of Europe. It was necessary to seek an enemy on their own level, such as the Crimean and Kazan Tatars," M. N. Po-

---

27. Solov'ev, *Istoriia Rossii*, bk. 3, p. 657.

krovskii confirms.[28] More surprisingly, R. Iu. Vipper, too, says the same thing: "In the conquest of the Volga region, the Muscovite mounted armies were engaged in battle with troops like themselves, and used extremely simple strategy and tactics. It was quite another matter to fight a Western war, where they had to confront the complex military art of the commanders of European mercenary armies: the Russian troops were almost always defeated on the open field."[29] Even S. V. Bakhrushin, who composed a no less triumphant hymn to Ivan the Terrible and the Livonian War than Vipper, admits with a sigh that "Russia in the sixteenth century was not yet prepared for a solution of the Baltic problem."

In the light of this unanimity, the conclusions which the fans of Ivan the Terrible draw from their premises seem quite insane. "One is therefore the more struck," Bakhrushin exclaims, for example, "by the penetration with which Ivan IV perceived the basic vital task of Russian foreign policy, and concentrated on it all the powers of his state."[30] Evidently the tsar consciously threw "the greatest empire in the world" into an obviously doomed adventure—or, as Vipper expresses it, "into the abyss of extermination"—merely in order to demonstrate his perspicacity to posterity. By involving the country in a national catastrophe, it seems, he demonstrated his statesmanship, and, Bakhrushin asserts, "anticipated Peter, and showed considerably more political penetration than [his opponents]."

6. The Last Compromise

"And again and again we importuned the tsar and counselled him either to endeavor to march himself or to send a great army at that time against the horde [i.e., the Crimea]," writes Andrei Kurbskii. "But he did not listen to us, for his flatterers, those good and trusty comrades of the table and the cups, his friends in various amusements, hampered us while helping him; and in the same way, he sharpened the edge of the sword for his kinsmen and fellows more than for the heathen."[31]

The Government of Compromise understood that its life was at stake. For if even later historians knew that "in almost all of the major confrontations with Western opponents on an open field the Muscovite troops lost," this must have been all the more striking to the

28. Pokrovskii, *Izbrannye proizvedeniia*, bk. I, p. 450.
29. Vipper, p. 69.
30. Bakhrushin, *Ivan Groznyi*, p. 84.
31. A. M. Kurbskii, *History of Ivan IV*, p. 126.

participants in these confrontations. And they could by no means be consoled by abstract considerations to the effect that their tsar was preparing to demonstrate his penetrating genius to posterity. For them the "turn on the Germans" meant, quite simply, disaster. And there is a reason to think that the tsar, too, understood this perfectly. Even in the years of the Oprichnina, he exclaimed in a letter to Kurbskii: "How can I not remember the endless objections of the priest Sil'vestr, of Aleksei [Adashev], and of *all of you* to the campaign against the German cities. . . . How many reproachful words we heard . . . from you, there is no need to recount in detail!" Further on, the tsar frankly admits: "Whatever bad thing happened to us, *it was all because of the Germans*" (he is speaking of the bitter conflict and confrontation which had arisen in the government over his decision to "turn against the Germans").

Apparently the government was trying to present the tsar with a fait accompli: it began a war in the South as early as 1556 with the Crimean expedition of the *d'iak* (civil servant, secretary) general Rzhevskii, who traveled down the Dnieper all the way to Ochakov, defeated the Tatars, seized their cattle and horses, and got away safely. The effect was electric. For the first time, the Tatars had been paid back in their own coin. Devlet Girei, who had been preparing to move against Moscow, immediately beat a retreat, and even agreed to release the Muscovite prisoners taken in the previous year's campaign. It was now that the tsar was "importuned and counselled . . . again and again" that the time had come for a new Ugra. But Ivan IV wanted to make war on Europe and not on the Tatars. And apparently he found strong allies in the Muscovite establishment, and perhaps in the government itself. At the begining of 1558, Adashev seems to have decided on a compromise: he tried to make war on two fronts. Despite the fact that, contrary to the traditional methods of Ivan III, no diplomatic or political preparations had been made for a war on Livonia, troops were dispatched against both Livonia *and* the Crimea.

After taking Narva, however, the Russian generals in Livonia halted their advance. "I had to send letters to you *more than seven times* before you finally took a small number of people and only after many reminders captured more than fifteen cities," Ivan the Terrible complained indignantly afterwards. "Is this a sign of your diligence, that you take cities after our letters and reminders, and *not on your own initiative?*"[32] At the first opportunity, when the king of Denmark of-

32. *Poslaniia Ivana Groznogo*, p. 317. Emphasis added.

fered to act as intermediary, Adashev petitioned for a truce with Livonia and got it.[33]

In the South, reminders and letters from the tsar were unnecessary. The war developed spontaneously there, and new allies joined in unasked—the Cossacks, refugees from Central Russia who wandered over the endless "Wild Field" and spent their energies and enterprise in banditry. Not only the Don Cossacks were involved. Hearing of the unexpected new prospects, the "chief of the Ukraine" and leader of the Dnieper Cossacks, Prince Dimitrii Ivanovich Vishnevetskii made an appeal to the tsar, declaring that he would be willing to repudiate his oath to Lithuania and enter Ivan's service if he were allowed to lead the Crimean campaign. A chain reaction developed. Not even waiting for the tsar's approval (he would never receive it), Vishnevetskii took the Tatar city of Islam-Kermen' by storm, and carried off its cannons to the camp which he had built on the island of Khortitsa in the Dnieper. Two Circassian princes in the service of Muscovy took two more Tatar cities, and the khan proved powerless to recover them. His attempt to storm Khortitsa ended, in S. M. Solov'ev's words, with his "being forced to retreat with great shame and loss."[34] In the spring of 1559, at the very moment of the truce with Livonia, Danilo Adashev, Aleksei's brother, seized two Turkish ships at the mouth of the Dnieper, made a landing in the Crimea, laid waste the settlements, and freed the Russian prisoners—and again the khan was unable to do anything about it.[35]

But the Crimea could not *be conquered*—put an end to, as an end had been put to Kazan'—by such raids. It was a matter of a difficult and long-drawn-out war, which might last for many years. The Crimea was hundreds of miles from Moscow. Kazan', which was much closer, had not fallen in a day—first, under Vasilii, the fortress of Vasil'sursk had had to be built at the halfway mark; then, under the Government of Compromise, Sviiazhsk had been erected opposite it on the other bank of the Volga to consolidate Muscovy's hold there. In the case of the Crimea, dozens of fortresses had to be built, a chain

33. Ibid., p. 603.
34. Solov'ev, *Istoriia Rossii*, bk. 3, p. 493.
35. In Karamzin's opinion, only the military help of the Turks saved the Tatars. "Devlet Girei trembled," he writes, "and thought that Rzhevskii, Vishnevetskii, and the Circassian princes were only the forward division of our troops. He was expecting Ivan himself, and petitioned him for peace, and wrote in desperation to the sultan that all was lost if he did not save the Crimea." The sultan saved it: "We . . . did not follow the indications of the finger of God, and gave the infidels time to recover. Vishnevetskii did not hold out at Khortitsa when numerous detachments of Turks and Wallachians, sent to Devlet Girei by the sultan, appeared" (N. M. Karamzin, pp. 253–54).

of cities stubbornly moving further and further into the southern steppe each year, conquering the land from the Tatars mile by mile, one frontier after another. The whole life of the country had to be subordinated to this "open frontier" strategy. The economic boom had to supply it with materials, and reforms and secularization of church lands had to yield financial resources; a modernized infantry had to balance cavalry manned by service gentry, since only new tactics and European technology could assure the Muscovite armies of decisive superiority over the Tatars.[36] For this struggle Muscovy needed to utilize European experience of military organization, as well as European trade and diplomatic ties—not the war with Europe for which the tsar had thirsted, but alliance. In modern language, détente.

7. The Autocrator's Complex

The great secretary Viskovatyi, the head of the Foreign Office, was a personal enemy of Sil'vestr. He may have impressed on the tsar the enormous difficulties involved in the anti-Tatar strategy. Metropolitan Makarii may have supported Viskovatyi (it is hard to believe that he would have missed such an opportunity to topple his mighty enemy from power). They may have introduced the tsar to the pamphlets of Peresvetov, which were circulating in Moscow, arguing the fatal danger of taking political decisions under the influence of "advisors."

We shall never know what the role of this whole complex network of personal conflicts and ideological influences was in the formation of the Oprichnina alternative to the Great Reform, in the victory of terror over compromise, of the Livonian War over the anti-Tatar strategy. But we do know what Viskovatyi and the Josephite hierarchs could not know—that they themselves were to be victims of the coup d'etat to which they had egged on Ivan IV. They paid for their victory

36. The main objection usually set forth against the feasibility of such an "open frontier" strategy is that a hundred years after the Livonian war, in the 1670s, Muscovy made an attempt to conquer the Crimea which ended in failure. Was it then possible for the Muscovy of the sixteenth century to have succeeded? My answer is essentially given in the introductory chapter of this book. What was indeed impossible for "weak, poor, almost unknown" pre-Petrine Muscovy, in a "state of nonexistence," was quite possible for pre-Oprichnina Muscovy, then at the height of its power. I am not speaking in terms of a single military operation, as in the 1670s, but of a national, long-range anti-Tatar strategy over a period of decades, which would have required détente with Europe as well as the continuation of the Great Reform, the reformation of the church, and the modernization of the army.

with their heads. The terror which they had helped to unleash had its own logic. In telling the tsar that all of his troubles came from "advisors," and that in relation to the *autocrator* all men were slaves, did they expect that, having rejected the advice of Sil'vestr and Adashev, he would be willing to be advised by Viskovatyi and the hierarchs? Were they not also the same kind of slaves as Kurliat'ev and Kurbskii? Why should they not also be skinned alive?

And, furthermore, in encouraging the tsar to believe that he was the only Orthodox (that is, true Christian) sovereign in the world, that he was descended in a direct line from the Roman emperor Augustus, and carried on the work of the Byzantine autocrators, how could they expect patience in international affairs and respect for the other European governments and monarchs from him? What diplomatic calculations could be required from the only genuine viceroy of God on earth?

The tsar was in the eye of the Russian political storm; his character therefore acquires enormous significance. Such was the opinion of classical historiography. According to the latest historiographic fashion, however, it is mistaken.

The most vivid and articulate proponent of this view of the matter is perhaps Edward L. Keenan, Jr., earlier famous for asserting that the cornerstone of the Russian political literature of the sixteenth century, the Ivan the Terrible-Kurbskii correspondence, is a forgery. To judge by his short essay in the *Harvard Magazine* in 1978, Keenan's suspicions are increasing swiftly. Now not only the correspondence of Ivan the Terrible, but even Ivan the Terrible himself, seems to him in a certain sense a forgery:

> A consideration of Ivan's medical record raises the question of whether he could even have been a functioning czar, let alone the volcanically energetic and Machiavellian prince of historical literature. . . . In my opinion, for most of his life he was not. . . . It seems impossible that he had any large role in the important events of his reign. . . . A traditional political system ruled by an oligarchy of royal in-laws and an administration run by professional bureaucrats required little intervention by the czar. . . . Nevertheless, the boyars and the bureaucrats *did* require that the czar be dynastically legitimate, capable of performing certain ceremonial functions and serviceable as the symbol and source of their own unquestioned power. Ivan—caring little for the hard work of politics and administration . . . —was for the most part quite suitable for his officials' purposes. Possibly they spread stories of his "terribleness" abroad to increase their own clout.[37]

37. Edward Keenan, "Vita: Ivan Vasil'evich, Terrible Tsar 1530–1584," p. 49.

Thus Keenan cuts the Gordian knot over which chroniclers and historians, dissertation writers and poets, have despaired for centuries. True, his account contradicts the testimony of numerous eyewitnesses—but this may also turn out to be forged, and the subject of a subsequent exposé. Unfortunately, however, it is not readily understandable why the all-powerful (according to Keenan) oligarchy of royal relatives and professional bureaucrats needed to unleash the train of events which resulted in their own ruin. Nor is it clear why the reign of this unfortunate invalid, who served only as a screen for the oligarchy, differs so strikingly from the epoch of "boyar rule" (during which the oligarchy was indeed powerful, and the child-sovereign was by definition a screen), which did not bring in its train either great reforms or revolution, and which was in general one of the most barren in Russian history. In fact, Keenan's thesis looks rather like a paraphrase of that submitted fifteen years previously by one of the most honest and bold (but, alas, not one of the most profound) of Soviet historians, D. P. Makovskii:

> It is not necessary to seek in the actions of Ivan IV any particular logic or consistency. Ivan IV—a mentally ill person—was always under the influence or suggestion of someone. The savage reprisals during the time of the Oprichnina were called forth, as contemporary sources note, by various adventurers (Basmanov, the Griaznyes, Skuratov, etc.) stimulating an unhealthy imagination and sadistic inclinations in Ivan, who did this in order to steal more goods and to enrich themselves.[38]

Keenan and Makovskii fail to notice the *revolutionary* character of the Oprichnina, which was not an extension of the previous structure of power, but its complete *reversal*. Or, rather, it was a triumph of the autocratic political tradition and at the same time a complete debacle for the absolutist tradition—a debacle which decisively changed the historical course of the nation.

Ivan the Terrible was unarguably mentally unbalanced, and the longer he lived, the more severe his illness became. But there was also something discernibly political to this illness which Keenan ignores. Just as in the case of Paul, Peter, or Stalin (who were no less indisputably ill), madness not only did not hinder the tsar from having his own personal political goals, but actually helped him to subordinate the strategy of the state to them.

The character and personal political goals of Ivan the Terrible were manifested vividly in the international relations of the Russia of

38. D. P. Makovskii, *Razvitie tovarno-denezhnykh otnoshenii* . . . (2nd ed).

that time, when the question of whether the country would adopt a European or an isolationist orientation was decided. Toward the end of the 1550s, R. Iu. Vipper notes,

> The haughtiness and caprices of [Ivan] the Terrible began to be reflected in the official diplomatic notes sent to foreign powers as soon as he himself began to direct policy. In the diplomatic correspondence with Denmark, the appearance of Ivan IV at the head of affairs was marked by a striking incident. Since the time of Ivan III, the Muscovite tsars had called the king of Denmark their brother, and suddenly in 1558 Shuiskii and the boyars found it necessary to reproach the king for the fact that he called "such an Orthodox tsar as the autocrat of all Rus' his brother; and previously there was no such reference.". . . The boyars are obviously telling an untruth. Certainly, nothing had been forgotten in Moscow and there had been no mistake, but the tsar had simply decided to change his tone with Denmark and behave more haughtily.[39]

In the 1560s, at the height of the Livonian campaign, when the efforts of Muscovy should logically have been concentrated on preventing Sweden from becoming involved in the war, Ivan the Terrible suddenly began a mortal quarrel with the Swedish king, too, because the latter was seized by an impious desire to call Ivan his brother in diplomatic papers. "The [Holy] Roman emperor and other great sovereigns are our brothers, but it is impossible to call you a brother because the Swedish land is lower in honor than those states," the tsar declared.[40]

Here, at least, it is hinted that there are other "great sovereigns," in addition to the emperor, who are permitted to call him brother. During the arguments of the 1570s, it becomes clear that these "other great ones" are a fiction. The number of candidates for brotherhood is reduced to two—the emperor and the Turkish sultan, who "are the preeminent sovereigns in all kingdoms."

In 1572, when the question of the candidacy of Tsarevich Fedor for the Polish throne arose, a hint was dropped in the tsar's letter to the Poles which showed that he was not against expelling the emperor himself from the narrow circle of the "preeminent":

> We know that the Holy Roman Emperor and the king of France have sent to you: but this is not an example for us, because other than us and the Turkish sultan there is in no state a sovereign whose house has

39. R. Iu. Vipper, p. 130.
40. M. D'akonov, *Vlast' moskovskikh gosudarei*, p. 151.

ruled for two hundred years without interruption . . . [we are] the sovereign of the state starting from Augustus Caesar, from the beginning of time, and all people know this.

Who was the Holy Roman Emperor but a mere elected official—a "functionary" for his own vassals? And, if it came to that, who was the Turkish sultan, a Mohammedan who had no claims to the heritage of Augustus Caesar? And what price the rest of the crowned rabble—the Polish king Stefan Batory, who until recently had been a miserable *voevoda*; the English queen Elizabeth, a "common maiden"; Gustav of Sweden, who, when the merchants came with goods to trade, personally put on gloves and measured out lard and wax "like the common people"; and all the other "functionaries," whether Hungarian, Danish, or French? This was the way Muscovite diplomats talked at the end of Ivan's life in the 1580s, on the brink of the catastrophe: "Even if old Rome and the new Rome, the ruling city of Byzantium, were compared to our sovereign, his Muscovite state would yield to none."

The crueller the blows which fate inflicted upon Ivan the Terrible's self-esteem, the paler his phantasmal star became, the more arrogant he grew. On his very deathbed he asserted that "by the mercy of God *no state* was higher than ours."[41] He was like one of the Fates—blind, unstoppable, and inhuman. In his own city of Novgorod, he behaved like a foreign conqueror; he treated foreign sovereigns like his own boyars: all are slaves, and nothing but slaves.

This was not simply the ridiculous bragging of a paranoid head of state; it was the logical behavior of an autocrator. Liberated from all limitations on power within the country, intoxicated by his own wild freedom, he came logically and inevitably to the thought of liberation from all limitations on earth. Such was, it seems, the pure political core of the tsar's mental illness, the method, one may say, of his madness.

Ivan the Terrible was the first of the Muscovite princes (unless we count the Tsarevich Dimitrii, who never ruled) to be crowned as tsar—that is, caesar. But it did not suffice merely to call himself this. In the official hierarchy of European sovereigns, he remained the prince of Muscovy—not even a king, let alone caesar. Such leaps on one's own initiative were not permitted. They had to be bought by first-class, generally recognized victories. Ivan learned from his tutors and intimates that he was "the great tsar of the greatest empire on earth" (and if he can hear after death, he has undoubtedly rejoiced to

41. Ibid., p. 156.

hear the same thing from both classical Russian and Soviet historians, the tutors and intimates of other autocrators). But he did not hear this from his peers, the "other great sovereigns." And he developed a kind of royal inferiority complex.

Peter ended the Northern War as an emperor. Ivan the Terrible was named tsar before the Livonian War, and even before the war with Kazan'. He wanted his own Northern War. The anti-Tatar strategy, perhaps requiring generations of painstaking effort, did not suffice. He needed the immediate and sensational rout of a European state, Livonia, in order to be considered a "preeminent sovereign." The arguments of the Government of Compromise for a sound national strategy, and a blow at the Crimea as the logical completion of the Kazan' campaign, finally routing the Tatars and freeing their Christian slaves, must have seemed to him naive and boring. His personal goals seemed to him infinitely more important. Rather, as to every patrimonial feudal lord, it must have seemed to him that the state simply could have no other goals than his own; by subordinating the country to these goals, he threw it "into the abyss of extermination."

Having conquered the kingdoms of the Volga in the middle of the century, supplied with Caspian silk and furs from the Urals (which were no less valuable than the treasures of India), swiftly urbanizing and expanding its wealth, trying to liberate itself by the Great Reform from the Tatar heritage, the young Muscovite state emerged onto the broad expanse of world politics, from the very beginning claiming a primary role in it. A quarter of a century later, sunk in an endless and fruitless war, unable even to protect its own capital from the assault of the Crimeans, Russia had been thrown back into the ranks of third-class powers, into the darkness of "nonexistence."

The dream of "preeminent rule"—to implement which it was found necessary to lop off all the heads in Moscow capable of thought—led, in complete accordance with the historical logic of autocracy, to the opposite result. It was obvious, even to a foreign observer, only four years after the death of Ivan the Terrible (the tsar died in 1584) that something terrible lay in store for this country. "And this wicked policy and tyrannous practice, though now it be ceased, hath so troubled that country and filled it so full of grudge and mortal hatred ever since that it will not be quenched, as it seemeth now, till it burn again into a civil flame," prophesied Giles Fletcher.[42] Thus ended the unfortunate, forgotten, and by now almost unbelievable, absolutist century in Russia.

42. G. Fletcher, *Of the Russe Common Wealth*, p. 34.

PART III

IVANIANA

Ivan IV transgressed the boundaries of evil established by the Almighty for his creatures.

ASTOLPHE MARQUIS DE CUSTINE

Ivan IV was a great and wise ruler, who guarded the
country from the penetration of foreign influence
and strove to unify Russia.

JOSEPH STALIN

Stalin is Ivan the Terrible plus electrification of the
entire country.

RICHARD LOWENTHAL

CHAPTER VII

THE DAWN

---

1. Methodological Problems

Intellectual history has its stereotypes. When we begin an analysis of
the evolution of ideas, we are primarily seeking forms of classification
by which we can most comfortably locate the proponents and opponents of various historical stratagems. For example, it is convenient
to divide them into "right-wingers" and "left-wingers," or into "con-
servatives" and "liberals," or into "ideologists" and "scholars." The
special and unprecedented difficulty of Ivaniana consists in the fact
that in this case not one of these conventional classifications works.
The Decembrist Ryleev, a "left-wing" dissident of the early nineteenth century, and the historian Pogodin, a "right-wing" reactionary,
fight on the same side of the barricades of Ivaniana; Ilovaiskii, a
member of the "Union of the Russian People," or Black Hundreds,
and Kavelin, a liberal of the first water, offer their hands to each other
across the decades; Bestuzhev-Riumin and Belov, declared in all the
Soviet texts on the subject to be representatives of "reactionary bour-
geois-and-nobility historiography," merrily run in tandem with the authors of the very works in which they are denounced, Bakhrushin and
Smirnov. How are we to explain these incongruities? Historians often
tried to avoid this difficulty by simply declaring the writing of their
predecessors, both of the left and of the right, to be unscientific. In
some cases this has meant that the opinions of the predecessors were
dictated more by emotions and prejudice than by analysis of primary
sources. In others, so the pious Marxists think, the predecessors were
infected with the ideology of obsolete classes, and therefore by definition incapable of having any communion with "genuine science."

Nowadays it is impossible, for example, to read K. D. Kavelin's review of M. P. Pogodin's article "On the Character of Ivan the Terrible" without smiling. Kavelin haughtily, not to say abusively, eluci-
dates the "unscientific nature" of the writings of his predecessor:

> Anyone who is at all acquainted with the course of our historical litera-
> ture knows how much material has now been printed which was un-

known and unavailable at that time [that is, in 1825, when Pogodin's article was written; Kavelin's review was published in 1846]. There were incomparably more prejudices. . . . In addition, at that time Karamzin's authority was still unlimited; he, for all his great and never-to-be-forgotten services to Russian historical scholarship, introduced into it completely unnatural views.[1]

From this it followed, naturally, that the more "material" was printed, and the fewer "prejudices" there were, and the faster "unnatural views" were replaced by "natural" ones, the closer we would be to the truth. An analogous point of view was held by Kavelin's contemporary and cothinker, S. M. Solov'ev, who explained the disagreements among historians in terms of the "immaturity of historical scholarship, and the common failure to pay attention to the correlation and sequence of phenomena. Ivan IV was not understood because he was separated from his father, grandfather, and great-grandfather." A half century later N. K. Mikhailovskii sarcastically noted that: "Solov'ev carried out this task, and connected the activity of Ivan with the activity of his father, grandfather, and great-grandfather, and pursued this connection even further into the depths of time, but the disagreements have not been terminated."[2]

After another half century, perhaps the most brilliant of the Soviet historians, S. B. Veselovskii, lamented: "The maturing of historical scholarship is proceeding so slowly that it may shake our faith in the strength of human reasoning altogether, and not only in the question of Tsar Ivan and his time."[3]

In the interim between these two pessimistic statements, all this did not, however, by any means prevent S. F. Platonov from presenting Ivaniana in 1923 as a triumph of "the maturing of historical scholarship":

> In order to survey in detail everything which has been written about [Ivan] the Terrible by historians and poets, one would need an entire book. From the *History of Russia* of Prince Mikhail Shcherbatov (1789) to R. Iu. Vipper's work *Ivan the Terrible* (1922), the understanding of Ivan the Terrible and his time has passed through a number of phases, and has attained significant success. It can be said that this success is one of the most brilliant stages in the history of our science—one of the most decisive victories of scientific method.[4]

1. K. D. Kavelin, *Sochineniia*, pt. 2, p. 112.
2. N. K. Mikhailovskii, "Ivan Groznyi v russkoi literature," p. 134.
3. S. B. Veselovskii, *Issledovaniia po istorii oprichniny*, p. 35.
4. S. F. Platonov, *Ivan Groznyi*, p. 5.

However, after Platonov died in exile, and the "appearance and dissemination of Marxism"—in the words of A. A. Zimin—"created a revolution in historical science,"[5] and "guided by the brilliant works of the founders of scientific socialism, Soviet historians received the broadest opportunities to make a new approach to the solution of basic questions of the history of Russia,"[6] everything became decidedly cloudy and got into a condition of even greater "immaturity" than was the case before Solov'ev. Whereas the latter had looked on Karamzin as a naive representative of "unnatural views" and a slave of idealistic "prejudices," the first leader of Soviet historiography thought even worse of Solov'ev than Solov'ev did of Karamzin: "Solov'ev's views were those of an idealist-historian,[7] who looks on the historical process from above, on the side of the ruling classes, and not from below, the side of the oppressed."[8]

Whereas Solov'ev, looking at the historical process from above, discovered that Ivan the Terrible "was indisputably the most gifted sovereign whom Russian history offers us before Peter the Great, and the most brilliant personality of all the Riurikids,"[9] for Pokrovskii, examining it from below, Ivan the Terrible represented a type of "hysterical and tyrannical person, who understood only his ego and did not wish to know anything except this precious ego—no political principles or societal obligations."[10]

But what happened later could not have been foreseen either by Solov'ev or by Pokrovskii: these mutually exclusive views were suddenly amalgamated, forming a monstrous explosive mixture, which haughtily continued to call itself "genuine science."

To begin with, the Soviet historian I. I. Polosin, from the prescribed perspective of "the oppressed classes," discovered that the social meaning of the Oprichnina consisted "in the enserfment of the peasants, in the enclosure of the communal lands characteristic of serfdom, and in the liquidation of St. George's Day."[11] But, not being able to resist the temptation of looking at matters "from the side of

5. A. A. Zimin, *Reformy* . . . , p. 31.
6. A. A. Zimin, *Oprichnina* . . . , p. 33.
7. The word "idealist" carries in Marxist discourse the special pejorative sense of a viewpoint or theory based on the assumption of the primacy of ideas or nonmaterial elements, rather than material factors, in the historical process and the formation of reality generally.
8. M. N. Pokrovskii, *Izbrannye proizvedeniia*, bk. 3, p. 239.
9. S. M. Solov'ev, *Istoriia Rossii s drevneishikh vremen*, bk. 3, p. 707.
10. Pokrovskii, bk. 1, p. 256.
11. I. I. Polosin, *Sotsial'no-politicheskaia istoriia Rossii XVI—nachala XVII v.*, p. 20.

the ruling classes" (reflecting, in his own words, the "powerful influence of contemporary reality"), Polosin all of a sudden discovered in that same Oprichnina "military-autocratic communism."[12] In other words, he equated communism with serfdom. Polosin obviously deserved punishment from both above and below for his infantile sincerity and reversion to Solov'ev's rehabilitation of the Terrible Tsar. But it was the wrong time for Polosin's colleagues to punish him. The rehabilitation picked up speed. It was transformed into a competition. One respected historian hastened to overtake the next. In the middle of the nineteenth century, Solov'ev, for all his bowing and scraping before the political achievements of the Terrible Tsar, had nevertheless condemned his depravity, crying out: "Let not the historian say a word in justification of such a person!"[13] In the middle of the twentieth century, this seemed to have been forgotten. Now the "idealist-historian" Solov'ev seemed to be looking at things "from the side of the oppressed," while the Marxist historians looked at them "from the side of the ruling classes." More than this, precisely this view was declared the only scientific one. R. Iu. Vipper asserted (in the second edition of his book) that only "Soviet historical science has restored the true figure of Ivan the Terrible as the creator of a centralized state and the major political figure of his time."[14]

This "historiographic nightmare" of the 1940s was evaluated by a participant, Veselovskii, in a book written during that time but published only many years after his death, in the 1960s:

> In recent times everyone who had occasion to write about Ivan the Terrible and his time began to say with a single voice that finally Ivan as a historical personality had been rehabilitated from the calumnies and distortions of the old historiography, and had risen before us in his full stature and correctly interpreted. S. Borodin, in his comment on the *Trilogy* [*Trilogiia*] of V. Kostylev, praised the author for having shown Ivan the Terrible as "a progressive statesman, who transformed the life of the country, firm in achieving his goals, farseeing and bold." S. Golubov in a critique of a new production of Aleksei Tolstoi's play at the Malyi Theater wrote that after many centuries of calumnies and slander by the enemies of Ivan the Terrible, "we see for the first time on the stage a true historical figure of a fighter for the 'bright kingdom,' a fiery patriot of his time, a mighty statesman." Academician N. Derzhavin expressed himself to approximately the same effect. . . . "Only relatively

12. Ibid., p. 14.
13. Solov'ev, *Istoriia Rossii s dreveneishikh vremen*, bk. 3, p. 713.
14. Vipper, p. 31.

recently have the events of the period of Ivan IV's reign received in our historical scholarship a correct and objective interpretation." Thus, the rehabilitation of the personality and political activity of Ivan IV is a novelty—the latest word in Soviet historical scholarship. But is this accurate? Can one believe that historians of the most varied tendencies, including Marxists, have been doing nothing for 200 years but confusing and distorting the history of their motherland?[15]

But why should we not believe this? Didn't Solov'ev and Kavelin say the same thing about Karamzin and Pogodin? And didn't Pokrovskii and Polosin say the same thing about Solov'ev and Kavelin (and also about Karamzin and Pogodin)? In this sense, Vipper and Derzhavin behaved in the traditional way, denying from the outset the "scholarly character" of Pokrovskii and Veselovskii (and at the same time of Solov'ev and Kavelin, and Karamzin and Pogodin).

Some of them had disclaimed their predecessors for neglecting the "factual material" and having "unnatural views." Others had attacked them for not looking at things from the angle at which a genuine scientist should. But why did the contemporaries of Veselovskii attack *all* of them?

In the first place, Veselovskii suggested, "the job of putting historians on the true path . . . was taken over by belles-lettrists, playwrights, dramatic critics, and film directors"—in a word, by laymen. But this was untrue. Academician Derzhavin, whom he had just finished quoting, was not a layman, but a professional historian. Academician Vipper, who four times, in the four editions of his *Ivan the Terrible*, sang a solemn hymn to the "major figure of a ruler of peoples and a great patriot," was likewise no layman. Professor Bakhrushin, who published three editions of his *Ivan the Terrible*, in which the tyrant is depicted as a democratic monarch, beloved by his people, was also a leading historian, who wrote the relevant sections in textbooks for schools and universities. The same went—and still goes—for the highly esteemed specialist Professor Smirnov, also the author of an *Ivan the Terrible*, who in his apologetic ecstasy went so far as to openly contrast scholarly analysis to "the power of the wisdom of the people, which evaluated and firmly held in its consciousness the truly progressive features of [Ivan] the Terrible. . . . The figure of the terrible tsar created by the people has stood the test of time."[16] Even Karamzin had known enough to separate the intellect of the nation

15. Veselovskii, pp. 36–37.
16. I. I. Smirnov, *Ivan Groznyi*, p. 5.

from its prejudices and, unlike the Marxist Smirnov, gave preference to the former.[17] Derzhavin, Polosin, Vipper, Bakhrushin, Smirnov, the major professionals of current Russian historiography, were the ones who contrasted "the wisdom of the people" to scientific analysis. Specialists, and not laymen, exclaimed in enthusiasm that "official historiography was in sharp contradiction with the numerous popular traditions, songs, and tales" in which "the terrible tsar appears not only as a historical personage, but precisely as a hero, whose deeds are praised and glorified."[18]

The first of Veselovskii's theses is thus not confirmed by the facts. "But the main thing perhaps," he writes in advancing his second thesis, "is the fact that scientific people, including historians, have long since lost the naive faith in miracles and know quite well that to say something new in historical science is not that easy, and that for this there is needed extensive and conscientious work on the primary sources, new factual material, and that inspiration is entirely insufficient, even when it is of the most benevolent kind."[19]

But, after all, Solov'ev said the same thing a hundred years ago. And, alas, his sermons did not protect the public consciousness from the recurrence of the "historiographic nightmare." Veselovskii was a brilliant and genuine scholar. I sincerely sympathize with his confusion. The fact is, however, that he had encountered a national drama occurring again and again over a period of centuries, and tried to treat it as an accidental and temporary deviation from "science." Even his opponents suggested to him that things were not that simple. Polosin wrote that Veselovskii "studied the Oprichnina from the position of Prince Kurbskii—an unreliable position, and, to put it bluntly, rotten through and through."[20] Veselovskii would never have

---

17. Karamzin ends volume 9 of his *Istoriia gosidarstva Rossiiskogo* with these words: "Ivan's good reputation has outlived his bad reputation in the memory of the people; the groans fell silent; the victims rotted away; and the old traditions were overshadowed by new ones; but the name of Ivan shone on the law code and reminded people of the acquisition of the three Mongol kingdoms. The documents proving the atrocities lay in the archives, and the people over the course of the centuries saw Kazan', Astrakhan', and Siberia as living monuments to the tsar-conqueror; they honored in him a famous proponent of the power of our state and of the formation of our social order; they rejected or forgot the name of Tormentor, which his contemporaries gave him, and from the obscure rumors of his cruelty, Ivan is now called only the Terrible, without distinguishing him from his grandfather, also so called in ancient Russian, more in praise than in reproach. History is more unforgiving than are the people" (p. 472).

18. Smirnov, p. 5.

19. Veselovskii, p. 37.

20. Polosin, p. 19.

agreed, but the criticism is valid, if you discard the abuse. Both Veselovskii and Kurbskii actually fought on one side of the barricades in the national debate on the nature of tyranny and its role in Russian history. They were both on the side of the intellect of the nation and against its prejudices in the historical battle taking place in the heart of one nation divided in two.

New apologias for Ivan the Terrible have arisen, and will continue to arise, independently of the "maturity" of historical scholarship in each new phase of pseudodespotism, each with a new Ivan the Terrible on the Russian throne. Society can outlive autocracy only in its historical experience. Historical scholarship, no matter how many new sources it discovers, is not capable of replacing this experience. But it can still do something: it can help or hinder a society in overcoming its autocratic tradition. Here we approach the real problem of Ivaniana. The opponents of Ivan the Terrible have been dissidents rather than oppositionists. In other words, they have argued, exposed, cursed, and been indignant, and they have been just and strong in their criticism—as long as criticism by itself was sufficient. But they have not thought out a positive alternative to autocracy. They have not seen it either in terms of theory or in terms of history. They have worked without depending on the ancient and powerful Russian absolutist tradition—on the tradition which gave them birth, *but which they were not able to make their tool.* On the other hand, their opponents—beginning with Ivan the Terrible himself, and ending with Ivan Smirnov—have based themselves on the equally ancient and mighty *autocratic* tradition, on the prejudices of a nation which lived through the Tatar yoke and the cultural revolution of the Oprichnina, on the powerful striving to justify the strong regime of the Boss. And they have not only based themselves on this tradition; *they have been able to make it their tool.* The dissidents of Ivaniana have never dared to recognize openly and fearlessly the tremendous power of this slave tradition, which seems to come from underground, from the very roots of the national consciousness. And for this reason they have been helpless against it. What good were primary sources and new "factual material," what good was the moral indignation and the martyrology of the victims of the Oprichnina against the terrible power of cultural stereotypes? This was like trying to storm an impregnable fortress armed with goose quills. The tradition of slavery could be destroyed only by an alternative tradition, only by recognizing its weaknesses, the mistakes which it made, and the reasons for its defeats. The dissidents of Ivaniana did not do this. For this reason they were defeated. I will try here to show how this happened.

2. At the Sources of Ivaniana

In 1564, Ivan IV's favorite, the boyar prince Andrei Kurbskii, a hero of the Kazan' and Livonian wars, fled to the protection of the king of Poland, leaving his wife and infant son in Derpt, where he had been governor. From Lithuania, Kurbskii wrote a sharp and reproachful letter to the tsar. The latter—himself a "master of rhetoric and written wisdom" in the eyes of contemporaries—replied with a lengthy epistle of self-justification. With the remarkable correspondence thus begun—which lasted, with long interruptions, from 1564 to 1579— commences what I call Ivaniana.[21]

The correspondence between Kurbskii and the tsar has been reinterpreted many times in the past 400 years. For declaring it apocryphal, Edward Keenan was given a distinguished prize not long ago.[22] Nonetheless, V. O. Kliuchevskii first perceived in it the fatal dichotomy in Russian political culture.[23] Paying tribute to Kliuchev-

21. V. O. Kliuchevskii, *Sochineniia* (2nd ed.), vol. 2, p. 164.

22. Keenan's *The Kurbskii-Groznyi Apocrypha* was awarded the first annual Thomas J. Wilson Prize. His point of view is based on a complex and inventive textological analysis, which a well-known émigré expert in the literature of this period has called "a fantastic pyramid of speculation" (N. Andreev, "Mnimaia tema," p. 270). A major Soviet expert comes to the conclusion that "the attentive reading of the sources promised by Keenan is reduced to an inaccurate and arbitrary interpretation of them, and the laws of probability serve as a bridge to unproved and fantastic speculations" (R. G. Skrynnikov, *Perepiska [Ivana] Groznogo i Kurbskogo. Paradoksy Edvarda Kinnona*, p. 123). I am prepared, however, to explain this strange coincidence by the prejudice of both reviewers. In any case, this is, as the saying is in Russia, after Pushkin, "a quarrel of Slavs among themselves"—a highly academic conflict between highly qualified textologists. What disturbs me is something else: as soon as Keenan goes beyond the limits of pure textology and addresses himself to the analysis of the content, his whole construction suddenly begins to sound somehow less than professional. Keenan is convinced, for example, that "Kurbskii . . . never really does make clear what he believes in, aside from his complaints against Ivan's personal tyranny, while Ivan, for the most part, is at pains to justify his own actions on personal and historical grounds, rather than by any consistent theoretical program" (p. 60). I would be prepared to agree with Keenan if he had said that Kurbskii did a poor job of defending his point of view. But unfortunately he does not analyze the political content of the correspondence at all. We shall see soon how complex, contradictory, and difficult to analyze this political content is. Keenan's refusal even to notice it rather compels me to agree with the conclusion of Professor Andreev: "What a pity Edward Keenan has thrown his enormous energy and tireless imagination into creation of an illusory theme" (p. 272). It is an even greater pity inasmuch as there are still so many real and difficult problems in the Russian history of this period which demand all of the attention and imagination of the few people working in the field. It is sad to contemplate a specialist playing with dolls, so to speak.

23. The classical stereotype has it that the dualism in Russian political life takes its origin from the "Westernist" modernization of Peter I (that is, from the second auto-

skii's role as trailblazer—but also because he is a brilliant writer, the Pushkin of Russian historiography—I will as far as possible set forth the essence of the correspondence in his words. "Kurbskii's text contains . . . political judgments resembling principles or a theory," he wrote.

He considers as normal only a structure of the state which is based not on the personal will of the sovereign, but on the participation of a "college"—a council of boyars—in the administration. . . . Furthermore the sovereign should share his royal concerns not only with highborn and just councillors: Prince Kurbskii also favors the participation of the people in the administration, and stands for the usefulness and necessity of an Assembly of the Land. . . . "If the tsar is respected by the kingdom . . . he must seek good and useful counsel not only from his councillors, but also from men of all the people, since the gift of the spirit is given not according to external wealth or according to power, but according to spiritual rectitude.". . . The prince stood for the governing role of the Council of Boyars and for the participation of the Assembly of the Land in the administration of the state. But he is dreaming of yesterday. . . . Neither the governing role of the Council of Boyars nor the participation of the Assembly of the Land in the administration was an ideal at that time, nor could it be a political dream. [They] were at that time political facts. . . . Thus, Prince Kurbskii stands for existing facts; his political program does not go beyond the limits of the existing structure of the state . . . while sharply critical of the past of Muscovy, [he] cannot think of anything better than this past.[21]

The reader might well conclude from this, as dozens of the most experienced experts have concluded before him, that Kurbskii stood for the status quo, and even for the past, which implies that his opponent, the tsar, was advancing something new, going "beyond the limits

cratic "revolution from above" at the beginning of the eighteenth century). Literally all historians of Russia, native and foreign, proceed from this stereotype. (The reader will find an excellent formulation of it, for example, in Dmitri Obolensky's "Russia's Byzantine Heritage," pp. 93–117.) In the mid-nineteenth century, the Slavophiles turned this stereotype into their ideological banner, calling the Russian elite "home" to pre-Petrine Russia. In the 1880s, their follower Konstantin Leont'ev laid bare the real essence of this appeal—the concept of "Russian Byzantinism," but since that time it has not entered anyone's head to doubt the validity of the stereotype itself. However, the dualism of Russian political culture goes back, as I have tried to show here, to roots in the structure of early medieval Russian society which have nothing to do with either "Westernism" or "Byzantinism" (which is not to deny important cultural influences from both sides). Two hundred years before Peter, this dichotomy was already an accomplished fact. The first decisive struggle between the two tendencies was the Oprichnina revolution of Ivan the Terrible.

24. Kliuchevskii, *Sochineniia* (2nd ed.), vol. 2, pp. 165, 166, 167.

of the existing structure of the state." Logically this should be so. Otherwise, what would they have to argue about? But

> let us look at the other side. The tsar . . . objects not to individual assertions of Kurbskii's but to the entire political mode of thought of boyardom, which Kurbskii has come forward to defend. "You," the tsar writes to him, "are always saying the same thing . . . turning this way and that your favorite thought, that slaves, not masters, should possess power"—although none of this is written in Kurbskii's letter. "Is it," the tsar continues, "contrary to reason not to wish to be possessed by one's own slaves? Is this glorious Orthodoxy—to be under the power of slaves?" All are slaves, and nothing but slaves. . . . All of the political thinking of the tsar is reducible to one idea—to the idea of autocratic power. For Ivan, autocracy is not only the normal order established from on high, but also the *original fact of our political life, proceeding out of the depths of time.* . . . The entire philosophy of autocracy is reduced to one simple conclusion: "We are free to show mercy to our bondsmen, and we are also free to execute them." Such a formula requires no effort of thought at all. The appanage princes came to the same conclusion without the help of an exalted theory of autocracy and even expressed themselves in almost the same words: "I, Prince So-and-so, am free to show mercy and also to execute whomever I like.". . . Such is the political program of Tsar Ivan.[25]

But if the appanage princes of two and three hundred years before Ivan the Terrible had already adhered to the same political philosophy, and even expressed it with the same words, then what, in essence, is new here? Nothing at all! says Kliuchevskii: "Both sides backed the existing order."[26] You will agree that here there is something inexplicable, or at least unexplained. Two irreconcilable enemies fight for long years, and on their banners there is inscribed the same thing: I am for the existing order.

Kliuchevskii, of course, feels something incongruous in this, and tries to explain the incongruity: "One feels . . . that some misunderstanding divided the two disputants. This misunderstanding consisted in the fact that in their correspondence, it was not two political modes of thought which came into collision, but two political moods." What the term "political mood" is supposed to mean is not very clear to me—nor, I am afraid, to Kliuchevskii. On the same page on which he comes to the conclusion that "both sides stood for the existing order," he suddenly declares: "Both sides were dissatisfied . . . with the structure of the state in which they acted, and which they even

25. Ibid., pp. 167, 169.
26. Ibid., p. 170.

led."[27] Unfortunately, I fail to see the logic of this conclusion, in which both sides went into battle for one and the same thing, while both were equally dissatisfied with it. I am afraid that Kliuchevskii failed too. Probably for this reason, he returns again and again to the topic which disturbs him, trying to explain his own thinking. In this, at least once, he succeeds superbly.

3. A Strange Conflict

"What in fact, was the Muscovite state in the sixteenth century?" Kliuchevskii asks.

> It was an absolute monarchy, but with an aristocratic administration. There was no political legislation which could have defined the boundaries of the supreme power, but there was a governmental class with an aristocratic organization, which the regime itself recognized. This regime grew together, simultaneously, and even hand in hand, with another political force, which limited it. Thus, the character of this regime did not correspond to the nature of the governmental tools through which it had to act. The boyars thought of themselves as powerful advisors of the sovereign of all Rus', while the same sovereign, remaining true to the views of an appanage prince, employed them according to ancient Russian law as his household servants, with the title of bondsmen of the sovereign.[28]

But here it is, the answer to the riddle which tormented Kliuchevskii and which he never solved. This answer consists in the fact that the political tradition of medieval Russia was *dualistic*—that it was a form of coexistence between two types of relationships between the "state" and the "land," which were not only different, but opposite. The first was the ancient relationship of an appanage prince to his household servants, who administered his *votchina*, and to the bondsmen who tilled the princely domain. This was a relationship of master to slave (precisely the relationship which Ivan the Terrible insisted on so fiercely in his letters). But the second relationship was no less ancient. This was the relationship of the prince as war leader and as defender of the land to his free retainers and the boyars of his council. It was just this relationship—which as a rule was contractual, but in any case was morally obligatory and fixed in the norms of customary law—which Kurbskii was insisting on.

Kurbskii's tradition was rooted in the custom of "free departure"

27. Ibid.
28. Ibid., p. 180.

of the boyars from the prince—a custom which gave the boyar a quite definite and strong guarantee against arbitrary behavior on the part of his sovereign, for a prince of a tyrannical turn of mind would soon lose military and thus political power. Therefore he either showed himself willing to make concessions, or he perished. Tyrants simply did not survive in the cruel and permanent war between princes. The competitive standing of the prince was a reliable guarantee of the political independence of his boyar councillors. Such were *the historical roots* of the absolutist tradition in Russia.

But it was not only that both these tendencies coexisted for many centuries; they also, Kliuchevskii observes, "grew hand in hand." This sharply contradicts the existing stereotype, according to which the absolutist tradition gradually but uninterruptedly weakened in Russia as the country was transformed from a conglomerate of princely domains into a unified state, and "if one left Muscovy, there was nowhere to go, or it was inconvenient." As the unified state was created, the boyars not only were not turned into bondsmen of the tsar, but quite the contrary, became "a governmental class with an aristocratic organization which the regime itself recognized."

The household of an "appanage prince" knew neither a governmental class nor an aristocratic organization: it contained either bondsmen or free retainers. Furthermore, the royal *votchina* was administered by bondsmen and not by retainers. Therefore, the aristocratization of the elite—that is, the transformation of free retainers into a governmental class—was a comparatively late phenomenon in Russia. The Russian aristocracy was thus formed precisely in connection with, and in the course of, the formation of the unified state. Moreover, *it was created by this very process.*

The boyars of the council of an appanage prince participated in political decisions mainly by taking advantage of the right of "free departure." In other words, their role in the formation of policy was at that time purely negative. Now, having lost the right of free travel between principalities, they had acquired in return something considerably greater: the privilege of participating in the adoption of political decisions, not only in a negative sense, as previously, but also positively. Thus, the Russian aristocracy was not an obsolete phenomenon, as the textbooks would have it, but a phenomenon which was developing and gathering strength. As early as the fourteenth century, the first conquerer of the Tatars, Dimitrii Donskoi, said on his deathbed to his boyars: "I was born in your presence, grew up among you, ruled as prince with you, made war with you in many countries and overthrew the heathen." He left this behest to his sons: "Listen to the boyars, and do nothing without their consent."[29] From here it was a long road to Article 98 of the law code of 1550, which juridically obliged the sovereign not to adopt any laws without the agreement of the boyars. In the course of two centuries, Russian boyardom *was transformed from a body of free retainers into a governmental class.* It compelled the regime to recognize its aristocratic organization. It learned to coexist with a new apparatus of executive power—*prikazy* (ministries) and secretaries (ministers), who were actually the heirs of the serf administrators in the appanage *votchiny.* In his doctoral dissertation, Kliuchevskii himself examined the mechanism of this coexistence in detail:

> The Duma supervised all new and extraordinary measures, but as the latter became customary through repetition, they passed over into the domain of the central bureaus. . . . The central bureaus were formed, so to speak, out of the administrative deposits gradually laid down from the legislative activities of the Duma having to do with extraordinary matters, which then passed into the order of clerical work."[30]

Thus, the Muscovite political machine in the mid-sixteenth century *combined single-handed leadership in the sphere of executive power* (which corresponded to the autocratic tradition) with *limited leadership in the sphere of legislative power* (which corresponded to the absolutist tradition).

In 1549, a new element was introduced—the Assembly of the Land, which potentially might have meant the institutionalization of broad-based legislative power (inasmuch as the Boyar Duma and the sacred synod of church hierarchs formed part of it). This third element was not an accidental phenomenon. The experience of the first half of the sixteenth century showed a need to correct an imbalance in the existing political machine.

In the absence of a law determining the mode of succession to the throne, the leadership was unstable. So was the relationship between the executive and legislative functions, which involved combining both unlimited and limited mandates in the person of the tsar. The reign of Vasilii (1505–33) had demonstrated that if the tsar aimed for a dictatorship, the Boyar Duma was an inadequate restraining factor. Vasilii had tried to concentrate the administration in the hands of the executive power he headed. In 1520 the boyar Bersen' Beklemishev openly accused Vasilii of violating the rules of the political game and deviating from the "conciliar methods" of Ivan III toward the adop-

29. E. A. Belov, *Ob istoricheskom znachenii russkogo boiarstva*, p. 29.
30. V. O. Kliuchevskii, *Boiarskaia duma* . . . , p. 162.

tion of decisions in camera with his secretaries. On the other hand, the epoch of "boyar rule" (1537–47) demonstrated that without a single leader the machine simply could not function: successive oligarchies practically paralyzed the political process.

Two opposed proposals to resolve the dilemma were in circulation in the middle years of the century. Ivan Peresvetov called for the complete removal of boyardom from power. Conversely, an anonymous pamphlet originating among the Non-Acquirers, the famous *Conversation of the Miracle Workers of Valaam*, proposed the summoning of a "universal assembly" of all estates from all the cities and regions of Russia, which would remain in session permanently, thus giving the tsar the opportunity to "question them well as to every kind of secular matter."[31]

Moscow of the 1550s was in transition toward the unknown. The traditional order of things was falling apart, changing its outline, disappearing before one's eyes. Kliuchevskii himself affirms this, when he says that "in the society of the time of [Ivan] the Terrible, the thought was abroad that it was necessary to make the Assembly of the Land a leader in the . . . cause of reforming . . . the administration."[32]

Who, ten or twenty years before, whether under Vasilii or under the "boyar government," could have imagined that such ideas would spring up in Muscovite society? Not a quarter century had passed since the last visit of the imperial ambassador Sigismund Herberstein, who noted of Muscovy's sovereign:

> He has power over both secular and clerical individuals and freely, according to his will, disposes of the life and property of all. Among the counselors whom he has, none enjoy such importance that they would dare to contradict him in anything or be of another opinion. . . . It is unknown whether the rudeness of the people requires such a tyrannical sovereign, or whether the tyranny of the prince made the people thus rude and cruel.[33]

Herberstein had not witnessed the short-lived flowering of the "Muscovite Athens" of the 1480s and 90s, and did not know that the tyrannical atmosphere of the court of Vasilii was the result of a political struggle which ended in the routing of the Non-Acquirers and the political trials of Bersen', of Maxim the Greek, and of Vassian Patrikeev. (All of whom had, inter alia, *contradicted the sovereign*—which was why they were convicted.) But if the political life of Muscovy

31. G. N. Moiseeva, *Valaamskaia beseda* . . .
32. Kliuchevskii, *Sochineniia* (2nd ed.), vol. 2, p. 392.
33. S. Herberstein, *Zapiski* . . . , p. 28.

could in such a short interval have risen to the idea of a national representative assembly, it could mean only that the existing order was changing swiftly. Not only did both sides in the dispute between Kurbskii and the tsar feel this change, but the fate of each of the social groups making up Muscovite society depended on it. The severity of the conflict is explained not by some elusive difference in "political mood," as Kliuchevskii thinks, but by the fact that the most profound and fundamental interests of the country were at stake.

Kliuchevskii's vast knowledge of the administrative structure of medieval Muscovy remains unsurpassed to this day.[34] It did not prevent him, however, from making contradictory statements. For example, he asserts that "neither the governing role of the Council of Boyars nor *the participation of the Assembly of the Land in the administration* was an ideal at that time nor could it be a political dream."[35] On the other hand, he tells us that "in practice the Assembly of the Land of the sixteenth century did not prove to be either universal [that is, representing all the estates] or a permanent gathering, convoked every year, and *did not take* into its hands the supervision of the administration."[36] The Assembly of the Land not only did not take supervision over the administration into its hands but—as can be seen both from Kurbskii's letter and from the behavior of the Government of Compromise—no one even had any real idea of how, concretely, this was to be done. The government was feeling its way in the dark. It did not even try to bring before the Assembly of the Land such fundamental conflicts as the secularization of church landholdings, or even the conflict over the immunities in which the decision of the assembly itself was violated by the church hierarchy. It did not try to address itself to the assembly in the decisive debate over foreign policy. In sum, it did not try to institutionalize the assembly as the supreme arbiter in its dispute with the tsar. This is why the only thing that Kliuchevskii can say in the government's defense is that *the thought was abroad* in the society that it was necessary to make the Assembly of the Land leader in the cause of correcting the administration. But can one seriously call this "wandering thought" a political fact—the more so since even in Kurbskii's letters it still "wanders," without ever growing

34. The well-known Soviet historian N. I. Pavlenko admits with a sigh that "about the Boyar Duma of the second half of the seventeenth century and the beginning of the eighteenth, we know no more than was known to Kliuchevskii almost ninety years ago. The situation with regard to the study of the Assemblies of the Land is equally unsatisfactory" ("K voprosu o genezise absoliutizma v Rossii," p. 54).

35. Kliuchevskii, *Sochineniia* (2nd ed.), vol. 2, p. 166. Emphasis added.

36. Ibid., p. 392. Emphasis added.

into a precise formulation? No political mechanism designed to secure the participation of the Assembly of the Land in the administration was even envisaged. And this is why it remained a political
dream.

Such was the extraordinary complexity of the Kurbskii-tsar correspondence which Vasilii Kliuchevskii found so difficult to analyze and
Edward Keenan failed to notice.

4. The First Attack of the "Historiographic Nightmare"

Until the publication of volume 9 of Karamzin's *History of the Russian State*, declared the Russian historian N. Ustrialov,

> Ivan was recognized among us as a great sovereign: he was seen as the
> conqueror of three kingdoms, and even more as a wise and solicitous
> legislator; it was known that he was hardhearted, but only by obscure
> traditions; and he was partly excused in many matters for having estab-
> lished a brilliant autocratic regime. Peter the Great himself wished to
> justify him. . . . This opinion was shaken by Karamzin, who solemnly
> declared that in the last years of his reign, Ivan did not run second ei-
> ther to Louis XI or to Caligula, but that until the death of his first wife,
> Anastasia Romanovna, he was the model of a pious, wise monarch, zeal-
> ous for the glory and happiness of the state.[37]

Ustrialov is both right and wrong. As early as 1564, Kurbskii quite
clearly divided the reign of Ivan the Terrible into the same two periods. Karamzin follows this division to the letter. More than this, following Kurbskii, he even divides his description into two volumes.
Volume 8, devoted to the "blue" period, ends thus: "This is the end of
the happy days of Ivan and of Russia: for he lost not only his wife but
his virtue."[38] Volume 9, devoted to the "black" period, opens with this
declaration: "We are approaching the description of terrible changes
in the soul of the tsar and in the fate of the kingdom."[39]

In Kliuchevskii's apt formula, "the tsar was split in two in the
thought of his contemporaries."[40] At the beginning he was great and
glorious, wrote one of them, "and then it was as if a terrible storm,
coming from a distance, disturbed the peace of his good heart, and I
do not know what upset his mind, great with wisdom, into a cruel dis-

---

37. Cited in Belov, p. 49.
38. N. M. Karamzin, *Istoriia gosudarstva Rossiiskogo*, vol. 8, p. 308.
39. Ibid., vol. 9, p. 5.
40. Kliuchevskii, p. 198.

position, and he became a mutineer in his own state." Even more decisive hostility to the "double tsar" was expressed in 1626 by Prince
Katyrev-Rostovskii, who described vividly how the tsar—"a man of
marvelous mind, skilled at book learning and eloquent"—suddenly
"was filled with wrath and fury" and "ruined a multitude of the people in his kingdom, both great and small." Finally, in the *Chronicle of
Ivan Timofeev*, the description of Ivan's evil deeds is brought out in
truly sculptural relief. It is true that as a motive for them only "poisonous fury" is cited, but it is said that the tsar suddenly "took a
hatred to the cities of his land, and in wrath . . . divided all the land
in his realm in two as though with a cleaver."[41] Iurii Krizhanich, with
whom we are already familiar, in his *Politics*, written in the 1660s, proposed a special term *"liudoderstvo"*[42] to define autocracy. Krizhanich
knew where this began in Rus':

> Who was the Russian Jeroboam [i.e., the beginning of evil]? Tsar Ivan
> Vasil'evich, who introduced extremely hard and merciless laws in order
> to rob his subjects. . . . That is how matters have gone in this king-
> dom from the reign of Ivan Vasil'evich, who was the originator of this
> *liudoderstvo*.[13]

Thus, contemporaries and immediate descendants clearly understood that there was something terrible in the activity of Tsar Ivan—
something which called forth a national disaster. For them, he was
Ivan the Tormenter and "a mutineer in his own state." We hear from
them no justifications of the tsar.

However, all these "dark legends" could not prevent the growth of
the "historiographic nightmare" in the first half of the eighteenth
century. The famous Russian scholar and poet Mikhail Lomonosov
wrote an ode "On the Capture of Khotin," in which Peter I says to
Ivan the Terrible, "Thy and my exploits are not in vain, that Russia
should be feared by the whole world."[44] (In fact, after Ivan the Terrible, Russia by no means inspired the world with fear, but rather with
contempt.) The historian Vasilii Tatishchev asserted that, "Ivan subjugated Kazan' and Astrakhan' to himself . . . and if the mutiny and
treason of a few good-for-nothing boyars had not prevented it, it

41. Cited in Zimin, *Oprichnina* . . . , p. 10.
42. This word cannot be literally rendered into English. It is derived from *liudi*
(people) and *drat'* (to tear, to skin), but as the text indicates, it means something more
than mere cruelty or atrocities, even of the most extreme kind.
43. Iu. Krizhanich, pp. 594, 597.
44. M. V. Lomonosov, *Izbrannye proizvedeniia*, p. 66.

would certainly not have been hard for him to conquer Livonia and a good part of Lithuania."[45] It was hard to blame Ivan's defeat on the Poles, the Germans, or the Jews (who would be blamed by Tatishchev's descendants and followers for other misfortunes of Russia). He was therefore forced to seek an internal enemy. His formula was brief: the boyars are guilty. They conspired, they mutinied, they betrayed. Thus even in the period of this first "historiographic nightmare," Kurbskii's view of the Oprichnina as a conflict between the tsar and the boyars was revealed as a stick with two ends.

The criterion used by Tatishchev and Lomonosov was the national power of Russia, understood exclusively as its potential for intimidation. All sacrifices were justified for the achievement of this result. To the credit of Russian historiography, it must be said, however, that the first "historiographic nightmare" did not last long. Prince M. M. Shcherbatov, the most prestigious representative of the conservative opposition in the time of Catherine the Great, branded the epoch of Ivan the Terrible a time when "love for the fatherland died out, and in its place came baseness, servility, and a striving only for one's own property."[46] Unlike Lomonosov and Tatishchev, Shcherbatov connected the decline of morality within the country with the catastrophic fall of its prestige abroad. He damned Ivan because the latter "made his name hated in all the countries of the world." And unlike the contemporaries of the tsar, he saw the source of these calamities neither in the tsar's character nor in his "poisonous fury," but in his striving for unlimited power: "Thus the unrestricted power, which autocrats only desire, is a sword serving to punish by cutting off their own glory, *even if nothing else happens.*"[47]

As we see, there was no lack of testimony to Ivan the Terrible's "baseness of heart," "poisonous fury," and striving for "unrestricted power" before Karamzin. But nevertheless, Ustrialov was partly right. For society remained deaf to this testimony. It did not hear it, did not wish to hear it, and having heard it, did not understand it. The curses in the chronicles and the investigations in the archives were one thing and the public consciousness was quite another. Lulled by dreams of the national might of Russia (as Catherine the Great's chancellor, Bezborodko, said, "Not a single cannon in Europe dare be fired without our permission"), it was inclined to believe Lomonosov rather than Shcherbatov. The truth could not become a fact of public con-

---

45. V. N. Tatishchev, *Istoriia Rossiiskaia s drevneishikh vremen*, bk. 1, pt. 2, p. 544.
46. M. M. Shcherbatov, *Istoriia Rossiiskaia s drevneishikh vremen*, vol. 2, p. 832.
47. Ibid. Emphasis added.

sciousness until Karamzin's time; by then Russia had experienced a brief, but fearful, parody of the Oprichnina of Ivan the Terrible under Emperor Paul, at the very end of the eighteenth century, when the frightful power of the state was again turned inward, against the society itself. And the latter, mortally frightened, "felt on its own skin" the immediate need to understand what the Russian Oprichnina really was.[48]

5. "Hero of Virtue" and "Insatiable Bloodsucker"

How to explain the contradictions in Ivan the Terrible's character? Shcherbatov reached the conclusion that "the inclinations of the heart [of Ivan the Terrible] were always the same," but that circumstances prevented them from being manifested before the Oprichnina. Precisely what these circumstances were, Shcherbatov does not exactly explain. He was inclined to think that it was primarily the gentleness of his first wife, Anastasia, which restrained the tsar.[49] But though we may accept this as an explanation of why Ivan *did not commit crimes* during his marriage to Anastasia, how is it that he *accomplished* great reforms and "sacred tasks" during this period? Again under beneficial feminine influence? Cherchez la femme? Neither Shcherbatov nor Karamzin (who in practice shares his predecessor's viewpoint as to Anastasia's role) is prepared to venture so gallant an explanation.

Karamzin, who was an adherent of "enlightened autocracy" (tyranny without a tyrant, so to speak), offers a subtler explanation for the "doubling" of the figure of the tsar, which permits him both to be condemned as a human being and justified as a political figure. Karamzin seeks to rehabilitate the autocracy by condemning the terror (in contemporary terms, he tried to do exactly what the Eurocommunists and Solzhenitsyn are now doing: the former would like to separate communism from the GULAG, and the latter would like to separate communism from traditional Russian autocracy). Karamzin writes:

> Despite all the speculative explanations, the character of Ivan—a hero of virtue in his youth and an insatiable bloodsucker in the years of his

48. Karamzin, who had begun his *History* during the Time of Troubles which occurred after the Oprichnina of Paul, was certainly aware of the need to prevent a new tyranny. As an adherent on principle of autocracy, he saw no better means of doing so than by threatening the potential tyrant with the "eternal curse of history" (vol. 9, p. 439).
49. Shcherbatov, vol. 5, pt. 3, p. 222.

maturity and his old age—is a riddle to the mind, and we would doubt
the truth of even the most reliable information about him, if the chronicles of other peoples did not reveal to us equally surprising examples:
that is to say, that if Caligula, the model sovereign and the monster, and
Nero, the pupil of the wise Seneca, the object of love, and the object of
loathing, had not ruled in Rome. They were pagans, but Louis XI was a
Christian, who yielded to Ivan neither in ferocity nor in the outward
piety with which they wished to smooth over their lawless acts: both
were pious out of fear, both were bloodthirsty and lecherous like the
Asiatic and Roman tormentors. Monsters outside the law, and outside
all the rules and probabilities of reason; such horrible meteors, such
wandering fires of unrestrained passions reveal to us across the extent
of the centuries the abyss of possible human wickedness, seeing which,
we tremble![50]

Karamzin goes even further, equating the reign of Ivan the Terrible with the Tatar yoke.[51] And still—despite all the sincerity of his
moral indignation—something holds him back from unconditional
condemnation of Ivan as a statesman. "But let us give even the tyrant
his due," he suddenly declares, right after the comparison of the
Oprichnina with the "yoke of Batu Khan."

Ivan, in the very extremes of evil, is, as it were, the ghost of a great
monarch, zealous, tireless, frequently penetrating in his political activity; although . . . he did not have even a shadow of courage in his
soul, he remained a conqueror, and in foreign policy followed unde-
viatingly the great intentions of his grandfather; he loved justice in the
court . . . and is famous in history as a lawgiver and a shaper of the
state.[52]

This unexpectedly conciliatory rider, after all Karamzin's curses,
has usually been overlooked by later historians, who have chiefly
quoted the famous phrase "a riddle to the mind." But in it there is
already contained, as in a seed, all the later drama of the Ivaniana.

6. Pogodin's Conjecture

Karamzin's craftiness did not escape his contemporaries. "In his history, refinement and simplicity show us, with no partiality at all, the
necessity of autocracy and the beauties of the knout," wrote Pushkin.[53] Nevertheless, after Karamzin, the mysterious duality in the
character of the tsar became one of the favorite topics of Russian lit-

50. Karamzin, vol. 9, pp. 438–39.   51. Ibid., p. 440.
52. Ibid., pp. 440–41, 443.
53. A. S. Pushkin, _Polnoe sobranie sochinenii_, vol. 1, p. 303.

erature. "Whereas historians like Kostomarov transform themselves for the sake of [Ivan] the Terrible into men of letters, poets like Maikov transform themselves for his sake into historians," Mikhailovskii observed.[54]

Vissarion Belinskii asserted that Ivan was "a fallen angel, who even after his fall revealed at times both the strength of an iron character and the strength of an exalted mind."[55] The Decembrist Ryleev, on the other hand, naturally brandished thunder and lightning against "the tyrant of our precious fatherland."[56] Another brilliant Decembrist, Mikhail Lunin, also unambiguously condemned tyrannical autocracy because "in its original form, it brought the Russians the mad tsar, who for twenty-four years bathed in the blood of his subjects."[57] In a great multitude of novels, plays, narrative poems, odes, and portraits, there appeared, in place of the real tsar,

> now a fallen angel, now merely a villain, now an exalted and penetrating mind, now a pedestrian person, now an independent figure consciously and systematically following great aims, and now some kind of rotten boat without a tiller or sails; now a person standing unattainably high over Rus', and now a base nature, alien to the best strivings of his time.[58]

The first voice to call a halt belonged to the well-known Russian historian Mikhail Pogodin. Pogodin was a rock-ribbed reactionary, even more convinced than Karamzin of the beneficial nature of the autocracy, but when it came to Ivaniana he was no less an iconoclast than Keenan is. Though even Kurbskii "praises Ivan for the middle years of his rule,"[59] Pogodin asserts that, "Ivan from 1547 onward became a completely passive figure and did not take any part in administration whatever."[60] The "blue period" of the reign simply did not belong to Tsar Ivan. "Obviously these were actions by the new party at court, unlike all the preceding ones, and the credit for them belongs to it, and to Sil'vestr, the founder and leader of it, and not to Ivan." Furthermore, Pogodin discovered an astonishing coincidence in the correspondence of the mortal enemies: Kurbskii attributed all of the "holy acts" of this period to the Chosen Rada (praising them, of course), and the tsar did the same (cursing them, of course). Ivan

54. N. K. Mikhailovskii, p. 130.
55. V. G. Belinskii, *Polnoe sobranie sochinenii*, vol. 4, p. 135.
56. K. F. Ryleev, *Polnoe sobranie sochinenii*, p. 155.
57. M. S. Lunin, *Dekabrist Lunin, sochineniia i pis'ma*, p. 80.
58. Mikhailovskii, p. 131.
59. M. P. Pogodin, *Istoriko-kriticheskie otryvki*, p. 251.
60. Ibid., p. 246.

never claimed to be the author of the law code, of the decisions of the church assembly of 1551, or of the administrative reform. "If Ivan did anything noteworthy during that time," Pogodin concluded from this, "he surely would not have neglected to speak of it in his letters to Kurbskii, where he tried to brag to him of his exploits." The conquest of Kazan'? "Ivan participated in it to the same extent as in the compilation of the law code and in the church assembly. . . . In the taking of Astrakhan', as in Siberia later on, and in the establishment of trade with England, he took no part whatever. . . . So what remains to Ivan in this so-called brilliant half of his reign?"[61]

Pogodin explains the transition from the "blue" to the "black" period by the machinations of the relatives of the tsaritsa, the Zakhar'ins, who skillfully played on Ivan's wounded self-esteem. He even lets slip an utterly heretical thought (which was not developed): "Was not the war with the Germans in Livonia a clever stratagem of the opposing party [i.e., the Zakhar'ins]?"[62] He refutes not only the opinions of Kurbskii and Karamzin, but also those of Tatishchev, who, it will be remembered, attributed the tsar's failures in his "black" period to the mutinies and treason of the villainous boyars. Pogodin replies that the measures undertaken by Ivan in the period of the Oprichnina had neither sound reasons of state behind them, nor even the most elementary common sense—that the boyars were not fighting against the tsar, and that his terror was therefore purposeless and itself the cause of the "mutinies and treason." "A villain, a beast—a pedantic chatterbox, with the mind of a petty bureaucrat—and that is all. Must it be that such a creature, who had lost the aspect even of a human being, let alone the exalted image of a tsar, should find people to glorify him?"[63]

Kurbskii, three centuries before, and Karamzin after him, had divided the tsar's reign into two periods. Pogodin—and this is his real merit—for the first time compelled historians to doubt the validity of such a division. Russian historiography was thus able to pass from the study of the character of the Terrible Tsar to analysis of the political crisis taking place in Muscovy of that time.

7. *The Political Crisis*

The logical extension of his hypothesis would scarcely have entered Pogodin's mind. Nevertheless, it was a remarkable breach in the

61. Ibid., p. 247.   62. Ibid., p. 256.
63. Cited in Mikhailovskii, pp. 160–61.

traditional model of the Muscovite political system, which presupposed that autocracy *already existed* in Russia in the mid-sixteenth century. For both the advocates and the accusers of Ivan IV, Russian history presented itself as a drama with a single actor surrounded by extras. To Lomonosov and to Ryleev, to Tatishchev and to Karamzin equally, the tsar was, to use Aristotle's terms, the dynamic "form" creating history, the society around him being inert and amorphous "matter." Psychological conflicts and crises could occur in such a system, but not political ones. However, if Pogodin was right, and the tsar did not institute the reforms (if, moreover, he denounced them as the "evil schemes" of "that dog Aleksei [Adashev], your boss"),[64] then who did? In other words, who made history in mid-sixteenth-century Muscovy and where was the autocracy?

Pogodin had not asked these questions, but by focusing on the strange parallel between Kurbskii's position and that of the tsar, he became the first to call attention to the political content of the correspondence, in which we can, perhaps, discern the actual logic of Ivan the Terrible's thinking. The tsar wrote:

> Woe to the city which is governed by many! . . . The rule of many, even if they are strong, brave, and intelligent, but do not have unified power, will be similar to the folly of women. . . . Just as a woman is not able to stick to one decision, but first decides one way and then another, so, if there are many rulers in the kingdom, one will wish one thing and another another. That is why the desires and plans of many people are similar to the folly of women.[65]

Obviously the tsar simply sees no alternative to autocracy but "the rule of many." And oligarchy brings with it the ruin of the country. "Think," he adjures Kurbskii (and, in fact, everyone who was able to read in Muscovy at that time),[66] "what kind of power was established in those countries where the tsars have listened to clerics and advisors, and how those states have fallen into ruin."[67]

Then where but in autocracy is the salvation of Russia? "What do you want," asks the tsar, repeating the thought of Ivan Peresvetov, "—the same thing that happened to the Greeks, who ruined their

64. *Poslaniia Ivana Groznogo*, p. 307.
65. Ibid., p. 299.
66. "The tsar's epistle," Ia. S. Lur'e writes, "is in fact directed least of all to 'Prince Andrei.' This epistle, as we can now say with confidence, was not even formally addressed to 'Prince Andrei.' Its address was 'the entire Russian kingdom'" (ibid., pp. 470–71). In other words, it was an open letter.
67. Ibid., p. 298.

kingdom and were given over to the Turks?"[68] More than this, for the tsar the corrosion of autocracy means not only the ruination of the state, but the ruination of the faith as well—that is, of the hope of eternal life. "And what they do say of godless peoples! Among them, the kings do not own their kingdoms, and as their subjects tell them, so they rule."[69]

One can, of course, look on all this as a clumsy attempt to justify the Oprichnina. But let us examine the political process which took place in the Kremlin in the 1550s, and, from the tsar's point of view, gradually transformed him into the chairman of the council of boyars. First, Adashev and Sil'vestr "began to take counsel with each other in secret from us." Then "Sil'vestr introduced into our council his cothinker, Prince Dimitrii Kurliat'ev . . . and they began . . . to carry out their evil plans." What plans? First of all, according to the tsar, rearrangements of personnel, which led finally to their actually forming a government, "not leaving a single power to which they would not appoint their supporters."[70] In other words, the tsar was gradually deprived of all the key positions in the government, and all the levers of real political power, including even the ancient prerogative of determining the makeup of the supreme state hierarchy: "They deprived us . . . of the right to distribute honors and positions among you, the boyars, and turned this matter to your desire and will." Little by little, Adashev, Sil'vestr, and Kurliat'ev "began to subject you, the boyars, to their will, and taught you to disobey us, and almost *made us equal to you*."[71] Ivan was convinced that they were attempting to turn him into a nominal head of state: "You and the priest decided that I should be the sovereign only in words, and you in fact."[72] Prohibiting the tsar from taking decisions single-handed was a usurpation of his power, and a sacrilegious violation of his "patrimonial" heritage: "You . . . took into your power the state which I had received from God and from my ancestors."[73]

Now we can see how unjust Pogodin was in characterizing this man as a "pedantic chatterbox with the mind of a petty bureaucrat—and that is all." For all his paranoia, the tsar appears to be an intelligent man, not only deeply convinced of the rightness of his position, but perfectly able to articulate it. For all we know, he describes the crisis in the Kremlin quite adequately. According to Kliuchevskii and Sergeevich, the political meaning of the reforms was chiefly reducible to

68. Ibid., p. 294.   69. Ibid., p. 288.

70. Ibid., p. 307. In translation by Lur'e, this reads "not leaving a single place." However, the original says "not leaving a single power."

71. Ibid.   72. Ibid., p. 295.   73. Ibid., p. 288.

two propositions: (a) the Assembly of the Land was to take the lead in improving the administration, which would *in fact* deprive the tsar of his unlimited mandate in the executive field, and (b) Article 98 of the law code deprived him *juridically* of his unlimited mandate in the legislative field. In other words, the latent and informal limitations on power were growing into juridical and institutional ones. But this is precisely what the tsar was trying to express in plain Russian by saying that his power was being replaced by the "rule of many."

The logical extension of Pogodin's hypothesis, whether he would like it or not, is that a political crisis was in full swing in Muscovy at the time of the reforms. Moreover, if we believe the tsar (and I do not know why we should not, inasmuch as Kurbskii, himself a witness, did not object to the claims quoted above), the autocratic tradition faced a grave challenge—if it was not, indeed, losing the game.

Thus, according to the logic of his own hypothesis, Pogodin was wrong in asserting that Ivan's terror was senseless and purposeless. On the contrary, it looks as though terror was the only means by which the autocratic tradition in Russia could avert its ultimate collapse. Nevertheless, Pogodin's contribution to Ivaniana was significant. It could in the 1820s have yielded results to which Ivaniana came only after many tortuous decades. It could have—but it did not.

8. Prolegomena to the Second Epoch

In 1815, a Russian emperor succeeded in doing what had remained an unattainable dream for Ivan the Terrible. He rode into Paris on a white horse as the conqueror of Napoleon, and the Cossacks held their morning promenade on the Champs Elysées. Russia had finally become a world power. Two decades after this, Pogodin could permit himself rhetorical flourishes such as: "I ask you, can anyone contend with us, and whom do we not compel to obedience? Is not the political fate of Europe, and consequently of the world, in our hands, if only we wished to decide it?"[74] The man who was to curse the tyranny of Ivan the Terrible then lauded the autocracy which had brought "the Russian sovereign closer than Charles V or Napoleon to their dream of a universal empire."[75] Was this one reason why in the next phase of pseudodespotism, the Nikolaian, the paths of Ivaniana again grew tortuous?

The following generation of historians became involved in pas-

74. M. P. Pogodin, *Sochineniia*, vol. 4, p. 7.
75. Ibid., p. 10.

sionate arguments between Westernizers and Slavophiles, in abstract disputes about the relations between the "state" and the "land" in Russian history. The second epoch of Ivaniana was destined to carry the dispute about Ivan the Terrible far from Pogodin's hypothesis. In this second epoch, the tsar would find defenders more prestigious than Lomonosov and Tatishchev—defenders who would need the Oprichnina of Ivan the Terrible to bring meaning and order into Russian history. These people would laugh at the bombast of Karamzin and the naivete of Pogodin, supremely confident that where these antediluvian moralists had been defeated, they would succeed in turning history into a science. This epoch was marked by such major names in Russian history as Kavelin and Solov'ev, Aksakov and Khomiakov, Chicherin and Kliuchevskii, who await us in the following chapter.

CHAPTER VIII

THE HYPNOSIS OF
"THE MYTH OF THE STATE"

1. Absolute and Relative Uniqueness

When Kavelin spoke of the "unnatural character of the views" introduced into Russian history by Karamzin he had in mind, among other things, the "impossible task of setting forth Russian history . . . from the point of view of Western European history."[1] In the 1840s, the uniqueness of Russia was the last word in historical scholarship. For the ideologists of Nikolaian autocracy, this conviction seemed natural: nationalism was the official ideology of the "gendarme of Europe." It was also natural for the powerful clan of nationalist dissidents of that time—the Slavophiles. But Kavelin was not one of the Slavophiles: on the contrary, he was perhaps the most influential and prestigious of their opponents, the Westernizers, unless we count Herzen and Belinskii. Belinskii, incidentally, also did not doubt the uniqueness of Russia for a minute. "One of the greatest intellectual achievements of our time consists in the fact," he wrote, "that we have finally understood that Russia has had its own history, not at all similar to the history of any other European state, and that it must be studied and be judged on the basis of itself, and not on the basis of the history of other European peoples which have nothing in common with it."[2] True, Belinskii was not a historian. As the saying is, he ate out of Kavelin's hands. And Kavelin simply could not recall his naive predecessors without a smile: "They looked at the ancient history of Russia from the point of view of the history of all kinds of western and eastern, northern and southern peoples, and no one understood it because it was not in fact like any other history."

Slavophiles and Westernizers stood thus on one and the same ground, proceeded from the same postulate, fought with the same weapon. However, the position of the Slavophiles was stronger, not

1. K. Kavelin, *Sochineniia*, pt. 2, p. 112.
2. V. G. Belinskii, *Sobranie sochinenii v trekh tomakh*, vol. 3, p. 644.

only because it is easier for nationalists to defend the uniqueness of a nation, but also because they, and only they, had at their disposal a fully worked-out theory of the uniqueness of Russia. The Slavophile theory was based on the fact that the overwhelming majority of the population of Russia lived in rural communes, and that the social structure of Russia was therefore based not on private property, as in the West, but on a kind of collective property. The Russian people, as they understood it, was primarily a nonstate people, something like a kin group, a family bound not by political ties, as were the European peoples, but by ties of blood and religion. On the intellectual level, the rationalism of the "Western spirit" was alien to the "Russian spirit." The latter was synthetic and integral in its nature, rather than analytical and one-sided, like its opposite. Accordingly, on the moral level, Russian life was not based on individualism and atheism, but on collectivism and Orthodox faith. The Russian people, the nation-commune, the "land" (as the Slavophiles called the society in contra-distinction to the state), was an independent and self-sufficient civi-lization. What was required of the state was not to interfere in the life of the land, not to violate its integral organic character, but to let it live by its own Russian laws and not by European ones. However, since Peter's time, the state had interfered. It had violated the struc-ture of folk life, corrupting the soul of the land. And since the land had offered resistance, the state had been transformed into a despo-tism, and had established its "yoke over the land." Under these condi-tions, the nonstate nature of the Russian people could be trans-formed into an antistate feeling, which threatened to destroy Russia.

Kavelin regarded this theory with alarm. It seemed to him that by too decisively separating Russia from Europe, the Slavophiles were depriving it of the capacity to develop, and thereby making it essen-tially indistinguishable from Asia. He insistently emphasizes that,

> Our history exhibits a gradual change of forms, not a repetition of them, and consequently it embodies a development, not as in the East, where from the very beginning up to the present day there has been an almost complete repetition of the same thing. . . . In this sense, we are a European people, capable of self-improvement, of development, which does not like . . . to remain for innumerable centuries on the same spot.[3]

But in this case, in what sense are we a non-European people? In what does our uniqueness consist? "All of Russian history is primarily

3. Kavelin, pt. 1, p. 308.

the history *of the state*, political history . . . the political and state element represents up to now the only living aspect of our history,"[4]
Kavelin answers. In other words, if, as distinct from the East, we develop, then as distinct from the West, the moving agent and embodiment of this development among us is the state (and not the land, as the
Slavophiles think). In the West society created the state, and in Russia
the state created society. If we take the state away from Russia, it transforms itself into China. If we take away Ivan the Terrible and Peter, it
"[will] stand for innumerable centuries on the same spot."

In challenging the Slavophiles on their own ground, Kavelin created the so-called "state school" of Russian historiography. Its origins
are to be found in Hegelian theory, but in the debate with the Slavophiles Kavelin modernized and Russified this so radically that he
should perhaps be called the Russian Hegel.

For Hegel, the development of mankind passes through three
phases: the "familial" phase, in which the individual is completely
swallowed up by the kin-collective; the phase of "civil society," in
which the individual is liberated from the bonds of the family and
does not recognize any authority other than himself; and the phase of
the "state," in which a negation of the negative takes place, and the
state establishes harmony between the individual and the collective.
Accepting this triune scheme in principle, Kavelin changes the sequence of phases in it, and also the phases themselves, as applied to
Russia.

First of all, he describes not a model for the development of mankind, but a model for the development of Russian state structure.
This begins with a "clan" phase, in which the country belongs to a single princely clan, which provides it with political unity, but shuns the
"element of the personality." It then passes into the "familial" (or "patrimonial") phase, destined to "destroy the political unity of Russia,"[5]
though still, however, without—as distinct from the phase of "civil society" in Europe—liberating the individual from the bonds of the
family. And, finally, this is replaced by the "state" phase, destined
both to recreate the political unity of the country and to "create the
personality."

Kavelin's theory aimed both at confirming the uniqueness of Russia *and* refuting the Slavophile validation of this uniqueness. On the
one hand, he attaches all of the negative elements in Russian history
(including the disintegration of the state and the denial of the "ele-

4. Ibid., pt. 2, pp. 454–55.
5. Ibid., pt. 1, p. 333.

ment of the personality") to the "familial" phase, dear to the heart of the Slavophiles. On the other hand, the Hegelian phase of "civil society," which showed that in the West the personality existed before the state, is omitted from Russian development. Hence, in Russia, the personality was created by the state. The Western peoples "were destined to develop a historical personality which they had brought with them into a human personality; we were destined to create a personality. For us and for them, the question is posed so dissimilarly that comparison is impossible."[6] I understand how murky such language may seem to a contemporary reader, but this was how they talked at the time.

Both "over there" and "among us," however, it is precisely the state which is the crown of history, its magnificent finale. Neither Hegel nor Kavelin even touches on the question of the political nature of this finale. The state as such, in the abstract—with no political specifications whatever—is for them both the goal of history and its demiurge. Everything which furthers its growth is progressive, all the sacrifices offered it are redeemed; all the crimes committed in its name are justified. The needs of the state (which coincide in some mysterious and inexplicable way with the "element of the personality") become the password which resolves all mysteries, all moral doubts, all contradiction.

And if there were still some holes and inconsistencies in Kavelin's theory, such first-class intellectuals and experts as S. M. Solov'ev, B. N. Chicherin, A. D. Gradovskii, N. P. Pavlov-Sil'vanskii, P. N. Miliukov, and G. V. Plekhanov came to the rescue. They thought up explanations for things which the Russian Hegel was unable to explain, resolved contradictions which he was unable to resolve. To nonspecialists—and to specialists as well—their arguments seemed irresistibly convincing. "Stone," Solov'ev would say,

> —for so mountains were called among us in the old days—stone split up Western Europe into many states. . . . In stone the western men built their nests, and from stone they held possession of the peasants; stone gave them independence, but soon the peasants also began to surround themselves with stone and to gain freedom and independence; everything firm, everything definite is thanks to stone. . . . On the gigantic eastern plain there is no stone . . . and therefore, there is one state of unheard-of extent. Here men have no place to build themselves stone nests. . . . The cities consist of wooden cottages; one spark, and in

6. Ibid., p. 321.

their place—a pile of ashes. . . . Hence the ease with which the ancient Russian abandoned his house. . . . and hence the striving of the government to catch and settle down and attach the people [to the land].[7]

"It is enough to look at its [Russia's] geographical position, at the huge areas over which the scanty population is scattered," Chicherin would say,

> and anyone will understand that life here must develop not so much the element of rights . . . as the element of power, which alone can fuse the inconceivable distances and the scattered population into a single political body. . . . The social structure which in the West was established of its own accord by the activity of the society . . . in Russia received existence from the state.[8]

"In studying the culture of any Western European state," Miliukov would say, "we have had to proceed from the economic system first to the social structure and only then to the organization of the state; relative to Russia it will be more convenient to take the reverse order [since] among us the state had a huge influence on the organization of the society, whereas in the West social organization determined the structure of the state."[9]

"The basic element of the structure of Russian society during the Muscovite period was the complete subordination of the personality to the interests of the state," Pavlov-Sil'vanskii would say. "The external circumstances of the life of Muscovite Rus', its stubborn struggle for existence . . . demanded extreme exertion from the people. . . . All classes of the population were attached to service or to the tax rolls."[10]

"In order to defend its existence in the struggle with opponents, economically far superior to it," Plekhanov would write,

> it [Russia] had to devote to the cause of self-defense . . . a share of its strength which certainly was far greater than the share used for the same purpose by the population of the Eastern despotisms. [If we compare] the sociopolitical structure of the Muscovite state with the structure of the Western European countries [and the Eastern despotisms], we will obtain the following result: this state differed from the Western ones by the fact that it enserfed to itself not only the lower agricultural, but also the upper service class, and from the Eastern ones, to whom it

7. S. M. Solov'ev, *Istoriia Rossii*, bk. 3, p. 664.
8. B. N. Chicherin, *O narodnom predstavitel'stve*, pp. 524–25.
9. P. N. Miliukov, *Ocherki* . . . , pp. 113–14.
10. N. P. Pavlov-Sil'vanskii, *Gosudarevy sluzhilye liudi* . . . , p. 223.

was very similar in this regard, by the fact that it was compelled to place a far more severe yoke on its enserfed population.[11]

All of these people argued fiercely among themselves. Some asserted that in Russia there was no feudalism, and others that there was. Some said that stone and wood lay at the basis of the political difference between Europe and Russia, and others denied this, pointing to the "woodenness" of medieval London and the "stoniness" of medieval Novgorod. Some said that Russia was "struggling for its existence" with its eastern neighbors, and others that it struggled with its western ones. However, despite their arguments, they all came out of Kavelin's school—in the sense that none of them had challenged his fundamental thesis that the Russian state, in the form in which it developed historically (i.e., the serf-holding autocracy), was the *sole possible form of the state under the given historical* (geographical, demographic, ecological, or economic, depending on inclination) *conditions*.

A wooden country with sparse population, scattered over a relatively infertile plain; a poor country, which had dozed away its youth in the "familial" phase, and had not developed a "historical personality," and had been the "patrimony" of its princes; a country like a besieged fortress, surrounded on all sides by enemies, which struggled for its national survival unceasingly over the course of centuries. What kind of state could develop here, other than serf-holding autocracy? *There was no alternative* to this autocracy. And therefore—however cruel and terrible it may have been—it embodied progress.

These writers did their job inventively and with brilliance. The conceptions they presented were remarkably well-ordered and artistically perfect. Only one reproach can be leveled at them: they were proving what was required to be proved by the assignment Kavelin had set for them in 1846, which was not to explain why serf-holding autocracy was the form of the Russian state structure, but why this autocracy was *historically necessary*.

2. A Symbol of Progress

It is not hard to guess that it was precisely at the fatal intersection between the "state" and the "familial" phases that Ivan the Terrible found his place in Kavelin's theory. It is also clear that boyardom occupied the negative pole of it (as the defender of obsolete "patrimonial" relationships), and the tsar the positive (as the first defender of the national state structure and of the "element of personality"). For

11. G. V. Plekhanov, *Sochineniia*, vol. 20, pp. 87–88.

Kavelin, the tsar became a key figure—the first step of progress on Russian earth. Could one, in the circumstances, resist the temptation of comparing him with Peter the Great? Kavelin could not. His pen distinguished "two extremely great figures of Russian history—Ivan IV and Peter the Great." And why not, indeed, if "both of them perceived with equal vividness the idea of the state and were its most noble and worthy representatives? . . . Separated by an entire century . . . they are remarkably similar . . . in the tendency of their activities. Both of them pursued the same goals. They are connected by some sympathy. Peter the Great deeply respected Ivan IV, called him his model and placed him higher than himself."

What did the similar nature of their "tendencies" consist of, in practical terms? Kavelin explains: Ivan the Terrible

> *wished to do away completely with the high nobility* and to surround himself with commoners, and even people of low birth, who were devoted, and willing to *serve him and the state* with no ulterior motives or personal calculations whatever. In 1565 he established the Oprichnina. This institution, slandered by its contemporaries and not understood by posterity, . . . was the first attempt to create a service elite and *to substitute it for the hereditary nobility*—to put the element of personal dignity in place of the element of blood and kinship in the administration of the state: a thought which later was carried out by Peter the Great in other forms.[12]

All of the three whales on which Kavelin's universe rests are revealed in this quotation with remarkable clarity. In the first place, the interests of the state are identified with the interests of the tsar (this, according to Aristotle, is the definition of tyranny). In the second place, the hereditary nobility is looked upon as the basic hindrance to the triumph of the "idea of the state," and as a barrier in the path of progress (and progress is therefore impossible without liquidation of the social limitations on power). In the third place, the interests of the "people" are identified with the interests of the tsar-state and the "new class" is presented as a bearer of "personal dignity." Speaking in my terms, the general direction of Russian history, according to Kavelin, is the transformation of absolutism into despotism, which is supposed to be the decisive condition for progress.

Remember that Kavelin wrote in 1846, at the height of the Nikolaian phase of "pseudodespotism," when the results of the work of both "extremely great leaders" were evident. The Slavophiles summarized the state of the nation as follows:

12. Kavelin, pt. 1, pp. 355, 362. Emphasis added.

> The current condition of Russia presents a picture of internal disarray covered by a conscienceless lie. . . . Everyone lies to each other, sees this, continues to lie, and no one knows how it will end . . . And on this internal disarray . . . there has grown up a conscienceless flattery, which assures people of its well being . . . the universal corruption and weakening of the morals in society has reached huge proportions . . . here we see the immorality of the entire internal structure. . . . The entire evil proceeds from the oppressive system of our government . . . the yoke of the state has been established over the land . . . the governmental system . . . which makes a slave of its subjects [has created in Russia] a type of police state.[13]

Let us add to this that the "people" was truly oppressed by serfdom, which had reached the stage of slavery, and in addition to everything else, there was no trace left of the "service elite," for the sake of whose establishment the "extremely great leaders" had so cruelly terrorized the country. It had been transformed in some way, inexplicable at least to Kavelin, into a "hereditary nobility," as if neither Ivan the Terrible nor Peter the Great had existed. Furthermore, it now took a form considerably worse than the Muscovite boyardom—that of a slave-holding aristocracy. In other words, if the path to progress and to the triumph of the personality lay precisely in the destruction of the "great lords," then by the mid-nineteenth century even a blind man must have seen that this path had ended in a cul-de-sac.

Indeed, Kavelin writes as though he were living not in a real police state, but in an imaginary country where there is neither slavery nor a new "hereditary nobility" and a boorish uprooting of the "personality," and as if the power of the Russian state redeemed and justified all of this. How does this differ from the position of Lomonosov and Tatishchev, which led to the first "historiographic nightmare"? The forerunners of the "state school" wrote all of this openly, nakedly. Kavelin's conception was intended to put rouge and powder on the ugly mug of autocracy and to hide it under the civilized wig of "the element of the personality," to make it acceptable to the progressives and liberals of the mid-nineteenth century. In spite of all its arrogance, the scholarship of the time did not demand comparison, analysis, and evaluation of the "state structure" of Ivan the Terrible according to its real results in the surrounding world. It was content with abstract analogies and symbolic parallels.[14] Between it and reality there lay an abyss.

13. *Teoriia gosudarstva u slavianofilov*, pp. 38, 39, 37, 9.
14. Otherwise how are we to explain the fact that Kavelin, guided by such a criterion of progress as "the complete destruction of the nobility," equally glorifies Ivan the

This permits us to make an approach to answering the question of how Kavelin was able to convince almost the entire Russian historiography of his time that he was right. In part, as we have seen, this is certainly explained by his opposition to Slavophilism. Kavelin introduced into Russian historiography the category of progress, and, to use his own words, represented "Russian history as a developing organism, a living whole, penetrated by a single spirit."[15] He was the only one who was, so to speak, able to contrast the Slavophile theory of the absolute uniqueness of Russia to a theory of its relative uniqueness. He introduced, too, a new and tragic dimension into the evaluation of Tsar Ivan's epoch. Whereas before Kavelin this epoch seemed the tragedy of the country, under his pen it appeared as the tsar's tragedy. From the "villain and beast with the mind of a petty bureaucrat," he was transformed into the lonely hero of classical antiquity, fearlessly throwing down a challenge to inescapable fate. Let us see how Kavelin does this.

Ancient, pre-Ivanian Rus' is presented as immersed in a way of life based on kinship. "There were no profound demands for another order of things, and where were they to come from? The personality, which is the sole fruitful soil for any moral development, had not yet emerged; it was suppressed by relationships of blood."[16] Tsar Ivan strove to arouse the country from the dangerous slumber which condemned it to eternal stagnation. What did he not do toward this end! He "destroyed the local rulers and placed the entire local administration under the complete control of the communes themselves."[17] This did no good. The boyars, excluded from local administration, concentrated themselves in the center, in Moscow. "The Duma was in their hands; they alone were its members."[18] The tsar tried to exclude them from the center. "The goal [of his reforms] was the same: to break the power of the great lords, and to give power and great scope to the state alone."[19] For this purpose, "All the major branches of the administration were entrusted to secretaries: they headed the government departments; the great lords were almost completely excluded from civil affairs."[20] Later, the tsar went after them in the Duma itself, "and introduced into it the new element of *personal* dig-

---

Terrible, who routed this nobility, and Catherine II who restored it? After all, they were working in opposite directions—from the point of view of Kavelin's criterion. They were united by another criterion of progress—also one of Kavelin's: the expansion of the might of the Russian state. The problem, however, lies in the fact that these two criteria contradict each other, which Kavelin does not even notice.

15. Kavelin, pt. 1, p. 310.   16. Ibid., p. 357.   17. Ibid., p. 361.
18. Ibid., p. 362.   19. Ibid., p. 361.   20. Ibid., pp. 361–62.

nity."[21] Again nothing happens: the tsar cannot appoint whomever he wants to whatever post he likes; the boyar tradition blocks his path, binds his hands, and nullifies all his efforts. There is no one who understands the tsar's grand design. There are no institutions: "The communes, however much Ivan tried to revive them for their own good, were dead; there was no public spirit in them because the former quasi-patriarchal way of life was continuing there."[22] Alas, the great tsar lived in an "unhappy time when no reform was capable of improving our way of life."[23] "Ivan sought for organs to implement his thoughts and did not find them; there was nowhere to take them from. . . . The elements for a better order of things did not yet exist in society itself."[24] How did this struggle end?

> Ivan lost his strength, finally, under the burden of a dull and quasi-patriarchal environment, which had already become meaningless, and in which he was fated to live and act. Struggling with it to the death over many years, and seeing no results, he lost faith in the possibility of realizing his great thoughts. Then life became for him an unbearable burden, a ceaseless torment, he became a hypocrite, a tyrant, and a coward. Ivan IV fell so far precisely because he was great.[25]

Do you see now where Belinskii's "fallen angel" came from? Do we not have before us a tragedy worthy of the pen of Shakespeare and Cervantes? A courageous Don Quixote, fatigued by the struggle with patriarchal dragons, is against his will transformed in the end into Macbeth—and since the role of Lady Macbeth is played by History herself, he is worthy not only of our sympathy but also of admiration. Furthermore, the mysterious dualism of the personality, which so tormented Shcherbatov and Karamzin, now receives both explanation and justification: the more bestialities Tsar Macbeth committed in his fall, the greater Tsar Don Quixote was at the height of his powers and hopes. From now on, the bestialities bear witness to greatness.

The jeremiads of Pogodin, based on simple common sense, could not compete with this monumental apologia, which transformed the mystery of the terrible tsar from an empirical problem into the fulcrum of the state and progress. The debate transcended historiography and acquired a philosophical significance affecting the very foundations of the individual Russian's weltanschauung. The concept of the nation-state was contrasted to the concept of the nation-family. The Slavophile "nation" was represented as a symbol of stagnation, Asiatic quietism, eternal marching in place, and cultural death. If you

21. Ibid., p. 362.   22. Ibid., p. 363.   23. Ibid., p. 361.
24. Ibid., p. 363.   25. Ibid., pp. 355–56.

are for the movement of History—so Kavelin persuaded his reader—
if you are for life and against death, then you are for the founder of
the Russian state, Ivan the Terrible, and you are for his Oprichnina.
The lamentations of moralists, like Karamzin, the slanders of reactionaries, like Pogodin, and the protests of advocates of stagnation,
the Slavophiles, cannot conceal the fact that progress in Russia owes
its existence to the state, and the state to the Oprichnina, and the
Oprichnina to Ivan the Terrible. Thus, for the second time in Russian
historiography, Ivan was transformed from a tsar-tormentor into a
hero, and—what is more important—into a symbol of Russian power.
But if the sentimental eighteenth century was content with this, for
the positivist nineteenth he became the symbol of progress as well.

3. The "Historical Necessity" of the Oprichnina

Kavelin developed only the points of departure for the construct
which Solov'ev clothed with flesh in his gigantic, multivolume *History
of Russia*. Of course, Solov'ev digressed from Kavelin's abstract models. Many things were dictated to him by the living material of history
which Kavelin allowed himself to disregard. Solov'ev had arrived independently at the contrast between the kin-based (old) order and
the state-based (new) order as early as his doctoral dissertation, *A History of the Relations Between the Russian Princes of the House of Riurik*,
published in 1847. True, Solov'ev's conception of this was oversimplified and primitive in comparison to Kavelin's. As originally formulated, it would have been easily destroyed by Pogodin, Solov'ev's former mentor, and subsequently his eternal enemy. Nevertheless, the
fact that the two conceptions were essentially the same shows once
again how much the air of Nikolaian Russia was infected by apologia
for Ivan the Terrible.

In his dissertation, Solov'ev's thesis was so marked by special plead-
ing that even Kavelin, in a review which took up 123 pages in three
issues of *Sovremennik* [*Contemporary*] (that is the kind of review they
wrote in those days!) was compelled to reproach him, even though
affectionately, with "a certain prejudice . . . in favor of Ivan the Terrible."[26] Solov'ev declared that,

> the opportunity of [free] departure, which was seen by some as a right
> . . . and by others as a sacred custom and tradition . . . was defended by
> the old society with all its strength against the state strivings of the Mus-
> covite grand princes, *who justly saw in it absurdity, lawlessness, treason*. This

26. Ibid., pt. 2, p. 597.

is the meaning of the struggle which began long ago in Northern Rus' but . . . reached its extreme point under . . . Ivan IV. If it is just to say, as many do, that Ivan IV was obsessed with treason, then at the same time it must be admitted that the old society was obsessed with [the right of] departure and free movement.[27]

"From these words it is clear how accurately the author views the significance of Ivan in Russian history," Kavelin comments. "We have not yet read anything about Ivan which so profoundly satisfied us."[28] And a little further on: "In Mr. Solov'ev, Ivan IV has found a worthy advocate for our time."[29]

In fact, the "right of departure," which in the fourteenth century had still been a precious guarantee for boyardom against the tyranny of princes, had long since lost its significance by the time of Ivan IV. The boyardom at that time was concerned with quite other problems. It was the peasantry for whom the right of departure had truly fateful significance in the mid-sixteenth century. Ivan III's St. George's Day, which was the legislative guarantee of this right, was now at stake. And for this reason its abolition, which Solov'ev depicts as a necessity of state, signified in plain language the enserfment of the peasants. And although Solov'ev does not say a word about the peasantry, he understands very well that it was by no means accidental that the "old society" was "obsessed with the right of departure." "Ivan IV," he says, "was not arming himself only against the boyars, for it was not only the boyars who were infected with the long-standing disease of old Russian society—the passion for movement and departure."[30] And Kavelin raises no fundamental objection to this. In other words, sympathy with the "necessity of state" proved so great in their liberal hearts that before it all other considerations, including hatred for slavery and revulsion against tyranny, retreated into second place. For Solov'ev, Kurbskii is, of course, the "advocate . . . of the ancient claims of the retainers, brought by them from ancient Rus'—[claims] to the custom of counselorship and to the right of free departure"— while Ivan the Terrible, full of "bright thoughts of state" and "clarity of political vision," displays "the great mind of a tsar . . . indefatigable activity . . . and judgment."[31]

27. S. M. Solov'ev, *Istoriia otnoshenii mezhdu russkimi kniaziami Riurikova doma*, p. 597. Emphasis added.

28. K. Kavelin, pt. 2, pp. 597, 596.

29. Ibid., p. 610.

30. Solov'ev, *Istoriia otnoshenii . . .* , p. 597.

31. Ibid., pp. 656, 645–46, 678.

For all that, Solov'ev was a historian. In his dissertation, he discussed the time of Tsar Ivan only in a concluding chapter, a kind of appendix, essentially unconnected to the basic theme, and he spoke of it on the basis primarily of the tsar's correspondence with Kurbskii. He still had to familiarize himself with the sources. And this was a terrible trial, which not even such principled adherents of autocracy as Karamzin and Pogodin were able to withstand. When, many years after Solov'ev, the remarkable Russian poet Aleksei Tolstoi familiarized himself with the sources, he admitted that as he read them the pen fell from his hand—not only because, as he wrote, such a monster as Ivan the Terrible could exist on Russian soil, but also because there could exist a society that could gaze upon him without indignation. Even so passionate an advocate of Ivan the Terrible as the well-known late-nineteenth-century reactionary from Khar'kov, Professor K. Iarosh, was compelled to admit, in reading the *Sinodik*—that is, the memorial to the victims of the Oprichnina, compiled at the order of the tsar himself—that,

> Blood spurted everywhere in fountains, and Russian cities and villages gave voice to groans. . . . With a trembling hand we turn the pages of the famous *Sinodik*, and pause with a particularly heavy feeling at the short and eloquent notations: let the Lord remember the soul of thy slave So-and-so—"with his mother, and his wife, and his son, and his daughter." [32]

S. B. Veselovskii, apparently a religious man, was shaken for his entire life by another aspect of the matter:

> The physical cruelty of the torturers and executioners seemed to Tsar Ivan insufficient, and he . . . resorted to extreme measures. . . . which, for the victims and their contemporaries, were more terrible than physical pain or even death, since they struck the soul for all eternity. So that the person would not have time to repent and make his final arrangements, he was killed suddenly. So that his body would not receive the benefits of Christian burial, it was chopped into pieces, pushed under the ice, or thrown out to be eaten by dogs, birds of prey, or wild beasts, the relatives and strangers being forbidden to bury it. In order to deprive the person of hope for the salvation of his soul, he was deprived of memorialization. [33]

32. K. Iarosh, *Psikhologicheskaia parallel'*, p. 31.
33. S. B. Veselovskii, *Issledovaniia* . . . , p. 336. True, in moments of repentance, the tsar ordered that the names of those of his victims who could be remembered be written down. But this was by no means always possible. Hence notations in the *Sinodik* of the type: "Remember, Lord, 50 [or 40 or 100] souls who perished in such-and-such

Not only to kill, but to exterminate your posterity to the last person, so that there should be no one to pray for your soul; not only to torment you here in this world, but to condemn you to eternal torment beyond the grave: such was the everyday practice of Kavelin's hero. And even with the all-saving "necessity of state," it was difficult to justify it, at least in the eyes of a person with a spark of humane instinct. Solov'ev simply could not keep consistently to Kavelin's abstract logic. "It is strange, to say the least, to see the historical explanation of phenomena confused with moral justification of them," he exclaimed.

> Ivan cannot be justified. . . . A person of flesh and blood, he was not aware of the moral and spiritual means for establishing law and order . . . instead of healing he intensified the disease, and accustomed us still more to tortures, the stake, the gallows. He sowed terrible seeds, and the harvest was terrible—the murder of his older son by his own hand, the killing of the younger one at Uglich, and the horrors of the Time of Troubles! Let not the historian pronounce a word in justification of such a person.[34]

It is all the more sickening, after this, to read the cold, mechanical reasoning of our contemporary I. I. Smirnov about the "inevitability of the Oprichnina terror," and the "objective necessity for physical extermination of the most prominent representatives of the hostile princely and boyar clans."[35] Unlike Solov'ev, Smirnov shows no awareness of the moral indecency of a policy which has the goal of physically exterminating people holding dissident opinions. Nonetheless, the idea of the "objective necessity" of the Oprichnina was introduced into Smirnov's mind by Solov'ev himself. By this logic, if the Oprichnina actually was the sole possible means of shaping the Russian state in the face of the treachery and rabid opposition of the forces of reaction surrounding the tsar, then the question is essentially solved, and one is left to argue only about the means. Solov'ev does not like terror as a means, but Smirnov does: it is just that he is not sentimental. On the same analogy, a historian who argued that Soviet Russia in the 1930s was indeed saturated with treason, that all the higher personnel of the country were conspiring against the state, and that the enserfment of the peasantry in the course of collectivization and the attachment of blue- and white-collar workers to their

---

votchina in such-and-such village." Unfortunately, moments of repentance were succeeded by new attacks of royal fury and, consequently, new hecatombs of nameless victims.

34. Solov'ev, *Istoriia Rossii* . . . , bk. 3, p. 713.

35. I. I. Smirnov, *Ivan Groznyi*, p. 93.

jobs was "historically necessary" to the survival of the state would be compelled to "justify morally" total terror and the GULAG. It seems that Veselovskii was right when he observed ironically that "all of Solov'ev's conclusions are reducible to the following reasoning: on the one hand, we cannot help recognizing, and on the other, we cannot help admitting." [36]

4. The Capitulation of Slavophilism

After Kavelin and Solov'ev, the second epoch of Ivaniana proceeded in three directions, the revisionist, the apologetic, and the "accidental." The first tried to offer resistance to the "myth of the state," which had suddenly evolved to the point of fetishism. The second directly developed the apologetic tendency of Kavelin, while decisively ridding itself of Solov'ev's tormenting moral doubts. The third tried to reduce the Oprichnina to a detail which, though monstrous, was random and nonessential. For our purposes, the most interesting figure in the first tendency was Konstantin Aksakov; in the second, Evgenii Belov; and in the third, Vasilii Kliuchevskii. The rest of this chapter will deal basically with them.

The revisionist tendency of Ivaniana was represented by the Moscow Slavophiles of the nineteenth century. Much has been written about them. Nevertheless, their political position seems strange, not to say exotic. How is one to react to people who saw the greatest evil in any kind of constitution, and, generally, in any attempt at juridical limitation on state power, and at the same time fought valiantly for unlimited freedom? "Unlimited power to the tsar; unlimited freedom of life and spirit to the people; freedom of action and law to the tsar, freedom of opinion and expression to the people." [37]

In fact, Slavophilism is not, in the broadest sense, a specifically Russian phenomenon, let alone one belonging exclusively to the nineteenth century. Wherever autocracy prevails, or autocratic tendencies predominate—whether France in the 1770s or Iran in the 1970s, ancient China or contemporary Russia—at the opposite pole there arises something like Slavophilism. And the power of this "Slavophilism" is directly proportionate to the power of the autocratic tendencies. Superficially, "Slavophilism" (in this broader sense) is a desperate attempt to organize a political structure in accordance with religious dogma, whether this be Russian Orthodoxy, Confucianism, or Islam. However, its true nucleus is not so much the Gospels, the

36. S. B. Veselovskii, p. 23.
37. K. S. Aksakov, *Sochineniia istoricheskie*, vol. 1, p. 284.

Koran, or some other religious revelation, as a completely secular *tra-dition* which presupposes that an ideal society existed at some time in the past and was then deformed by an autocratic catastrophe analo-gous to the Biblical flood. Thus, the essence of "Slavophilism" is a ro-mantic belief that, having stripped away the false upper stratum of modern political reality, we will find the eternal and immutable core of Absolute Good—free from the corrupt politicians with their artifi-cial laws and stupid constitutions, free in short from all the "cunnings of reason," as Hegel had it. We can see this belief equally clearly in Confucius and Baudeau, in Homeini and Solzhenitsyn.

Let us remember that at approximately the same time—around 500 B.C.—there evolved at the opposite ends of the known world two opposed world-views. The culture of the ancient Greek polis de-veloped the classical concept of the law as a political limitation on power—a means of *control by the system over the administration*. The cul-ture of the ancient Chinese city-states developed the concept of *Fa*—of the law as a means of legalization of the arbitrary conduct of the government, or, in other words, of *control by the administration over the system*. Only by understanding this fundamental difference can we ap-preciate the revulsion which Confucius felt for *Fa*, in contrasting to it *Li*—the traditional system of moral and cultural values. Paradoxical as it may sound, the first historical variety of "Slavophilism" was thus, from my point of view, early Confucianism.

Was it by accident that in the middle of the eighteenth century, when Montesquieu predicted that France was slipping irreversibly into the abyss of despotism, there was a trend of thought one of whose representatives, the Abbé Bodeaux, considered the Chinese empire to be the ideal monarchy, contrasting it to ancient Greek de-mocracy whose "chronicles present only a horrible spectacle of horri-ble violations against the peace and happiness of mankind"?[38]

Confucianism as a form of absolutist opposition had practically ceased to exist as early as the 2nd century B.C. On this basis we can hypothesize, without even addressing the specialized works, that the period from the 5th to the 2nd century B.C. in China was an epoch of fierce struggle between *Fa* and *Li*—that is, between autocratic and ab-solutist cultures—which ended with the complete defeat and dissolu-tion of early Confucianism in a uniform and lifeless *Fa* culture.[39]

French history of the eighteenth century presents an analogous

38. Cited in E. V. Tarle, *Padenie absoliutizma*, p. 99.
39. V. Rubin, *Ideologiia i kul'tura drevnego Kitaia*, p. 84. The conception of the destiny of the doctrine of Confucius given here is that of the author of this book, which is re-markable in many respects.

model, but with the opposite result. After the collapse of the Turgot government in the remarkable two-year period 1774–76, which showed the utopian nature of the absolutist opposition, France responded to the autocratic tendencies with a revolution.

In other words, in the Far East, the collision between *Fa* and *Li* led to the fruitless triumph of despotism; in the West, it led to revolution; and on the gigantic Eurasian continent of Russia, to a symbiosis of both cultures, which over the course of centuries generated Slavophilism. For this reason, what turned out to be only a passing episode in the political history of France and China, survived all reforms and revolutions in Russia.

For nineteenth-century Russian Slavophiles, monarchy was the natural, traditional form of political organization; on the other hand, "freedom of life and of the spirit" (or what I would call latent limitations on power) was also sanctified by tradition. The problem of the ideal political structure consequently consisted not in destroying the original harmony of both traditions in order to achieve constitutional limitations on power, but, on the contrary, in preserving their mutual trust and harmony. How was this to be done? Just as it was done in a family or in a peasant commune. Did children or peasants seek constitutional limitations on the power of the father or head man? Could a constitution be a real guarantee against the abuse of power, whether in a family, in a commune, or in a nation? Who would guarantee this guarantee?

"Look at the West," exclaimed Aksakov, "the peoples . . . have begun to believe in the possibility of a perfect government and have made up republics and devised constitutions . . . and have become poor in spirit. . . . [The societies] are ready to collapse . . . at any moment."[40] In a fatal fit of mindlessness, the European peoples had destroyed what Confucius called *Li*, and what Aksakov called "the union between the land and the state." The price exacted for this would be terrible. Nihilism and anarchy, general hostility and distrust, enfeeblement and degradation awaited the West. What was the major task of the Russian state from this point of view? Did it not consist in closing tight the doors of its fortress and not permitting into the country the fatal infection of Western civilization? The Russian state in the person of Peter I acted in precisely the opposite way. Thus the "government [was] separated from the people and made alien to it."[41] The "yoke of the state over the land" was established and "the Russian land became, as it were, conquered, and the state the con-

40. *Teoriia gosudarstva u slavianofilov*, p. 31.
41. Ibid., p. 38.

querer. The Russian monarch took on the status of a despot, and the free subject people, the status of a captive slave."[42] As Aksakov explains it: "The state accomplished a coup d'etat, dissolved the alliance with the land and subordinated it to itself."[43]

How was Russia to be purified of pollution and return to the national tradition? The reader will probably not be surprised now to learn that the political recommendations of the Slavophiles coincided word for word with the "political dream" of Prince Kurbskii and the author of *The Conversation of Valaam*—the calling of an Assembly of the Land with which "the tsar could every day take counsel as to the affairs of the realm." The nineteenth-century descendants of the medieval oppositionists, trained in Europe (which they cursed in contemporary philosophical language, invoking Schelling and attacking Hegel), proposed the same thing as their slandered ancestors. More than this, in 1881 they were literally a step from a repetition of 1549. Only the Oprichniki of a new tyrant (this time Alexander III) prevented their dream from becoming a political fact.

Despite their new philosophical ammunition, Aksakov's Slavophiles proved weaker than their medieval ancestors. The "myth of the state" was an apologia for despotism, which they should have rebelled against and revised. But like their twentieth-century descendents, the new Russian right (Solzhenitsyn being a best example), they counterposed to the "myth of the state" not analysis but a myth of their own, which I would call the "myth of the land." And just as the modern Slavophiles appeal from the alien Marxist state to the prerevolutionary "enlightened authoritarianism" of the tsars, their predecessors appealed from the alien police state of the tsars to the "enlightened authoritarianism" of pre-Petrine Russia. And again, like the modern Slavophiles, who associate the origin of autocracy, i.e., serfdom and despotism, with Lenin, their predecessors, contrary to facts generally known, connected the origins of serfdom and despotism not with the time of Ivan the Terrible but with that of Peter. How indeed could Russians have enslaved their compatriots when the "land" was still firmly closed to the penetration of Western influences? As far as the myth was concerned, serfdom and despotism simply could not exist in Russia before Peter.

If Ivan the Terrible, who had no smell of Europeanism about him, had appeared after Peter, everything would have been all right, but he preceded Peter. The Slavophiles accordingly declared the Oprich-

---

42. *Rannie slavianofily*, p. 86.
43. Aksakov, p. 50.

nina to be, as it were, the first draft of an attempt to break up the union of the land with the state, a kind of rehearsal for the Petrine coup d'etat. But this meant that the Petrine catastrophe was not a freak of fate, that long before Peter, without any alien influences, the national tradition had showed such deep crevices as to compel one to doubt the very existence of the union between the land and the state. Here the Slavophiles turned to the saving "human formula" of the first epoch of Ivaniana. Kavelin had been the first to resort to it when he wrote of Ivan and Peter that "both of them were equally keenly aware of the idea of the state . . . but Ivan was aware of it as a poet, and Peter the Great as a man of primarily practical concerns. In the first, imagination predominated, and in the second, the will."[44] The Slavophiles tried to pay him back in his own coin. Yes, Ivan was an "artistic nature," they agreed. His acts were therefore dictated not by reason, for which Kavelin and Solov'ev praised him, but by the play of imagination. He was impulsive; he uttered good and evil, without plan or comprehension or system. And in the process of this spontaneous amateur artistic activity he among other things accidentally hit upon the institution of the "police state." This was the way the Slavophiles tried to avoid the connection between Ivan and Peter which was fatal for their myth, and which Kavelin emphasized.

Is it surprising, after this, that the Slavophiles had nothing essentially to say in reply to Kavelin? Their revisionism was destined to choke on the same sentimental indignation toward the "fierce bloodsucker" with which we are already familiar from the works of Karamzin. This was obvious from their first sally—the article by M. Z. K. . . . (the pseudonym of Iu. Samarin) "On the Historical and Literary Opinions of the Journal *Sovremennik*" in Pogodin's magazine *Moskvitianin*. "In [Kavelin's] words," wrote Samarin,

> a thought which is offensive to human dignity emerges without his knowing it . . . namely that there are times when a man of genius cannot help becoming a monster and when the corruption of his contemporaries . . . absolves the person who is aware of it from the obligations of the moral law, or at least reduces his guilt to the point where his descendants can only sympathize with him, and the heavy burden of responsibility for his crimes is unloaded onto the heads of his victims.[15]

Those psychological exercises were laughable to a diehard like Kavelin. He had come too far from the sentimental epoch of Karamzin.

44. Kavelin, pt. 1, p. 355.
45. Iu. Samarin, "O mneniiakh *Sovremennika* istoricheskikh i literaturnykh," p. 163.

"This is not an argument against me," he parried carelessly. "One must intentionally close one's eyes in order not to see that history is filled with such situations offensive to human dignity."[46] And he condescendingly added, "From the horror of that period there remains to us the cause of Ivan, and it shows how much higher he was than his contemporaries."[47] The polemic proceeded in this key. The Slavophiles read moral sermons to the "statists," who haughtily rejected them. Solov'ev contemptuously called the Slavophiles "Buddhists" in history. And, as though recognizing their impotence, the latter tried to avoid the theme of Ivan the Terrible. In their extensive historiographic legacy, we do not even find articles especially devoted to him, let alone books. There was no counterattack—only partisan raids, powerless against the regular army of the state school. Just as the conservative absolutist opposition had capitulated before Ivan the Terrible in the sixteenth century, so its heirs and successors capitulated before his apologists three hundred years later.

5. The "Old" and the "New"

The representatives of the apologistic tendency reveal their school by open glorification of their teachers. S. Gorskii, who in Kazan' wrote a fat book, *The Life and Historical Significance of Prince A. M. Kurbskii* (the sole monograph on the patriarch of the Russian opposition, which unfortunately is sadly reminiscent of a poor joke), writes as follows: "Not taking upon myself the boldness to claim complete independence for my work, I will say openly that the works of Messrs. Solov'ev, Kavelin, and other prominent figures in the field of native history have guided me."[48] In fact, Gorskii has a single idea on his mind, one let fall by Solov'ev in the sixth volume of his *History of Russia*. It would hardly be worthwhile discussing, were it not that it became the leitmotif of all the subsequent apologetics for Ivan the Terrible. Certainly, the apologists make every effort to conceal their relationship to the most stupid of the reactionaries of the last century (as a rule they do not even mention Gorskii's book), but their language irrefutably betrays them:

> Ivan was concerned that the idea of the state should triumph over the elements opposed to it, and wished to see it prevail in Russian society, because he saw in it the guarantee of the glory and prosperity of the

46. Kavelin, pt. 1, p. 410.
47. Ibid., p. 412.
48. S. Gorskii, *Zhizn' i istoricheskoe znachenie kniazia A. M. Kurbskogo*, p. 15.

fatherland. . . . This idea placed Ivan above the conceptions of the century; it raised him to a height inaccessible to his contemporaries, and therefore it is not surprising that they . . . began a life-and-death struggle with Ivan. . . . *The old* does not give way to *the new* without a struggle. . . . Boyardom strove to retain *the old.* This was chiefly what the ideology of boyardom consisted of. . . . The epoch of the creation of the Russian national state appears before us as a time of acute and tense struggle: *of the old and the new.*[49]

Gorskii wrote only part of this passage. The rest is the inalienable property of our distinguished contemporaries, D. S. Likhachev and I. I. Smirnov, and was published a century after the appearance of Gorskii's book. The reader will perhaps succeed in finding an essential difference in these quotations; I did not.

Asking whom we are to believe in the dispute between the tsar "standing on an inaccessible height," and the traitor making a brave front abroad, Gorskii answers, "It is better to believe a tsar than a traitor who is unscrupulously slandering his sovereign."[50] But what was simple for a primitive monarchist (who was, furthermore, a captive of the stereotypes of the "state school") becomes complicated for our contemporaries. And for that matter, for Gorskii's own contemporaries it was far from clear-cut. As Kurbskii's nineteenth-century successor, Aleksandr Herzen, who also fled his country and struggled in exile against its autocracy, explained: "We are not slaves to our love for our country, any more than we are slaves to anything else. A free person cannot admit a dependence on his native land which would compel him to participate in matters contrary to his conscience."[51]

Here we touch upon the most sensitive spot in Ivaniana. The "myth of the state" arose in the epoch of Ivan the Terrible, and Ivaniana—that is to say, the argument over Tsar Ivan—is the form in which it has developed. But in its hypnotic and almost mystical power, the myth goes far beyond the limits of this argument, and influences the Russian world-view itself. In no other area, perhaps, does this dictatorship of the myth manifest itself so vividly as in attitudes toward the political opposition as a whole and political emigration in particular. This is the test for freedom of thought; here lies the bad con-

49. Ibid., p. 412; D. S. Likhachev, "Ivan Peresvetov i ego literaturnaia sovremennost'," p. 35; I. I. Smirnov, p. 18. Emphasis added.

50. S. Gorskii, p. 373.

51. Quoted from A. Yanov, "Al'ternativa," p. 72. This article, in which the struggle of the émigré Herzen was represented as the only worthy alternative to the pseudopatriotism of the "slavish majority," was one of the causes of my own expulsion from Russia, and the issue of *Molodoi kommunist* in which it appeared was suppressed.

science of all of Russian historiography. And we must be grateful to Gorskii for having posed this question so openly—even if he did so out of stupidity.

For Gorskii and the majority of his coevals, Herzen was the same kind of traitor as Kurbskii—"the power of darkness, which undermined the most precious foundations of our state structure," as one of them put it.[52] Down the centuries, from Ivan the Terrible to Josef Stalin and beyond, whenever confrontation has arisen between the individual and the state, the majority takes the side of the state, and the political émigré is open to an accusation of treason. Herzen understood this quite well. Protesting against the bloody suppression of the Polish insurrection of 1863, he wrote:

> If no one makes this protest, we will be alone in our protest, but we will not abandon it. We will repeat it in order that there be witness to the fact that in a time of general intoxication with narrow patriotism, there were still people who found the strength to separate themselves from a rotting empire in the name of the future Russia which was coming to birth, and found the strength to subject themselves to the accusation of treason in the name of love for the Russian people.[53]

Not only Herzen, but hundreds of Russian oppositionists took this stand—from the Narodniks to the Bolsheviks. The most eminent of these were Georgii Plekhanov, who spent almost his entire conscious life in exile, and Vladimir Lenin, who struggled abroad for the defeat of his own government, and therefore—by the logic of the "statists"—of his nation, in the wars with Japan and Germany. All of these people were traitors in the eyes of the majority. All of them were judged as Gorskii judged Kurbskii. Then the revolution of 1917 occurred.

Everything, it seemed, had changed. The opinions of the old majority were rejected and mocked by the new majority. Herzen, Plekhanov, and Lenin were turned from traitors into saints. Only one verdict remained in force as if there had been no revolution. And this was the verdict on Kurbskii. Even in our time, Academician D. S. Likhachev, closely following Gorskii, placidly called the correspondence between Ivan the Terrible and Kurbskii "correspondence between the tsar and a traitor."[54] Professor Ia. S. Lur'e, quoting Tsar Ivan, also called Kurbskii and the entire group of political émigrés in

52. Ibid., p. 74.
53. Ibid., p. 71.
54. Cited in *Poslaniia Ivana Groznogo*, p. 459.

Lithuania (Vladimir Zabolotskii, Mark Sarykhozin, the Elder Artemii, Timofei Teterin) "traitors to the sovereign."[55] And very recently, in the 1970s, Professor R. G. Skrynnikov has had no words for Kurbskii except "a history of treason," "treasonous negotiations," and "treasonous relations."[56] Destiny was truly merciless toward Kurbskii. For 400 years, both before the revolution and after it, no one has been found willing to raise their voice in defense of him.[57] But whom should anyone who was so bold refute? Skrynnikov, who borrowed his opinion from Gorskii? Gorskii, who borrowed his opinion from Kavelin? Kavelin, who borrowed it from Karamzin? Karamzin, who borrowed it from Tatishchev? Tatishchev, after all, had it from Tsar Ivan himself, who first called Kurbskii a "traitor" and "oath-breaker." Only by tracing back this chain, unbroken for centuries, do we come finally to the original inspiration of all of these ideologists and historians—to the true founder of the "state school" in Rus'. Before Tsar Ivan, the Muscovite government stood, at least officially, for freedom of political choice, decisively rejecting—even if for selfish reasons— the treatment of political emigration as treason. Ivan was the first to put the question in the terms in which it is phrased to this day. His credo ran: "He who opposes the regime opposes God. . . . Children should not oppose their parents nor slaves their masters." The tsar cited Saint Paul, forgetting that the apostle was speaking of slaves. Kurbskii was a famous general, a boyar, and an advisor to the tsar. He felt himself to be a free man.

The alternative to emigration which the tsar proposed to him was: "If you are just and pious, why do you not desire to suffer and acquire a martyr's crown from me, the obstinate ruler?"[58] Kurbskii preferred exile and struggle against the tyrant to slavery and the martyr's crown, a choice for which Russian historians have unanimously pro-

55. Cited in ibid., pp. 469, 471.

56. R. G. Skrynnikov, *Perepiska [Ivana] Groznogo i Kurbskogo*, pp. 57, 59.

57. One honorable exception should, however, be mentioned. In a remarkable poem published the year (1968) of the Prague Spring, when the discussion of Russian absolutism analyzed above was aboil, a young poet (not a historian, a poet!) actually defended Kurbskii: "How but by infidelity can you repay the tyrant when this tyrant is ruining your state?" asked Oleg Chukhontsev, with these words ruining his own career in official literature and winning admiration from the Moscow intelligentsia ("Povestvovanie o Kurbskom'," p. 29). According to Grigorii Svirskii, the official response was crushing. Among other things, a group of Soviet generals wrote a letter to the Party Central Committee, asserting that Chukhontsev had "called our youth to treason." Not a single historian since has let fall a word in defense of the poet (Grigorii Svirskii, *Na lobnom meste*, p. 431).

58. *Poslaniia Ivana Groznogo*, p. 286.

nounced him to be a traitor, thereby recognizing Ivan the Terrible's alternatives, slavery or martyrdom, as the rational ones, and coming down on the side of the autocrator. But it is not so much the medieval sermons of the terrible tsar which astonish, as the slavish concurrence of modern Russian commentators.

Karamzin called one subsection in his *History* "The Treason of Andrei Kurbskii." This was not as easy for him as it was for Gorskii. A few pages earlier, he describes the situation preceding Kurbskii's flight: "Muscovy was paralyzed with fear. Blood poured out; in the dungeons and the monasteries the victims groaned; but . . . the tyranny was still maturing; the present was horrified by the future."[59] In a situation of total terror, when the fate of a person no longer depends on his or her behavior, but only on the caprice of the tyrant, on dark rumors, on evil reports—how in this situation, are we to judge a person who does not wait for the executioners to come after him? Karamzin does not judge: "He [Kurbskii] could without qualms of conscience seek refuge from the persecutor in Lithuania itself." There is another thing, however, for which he cannot forgive Kurbskii: "Regrettably, [he] did more: he joined the enemies of the fatherland. . . . He committed [to the king of Poland] his honor and his soul, and advised the king on how to ruin Russia."[60] But why Russia?—we might ask Karamzin. Why not the terroristic dictatorship of Ivan the Tormentor—a dictatorship which truly ruined Russia? We would ask this in vain of Karamzin, for whom the autocracy was the soul of Russia and struggle against it equivalent to struggle against the fatherland.

For Skrynnikov today, we must assume, the autocracy is no longer a synonym for the fatherland. However, he goes even further than Karamzin. He not only associates himself with Gorskii, but judges the "traitor" even more severely than does Tsar Ivan himself: "The viceroy of Livonia [Kurbskii] had been bribed by the Lithuanians, and was driven from his country by the fear of exposure. Kurbskii was not subject to direct persecution at home. To the last day he enjoyed power and honor."[61] A little further on, Skrynnikov writes of the "insolent reproach [by Kurbskii] to the tsar, [whom he] compared to a fierce and bloodthirsty beast," who had embarked on the "universal ruination" of his governors and counsellors.[62] Well, does Skrynnikov refute this "insolent reproach"? Not at all. "Kurbskii's words," he writes,

59. N. M. Karamzin, *Istoriia* . . . , vol. 9, p. 23.
60. Ibid., p. 68.
61. R. G. Skrynnikov, *Perepiska* . . . , p. 61.
62. Ibid., p. 53.

had a quite real historical basis. On the eve of his flight, the tsar's wrath and punishment lost their usual personal character and began to affect entire families. After the death of A. Adashev, the tsar ordered his brother Daniil [the hero of the Crimean campaign of 1559] killed, with his son and his relatives—P. Turov, I. Shiskin, the Satins, and others. In precisely the same way he confined in a monastery the boyar Prince D. Kurliat'ev, his wife, his son, and his daughters.[63]

Furthermore, Skrynnikov understands the meaning of these events excellently: "The execution of famous war leaders symbolized the end of an entire period. . . . Under the 'liberal' regime of Adashev, the death penalty was not once applied to a boyar. . . . The first executions of boyars in 1564 signalized the onset of the Oprichnina terror against the boyardom." Why does Skrynnikov think that the boyar Kurbskii, a member of the Government of Compromise, understood what was happening less well than he himself does? In fact, Skrynnikov does not think anything of the kind. "Kurbskii understood well the meaning of the events taking place before his eyes," he tells us.[64] What is there surprising, then, about the fact that "in a letter to the tsar, the refugee boyar undertakes the role of intercessor for all people suffering in Rus'"?[65] Why is Kurbskii's flight necessarily explained by an ignoble bribe, and not by a noble attempt—which under the conditions of total terror is the only possible one—to "intercede for all the people suffering in Rus'"? Why does this simple and apparently self-evident explanation not even enter Skrynnikov's head—just as it did not enter the head of Likhachev or Lur'e, or Solov'ev or Kavelin, not to speak of Karamzin? And why, if he asserts that the political émigré Kurbskii was bribed by the Lithuanians, is Skrynnikov offended when he is told that the political émigré Lenin was bribed by the Germans?

We will never find the answer to these questions unless we return to poor Gorskii, with his stereotype about the struggle of "the old" and "the new." Let us remember how he reasons: "The old for Kurbskii was second nature; it was his flesh and blood, a vital necessity. . . . He considers the restoration of the old tradition the main task of his life." What "old tradition" is Gorskii talking about? And what is bad about it? "What advantage for Russia could be expected from the restoration of the custom of boyar council? . . . What advantage could it obtain from its old-fashioned politics"? Gorskii asks indignantly, revealing in his simplemindedness the horrible secret of the entire apologia for Ivan the Terrible. And he answers: "Nothing but

63. Ibid., p. 47.   64. Ibid., p. 52.   65. Ibid., p. 47.

ruin and harm."[66] Here we see quite clearly what, precisely, it is that
Gorskii (and his Soviet pupils) cannot forgive the opposition of that
time, and why it is that they hate Kurbskii: the struggle for limitations
on power, for the custom of the boyar council and the Assembly of
the Land, for social control over the administration. Why was the
ruin in England not brought about by the existence there, even in the
darkest times, of the custom of Parliament? Why was France not
ruined by the provincial Estates-General? Why was Sweden not
ruined by the Landtags, why did Denmark get only good out of its
"old-fashioned politics"? Why is it that what was possible for them
was not possible for us? No one, beginning with Tatishchev and ending with Skrynnikov, has an answer to this question. For that matter,
no one ever asked it. Autocracy is the imperative for Russia, a historical necessity, its destiny.

　　In fact, the church immunities, the custom of the boyar council,
the custom of taking fixed taxes from the peasants, "by tradition," "as
they were received by the previous landowners," the mobility of peasants, guaranteed as a matter of law by St. George's Day, and everything else that Ivan the Terrible destroyed, were old fashioned and
essentially feudal forms of limitation on power. Many of them really
had outlived their time, and required modernization. But, after all,
this was what the Government of Compromise was doing. One need
only briefly list what it did, or tried to do, in order to make this clear.
What were the replacement of the vicegerents by a local government,
and the introduction of trial by jury, and the creation of a new code of
law, and the calling of an Assembly of the Land, and the attempt to
introduce an income tax and restrict the immunities, if not a *modernization of the limitations on power*? By modernizing the traditional limitations on power, the Government of Compromise was following in the
line of contemporary European absolutism. The Oprichnina of Ivan
the Terrible, however, questioned not the *form* of the limitations on
power, but their *existence*.

　　In the Criminal Code of contemporary Russia there is an article
which defines "flight abroad or refusal to return from abroad" as
treason to the motherland. This is a most precise indicator of what
the victory of Ivan the Terrible over Kurbskii turned Russia into.
Kurbskii's French contemporary, Duplesis-Mornay, in his famous
Suit Against Tyrants, says almost word for word the same thing as the
Muscovite exile. The tyrant, he says, destroys his counsellors ("the

66. S. Gorskii, p. 413.

strong men in Israel," as Kurbskii calls them). The tyrant does not take counsel with the estates and the land ("he is not a lover of counsel," says Kurbskii). The tyrant counterposes to them hired mercenaries ("he creates a seed of Abraham out of stone," says Kurbskii). The tyrant steals the property of his subjects ("he ruins them for the sake of their miserable *votchiny*," says Kurbskii). One might think that Duplesis-Mornay was describing Ivan the Terrible. And although he was also a political émigré, it is hardly likely that any modern French historian would call him a traitor. For they do not consider a struggle against tyranny to be treason. But the Russian historians—from Gorskii to Skrynnikov—do. They have chosen the autocrator's alternative: as distinct from Kurbskii, they have preferred slavery.

The myth of the state is cunningly constructed. In it the apologia for tyranny is skillfully interwoven with patriotism, the justification of terror with national feelings. In raising one's hand against tyranny, one therefore risks dealing a blow to patriotism; in protesting against terror one may offend national feelings; in struggling for limitations on power, one turns into a traitor to one's country.

6. *The Bugbear of Oligarchy*

Evgenii Belov's *On the Historical Significance of Russian Boyardom* endeavors to show what Russia might have turned into if Kurbskii and the boyardom had prevailed, if Ivan the Terrible had not found a power base for the Oprichnina in the bureaucracy. Belov is, as far as I know, the only Russian historian prepared to praise the Muscovite bureaucracy, whose contemptible and fiercely grasping nature has become proverbial. In his opinion, the bureaucracy preserved Russia from "oligarchical intrigues" which had marked its entire history before the Oprichnina.

Belov uncovers the first oligarchical intrigue as early as 1498, when, he believes, the boyar opposition compelled Ivan III to crown as his heir-apparent not his son Vasilii (the father of Ivan the Terrible), but his grandson Dimitrii. The intrigue against Tsar Ivan thus began before he had even had time to be born. The counterconspiracy in favor of Vasilii, Belov asserts, "did not contain a single boyar." The only ones who acted in defense of the traditional structure of power, which was on the point of disintegration, were the "secretaries [*d'yaki*] of the party of Sof'ia." Everything in subsequent Russian history proceeded according to the same model: selfless scions of the people in the shape of the secretaries were constantly thwarting the cunning intrigues of the boyar oligarchs—right until 1565, when the tsar was finally able to unseat the latter. "[Ivan] the Terrible is the retribution on the boyardom for its narrow and egoistic policies. . . . [Ivan] the Terrible diverted Russia from the danger of oligarchical rule. [Had it not been for the Oprichnina] Russia would have been transformed into a second Poland."[67]

This, in brief, is Belov's concept of things. Only at first glance does it seem to be worthy of the pen of a Gorskii. In fact, Belov is doing the same thing as Kavelin, but from the other side. He was the first in Russian historiography to pose the question of an alternative to autocracy. Other than oligarchy and transformation into a second Poland, he declared, no such alternative existed. Poland symbolized political disintegration and, in the final analysis, the loss of national existence. If this was the sole alternative, then the autocracy of Tsar Ivan, as also the messianic role of the Muscovite bureaucracy, could be considered justified. Not only Soviet historians, such as A. N. Sakharov, but also such classic Russian historiographers as V. O. Kliuchevskii, fell into this trap.

Belov's argument is most conveniently considered by comparison of the "maintenances" (*kormleniia*) held by vicegerents in the Polish-Lithuanian state and in Muscovy. In the first case, such maintenances provided the vicegerents with a nucleus for creating their own political bases in the regions. The vicegerents subsequently represented "their" districts in the Duma (or "Rada" as it was called in the Polish-Lithuanian kingdom) and were practically uncontrolled rulers of them. As Kliuchevskii says, "the most influential force in the Rada— the 'front' or 'higher' Rada—was made up of the major regional rulers." In other words, the political basis of the oligarchy was the division of the country in practical terms among semiautonomous governors, who, although they were formally subject to the central power, appeared in effect as overlords of the regions which "maintained" them: "The economic and administrative strings of local life were in their hands, and the Rada served them only as the conductor, and not as the source of their political influence. Its members were not mere state counsellors, but actual rulers."[68]

The political process in sixteenth-century Muscovy proceeded, as we have seen, in precisely the opposite direction. Not only the maintenances, but also the district vicegerencies themselves were abolished. The local elected governments, which replaced them, were

67. E. A. Belov, *Ob istoricheskom znachenii russkogo boyarstva*, p. 69.
68. V. O. Kliuchevskii, *Boiarskaia duma . . .* , p. 296.

directly subject to the central government offices. Paraphrasing Kliu-chevskii, we may say that in Muscovy the boyars were "not actual rulers but mere state counsellors." As the experience of the "boyar govern-ments" of 1537 to 1547 showed, they *never* claimed more than this. Thus, on the eve of the Oprichnina there were no oligarchical tenden-cies in Muscovy, even in embryonic form.

But if this is so, the oligarchy turns out to be only a bugbear thought up by Belov to justify the autocracy—a bugbear in con-firmation of which he was not able to cite a single argument which would stand historical criticism. The problem, however, was not in his arguments, but in the fact that Russian historiography, as we shall see presently, did not have at its disposal any *other* alternative.

7. Kliuchevskii's Premise

The Muscovite state in the sixteenth century was an absolute mon-archy with an aristocratic governing class, Kliuchevskii tells us. "The boyars thought of themselves as powerful counsellors of the sover-eign of all Rus'," while Ivan IV, on the other hand, rewarded them with the status of "bondsmen of the sovereign," he continues.

> Both sides felt themselves in an unnatural relationship to each other, which they, it seems, had not been aware of while it was developing, and did not know what to do with when they noticed it. . . . Boyardom did not know how to set itself up and to set up the order of the state without the power of the ruler, to which it was accustomed, and the sovereign did not know how to deal with his kingdom in its new boundaries with-out the help of the boyars. *The two sides could neither get along with each other nor do without each other.* Not knowing either how to get along or how to part, they tried to separate, and to live side by side but not to-gether. The Oprichnina was to be a way out of this difficulty.[69]

But this attempted compromise misfired, because "in the Oprichnina, he [the tsar] felt at home, like a real ancient Russian liege lord among his serf-henchmen, and could without hindrance exercise his per-sonal rule, which was hampered in the Zemshchina by the morally obligatory respect for traditions and customs which were honored by all."[70] The tsar "assigned to the Oprichnina a task for which in the government of that time there was no special institution. The newly created appanage office was supposed to become also the highest in-stitution for protecting the order of the state from sedition, and the

69. V. O. Kliuchevskii, *Sochineniia* (1st ed.), vol 2, pp. 192–93. Emphasis added.
70. V. O. Kliuchevskii, *Boiarskaia duma . . .* , p. 340.

detachments of the Oprichnina were to be a corps of gendarmes and also an execution squad in cases of treason."[71] As a result, "the Oprichnina, in ridding the country of sedition, introduced anarchy, and in protecting the sovereign, shook the very foundations of the state."[72]

A monstrous parody of a German knightly order—but without any conception of the code of chivalry—the Oprichnina simultaneously fulfilled the functions of a political party and a political police. Called into being, according to Kliuchevskii,

> by a collision the cause of which was the system, and not persons, it was directed against persons, and not against the system. The Oprichniki were put, not in the place of the boyars, but against the boyars; by their very role, they could not be the rulers, but only the executioners of the country. . . . This means that for the direction which the tsar gave to the political encounter, his personal character is greatly to blame, and therefore it takes on certain significance in the history of our state.[73]

Thus, the premise for all of Kliuchevskii's reasoning is that "absolute power" and the boyardom "could not get along with each other." From this it follows that the Oprichnina, being incapable of resolving this conflict, takes on the aspect of a savage and bloody, but nevertheless historically accidental, episode in Russian history, due primarily to the personal character of Tsar Ivan. It is this, properly speaking, which constitutes the "accidental" thrust of Kliuchevskii's conception.

8. An Impossible Combination?

It seems to me that Kliuchevskii's error arises out of the fact that he does not attempt to analyze the category of "absolute power" (which in turn prevented him from distinguishing absolutism from despotism). Authoritarianism presented itself to him—and to his contemporaries as well—as a single, undifferentiated phenomenon. "Absolute power" is a synonym for "unlimited power." He conceived of limitations on power, as was customary for the "state school," exclusively as political (juridical) limitations. The category of latent limitations on power, which was the paradoxical core of the "limited/unlimited" structure of absolutism, did not exist for him. And here a riddle arose: how and by what means could there nevertheless be in pre-Oprichnina Russia "absolute power . . . with an aristocratic administration," if from the very beginning, even under Ivan III, "the

71. Kliuchevskii, *Sochineniia* (1st ed.), vol. 2, p. 197.
72. Ibid., p. 195.
73. Ibid., p. 198.

character of this power did not correspond to the nature of the governmental tools through which it had to act?"[74]

Kliuchevskii sees the answer to this question as twofold: first, this impossible combination was possible only as long as its impossibility was not recognized, and as long as the conflict between the two political forces had not come out into the open; secondly, the "personal character of Tsar Ivan" comes into play here. It turns out that,

> Having acquired an extremely exclusive and impatient, purely abstract idea of supreme power, he decided that he could not rule the state as his father and grandfather had done, with the collaboration of the boyars . . . and he incautiously raised the old question of the relationship between the sovereign and the boyardom—a question which he was not in a position to answer and which, therefore, he should not have raised.[75]

Kliuchevskii admits that until Tsar Ivan "raised the question," the collaboration of the single leadership ("absolute power") with the boyar Duma (the "aristocratic personnel") proceeded relatively smoothly, and the disagreements which arose between the tsar and the Duma were smoothed over without reaching the level of political confrontation.

> Its [the Duma's] structure, authority, and customary order of business seemed to be based on the assumption of an unshakable mutual confidence between its chairman and the counsellors, and bore witness to the fact that between the sovereign and his boyars there could not be a conflict of interest, and that these political forces had grown together, and become accustomed to acting in concert, hand in hand, and could not—did not know how to—proceed otherwise. There were collisions . . . and arguments, but about business, not about power; opinions about business came into conflict, but not political claims.[76]

And even the development of "bureaucratic governmental personnel," which was natural as the state grew and became more complex, could not destroy this order of things: being directly subject to the tsar, the bureaucracy in the government departments was transformed into an apparatus of executive power, which did not claim to take part in legislation and the adoption of political decisions. Thus, both the aristocratic and the bureaucratic personnel in this system of absolute monarchy had their own separate and nonintersecting functions, which did not contradict each other.

But all this was true only so long as the conflict was not discerned.

74. Kliuchevskii, *Sochineniia* (2nd ed.), vol. 2, pp. 180–81.
75. Ibid., p. 197.
76. Ibid., p. 348.

Once having arisen, it had to grow into a confrontation to the death, a war of annihilation, what is now called a zero-sum game. This had to be, because the organic incompatibility was, as Kliuchevskii liked to say, a political fact. There was no getting away from it. Had it not been Tsar Ivan, some other tsar would have detonated this delayed-action bomb built into the Muscovite political mechanism.

Muscovite political practice and theory compel us in equal degree to doubt Kliuchevskii's premise. In the first place, the conflict in the Muscovite absolute monarchy arose long before the birth of Tsar Ivan. As early as the 1520s, his father, Vasilii, had tried to establish a personal dictatorship by contrasting executive power to the boyar Duma. But, contrary to Kliuchevskii's supposition, this conflict did not lead to a fatal confrontation. Quite the contrary: under the Government of Compromise, boyardom, revealing an indubitable capacity to learn, responded with Article 98 of the law code and the calling of an Assembly of the Land. In other words, the Muscovite political machine turned out to be sufficiently adroit to leave room for political maneuvering. This was still an open system, on its way to achieving new political forms.

True, the attainment of these new forms ran counter to the interests of important social groups (in the first place, the church hierarchy). The political base of the government appeared to be divided, and the entire Muscovite political machine started to skid. And it was precisely because of this unstable equilibrium of forces—and not because of the "impossible combination" of absolute power with the aristocratic administration, as Kliuchevskii had it—that the character of the tsar emerged into the foreground. History, it seems, created three possible roles for this man. He could join the government in its efforts to crush the resistance of the church hierarchy, thus leading and actualizing the absolutist coalition of Non-Acquirers, boyardom, and the proto-bourgeoisie; in this role he could speed up the Europeanization of Russia. Or he could maneuver between the opposing forces in the Muscovite establishment, acting in the role of arbiter, and thus giving the system time to grow naturally in the same direction. Or, finally, he could go for a coup d'etat, creating his own political base in the shape of a "new class," and thereby putting an end to the process of Europeanization. For the reasons discussed above, he chose the third role.

Thus, because of his incorrect premise, Kliuchevskii was destined to become a prisoner of the artificial dichotomy of his opposite, Belov: either the aristocracy established the order of the state without leadership being vested in any one person (oligarchy), or the leader ruled without the collaboration of the boyars (autocracy). In this view, there was no third alternative, inasmuch as the latent conflict between "absolute power" and aristocracy had been dragged to the surface and exposed.

But there *was* a third alternative. The entire history of medieval Europe is a proof of this. It was precisely this conflict, now hidden and now open, which was the *norm, the law of existence,* and, we may say, the *natural condition of all absolutist states.* What was unnatural was the liquidation of the struggle, and the autocratic metamorphosis experienced by Russia in the course of the Oprichnina—the creation of the "new class" and the ensuing establishment of universal service.

We reach the same results in considering Kliuchevskii's premise from a theoretical point of view. The establishment of absolute monarchy did not by any means signify, as Belov thought, the mere substitution of the bureaucracy for the aristocracy as governmental personnel. It did not signify this, since absolute monarchy was an incomparably more complex system than the conglomerate of feudal princedoms which preceded it. And the complexity of the system demanded not simplification, but corresponding complication of administration. Therefore, absolute monarchy—whose specific character consists precisely in the heterogeneity of its political elite—is constructed of two elements which differ in their significance and in their origin: of bureaucratic and aristocratic personnel, of the combination of these in the most various proportions, and of political compromise between them.

Of course, the setting up of an aristocracy within an absolute monarchy is a painful and contradictory historical process, inevitably fraught with numerous conflicts. Certainly, in the course of these conflicts, the single leadership—as the Scandinavian experience, for example, shows—could base itself not only on the bureaucracy, but also on the city dwellers, the service landholders, and even on the peasantry. The aristocracy in its turn could seek political allies in various social strata. The compromise between them could take various forms. However, what is important for us here is that both the single leadership and the aristocratic personnel were elements in a single system of absolute monarchy, and as a rule set themselves the goal not of destroying each other, but merely of finding an advantageous form of compromise. I say "as a rule," because when in the France of the late Bourbons, the kings in fact tried to rid themselves of the political interference of the aristocracy, the absolute monarchy, as Montesquieu noted, began to degenerate into despotism. But, I repeat, as a rule the argument between absolute monarchy and aristocracy concerned the *form of coexistence* and not life or death—this is the essence of the matter. Nowhere in medieval Europe, except in Russia, had a "new class" *replaced* the old elite, thus creating, instead of absolutism, a political structure which was unique at that time, the autocracy.

In other words, contrary to Kliuchevskii's premise, absolute monarchy *was* in principle compatible with aristocracy as a guarantor of the social limitations on power. And it was not absolutism but autocracy, therefore, which required the total replacement of an aristocratic governmental class by a system of universal service.

But if Kliuchevskii's premise was incorrect, his conclusions also became dubious. This applies to the idea that "the life of the Muscovite state even without Ivan would have been set up in the same way in which it was set up before him and after him,"[77] and that the Oprichnina was a random and arbitrary historical accident, connected with the personal character of Tsar Ivan.

The connection of the Oprichnina with the Russian political tradition is demonstrated very easily by Kliuchevskii's own analysis— which, alas, entirely contradicts his own conclusions. Does he not assert that "the sovereign, *remaining faithful to the views of an appanage prince holding patrimonial properties, according to the ancient Russian law*, treated them [the boyars] as his household servants with the title of bondsmen of the sovereign"? Does he not quite clearly formulate the historical character of the Oprichnina, saying: "In the Oprichnina, he [the tsar] felt at home—*a real ancient Russian liege lord* among his serf-henchmen"? Therefore, not the tsar's personal character was the essence of the matter, but rather the ancient "tradition of the appanage prince holding patrimonial estates," which Ivan the Terrible in the course of the Oprichnina made universal.

It is another matter entirely—contrary to the opinion of the despotists, who see nothing but this tradition of the patrimonial appanage prince in Russian political history—that it not only did not dominate in sixteenth-century Muscovy, but hewed a path for itself only at enormous cost and with a great many victims. The Oprichnina itself is proof of this. If the Muscovite kingdom of the sixteenth century in fact merely reproduced the characteristic features of the Eastern Roman Empire, as Toynbee postulates, why, for example, did the despot need a coup d'etat, renunciation of the throne, manifestos to the people, a division of the country into two parts, an agreement with the boyars and the clergy, mass terror, a second capital, and a

77. Ibid., p. 198.

parallel apparatus of administration? According to the account of contemporaries, the tsar returned to Moscow after the revolution quite grey at thirty-five years of age. A Byzantine autocrator would simply have compiled lists of proscriptions, and one fine night, as the saying goes, have taken his opponents from their beds with his bare hands. Why did Tsar Ivan behave differently? Why did he need a revolution in place of a "night of the long knives," if not in order to break up the existing order of the state, created by a different, competing absolutist tendency?

Here, it might seem, is just the place to catch me up. For, objecting to Toynbee, I assert that Byzantinism—if by this we mean autocracy—was a fundamentally new phenomenon in sixteenth-century Russia; and, objecting to Kliuchevskii, I assert the reverse—that it was a traditional phenomenon. This is not a logical contradiction, however, but an ontological one. It reflects the fundamental dualism of Russian political culture itself, which already existed in Kievan Rus'. Before Ivan the Terrible—even despite the Tatar influence—absolutist (European) tendencies predominated; after him they passed over into the opposition, yielding the historical proscenium to the victorious autocracy.

9. Platonov's Argument With Kliuchevskii

In nothing else, perhaps, does the dualism of Russian political life appear so strikingly as in the events of the first Time of Troubles, which followed the death of the tyrant and reached its height in the national crisis of 1605–13. And in nothing else has the transfixing of Russian historiography in the hypnosis of the "myth of the state" manifested itself so vividly as in its inability to explain these events. I cannot discuss the Time of Troubles in detail here. Let us merely consider one example.

When the new tsar, Vasilii Shuiskii, ascended the Russian throne on May 19, 1605, the first thing he did was to make a public declaration in the cathedral Church of the Holy Virgin: "I kiss the cross before the whole world that I will take no action against anyone without the approval of the assembly; and that if the father is guilty, I will take no action against the son; and if the son is guilty, no action against the father." One need only remember the *Sinodik* of Tsar Ivan, with its requests to remember the soul of so-and-so, killed "along with his mother, and his wife, and his sons, and his daughters," for it to become entirely clear what the new tsar is promising the people. He does not intend to continue the autocratic policy of Ivan the Terrible. On the contrary, he publicly and solemnly renounces it. Physical safety, an end to terror, the introduction of the category of "political death"—this is what he promises in his declaration, which is a medieval analog to the famous secret speech of Nikita Khrushchev at the 20th Congress of the Communist Party of the Soviet Union in 1956. But Shuiskii goes further: in the memorandum which he distributed to all the cities in the Russian land, we read,

> I, the tsar and great prince Vasilii Ivanovich of all Rus' have kissed the cross that I, the great sovereign, will not give over to death any person *not judged by a true court* made up of my own boyars and will not take his patrimony and his house and his property from his brother and his wife and his children. . . . Likewise, I will not take houses and stores and property *from merchants and trading people and peasants.* . . . Likewise, I, the great sovereign, will not listen to false information and will try all cases well, by face to face contact, so that guiltless Orthodox Christians will not perish.[78]

An end to denunciations, confiscations, executions of entire families, mass plundering, murder without trial and investigation, an end to unlimited arbitrary rule—this is what the tormented Russian land cries for through the mouth of the tsar. It was not a matter of the liquidation of absolute monarchy. It was not a matter, consequently, of political limitations on power. This did not enter anyone's head. It was only a matter of elementary guarantees of life and property—of the latent limitations on power, in my terms—that is, a matter of restoration of the absolutist spirit of Ivan III and the Government of Compromise. And Russian historiography proved unable to explain this, which is like not being able to explain the difference between Khrushchev and Stalin.

Kliuchevskii, though, with his fine historical intuition, felt something unusual and historically significant in the declaration of the new tsar. He says: "The crowning of Prince Vasilii marked an epoch in our political history. On ascending the throne, he limited his power and officially set forth the conditions of this limitation in a document distributed to all the regions, on which he kissed the cross on being crowned."[79] This assertion of Kliuchevskii's called forth a protest by another classical figure in Russian historiography—Academician S. F. Platonov, with whom we shall have occasion to become familiar in more detail in the next chapter. In his famous *Outlines of the History of*

78. Cited in N. V. Latkin, *Zemskie sobory drevnei Rusi,* p. 104.
79. Kliuchevskii, *Sochineniia* (1st ed.), vol. 3, p. 37.

the Rebellions in the Muscovite State of the Sixteenth and Seventeenth Centuries, Platonov inserted a subsection entitled "The Cross-Kissing Document is Not a Limitation." His commentary deserves to be reproduced:

> In all this it is very difficult to see an actual limitation of the tsar's power, and one may see only an abandonment of unworthy means of manifesting these powers. Here the tsar does not yield any of his rights. . . . He only promises to refrain from arbitrary personal caprice, and to act through the court of boyars, which existed equally in all periods of the Muscovite state and was always a law-enforcing and legislative institution, without, however, limiting the power of the tsar. In a word, in the memorandum of Tsar Vasilii one cannot find anything which would essentially limit his power and would be juridically obligatory for him.[80]

To this Kliuchevskii (shrewdly foreseeing the objections of his opponent) notes:

> The oath denied the very essence of the personal power of the tsar in the previous dynasty, which had developed out of the appanage relationships of a liege lord. Do heads of households swear oaths to their servants and tenants? Along with this, Tsar Vasilii renounced three prerogatives in which the personal power of the tsar was most clearly expressed: (1) "disgrace without guilt"—the tsar's punishment without adequate occasion, and by personal decision; (2) the confiscation of property from the family and relatives of a criminal who were not involved in the crime. . . . (3) extraordinary trials by police and other investigative agencies, calling upon denunciation, with tortures and slanders, but without face-to-face confrontation, examination of witnesses, and other means of normal legal process. These prerogatives constituted an essential part of the contents of the power of Muscovite sovereigns. . . . By divesting himself by oath of these prerogatives, Vasilii Shuiskii transformed himself from the sovereign of bondsmen into the legitimate tsar of subjects, ruling according to law.[81]

By what law? No constitution existed in the country which specified the interrelationships of executive and legislative power, to say nothing of judicial power. These relationships were dictated by tradition and political practice, but not by law. Shuiskii promised a "true court," but where were the guarantees that he would fulfill his promises? Therefore it seems that Platonov is right in asserting that "in the memorandum of Tsar Vasilii one cannot find anything which . . . would be juridically obligatory for him."

80. S. F. Platonov, *Ocherki po istorii smuty v Moskovskom gosudarstve XVI–XVIII vekov*, p. 230. Emphasis added.

81. V. O. Kliuchevskii, *Sochineniia*, 1st ed., vol. 3, p. 40.

However, is not Kliuchevskii right in saying that the tsar renounced the autocratic prerogatives which gave him the opportunity to treat his subjects as slaves? True, these prerogatives proceeded "from the appanage relationships of a liege lord." But after all, Ivan the Terrible had tried to extend them over the entire state by means of mass terror. Vasilii Shuiskii renounced them, and therefore, it seems, actually did limit his power.

Thus it turns out that both Platonov and Kliuchevskii were right. Kliuchevskii was right, in insisting on the fundamental novelty of Shuiskii's antiautocratic manifesto. And Platonov was right in emphasizing its traditional, absolutist character. Both were right, for the restoration of absolutism declared by Tsar Vasilii was an antiautocratic and anti-Oprichnina action.

But at the same time, both were wrong.

10. The Argument With Platonov and Kliuchevskii

For Platonov, who understood the Oprichnina as a revolution by the tsar which liberated him from the tutelage of the reactionary aristocracy, Shuiskii's manifesto was a kind of credo for the restoration of the "old order." The overthrown aristrocracy once again ruled in Moscow, cunningly *taking advantage for this purpose of the abuses of the Oprichnina*:

> The old nobility once again occupied first place in the country. Through the mouth of *its tsar* it solemnly renounced the system which had just been in operation, and promised "true judgment" and protection from "all violence" and injustice, of which it accused the previous regime. . . . Tsar Vasilii said and thought that he was reestablishing . . . *the old order*. This was the order which had existed *before the Oprichnina*. . . . this, it seems to us, was the true meaning of Shuiskii's memorandum: it announced . . . not the reduction of the power of the tsar, but the return to its former moral height.[82]

But what is bad about the "return of the regime to its former moral height," and why is Platonov convinced that it was only the "old nobility" which had a stake in "protecting from all violence"? Was not "true judgment" in the interests of the society as a whole? And wasn't this precisely what Shuiskii promises, in obligating himself "not to take from the merchants and the trading people and the peasants . . . their houses and shops and their property"? Isn't it more natural to assume that the manifesto of Tsar Vasilii (like Khrushchev's secret

82. Platonov, pp. 231–32. Emphasis added.

speech) reflected only the simple truth: the boyardom was aware that it could not protect its own privileges without at the same time extending the elementary guarantees of life and property to the whole nation? Strangely enough, Platonov did not notice this. But after all, is this really so strange? Platonov was not the first Russian historian or the last for whom the hypnosis of the "myth of the state" cut off the path to the understanding of the dualism of Russian political tradition.

But, at the same time, it is difficult to agree with Kliuchevskii that "the ascent of Tsar Vasilii to the throne marked an epoch in our political history." It might have marked an epoch if it had occurred before the Oprichnina, on a wave of absolutist reforms by the Government of Compromise, as an element of these reforms and their logical development. But it occurred after Ivan the Terrible—after the absolutist structure of the state had collapsed to the ringing of the Oprichnina's bells and in the light of its bonfires, and after the leaden cloud of serfdom had gathered over it. Ivan's "new class" was still there and the problems facing the country had not been mitigated, but, on the contrary, had been sharpened. Mortal battle was raging. This was a time for deeds, and not only kissing of crosses. How could the country be saved from the inexorably advancing autocracy? Could this be done at all? Who knows? But if it was at all possible, it required something considerably more than manifestos—the immediate convocation of an Assembly of the Land, a solemn restoration of St. George's Day, an alliance with the "best people" of the peasantry and of the cities, the organization and arming of a new political coalition, and a strategy of reform going far beyond that of the pre-Oprichnina Government of Compromise. But this was not what the new tsar had in mind—and for this reason Vasilii Shuiskii was destined to play only a walk-on part in political history, as Alexander Kerensky did in 1917.

CHAPTER IX

AGAIN AT THE CROSSROADS

1. At the Boundary of the Ages

An observer who around the year 1900 undertook to make a prognosis of the further development of Ivaniana would have had to report, first of all, that the political (to say nothing of the moral) reputation of the terrible tsar had been ruined. As debatable as Kliuchevskii's methodological premise might be, his verdict on the Oprichnina was, on the face of it, not open to appeal. Whatever new facts were discovered by twentieth-century historians, and whatever new conclusions they might come to, Ivan the Terrible and his Oprichnina were not suited to rehabilitation. Consequently, a new repetition of the "historiographic nightmare" appeared to be excluded. There would be neither new Tatishchevs nor new Kavelins. Lomonosov's arrogant bravado, Karamzin's sentimental indignation, and the servile enthusiasm of Gorskii, all equally must now have seemed the product of a dark, archaic, almost mythological era of Ivaniana.

In fact, a third "historiographic nightmare," the dimensions of which exceeded anything which had occurred up to that time, lay just around the corner. I am not speaking now of the shameless hymns to the "commander of the peoples" and the "great and sagacious statesman" which the coming generation of Russian readers was destined to hear from the coming generation of Russian historians—hymns which would reduce Veselovskii to despair. Nor am I speaking of the fact that the irrationality of the Oprichnina was once again rationalized, and the unjustifiable justified. How all this happened, we shall see presently. But never during the preceding "historiographic nightmares" had a Russian historian openly justified serfdom, the greatest evil which the Oprichnina brought down on Russia. In the 1940s, however, serfdom was to be declared progressive. I. I. Polosin would write: "The strengthening of serfdom at this time—in the sixteenth century—signified the strengthened and accelerated development of the country's productive forces. . . . Serfdom was a natural, spontaneous necessity, morally offensive, but economically inevitable."[1]

1. I. I. Polosin, *Sotsial'no-politicheskaia* . . . , p. 132.

2. The Economic Apologia for the Oprichnina

The "state school" died quietly at the beginning of the century. Despite the writings of P. N. Miliukov and G. V. Plekhanov, its triumphs were behind it. The formulas which had once prevailed—whether the "struggle of the state with the clan," the "struggle with the steppe," or the "enserfment of the society by the state"—came to provoke in many experts only a condescending smile. S. F. Platonov admitted with mocking academic politeness that "the scientific method of the historical-juridical [state] school exercised a strong influence on the development of the science of Russian history." He had in mind, however, only the "quantitative and qualitative growth" of the works of Russian historians.[2] He spoke of the "hyperboles" of the founder of the school, Kavelin, with the same contempt for archaic dilettantism with which Kavelin in his time had spoken of Karamzin's metaphors. M. N. Pokrovskii was not even polite: he openly laughed at the old models. In the writings of the historians of the state school, he observes,

> there is developed a grandiose picture of how the "struggle for the steppe" forged and created the Russian state. The steppe people, like wild beasts, attacked Rus'; in order to save itself from these raids, the entire state was constructed along military lines: half of it—the service landholders [*pomeshchiki*]—had to live in constant readiness for battle; the other half—the taxable people [merchants, craftsmen, and peasants]—were supposed to support the first. . . . Thus the state, in the name of the common interest, *enserfed* the society *to itself*; but when the struggle for the steppe ended in the victory of the Russian state, emancipation began: first, in the eighteenth century, the military obligations of the nobility were lifted, and then in the nineteenth century, serfdom for the peasants also fell. . . . This grandiose picture has one defect: it does not correspond at all to historical reality. The most intense struggle with the steppe came in the eleventh to thirteenth centuries . . . but it was not just then that the unified state was formed . . . and there was no enserfment. . . . And in the sixteenth to eighteenth centuries, when both the Muscovite state and serfdom originated, the Tatars had already grown so weak that they could not dream of conquering Rus'.[3]

The "state school" continued to reign but, like the queen of England, it had ceased to rule. A coup d'etat (one might call it an "agrarian coup," because the mythology of the "state school" was replaced by the mythology of the "agrarian school") had taken place in Ivaniana.

2. S. F. Platonov, *Ivan Groznyi*, p. 19.
3. M. N. Pokrovskii, *Izbrannye proizvedeniia*, vol. 3, pp. 239–40.

The nineteenth century had been tormented by the riddle of the *strength* of the Russian state, which raised Russia from the "darkness of nonexistence" to the rank of a superpower. The twentieth century began with the riddle of the *weakness* of the Russian state, which hung over a precipice and threatened once again to plunge Russia into the "darkness of nonexistence." Central to the problem was the "agrarian question"—the question of the redistribution of land resources. As may be supposed, the right wing of Russian historiography favored strengthening the monarchy by giving land to the peasants and thereby creating a strong conservative social base. The left wing, on the other hand, hoped to destroy the monarchy by rousing the land-hungry peasants against it. For both, the aristocracy surrounding the tsar was a hostile force. It was perhaps for this reason that the "agrarian coup" in Ivaniana was carried out by an unnatural coalition of right-wingers (led by the monarchist Platonov) and left-wingers (led by the Marxist Pokrovskii).

The monarchist K. Iarosh—who, if the reader remembers, was horrified by the *Sinodik* of Ivan the Terrible—nevertheless justified the tsar's destruction of his advisors. In the middle of the sixteenth century, in his opinion, the tsar "understood that the sole danger in terms of the establishment of cordial relations between the Russian people and the throne consisted of these importunate 'councillors' holding letters patent. Ivan wanted to reduce them entirely to the ranks of ordinary citizens of Russia and servants of the fatherland."[4] And since they did not wish to be "reduced," he destroyed them. This was a recommendation to Nicholas II to head a new Oprichnina.

Thus, the dramatic quality of the times entered into Ivaniana. Ancient history returned, as it were, to modern Russia. The dead seized the living. A contemporary civilized country, which had succeeded in astonishing the world not only with its military might, as in the time of Lomonosov and Kavelin, but also with its great literature—a country to whose greatest historian, Kliuchevskii, the Oprichnina had quite recently seemed "purposeless"—stood again on the point of undergoing a medieval spasm.

Platonov, an infinitely more serious and subtle scholar than Iarosh, depicted the sources of the Oprichnina in this way: "[Ivan] the Terrible felt around himself the danger of an opposition, and of course understood that this was a *class opposition*, a princely opposition, led by the political memories and instincts of formerly sovereign princes 'who desired by their traitorous custom' to become appanage 'lords'

4. K. Iarosh, *Psikhologicheskaia parallel'*, p. 28.

along with the Muscovite sovereign."[5] Thus, Platonov refused to consider the conflict which led to the Oprichnina in the traditional terms of Solov'ev and Gorskii—in the terms of a "struggle of the service nobility (the new) with the boyardom (the old)." For him the matter was much more serious: the might of the formerly sovereign princes was so great that it threatened the very existence of the centralized Russian state, which might perhaps collapse again into a collection of appanage principalities. For this reason I will call his view the "appanage" conception.

Pokrovskii was even more adamant in refusing to accept the oversimplified scheme of the "state school." Platonov gave the "class of formerly sovereign princes" the center of the stage. Pokrovskii placed the "class of the bourgeoisie" there. Whereas for Platonov, the Government of Compromise accordingly represented this "class of formerly sovereign princes," for Pokrovskii it represented a class alliance of the bourgeoisie with the boyardom. For Platonov the essence of the Oprichnina consisted in the fact that the tsar took land away from the formerly sovereign princes, who had a great deal, and gave it to the service landholders, who had little, and thereby strengthened his power. For Pokrovskii its essence consisted in more or less the same thing—with the difference that the tsar himself appeared in this conflict as the tool of the bourgeoisie, which, having repudiated its class alliance with the boyardom, had chosen a new partner, the service landholders. For Pokrovskii, "the whole coup was a matter of establishing a new *class* regime, for which the personal power of the tsar was only a tool, and not at all a matter of freeing [Ivan] the Terrible personally from the tutelage of the boyars which hindered him."[6]

But for both Platonov and Pokrovskii, the basis of the conflict was the redistribution of the land and the agrarian crisis, that is, the economic revolution. Both of them, in trying to replace the old models with their own, even more fantastic ones, suffered defeat. At the same time, both triumphed: the mongrel "agrarian school" born of their unnatural alliance prevails to this day in Ivaniana.

3. Platonov's Contradiction

Platonov's attitude towards the Oprichnina was no less complex than Solov'ev's. On the one hand, he declares just as categorically as Solov'ev that "the meaning of the Oprichnina had been thoroughly ex-

5. Platonov, p. 125. Emphasis added.
6. Pokrovskii, vol. 1, p. 313.

plained by the scholarly studies of recent decades."[7] And we already know that this meaning consisted, according to Platonov, in the confiscation of the lands of the formerly sovereign princes. But on the other hand, the blood and bestialities of the Oprichnina provoke exactly the same revulsion in the new classical writer as they did in the old one. And Platonov makes the qualification that "the goal of the Oprichnina could have been achieved by less complex means," since "the means which were used by [Ivan] the Terrible, although they proved effective, brought with them not only the destruction of the nobility, but also a number of other consequences which [Ivan] the Terrible can hardly have wished or expected."[8]

But in that case, what was the alternative to the Oprichnina? How otherwise could the tsar have acted in the face of the disintegration which threatened the country? What could he have done if the Muscovite government itself (or the "Chosen Rada," as Platonov by tradition called it) had taken the side of the formerly sovereign princes? The historian, after all, himself notes that "the Rada, we must suppose, was made up of princes, and its tendency was apparently also in accordance with their interests. The influence of the 'priest' and his 'collection of dogs' in the first years of their activity was very strong. . . . The entire mechanism of administration was in their hands."[9] Was the tsar's victory conceivable without the Oprichnina—that is to say, without a coup d'etat, without the creation of his own army and police, free of the influence of the formerly sovereign princes, without mass terror and all those atrocities which were so repugnant to Platonov? In the final analysis, Platonov himself, almost 400 years later, is unable to think up any alternative to the Oprichnina. Moral lamentations appear to be of no more help to him than they were to Solov'ev: his logic leads inexorably to justification of the Oprichnina.

But this is only half the problem. The real trouble begins when the reader recognizes to his astonishment that despite his loud declarations, Platonov is, in fact, not even sure of his main thesis that the Oprichnina was directed against the formerly sovereign princes and not against the nobility in general.

The touchstone, which gives an appearance of novelty to Platonov's deductions, is "expulsion." "The father and grandfather of [Ivan] the Terrible, following the old custom, when they conquered Novgorod, Pskov, Riazan', Viatka, and other places, expelled the leading strata of the population, which were dangerous for Muscovy, to the internal districts of Muscovy, and placed settlers from central

---

7. Platonov, p. 119.		8. Ibid., p. 133.		9. Ibid., pp. 124–25.

Muscovy in the newly conquered districts," Platonov says. True, the father and the grandfather applied "expulsion" to the conquered districts; but the grandson applied it to the Muscovite heartland. This, Platonov solemnly declares, however, is precisely what the grandson's political innovation consisted in: "That which succeeded so well with external enemies, [Ivan] the Terrible thought of trying with internal enemies."[10] In other words, the tsar, just like Lenin, applied the methods of international war to class war. But the question still remains: Who were these sinister "internal enemies" who were expelled?

Platonov gives two answers. "On the one hand," he tells us in his book *Ivan the Terrible*, in full accordance with his "appanage" concept, "the tsar decided to remove from the hereditary *appanage* lands their owners, *the formerly sovereign princes*, and to settle them in places distant from their former residence, where there were no *memories of appanage conditions* or conditions conducive to opposition."[11] His formulation of the role of the Oprichnina in his *Outlines of the History of the Rebellions* supports this: "The Oprichnina systematically broke up the land tenure of the *service princes*."[12]

The following page of *Ivan the Terrible*, however, contains something more reminiscent of Gorskii than of Platonov: "This operation . . . of removal of landowners took on the character [of] replacement of *large-scale votchina* [hereditary] land tenure by *small-scale service-estate* [conditional] land tenure."[13] As we see, there is no talk here of "formerly sovereign princes" and "memories of appanage conditions." Likewise in the *Outlines* another formulation with respect to the Oprichnina supports Gorskii: "The Oprichnina was the first attempt to resolve one of the contradictions of the structure of the Muscovite state; it destroyed the land holdings of the *nobility* in the form in which they had existed from old times."[14] Here everything is simple: the tsar is against the aristocracy.

It was not for nothing that Platonov vacillated between the "appanage" and "state" explanations of the Oprichnina. In fact, the "scholarly studies of recent decades" by no means furnished him with data to support the hypothesis of the tsar's struggle with the "class of formerly sovereign princes"—a hypothesis which he incautiously presented as an unconditional fact. When so powerful and scrupulous an investigator as S. B. Veselovskii undertook to verify Pla-

10. Ibid., p. 120.
11. Ibid., p. 121. Emphasis added.
12. Platonov, *Ocherki* . . . , p. 157. Emphasis added.
13. Platonov, *Ivan Groznyi*, p. 122. Emphasis added.
14. Platonov, *Ocherki* . . . , p. 157. Emphasis added.

tonov's hypothesis, it proved to be simply a fiction. "In a search for effective and striking lectures, S. F. Platonov abandoned his characteristic caution of thought and language, and presented a conception of the policy of Tsar Ivan . . . which was filled with flaws and factually inaccurate assertions," Veselovskii says. Calling Platonov's interpretation downright "pseudoscientific" and even "a circuitous maneuver to rehabilitate the monarchy," Veselovskii somberly states that "the idea that the Oprichnina was directed against the old land holdings of the formerly sovereign appanage princes must be recognized as a misunderstanding through and through."[15] This conclusion is fully shared by the leading (after A. A. Zimin) contemporary Soviet expert on the Oprichnina, R. G. Skrynnikov, who also asserts that "the Oprichnina was not a special measure against the appanage. . . . Neither Tsar Ivan nor his Oprichnina Duma ever emerged as consistent opponents of appanage landholding."[16]

4. Pokrovskii's Paradox

All of this, however, only became clear many decades afterwards. For Pokrovskii, who at the beginning of the century revised Russian history from a Marxist point of view, and therefore needed an economic explanation of its fundamental phenomena, Platonov's hypothesis was a gift from heaven. For Platonov was the first to depict the drama of the Oprichnina neither as an empty battle of "the new" against "the old" nor as the destruction of the "oligarchy," but as the embodiment of class struggle and of indomitable economic progress. And the atrocities of the Oprichnina did not confuse Pokrovskii as they had confused Karamzin and Solov'ev. Because what is progress after all? When you chop wood, the chips fly. If the liberal Kavelin was not ashamed to use the nineteenth-century vogue for "the progress of the state idea" as a justification of the Oprichnina, then why should the Marxist liberal Pokrovskii hesitate to use the twentieth-century vogue for "economic progress"? Relying on Platonov's hypothesis, Pokrovskii invented what I would call the economic apologia for the Oprichnina. He introduced it at the very point when Tsar Ivan was apparently being irrevocably banished from contemporary political reality to the obscurity of the Middle Ages to which he belonged. The Oprichnina suddenly acquired a rational economic underpinning. It was no longer "purposeless," as Kliuchevskii had asserted. It fulfilled a necessary

15. S. V. Veselovskii, *Issledovaniia po istorii oprichniny*, p. 32.
16. R. G. Skrynnikov, *Oprichnyi terror*, pp. 214–15.

function in Russian history by destroying the aristocratic latifundia and making room for the "progressive economical type" of service landholding, which was supposed to bring with it the replacement of obligations in kind by commodity-and-money relationships. Tsar Ivan proved to be a tool of Marxist Providence. Against this, what were Kliuchevskii's highbrow speculations about the struggle of the "absolute monarchy" with the "aristocratic governmental personnel"? What use was moral indignation? All these were disorderly "superstructural" sentiments. Thus Ivan the Terrible, unexpectedly elevated to a pedestal by economic determinism, again underwent rehabilitation.

But, in order to support this rehabilitation, one had still to demonstrate that the Oprichnina actually pursued a progressive economic role; and, in the second place, that the aristocratic latifundia had in the sixteenth century actually become a reactionary bastion in the path of progress; and, finally, that service landholding somehow corresponded to this sought-after progress. Pokrovskii fearlessly undertook the task:

> Two conditions led to the swift liquidation of the Muscovite latifundia of that time. In the first place, their owners rarely possessed the ability and the desire to organize their operation in a new way. . . . In the second place, the status of a feudal noble carried "obligations" with it, at that time as later: a great boyar . . . had by tradition to keep an extensive "household," a mass of idle attendants and retainers. . . . As long as all these lived on grain gotten free from the peasants, the boyar might not notice the economic burden of his official prestige. But when many things had to be bought for money—money whose value was falling from year to year as the Muscovite economy developed—it became a heavy burden on the shoulders of the large landowners. . . . The small vassals were in this case in a considerably more advantageous position. They did not spend money on their service, and in fact received money for it. . . . If we add to this that the small estate was considerably easier to organize than the large ones . . . and that the small landowner was better able to supervise personally the work of his corvée peasants and slaves, while the large landowner had to do this through an overseer, we see that when the battle between the large and middle-sized landholdings began, all the economic benefits were on the side of the latter . . . by expropriating the rich *votchina* boyar, the Oprichnina followed the path of natural economic development.[17]

Here we have both proofs at once—of the reactionary nature of boyar *votchina* and the progressive nature of service landholding.

17. Pokrovskii, vol. 1, pp. 271–73.

True, the "economic" character of both provokes some doubt, to say the least. For, having to do chiefly with "the burden of official prestige" and "a lack of desire to organize the economy in a new way," we still remain primarily in the sphere of social psychology. The only properly economic consideration here seems to be the fall in the value of money, and the consequent rise in the price of grain. However, this "price revolution" was by no means specifically Russian, but was a phenomenon common to all of Europe. Even in Pokrovskii's time this was known to every student. But if this is so, why is it that the progressive "agrarian revolution" in favor of the small vassals, which was connected with this in Pokrovskii's opinion, was successful only in Russia and in Eastern Europe, and did not become widespread anywhere in the West? Were the Western seigneurs more willing than the Muscovite boyars to "organize their economy in a new way"? Or perhaps their "feudal noble status" carried fewer obligations and it was, therefore, easier for them to bear the "economic burden of their official prestige"? Unfortunately there is no answer to these questions to be found in the economic apologia for the Oprichnina. And there are also others.

As we already know, the Oprichnina, according to Pokrovskii, although it was "the state of the service-landowning class,"[18] was not only formed "with the participation of [commercial] capital,"[19] but proved essentially to be a stepping stone to the ascent to the throne of Muscovy of "commercial capital wearing the cap of Monomakh." We might call it in this sense a Russian equivalent of the Western bourgeois revolutions. So interpreted, Muscovy ought perhaps to contend with the Netherlands for the role of pioneer on the path of European economic development. If the triumph of the small vassals in fact embodied the march of progress, then Eastern Europe, and especially Russia, should have gained a decisive advantage over the countries of the West, which did not allow so progressive a process among themselves. The West was in that case doomed to lag behind, and the Muscovy of Ivan the Terrible should have become the torchbearer of world progress.

Only one thing remained incomprehensible: What was one to do with the subsequent four centuries of Russian history? How was one to explain why all these wonders somehow did not take place? More than this, that precisely the reverse occurred: Russia was thrown down into "the darkness of nonexistence," and the "progressive service-landowner" suddenly became the organizer of feudal slavery.

18. Ibid., p. 313.   19. Ibid., p. 307.

Pokrovskii was a scholar first and then a Marxist: apparently the bourgeois leavening was still too strong in him. In any case, he did not even try to distract the reader's attention from the metamorphosis of the service landowner, which made nonsense of his whole conception. This metamorphosis always remained mysterious and inexplicable for Pokrovskii:

> His [the service landowner's] victory should have signified a major economic success—the final triumph of the "monetary" system over the "subsistence" one. *In fact, we see something quite different.* Obligations in kind, crystallized into a complex whole known under the name of "serfdom," again take center stage and are maintained, this time firmly and for a long interval. . . . Having suppressed the feudal *votchina* owner in the name of economic progress, the service landowner very swiftly himself becomes a backward type: this is the paradox with which the history of the Russian economy of the epoch of [Ivan] the Terrible concludes.[20]

However, this paradox did not compel Pokrovskii to review the economic apologia for the Oprichnina or to doubt the Marxist understanding of history. He doubted himself; he doubted the possibilities of the scholarship of that time, pinning his hopes on the idea that the "followers in the cause of applying the materialist method to the data of the Russian past will be more fortunate."[21] Such was the testament of the patriarch of Soviet historical scholarship.

5. The Political Meaning of "Collectivization"

On the ruins of Platonov's "misunderstanding through and through" and Pokrovskii's "paradox," there developed—and it is functioning prosperously to this day—the so-called "agrarian school" of Soviet historians. By the authoritative testimony of N. E. Nosov, "it is precisely this point of view which is brought forward in the works of B. D. Grekov, I. I. Polosin, I. I. Smirnov, A. A. Zimin, R. G. Skrynnikov, Iu. G. Alekseev, and it is perhaps the most widespread up to the present time."[22] Almost all of the luminaries of Soviet historiography are mentioned in this list.

This looks all the more paradoxical inasmuch as the Soviet historians themselves showed that there was no "paradox" in the economic results of the "revolution from above." In the first place, large-scale

20. Ibid., pp. 317–18. Emphasis added.
21. Ibid., p. 319.
22. N. E. Nosov, *O dvukh tendentsiiakh* . . . , p. 5.

landholding in medieval Russia by no means corresponded to large-scale farming. Quite the contrary: the former was only an organizational form, the protective envelope within which the truly progressive process of peasant differentiation took place. Here, as Nosov says, "development proceeds along a new, bourgeois, and nonfeudal path. We have in mind the social differentiation of the countryside, the buying up of land by the rich . . . the development of commercial and industrial capital by peasants. But it was precisely this process that was sharply slowed down, and then totally stopped, on service landholdings."[23] Academician S. D. Skazkin describes the metamorphosis of the "*votchina*" farm into a service farm in precisely the same way: "The landlord's land is transformed into a large-scale, purely entrepreneurial operation. In connection with this, the significance of the peasant farm also changes. . . . The peasant farm becomes a source of unpaid labor power, and for the peasant himself, his allotment and farm become, as Lenin expressed it, 'wages in kind.'"[24]

One would have to be very incurious not to wonder what Skazkin and Nosov are actually describing—the economic results of the "Oprichnina of Ivan" in the 1570s, or those of Stalin's "collectivization" in the 1930s. Did not the real meaning of this "collectivization" consist in the same "change in the significance of the peasant farm" of which Skazkin is speaking? In the same transformation of the household plot, left in the possession of the peasant as his "wages in kind," of which Lenin spoke? In the same transformation of the peasants' labor into "unpaid labor power" for the working of the "landlord's land" of the collective farms? Is it not true that the economic significance of "collectivization" consisted in the violent arrest of the process of peasant differentiation, and in the scattering and robbing of the "best people" of the Russian countryside (which in Stalin's time was called "dekulakization"), of which Nosov speaks?

The analogy between the "collectivization" which destroyed Russian agriculture in the 1930s and the "agrarian revolution" of the 1570s is inescapable. In both cases, the economic result of the Oprichnina was autocratic reaction, which put an end to the process of bourgeois differentiation of the peasantry, and thereby destroyed not only the fruits of previous development, but also the potential it embodied. The Oprichnina rises before us as a monstrous embodiment of reaction, in both the sixteenth and twentieth centuries, in the eco-

23. Ibid., p. 12.
24. S. D. Skazkin, "Osnovnye problemy tak nazyvaemogo 'vtorogo izdaniia' krepostnichestva v Srednei i Vostochnoi Evrope," p. 104.

nomic sense no less than in the political. And this is the real answer to "Pokrovskii's paradox"—one delivered not by the logic of the historians but by the logic of history itself.

6. The Militarist Apologia for the Oprichnina

In the 1930s, the so-called "Pokrovskii school" collapsed. The maturing regime no longer needed a "revolutionary" historiography. It thirsted rather for stabilization and national roots. It needed a historiography which would unify it with the Russian historical tradition, not one which cut it off from that tradition. And, for this purpose, it was willing to make sacrifices, and prepared to prefer old professors to new revolutionaries. R. Iu. Vipper, for example, who first published his book on Ivan the Terrible in 1922, when there was no smell of Marxism about him (in fact, Vipper, along with Platonov and Iarosh, belonged to the right wing), was able twenty years later to write proudly in the preface to the second edition of this book: "I am glad of the fact that the basic positions of my first work have remained unshaken and, it seems to me, have been confirmed once more by the studies of highly authoritative scholars in the past two decades."[25] Vipper was entitled to be triumphant: the Marxists had come to him, and not he to the Marxists. And once again, like Kavelin in the 1840s and Platonov in the 1920s, he advanced the standard and invincible justification of "the studies of the past two decades."

But even taking all this into account, it is difficult to explain the solemn manifestations of loyalty to Ivan the Terrible—the new coronation of him in Russian historiography—which occurred in the 1940s. It would probably have been unimaginable if Russia had not, during the previous decade, entered the most severe phase of pseudodespotism in its history, with all the traditionally characteristic attributes: a "new class," an explosion of modernization, total terror, a militarist-nationalist delirium, and, of course, a new Ivan the Terrible. Once again, its traitorous boyars and the opposition (who were now called "the Right-Trotskyist bloc") were eliminated on a national scale. Once again, its Kurbskiis fled the country (having, incidentally, no notion of their medieval predecessors), and some of them (for ex-

---

25. R. Iu. Vipper, p. 3. On the importance of the legitimizing function of historical studies in the Soviet context, Nancy Whittier Heer notes correctly: "Historical writings in the Soviet Union have come to perform vital sociopolitical functions of a degree and scope perhaps unique and certainly beyond those found under other political systems" ("Political Leadership in Soviet Historiography," p. 12).

ample, Fedor Raskol'nikov)[26] wrote desperate letters to the tsar from abroad. Once again, serfdom was introduced, and once again, the Baltic had to be conquered.

Stalin's Oprichnina had to be historically legitimized; not only force, but the memory and tradition of the nation had to be mobilized towards its justification. Folksongs about Ivan the Terrible surfaced—a conclusive argument in the dispute with the opponents of the tsar. Serfdom was rehabilitated. "The Oprichnina in its class expression," wrote I. I. Polosin,

> was the formation of serfdom, the organized robbing of the peasantry. . . . The survey book of 1571–72 tells how the members of the Oprichnina drowned the peasant rebels in streams of blood, how they burned whole regions, how those of the peasants who survived after the . . . punitive expeditions wandered "in the world" and "between the houses" as beggars.[27]

We have again before us a picture of the collectivization of 1929–33. And what, other than indignation and grief, could this picture of the extermination of one's own people provoke? In a Soviet historian, it provoked a prideful declaration that serfdom was an absolute necessity for the "intensified and accelerated development of production."

This may seem an open revision of Marxism, not to say cynicism. But in the 1940s it seemed to be filled with Marxist fire and pioneer enthusiasm. In the new "myth of the state" created by the new Ivan the Terrible, the first postulate was that the history of society is primarily the history of production. And the second postulate was that as this society-production develops, both the treason within it and the danger from outside grow. The third postulate, that terror ("the struggle against treason") and the cultivation of military might are the sole guarantees of "the intensified and accelerated development" of society-production, flowed logically out of this. Two general motifs, "treason" and "war" and "war" and "treason," are inextricably bound up together.

The new Ivan the Terrible himself spoke of his predecessor in con-

---

26. Fedor Raskol'nikov, one of the leaders of the Bolshevik Party, was Soviet ambassador to Bulgaria during the 1930s. In 1937, he, like the then Soviet ambassador to Greece, A. Barmin, refused to return to Moscow to certain death, and instead wrote Stalin a sharply denunciatory letter from abroad. An analogous letter, incidentally, was written two days before his arrest by Nikolai Bukharin, who, unlike Kurbskii and Raskol'nikov, returned from abroad in 1936, to receive a martyr's crown from the hands of tyrant, as Ivan the Terrible had presaged.

27. I. I. Polosin, p. 132.

sistent terms. His conversation with the actor N. K. Cherkasov, who played the part of Ivan the Terrible in Eizenshtein's film, has preserved this precious testimony for posterity:

> Speaking of the statesmanship of [Ivan] the Terrible, Comrade I. V. Stalin noted that Ivan IV was a great and wise ruler, who guarded the country from the penetration of foreign influence and strove to unify Russia. In particular, speaking of the progressive activity of [Ivan] the Terrible, Comrade Stalin noted that Ivan IV was the first to introduce into Russia the monopoly of foreign trade, and that Lenin was the only one to do so after him. Iosif Vissarionovich also noted the progressive role of the Oprichnina. . . . Referring to the mistakes of Ivan the Terrible, Iosif Vissarionovich noted that one of his mistakes consisted in the fact that he was not able to liquidate the five remaining large feudal families, and did not complete the struggle with feudalism: if he had done so, there would have been no Time of Troubles in Rus'.[28]

Of course, a Marxist historian would have to shudder at this way of putting the question. The contradictions in it are obvious. Was it actually possible in the sixteenth century to "complete the struggle with feudalism," if, as we have just seen, even the Oprichnik Polosin justifies the "economic inevitability of serfdom" precisely by the fact that "sixteenth-century Russia was built and could be built *only* on the basis of feudal and serf production"?[29] But for Stalin, who confused the Turks with the Tatars, and whose reading in Russian history never went higher than the level of the junior grades of a Georgian theological seminary, such subtleties were immaterial. To Stalin "completing the struggle against feudalism" meant only the need to finish murdering the "five remaining feudal families." For, unmurdered, they ruined all the achievements of Ivan the Terrible in "guarding the country from the penetration of foreign influence." In other words, the cause of the catastrophe which overtook Russia in the sixteenth century lay in the inconsistency and insufficiency of the terror. This, for a fact, was Ivan the Terrible's language.

There was no one around to shudder: the historians, as if enchanted, accepted the new idol. Let us return to their texts:

> [New evidence] explains the terror of the critical epoch of 1567–72, and shows that the dangers which surrounded the cause and the person of Ivan the Terrible were still more menacing, and the political atmosphere still more saturated with treachery than might have been as-

---

28. N. Cherkasov, *Zapiski sovetskogo aktera*, p. 308. The authenticity of the quote is beyond doubt, since the book was prepared for the press during Stalin's lifetime.

29. Polosin, p. 132.

sumed on the basis of the sources hostile to the Muscovite state which were known earlier. Ivan the Terrible cannot be accused of excessive suspicion; on the contrary, his mistake consisted, perhaps, in having been too trusting . . . [and] in inadequate attention to the danger which threatened him from the side of the conservative and reactionary opposition, and which he not only did not exaggerate, but even underestimated. . . . After all, it was a matter of treason . . . highly dangerous for the Muscovite state. And at what moment did it threaten to break out? Among the difficulties of a war for which the government had mobilized all the means possessed by the state, had gathered all military and financial reserves, and had demanded from the population the greatest possible patriotic inspiration. Those historians of our time, who, speaking in chorus with the reactionary opposition of the sixteenth century, would insist on the objectless cruelty of Ivan the Terrible . . . should have thought about how antipatriotic and antistate was the mood of the upper classes in that time. . . . The attempt on the life of the tsar was very closely connected with the yielding up to the enemy not only of the newly conquered territories but also the old Russian lands. . . . It was a matter of internal subversion, of intervention, of the division of a great state![30]

This is no longer Stalin—or even the state prosecutor at the trial of the boyar opposition of the "Right-Trotskyist bloc." This is the historian Vipper anticipating Stalin's argument about the unmurdered families.

But the main thing for Stalin was nevertheless not serfdom or terror as such. These were merely means. What was really needed was the transformation of the country into a colony of the military-industrial complex, as an instrument of world dominion. It was precisely this, the main thing, which had to be suitably legitimized by the tradition.

For all his ignorance of Russian history, Stalin intuitively picked out from the multitude of Russian tsars his most appropriate predecessors. And they—what a strange coincidence!—proved to be the same ones whose exploits, in the opinion of Lomonosov (during the period of the first "historiographic nightmare"), had made it possible "that Russia should be feared by the whole world." They proved to be the same "two extremely great statesmen," who in the opinion of Kavelin (during the period of the second "historiographic nightmare") "were equally keenly aware of the idea of the Russian state." And Stalin openly valued them for the same thing—their Northern Wars. The main hangman of the Oprichnina, Maliuta Skuratov, that medi-

30. Vipper, pp. 113–14.

eval Beriia, he called "a great Russian commander, who fell heroically in the struggle with Livonia."[31] He valued Peter because the tsar "feverishly built factories and workshops to supply the army and to strengthen the defense of the country."[32]

However, Stalin had much to do besides rehabilitating Ivan the Terrible and Peter. He entrusted the concrete working out of a new militarist apologia for the Oprichnina to experts.

One of the first to recognize this patriotic duty was the prominent student of the Oprichnina, P. A. Sadikov (on whose works Platonov had constructed his unfortunate hypothesis). Sadikov introduced a completely new note into Platonov's canonical interpretation. In his opinion,

> having been thrust like a wedge into . . . the Muscovite territory, "the appanage of the sovereign" [the Oprichnina] was supposed, according to [Ivan] the Terrible's plan, not only to be a means for decisive struggle with the feudal princes and the boyardom by rearranging their landholdings, but also to become an organizational nucleus for creating the possibility of struggle against enemies *on the external front.*[33]

Thus, the Oprichnina outgrew the infantile tasks in internal policy on which Russian historians had concentrated for centuries, and revealed a completely new military-mobilizational function, which had previously remained in the shadows for some reason. It is no accident that Vipper comments as follows on this discovery by Sadikov:

> If, like the malcontents of the princely and boyar opposition, the historians of the nineteenth century liked to speak easily of the disorderly plundering by Ivan the Terrible and his Oprichniki of the entire Trans-Muscovite region, a historian of our time has contrasted to these unsubstantiated assertions documented facts which show . . . the constructive work which was performed within the limits of the territory of the Oprichnina.[34]

And the constructiveness of this work is seen by Vipper no longer, as Platonov did, in the quarrel with the "formerly sovereign princes," or, as Pokrovskii did, in the "class struggle" (the category of class struggle is completely replaced in his work by "the struggle with treason"), but in the fact that Ivan the Terrible began the transformation of the country into a *"military monarchy."* For this reason, the Oprichnina was

31. N. Cherkasov, p. 380.
32. I. V. Stalin, *Voprosy leninizma* (9th ed.), p. 359.
33. Cited in Vipper, p. 123. Emphasis added.
34. Ibid.

for Vipper primarily a "measure of a *military-organizational* character."[35] (While I disagree totally with Vipper in the evaluation of this
"measure," I am in full agreement with him, and with Sadikov, on the
principle: contrary to what the "despotists" think, Ivan the Terrible
actually did *begin* the history of the autocracy, which was militaristic
and mobilizational in nature, using the Oprichnina as a tool, a school,
and a laboratory for the total militarization of the country.) From this
point of view, however, the war in whose name, according to Sadikov
and Vipper, the Oprichnina transformation of Russia was undertaken, assumes a completely different significance.

The founders of the "agrarian school" (like their predecessors, the
"statists") stood entirely on the tsar's side in the strategic argument
with the Government of Compromise. Platonov wrote that "the times
called Muscovy to the West, to the shores of the sea, and [Ivan] the
Terrible did not let pass the moment to state his claims to a part of the
Livonian heritage."[36] Pokrovskii noted that "the Oprichnina terror
can be understood only in connection with the failures of the Livonian War."[37] However, for them, the Livonian War, and the terror, were
only elements in the great "agrarian revolution." For the "militarists,"
the "agrarian revolution" was merely an element in the war.[38] The
war itself ceased to be for them a prosaic adventure of conquest, a
mere claim to "a part of the Livonian heritage," as it had been for
Platonov, or a "war over trade routes—that is, indirectly over markets,"[39] as it had been for Pokrovskii. It became a crusade, a sacred
task taking on features of national, historical, and almost mystical significance. "In the second half of the 1560s, Russia was solving complex questions of foreign policy," writes Polosin.

> This was a time when the struggle for Lithuania, the Ukraine, and Be-
> lorussia became especially acute. This was a time when the question of
> the kingdom of Livonia was being decided. . . . This was a time when
> the Vatican was going over to the offensive. From behind the backs of
> the king of Poland and the archbishop of Riga, the figure of the pope,

35. Ibid., p. 75. Emphasis added.
36. Platonov, *Ivan Groznyi*, p. 105.   37. Pokrovskii, vol. 1, p. 302.
38. For P. A. Sadikov the "formation of the Oprichnina corps" was directly "dependent on the conditions of military defense." Furthermore, quoting the testimony of
eyewitnesses, Taube and Kruze, he confirms that the service landholders were considerably less competent farmers than the boyars: "the lack of skill of the Oprichniki in farming on their new holdings" led to the fact that "huge properties were destroyed and
plundered in such a short time that it seemed as if the enemy had passed through"
(P. A. Sadikov, *Ocherki po istorii oprichniny*, p. 113).
39. Pokrovskii, vol. 1, p. 319.

who had closed the Council of Trent in order to develop the attack of Catholicism more energetically, revealed himself. Not only Latvia and Lithuania were under threat, but also the Ukraine and Belorussia. . . . It was with complete justification that [Ivan] the Terrible considered the Vatican his major enemy, and it was not without reference to the papal orders that the Oprichnina was organized.[10]

What price, then, the Tatar threat or the struggle with the "aristocratic personnel" propounded by the naive Kliuchevskii, or even the struggle against the "class of formerly sovereign princes" mooted by the now hopelessly obsolete Platonov? All of Eastern Europe was under mortal threat of a "Catholic offensive," it turns out, with Muscovy defending Latvia and Lithuania, not to speak of the Ukraine and Belorussia, with its own breast. A general European Catholic conspiracy was developing, if not a worldwide one, and Muscovy somehow turned out to be the only force able to withstand it. In trying to seize Livonia, Tsar Ivan was performing not only a patriotic duty, but a kind of great religio-political mission. He was suddenly transformed "into one of the most significant political and military figures of European history in the sixteenth century."[41]

The contours of the assignment given to Russian historiography by Stalin are starting to become clear. This was at the same time an aggressive and a defensive spirit, both justifying conquests and affected by an inferiority complex—a monstrous amalgam of persecution mania and striving for absolute dominance. It was the same mixture which had compelled Ivan the Terrible to seek salvation from the boyar conspiracy which surrounded him (or so it seemed to him) in the physical destruction of his opponents. In the speeches of a modern Tsar Ivan and in the interpretations of the contemporary Oprichniki, the old boyar conspiracy grew to the dimensions of a world conspiracy, inspired now by the Tatars, now by the papacy, now by imperialism, but always pursuing one and the same goal—to deprive Russia of its independence, to turn it into a colony, and to prevent it from fulfilling its historical mission. It was now no longer sufficient, in order to make absolute the power of the tyrant as the instrument of Russia's salvation, merely to exterminate internal opponents. Now, for this purpose, one had to exterminate the organizers of the world conspiracy, and, therefore, upset not only Russia, but the whole planet. This is how the twentieth-century Ivan the Terrible formulated the task: "We are doing a job which, if it succeeds, will turn the

40. Polosin, p. 137.
41. Vipper, p. 174.

whole world upside down."[42] And what was the alternative to the success of this job? "Do you want our fatherland to be beaten and to lose its independence?"[43]

Either we "turn the world upside down," or "we lose our independence." There is no middle road. On the one hand Stalin asserted that the history of Russia consisted in her being beaten (and, consequently, that the time had finally come for her to be avenged for the humiliations of the past), and on the other hand he called down the blessings of the victorious tsars on the Russian banners.

As applied to the epoch of Ivan the Terrible, Stalin's approach went: if the tsar had not attacked Livonia, Russia would have been the prey of the Mongols. As applied to the period of Peter: if Peter had not conquered the Baltic, Russia would have been a colony of Sweden, etc., etc. This was not said by Stalin. This was said by experts. In the officially approved textbook of N. Rubinshtein, *Russian Historiography*, designed for students in the historical faculties of the Soviet universities in the 1940s, we read:

> The development of the multinational centralized state in Russia in the sixteenth century was the beginning of the transformation of Russia into a prison of people. But if this had not occurred, Russia would have been the prey of the Mongols or of Poland. . . . The policy of Peter I laid a heavy burden on the peasants, [but] saved Russia from the prospect of transformation into a colony or semicolony of Sweden, which threatened it.[44]

What Mongols could have threatened Russia in the sixteenth century? Who does not know that it was not the Swedes who attacked Russia under Peter in 1700, but Russia which attacked the Swedes? Stalin could permit himself to say those things—out of ignorance, from political calculation, or because of the paranoia which convulsed him. But how could the professional experts permit themselves this? And yet they did so. Russian historiography suddenly began to speak with the voice of Ivan the Terrible. With the new, militaristic apologia, a third "historiographic nightmare" rolled down on Ivaniana. Forgotten was S. M. Solov'ev's injunction: "Let not the historian say a word in justification of such a person." This person was justified. Forgotten was A. K. Tolstoi's horror in the face of the fact that "there could exist a society which could gaze upon him without indignation." Such a society existed.

42. I. V. Stalin, *Voprosy leninizma* (11th ed.), p. 329.
43. Ibid., p. 328.
44. N. L. Rubinshtein, *Russkaia istoriografiia*, p. 634.

7. A Medieval Vision

How could this happen? I understand that this is to some extent a personal question. It concerns not so much the explanation of historical circumstances as the moral collapse of Russian historiography—a phenomenon which in religious parlance would probably be called a fall from grace. For a Western author, the question would presuppose an objective analysis of what in fact did happen. What did not happen, he would leave out of account. I cannot allow myself that luxury. For me, this is a piece of life, and not only the subject of academic consideration. I feel myself infinitely humiliated because this happened to my country in my generation. The problem for me is not only one of describing the past, but of coming to terms with it. For this reason, everything I here offer the reader is closer to personal confession than to scholarly analysis. Those indifferent to historical reflection and inclined to think that "facts are facts and the rest is belles lettres," as one great Russian poet used to say, can quietly skip this subsection.

One cannot come to terms with the fall from grace of a nation without coming to terms with it in one's self. In me, as in every offspring of Russian culture, two souls coexist. But not peacefully: they fight to the death—exactly as its two cultural traditions contend in the consciousness of the nation. Each of these has its own hierarchy of values. The highest value of the one is order (and, correspondingly, the lowest is anarchy or chaos). The highest value of the other is freedom (and, correspondingly, the lowest is slavery). I fear chaos and hate slavery. I feel the temptation to believe in "a strong regime" able to defend the humiliated and aggrieved, to dry all tears and console all griefs. And I am ashamed of this temptation. Sometimes it seems to me that freedom gives birth to chaos (as it seemed to Solov'ev, who saw the major evil of Russian life in "the freedom of movement"). Sometimes it seems to me that slavery gives birth to order (as it seemed to Polosin, who justified serfdom). It is precisely in the epoch of the "historiographic nightmare" which we are considering, that the fundamental incompatibility of both traditions comes to light with ultimate clarity. The time has come to choose between them.

For almost 400 years the gigantic shadow of its first autocrator has loomed over Russian history, now losing his crown, and now raised again to imperial dignity. Never until now, however, has his terrible heritage threatened the very existence of the nation as a moral union. I am not speaking only of the fact that we have lived through the nightmare of the GULAG, but also of the impossibility of living any longer with the consciousness that this nightmare may be repeated, that the most honored and learned preceptors of our nation will again abase themselves—and abase the nation—by justifying serfdom, terror, and aggression. That once again they will help the tyrant to legitimize slavery by legitimizing the tradition of slavery.

It would be infinitely easier for me if I could simply say that this was the price at which the historians of Stalin's time bought their lives and well-being in an epoch when the struggle for physical survival ruled: after all, all countries and all ages have had their collaborationists. This would be easier, but it would be false. It is sufficient to read the works of Sadikov, Polosin, Bakhrushin, Vipper, or Smirnov, to be convinced that this is not bureaucratic prose or official rhetoric. A profoundly personal impulse is present here, a clear certainty of being in the right.

Polosin wrote: "The Oprichnina . . . received its scientific and historical *justification* only in Soviet scholarship."[45] Bakhrushin wrote: "The true significance of Ivan the Terrible becomes clear only in our time . . . *in the light of Marxist methodology.*"[46] They were convinced of this. If this was a false faith, it was a faith nevertheless.

The mighty autocratic tradition of Russian historiography was speaking through their mouths. Lomonosov, Tatishchev, Kavelin, Gorskii, Belov, and Iarosh were speaking. All of those who, without any connection with the "light of Marxist methodology," had justified the Oprichnina long before Polosin, because somewhere in the dark depths of their souls, almost unconsciously, they were convinced that "freedom of movement" creates chaos, that opposition gives rise to anarchy, and that Paris is worth a mass—that is, that "order" is worth the price of slavery. The tradition of slavery spoke through their mouths, and it was tradition—not personal cowardice, or timeserving, or the desire for a good life—which compelled them to lie, and to believe their own lies, and inventively to justify atrocities by reference to "documented facts," wrapping themselves in the cardboard armor of the "Marxist-Leninist ideology." This was not so much their fault, as their calamity.

What happened, happened. If the behavior of Ivan the Terrible's Oprichniki can still be interpreted in various ways, the behavior of Stalin's Oprichniki does not permit two opinions. In order to evaluate it, we do not need either "documented facts" or "the light of Marxist methodology." We were there. We know that we have before us not

---

45. Polosin, p. 182.
46. S. V. Bakhrushin, *Ivan Groznyi*, p. 5.

only beasts and hangmen, but also people to whom the tradition gives a basis for being proud of their corruption.

If we actually are faced by a mighty tradition, and if this tradition actually does lead us to such depths of humiliation, then are we entitled to wait passively for the hour of humiliation and corruption to strike again for us, or for those who come after us? This is no longer a question of national pride, as it was in the time of Lomonosov and Shcherbatov, nor is it a question of national self-respect, as it was in the time of Kavelin and Kliuchevskii. This is a question of national existence. After all, three successive "historiographic nightmares" have demonstrated unmercifully that the tradition of collaborationism is not simply implanted by the police. It is not a force external to us, it is within us. And it is killing us from within. Will we survive a fourth "historiographic nightmare"? And, if we survive, will we still be human beings?

The structure of the "myth of the state" is elementary. On what premises, in fact, does the tsar justify his position in his letters to Kurbskii? In the first place, by identifying the goals of the leader with those of the state. In the second place, by identifying the goals of the state with those of the nation. The whole essence of the matter, in my view, is contained in this formula of double identification. To suggest that the leadership proceeds from goals and interests distinct from the interests of the state, and still more from those of the nation, is to be a traitor and an enemy of the people. This was Ivan the Terrible's fundamental postulate, so obvious to him that he does not even state it directly. Behind this postulate stands the vision of an absolutely consensual society-family, the head of which sees everything, knows everything, is concerned for everyone, and by definition cannot have any other interests than those of the members of his household.

This was an essentially medieval vision, symbolized and confirmed by the divine mandate of the suzerain. But, surprisingly, in the nineteenth century it was again reborn in Russian historiography. Only now justification was provided in the shape of the alleged need to destroy the "clan element," or by the postulate of a poor nation, deprived of "stone," or of a nation threatened by the fate of Poland. And once again it seemed that Russia could not overcome these obstacles without an Ivan the Terrible. In other words, the "myth of the state" took on the scholarly form of the state school, but it was based as before on the vision of the consensual society, in which the administration performed the necessary historical function of organizing and defending the system, of saving it—whether from the clan element, from aggressive neighbors, or from the oligarchy. For this reason, the interests of the administration not only could not differ from the interests and goals of the system, but properly speaking, the latter did not even exist in and of themselves. The system and the administration were one—undivided and indivisible.

When later, in the twentieth century, the time came for the "agrarian school," with its "class struggle" and its "economic revolution," it seemed that the time to part company with the vision of the consensual society had finally arrived. The "class struggle" itself presupposed that the society is neither a family nor a homogeneous unit, that the interests of its various groups not only differ, but are opposed to each other. And still, in some strange way, it again turned out that the goals of the state coincided with the goals of a "progressive" class, and thereby, just as in the time of Ivan the Terrible, were indistinguishable from the goals of the society.

Once again—for both "agrarianist" and "militarist" historiography—the state is perceived as having saved the nation: in the one case from the "class of formerly sovereign princes," from the reactionary latifundia, and the opponents of commodity-and-money relationships; and in the other from the "Catholic assault," from military backwardness, from the world conspiracy of the Vatican. The oppositionists remained "enemies of the people."

None of these historiographic schools, which successively replaced each other, admitted that there could exist a divergence between the goals of the administration and those of the system, that the leader could pursue his own interests, opposed to the interests both of the state and of the nation. The medieval vision of the consensual society hung over both the "left-wingers" and the "right-wingers." Even the Marxists, for whom the state in theory constituted "the organization of the ruling class," could not keep from officially proclaiming it "the state of all the people"—that is, capitulating before the thesis of the bourgeois state school.

However, history has confirmed Aristotle, who, as we have seen, argued 500 years before the birth of Christ that divergences between the goals of the administration and those of the system are in the nature of things, and, consequently, that consensual political structures are simply not found on earth. It was already clear to him that "deviations"—that is, the striving of the state to subject the society to the interests of particular groups or to the personal interests of the leader—were politically inevitable. The problem, therefore, consists not in preserving a mythical consensus, but in making society capable of correcting the "deviations" of the state. And the sole means of such correction invented by the political genius of mankind—the sole

means of preventing destructive revolutions which sow chaos and anarchy—is the very opposition which in Russian historiography is traditionally branded "treason." In this sense, the political history of
mankind can be summed up as the history of the legalization and le-
gitimization of the opposition.

It was neither the heritage of the primeval clan which threatened
the integrity of the nation, as the "statists" thought, nor feudal eco-
nomics, as the Marxists had it. With these the nation was learning to
cope; but there was something against which it was, and still is, helpless: the elemental force embodied in arbitrary state power, which
was, and still is, fraught with the like of Ivan's Oprichnina and Stalin's
Gulag. It is this force which thus proves to be the real source of chaos
in social systems, and the only tool for curbing its terrible power (that
is, for preserving the much-desired "order") is the free functioning of
the opposition. We thus come to the heretical and—from the viewpoint of the "myth of the state"—criminal conclusion that the basis of
order is freedom. A historiography which depicts opposition as treason falls inevitably—and always will fall—into a logical trap, the only
escape from which is in lies, collaborationism, and Stalinization.

Open the well-known trilogy by V. Kostylev, which received not
only the Stalin Prize, but an enthusiastic review by so experienced an
expert as Academician N. Druzhinin.[47] Russians would rather forget
about this shameful matter. But this is precisely what one should not
do. To remember, to remember as much as possible—this is the only
thing which can save us from ourselves. The whole meaning of Ivaniana lies in compelling us to remember. In Kostylev's trilogy the tsar
speaks in garbled quotations from his letters to Kurbskii, and his
Oprichniki in quotations from Vipper, but let us leave it to the literary
critics. Across its pages there walk disreputable, stinking, bearded
boyars, occupied exclusively with oppressing the peasants and com-
mitting treason. The Oprichniki, on the other hand, are all as if specially selected, stalwart young men out of the epic ballads, real scions
of the people, liberating it from bloodthirsty exploiters, and eradicat-
ing "the enemies of the people," without regard to the danger to their
own lives. These Oprichniki have warm hearts, cool minds, and clean
hands, just as the modern official version depicts the *"Chekisty"*[48]—

47. V. I. Kostylev, *Ivan Groznyi.*
48. *Cheka* is the Russian abbreviation for the Extraordinary Commission for Combatting Counterrevolution, Sabotage, and Speculation, the main political police organ
of the early revolutionary period, which functioned from 1917 to 1922. The derivative
of this dreadful term, *"Chekisty,"* is an honorary title for all the successors of the *Cheka,*
that is, all members of the Soviet political police to this day.

that is to say, Stalin's Oprichniki. Let us accept this picture as sound. Let us even accept, further, the entreaties of Kostylev and Vipper not to believe the oppositionists, explaining all the shadows cast upon the tsar exclusively by their sinister influence. "The failures in the external war," Vipper complains,

> the bloodshed of the internal war—the struggle with treason—overshadowed even for the immediately following generations the military triumphs and military achievements of the reign of [Ivan] the Terrible. Among the subsequent historians . . . the majority were subject to the influence of sources originating from oppositionist circles: in their eyes, the significance of his personality was diminished. He was included in the list of "tyrants."[49]

If we remember that even Karamzin, who was precisely the one who included the tsar "in the list of tyrants," not only did not deny, but even glorified his services to the state, we will see immediately that Vipper is lying (or does not know his subject). But this is not what is important. Let us turn to sources free of the "influence of oppositionist circles"—to the sources which Vipper himself recommends. Who, in the Russia of that time, was free from "influence"? Naturally, Ivan the Terrible's Chekist, the Oprichnik Heinrich Staden. True, he was a German, and, of course, a low-life—this much Vipper willingly admits. But his testimony is precious (we already know for what reason) to such a degree that in Vipper's eyes he is quite qualified to be a defense witness. His *Notes on Muscovy* "may boldly be called a first-class document of the history of Moscow and the Muscovite state in the 1560s and 1570s."[50]

Let us agree that "opposition circles" were wrong in characterizing the Oprichnina of Ivan the Terrible as riffraff gathered by the tsar from all corners of the country and even hired from abroad in order to destroy its elite. Let us agree that the Oprichniki were the most honorable servants of the tsar, who helped him in the fateful struggle with treason, which was beyond his own powers. Now let us see what the defense witness says about the fate of these devoted "hounds of the sovereign." In 1572 the tsar suddenly "began to take reprisals against the top people of the Oprichnina," Staden writes.

> Prince Afanasii Viazemskii died . . . in iron shackles. Aleksei [Basmanov] and his son [Fedor] with whom [the tsar] practiced depravity were killed. . . . Prince Mikhail [Cherkasskii], brother-in-law [of the tsar] was hacked to pieces by *strel'tsy* [musketeers] with axes. . . . Prince Vasilii

49. Vipper, p. 174.
50. Ibid., p. 105.

Temkin was drowned. Ivan Zobatyi was killed. Petr [Shcheniat'ev?] was hanged on his own gates in front of his bedroom. Prince Andrei Ovtsyn was hanged at Oprichnina headquarters in Arbatskii street; a live sheep [Ovtsyn's name recalls the Russian word for sheep (*ovtsa*)] was hanged together with him. The marshal Bulat wished to make a match between his sister and [the tsar] and was killed, and the sister was raped by 500 *strel'tsy*. Kuraka Unkovskii, head man of the *strel'tsy*, was killed and pushed under the ice.[51]

What are we to conclude from this "defense testimony"? Were the Oprichniki actually the most honorable of men, as Kostylev suggests to the mass reader in a large edition of books, with Druzhinin's blessing? What are we, then, to say of the tsar who hanged them upon the gates of their own houses, as he did "enemies of the people"? What are we to say of the tsar who after 1572 forbade the very use of the term "Oprichnina," threatening its users with the severest penalties? And if the Oprichniki really did deserve such punishment, who was right—the "oppositionist circles" or the respected scholars?

Let us assume that the writer Kostylev was deceived by his capricious muse. But it was harder to fool experts who had read the primary sources. Bakhrushin, one of the major Russian historians of the twentieth century, knows quite well what went on in the Oprichnina. He knows, for example, that "the service landholders were interested in having on the throne a strong tsar, capable of satisfying the need of the service class for land and serf labor," while "on the other hand, the boyars were interested in protecting their lives and property from the arbitrary behavior of the tsar."[52]

What, one wonders, is so bad about defending one's life and property from the arbitrary behavior of the tsar? Why did such a natural human desire make the boyars "enemies of the people"? And why were the service landholders, who needed the serf labor of the people, their friends? Why does the author take this need of theirs so much to heart? Why is the "arbitrary behavior of the tsar" so dear to him that he is prepared to justify it by declaring the terror "inevitable under the given historical conditions"? Here is the concluding characterization of the tsar given by Bakhrushin in his book *Ivan the Terrible*:

There is no need for us to idealize Ivan the Terrible. . . . His deeds speak for themselves. He created a mighty feudal state. His reforms, which *assured order* within the country and its defense from external en-

51. Cited in ibid., pp. 121–22.
52. Bakhrushin, pp. 52, 54.

emies, met with warm support from the Russian people. . . . Thus, in the person of [Ivan] the Terrible we have not an "angel of virtue" and not the mysterious villain of melodramas, but a major statesman of his period, who *correctly understood the interests and needs of his people, and struggled to see them satisfied.*[53]

This picture plainly shows that Russian historiography even in the twentieth century is still in the paws of the Middle Ages. But if this is so, then a completely different question arises: how did it happen that Russian historiography was not transformed into an undifferentiated heap of lies? The only answer consists, I believe, in the fact that, along with the tradition of collaborationism, there exists in Russian historiography another, parallel tradition, deriving precisely from the "oppositionist circles" which Vipper damns—one which I would call the tradition of Resistance, which passed like a torch from Kurbskii to Krizhanich, from Shcherbatov to Aksakov, from Lunin to Herzen, from Kliuchevskii to Veselovskii. There has never been an epoch when the tradition of Resistance was not present in Russian historiography. Even in the somber years of the "historiographic nightmares," this torch flickered before our eyes, even if it did not exactly shine. In this, in our capacity for opposition, is our real hope. Every oppositionist, individually, is easy to slander as an "enemy of the people," to throw into prison, to exile, or to slay—"with his wife and his sons and his daughters." But for some reason there always remain five families which have not been murdered, and perhaps thanks to this, it has been impossible to murder completely the tradition of Resistance. Russia lives by it, and Russian historiography lives by it.

8. The Mutiny of Dubrovskii

This tradition did not die out in Ivaniana even under the ice of Stalin's Oprichnina. Exactly as the terrible tsar was exposed after his death by M. Katyrev and I. Timofeev during the first Russian Time of Troubles, so S. Dubrovskii and V. Sheviakov rebelled against the heirs of the Oprichnina during the seventh Time of Troubles. "Ivan IV must be considered . . . as the tsar of the serfholding service landholders," declared the rebels. "The personality of Ivan IV has overshadowed [in Soviet historiography] the people, and overshadowed the epoch. The people have been allowed to appear on the historical scene only in order to show 'love' for Ivan IV and to praise his actions."[54]

53. Ibid., p. 90. Emphasis added.
54. S. Dubrovskii, "Protiv idealizatsii deiatel'nosti Ivana IV," pp. 123–29.

Professor Dubrovskii sincerely believed that he was combatting Vipper, Bakhrushin, and Smirnov. But, as we have seen, they were not his only opponents in this battle. Karamzin, Kavelin, Platonov, and the entire mighty collaborationist tradition stood against him. It could not be overcome simply by appeals to obvious facts and common sense. The rebellions of Pogodin and Veselovskii had already shown this. Facts were powerless against the hypnosis of the myth. Dubrovskii could rely on the tradition of the "oppositionist circles," on Kurbskii and Krizhanich in the attempt to create an alternative conception of Ivaniana. But are we entitled to demand so much of him? After all, he came out of the same school as the collaborationists. He himself considered autocracy—"the dictatorship of the serf holders," as he called it—an inevitable and natural dominant feature of Russian history. He himself had grown up with the traditional contempt for "reactionary boyardom." And for this reason an instrumental apparatus different from the one with which his opponents, the collaborationists, worked was simply not available to him. And this was easily demonstrated by I. I. Smirnov in a rebuff (which I would rather call a punitive expedition) that deserves description. If the reader finds this rebuff to be a terrible oversimplification, full of logical and factual errors, I would agree with him completely. But I am here only the modest reporter of a discussion which actually took place in Moscow, in the summer of 1956 (that is, in the middle of the post-Stalinist thaw).

Was the liquidation of the feudal fragmentation, and the centralization of the country, not a current necessity of state in the epoch of Ivan the Terrible? Smirnov asked. Was the absolute monarchy not an inevitable phase in the history of feudal society, and did it not play the role of the centralizing element in the state? Did all the European countries in the Middle Ages not know a "terrible, bloody struggle" (compare the Wars of the Roses in England, the Massacre of St. Bartholomew in France, the Stockholm Bloodbath, etc.)? From this collection of clichés Smirnov drew the conclusion—as simple as two times two equals four—that the Oprichnina was an inevitable form of the struggle of absolute monarchy for the centralization of the country against the reactionary boyars and formerly sovereign princes. As for the "cruel form" which was taken by this struggle for centralization in the epoch of the Oprichnina, and as for the enserfment of the peasants and the atrocities of the terror, on these questions Smirnov was excellently prepared—once more, with Kavelin. Alas, he replied, such is the price of progress and of liberation from "the forces of reaction and stagnation."

It made no difference that the "progress" in question, for which such an immoderate price had been paid, turned out to be the impenetrable darkness of the same "reaction and stagnation" of which it was supposed to free the country. It made no difference that besides serfdom and permanent backwardness, the Oprichnina also established a serflike cultural tradition, of which Smirnov himself—together with his opponents, unfortunately—was a victim.

For Dubrovskii, like Kliuchevskii before him, did not reflect on the content of the concept of "absolute monarchy," which beat him over the head like a club. He was unable, therefore, to object that absolutism and despotism and autocracy are all of them forms of "absolute monarchy," and that what is important in Ivaniana is not so much their similarity as their differences.

In 1956, after all of the triumphs of "genuine science," Dubrovskii found himself in the same position in which the primeval and "prescientific" Karamzin had found himself in 1821. And, just like Karamzin, he had nothing with which to respond to his opponents but emotional protest and wounded moral feelings. His defeat was built into his methodology. Of course, this by no means diminishes what he had done: on the contrary, we must pay tribute to his courage. The apparently indestructible ice of the "militarist apologia" had indeed been cracked. By the end of the 1950s, there was no trace of it left. And if, in 1963, A. A. Zimin was able to write, in his *Oprichnina of Ivan the Terrible*, that "in the works of a number of [Soviet] historians, an idyllic image of Ivan IV and a prettied up representation of the Oprichnina have been given," this is indisputably to the credit of Dubrovskii. And if Zimin added: "This was facilitated to no small degree by the statements of I. V. Stalin, who praised Ivan the Terrible without restraint, forgetting about those innumerable calamities which the spread of serfdom in the sixteenth century brought to the people,"[55] this sounded like a mere echo of Dubrovskii, who was the first to draw attention to this strange—or so it seemed at the time—emotional attraction of one tyrant to another.

But on closer examination, it is not hard to see that Dubrovskii's opponents had not retreated very far. They had withdrawn, as the military expression has it, to previously prepared positions—and, furthermore, to ones established a long time ago and with no help whatever from Marxism. They had retreated to Solov'ev's position: moral condemnation was the only price which they would agree to pay for the political rehabilitation of Ivan the Terrible. Hardening

55. A. A. Zimin, *Oprichnina Ivana Groznogo*, pp. 4–5.

their hearts, they agreed that the moral qualities of the tyrant did not deserve to be "idealized"; on the other hand, they came unanimously to the defense of Ivan's terror as a means of "centralization." This is immediately apparent in the commentaries to volume six of Solov'ev's *History of Russia* published in 1960 under the editorship of Academician L. V. Cherepnin, which, as it were, summarize the discussion called forth by the mutiny of Dubrovskii. Here, among other things, it is said that "no matter how great the actual cruelties by which Ivan IV implemented his policy, they cannot conceal the fact that the struggle against the princely and boyar elite was *historically conditioned, inevitable, and progressive*." Furthermore, the authors of the commentaries say, "the government of Ivan IV *was compelled* by the objective situation to act primarily by *violent methods* in the struggle to centralize the power in the state." As regards the critique of the "rebels" of 1956, Dubrovskii and Sheviakov, the commentary says, with implacable bureaucratic haughtiness: "Having correctly noted the inadmissibility of the idealization of Ivan IV, the authors of these articles were *unable to argue* for their proposed reconsideration of the policy of Ivan IV in the direction of regarding it as reactionary and even historically meaningless."[56]

The de-Stalinization of Ivaniana did not take place. After the thunderous explosion of the militarist apologia and a Kavelinist outburst of "idealization," genuine science had peaceably returned to the accustomed, cozy swamp of Solov'evian "centralization"—of course, with the obligatory addition of Platonov's "agrarian revolution." The place of the solemn hymns of Vipper-Bakhrushin is taken by the grey consensus of Cherepnin-Likhachev. Whereas before the revolt of Dubrovskii, the position of genuine science in Ivaniana was an eclectic blend of Platonov and Kavelin, after that revolt, it was transformed into a cocktail mixed from the ideas of Platonov and Solov'ev. It remained essentially what it had been before—a symbiosis of the "agrarian" and "state" schools of Ivaniana. Thus, out of a mixture of two "bourgeois" ideas, we get Marxism-Leninism as the sum. Alas, despite its revolutionary promises, Marxism has not saved "genuine science" from enslavement to the "myth of the state."

Even if we did not have any other indicators of this slavery, one—and the most important—still remains: its attitude towards the political opposition. In the year in which Dubrovskii rebelled, his colleague Likhachev repeated *literally* what had been written in 1856 by Solov'ev's pupil Gorskii. At the risk of exhausting the reader's patience,

56. Cited in S. M. Solov'ev, *Istoriia Rossii*, bk. 3, pp. 756–57.

I will again double up the quotations. Try to separate the revelations of the 1956-model Marxist from those of the 1856-model monarchist. Here is what they wrote:

> In arguing for the old tradition, Kurbskii was led not by the interests of the fatherland, but only by purely selfish considerations. . . . His ideal was not in the future, but in the past. In the person of Kurbskii, the reactionary boyars and princes had found themselves a bard and a philosopher. . . . To this reactionary ideology, Ivan the Terrible counterposed . . . the principle of the construction of a new state . . . branding Kurbskii as a criminal and a traitor to his fatherland. . . . He [Kurbskii] in vain spent his efforts in the struggle against the innovations. . . . Before this severe judgment of posterity he is the defender of the immobility and stagnation, which went counter to history and counter to the development of the society.[57]

9. The Sacred Formula

"The centralization of the state" thus proves to be the last word of genuine science. The formula does not rest on any characterization of the state, whether social or political. It is completely amorphous, and, therefore, fruitless, since a democratic state can be no less centralized than an autocratic one. If sacrifices to this heathen idol are forgivable in the "bourgeois" Solov'ev, who reasons in abstract terms about the struggle between the "state" and the "*votchina*" elements, how are they to be explained in the works of historians who call themselves Marxists? However, the abstract nature of the sacred formula is only half the trouble. The other half is that for the sixteenth-century Russia of Ivan the Terrible and the Government of Compromise, to which they apply it, it is simply false.

It is false because centralization—to the degree to which this was possible in a medieval state, and in the sense in which Soviet historians use this formula, i.e., the administration of all the regions of the country from a single center—had already been completed in the fifteenth century. The publication of the law code of 1497, which signalized the juridical unification of the country, was the *concluding* accord of this centralization. For two centuries, the House of Rurik, like the French Capetians, had been gathering together northeastern Rus' piece by piece, through intrigues and flattery, threats and violence. Their will had become law from one frontier to another. They could

---

57. S. Gorskii, *Zhizn' i istoricheskoe znachenie kniazia A. M. Kurbskogo*, p. 414; D. S. Likhachev, "Ivan Peresvetov i ego literaturnaia sovremennost'," p. 35.

dictate from the Kremlin how to give judgment, how to farm, and how to live, whether in Novgorod, in Tver', or in Riazan'. No one, either in the country or outside it, doubted the right of Muscovy's grand prince to rule over the entire area from the White Sea to Putivl', to make laws as he thought best, to appoint and depose vice-gerents, or to destroy altogether the institution of vicegerents. The administrative center of the system had been created. And the periphery recognized it as the center. Unity of will and unity of program had become a political fact in the Muscovite state. What more centralization was needed?

What passed on unsolved to the heirs of Ivan III was quite another task, completely different from the "gathering-in" and infinitely more complex than "centralization"—the *integration* of the newly centralized state: the transformation of its external, administrative, and juridical unity into an internal, moral, and economic unity.

This integration could be absolutist or autocratic in nature. It could proceed from elements in the state program of Ivan III (envisaging the formation of juridical and cultural guarantees of security of life and property for the citizen) or from the opposite elements in the program of Ivan IV (which negate these guarantees). After all, we must not forget that this was only the *beginning*, that the cultural norms were only just being formed. By violently splitting the country into two parts, destroying all the limitations on the arbitrary behavior of the "administrative center," legalizing the disorder in the state as order, causing the rebirth of the appanage morality, setting Moscow against Tver' and Novgorod, the service landholders against the boyars, the Muscovite boyars on the formerly sovereign princes of Suzdal', the "plebs" on the patricians, the Oprichnina on the Zemshchina, by abolishing St. George's Day and thereby clearing the road for serfdom—Ivan the Terrible *disintegrated Russian absolutism by integrating autocracy.*

He sowed terror of the state, and not sympathy with the national idea. If, after all he had done to it, the country did not fall to pieces, this only shows that the work of centralization had so thoroughly been worked out by the sixteenth century that even the royal hangman and his Oprichnina "centralizers" were not able to break it up.

10. The Attacks of the 1960s

What happened in Ivaniana subsequently simultaneously demonstrated two opposite things: the fragility of the gray consensus reached in the 1960s and the power of the shaken, but unshattered, "myth of the state." A. A. Zimin furiously attacked the consensus, blasting its fundamental postulates one after another. He rejected the main thesis of the "agrarian school," asserting that "the counterposition of the *votchina* boyars to the landholding service nobility is untenable."[58] He denied the very existence of the "reactionary boyar ideology" rehabilitating not only Vassian Patrikeev and Maxim the Greek, but apparently even Kurbskii himself: "It is now impossible to point to *a single* Russian thinker of the sixteenth century whose views can be evaluated as reactionary and boyar."[59] He fearlessly invaded the very holy of holies of the consensus—the postulate about the alleged struggle of the feudal boyars against "centralization." "We can speak," he declared, "only of a struggle for *different paths* towards the centralization of the state."[60] What, it would seem, could be more radical than this critique? Since Pokrovskii's time, no one had dared to declare that "the time has come for a radical reinterpretation of questions of sixteenth-century Russian political history."[61] And this critique was based on entirely sound reasoning, which would have done honor even to Kliuchevskii himself. Although "the elite of high lords was not inclined to yield its enormous latifundias for the benefit of the small holdings of the service landholders," neither did the boyardom "strive for the immediate liquidation of the freedom of peasant movement." From here it was only one step to the recognition of the fundamental point that the boyardom shielded peasant differentiation from the serfholding aggression of the service landholders, and that the political rout of the boyardom was, therefore, only a prelude to the economic and social rout of the peasantry.

And Zimin takes that step—but, to our surprise and disappointment, it is in the opposite direction. "The need for further attack of the feudal elite was obvious," he says, "and was perceived by such far-sighted thinkers as I. S. Peresvetov."[62] What can this mean? After all, what he has said implies a completely opposite conclusion. Alas, it turns out that this furious attack on the new Marxist-Solov'evist consensus has been undertaken only in order to replace it with the old, equally fruitless Marxist-Platonovist consensus. Zimin rehabilitates the boyardom only in order to again accuse the unfortunate "formerly sovereign princes" (and thereby again to justify the Oprichnina). He is convinced that

58. A. A. Zimin, "O politicheskikh predposylkakh vozniknoveniia russkogo absoliutizma," p. 22.
59. Ibid., p. 27. Emphasis added.   60. Ibid., p. 23.   61. Ibid., p. 21.
62. Ibid., p. 41.

the basic hindrance to the socio-economic and political progress of Russia at the end of the fifteenth and in the sixteenth centuries was not the boyardom but the real heirs of feudal fragmentation—the last appanages. . . . Hence, naturally, it is not the notorious collision of the service nobility with the boyardom, but the struggle with the remnants of fragmentation that constitutes the basis of the political history of that period.[63]

Once again, despite Veselovskii's annihilating critique, Platonov's paradigm arises from the grave, freshly rouged and modernized. Zimin's junior competitor, R. G. Skrynnikov, subjected him to devastating criticism, literally dismantling the new edition of the "appanage" revision of the myth stone by stone. Skrynnikov, in fact, did more. His works actually did bring a breath of fresh air into Ivaniana.[64] He was the first to study in detail the *mechanism* of the Oprichnina terror, and in the picture emerging from his studies the reader encounters something oddly familiar. Of what does the endless chain of "cases" arising one out of another (the "case of Metropolitan Filipp," the "Moscow case," the "Novgorodian case," the "case of Vladimir Staritskii," etc.) remind us? What does the wave of falsified show trials—with the confessions of the accused exacted by torture, with a bloody spiderweb of mutual slanders, with the boorish triumph of "state prosecutors," and with the horrible jargon of the hangmen (instead of "kill" they said "do away with," writing that in one place 50 people were "done away with" and in another place 150)—call to mind? There's no doubt that in describing the "great purge" of the 1560s, Skrynnikov is recounting the history of the "great purge" of the 1930s. But what is surprising is that Skrynnikov tells us this not only without hinting at the Stalinist terror, but perhaps even without thinking of it. He is a medievalist, a scrupulous historian of Ivan's Oprichnina, and he speaks only of this. Let us pause for a moment to consider it.

Among the first victims of the Oprichnina was one of the most influential members of the Duma, the conqueror of Kazan', Prince Gorbatyi. The most prominent of the Russian military leaders, he was suddenly beheaded, together with his fifteen-year-old son and his father-in-law, the *Okol'nichii* Golovin. Immediately after him, the boyar Prince Kurakin, the boyar Prince Obolenskii, and the boyar Prince Rostovskii were beheaded. Prince Shevyrev was impaled on a stake.

63. Ibid., pp. 27, 20.
64. It is sufficient to mention his well-known works: *Nachalo oprichniny, Oprichnyi terror*, and *Ivan Groznyi*.

The idea involuntarily occurs to one that this is a purge of the last of the "right opposition" from the Politburo-Duma (perhaps members or fellow travelers of the Government of Compromise), and that it was supposed to be the prelude to some kind of broad social action. In fact, it was followed by the confiscation of the lands of the titled aristocracy (formerly sovereign princes) and the expulsion of princely families to Kazan', which in the Russia of that time fulfilled the function of Siberia. The confiscation was accompanied, of course, by robbery and ruination of the peasants living on the confiscated land, and spoliation of the lands themselves. In a word, this was a medieval equivalent of what in the 1930s was called "dekulakization." The fixed quitrent paid by the peasants "by the old ways" was liquidated, and along with it whatever legal or traditional limitations on arbitrary behavior of the landowners might have existed. This was the beginning not only of mass famine and devastation in the central regions of Russia, but essentially also of serfdom (since, as Academician B. D. Grekov would say later, "the government of the service landholders could not be silent" in the face of the "great ruin" which threatened its social base).[65] But the main analogy, in any case, is the mechanism of the purge: first phase—removal of a faction in the Politburo-Duma representing both a particular social group and an intellectual current within the elite; second phase—removal of this social group itself; third phase—mass "dekulakization" of the "best people" (which is to say those who have something which can be stolen).

After the division of the country into the Oprichnina and the Zemshchina, power in the Zemshchina fell into the hands of a stratum of untitled boyars which in a certain sense was sympathetic to the tsar (and sometimes helped directly in the struggle with the "right opposition" and the Government of Compromise). Whatever the attitude of these people to the formerly sovereign princes and to the methods used by the tsar may have been, however, now, when they were actually at the wheel, they must have thought: this is enough! They had already made their revolution. The continuation of the terror became not only meaningless, but also dangerous for them. It must be supposed that it was not without their influence that the seventeenth congress of the party was held in the spring of 1566—the "congress of the victors" (I mean, of course, the Assembly of the Land, which, incidentally, was the most representative in the history of Russia). The delegates to the congress tactfully indicated to the tsar that

65. Grekov, *Krestiane na Rusi*, vol. 1, p. 297.

it was now time to put an end to the Oprichnina. Others, more realistic, conceived a plan for putting up a Kirov (in the shape of Prince Vladimir Staritskii, the tsar's cousin) against Ivan the Terrible. The matter never came to a conspiracy, but conversations were enough for the tsar. The following blow was against this group. "When this stratum became involved in the conflict," Skrynnikov notes, "the transition from limited repressions to mass terror became inevitable."[66]

Terror has its own logic. One after another, the leaders of the Duma of the Zemshchina, the last leaders of boyardom, perished. Next came the turn of the higher bureaucracy. One of the most influential opponents of the Government of Compromise, the Muscovite minister of foreign affairs, the great secretary Viskovatyi, who had undoubtedly lent a hand in the fall of Sil'vestr, was first crucified and then chopped into pieces. The state treasurer Funikov was boiled alive in a kettle. Next came the leaders of the Orthodox hierarchy, then Prince Staritskii himself. And each of these drew after them into the maelstrom of terror wider and wider circles of relatives, sympathizers, acquaintances, and even strangers, with whom the Oprichnina settled accounts. When the senior boyar of the Duma of the Zemshchina, Cheliadnin-Fedorov, laid his head on the block, his servants were hacked to bits with sabers, and all his household members were herded into a barn and blown up. (The *Sinodnik* carries the notation: "In Upper Bezhitsk, sixty-five people were done away with . . . and twelve people were beheaded with swords.")[67]

I will spare the reader and myself any more, for I am not writing a martyrology of the Oprichnina. Suffice it to note that, just as in the 1930s, the leaders of the Oprichnina apparently did not notice that the circles of terror were coming ever closer to them. Aleksei Basmanov, that medieval Yezhov, already seemed a dangerous liberal to the favorite of Stalin and Ivan the Terrible, Maliuta Skuratov, who personally strangled Metropolitan Filipp. Prince Afanasii Viazemskii, who had organized the reprisals against Gorbatyi and Obolenskii, was himself already under suspicion when his appointee, Archbishop Pimen, a rabid supporter of the Oprichnina, perished during the sack of Novgorod. "Under conditions of mass terror, universal fear, and denunciations, the apparatus of violence created in the Oprichnina acquired an entirely overwhelming influence on the political structure of the leadership," Skrynnikov relates with horror. "In the

66. Skrynnikov, *Ivan Groznyi*, p. 114.
67. Cited in ibid., p. 138.

final analysis, the infernal machine of terror escaped from the control
of its creators. The final victims of the Oprichnina proved to be all of
those who had stood at its cradle."[68]

As we see, Skrynnikov knows perfectly well what was happening in
Russia during the 1560s. He does not show the slightest desire to justify this horrible rehearsal for Stalin's purges as the "struggle against
treason," as Vipper and Polosin had done twenty years before him.
And although he notes that in pre-Oprichnina Muscovy, "the monarchy had become the prisoner of the aristocracy,"[69] he does not seem
inclined to justify the terror as the "objective inevitability of the physical extermination of the princely and boyar families," as his teacher
Smirnov had done. More than this, he does not hide from himself (or
from the reader) that, in the first place, "the period of the Oprichnina
is marked by a sharp intensification of feudal exploitation," which
preconditioned "the final triumph of serfdom." In the second place,
he notes, "the pogroms of the Oprichnina, and the indiscriminate
bloody terror, brought deep demoralization to the life of the country."[70] And then what?

Working with his eyes open, and having before him the horrifying
facts, many of which he himself introduced into scholarly discourse,
does he make an attempt to reinterpret the Oprichnina? Unfortunately, once again, as in the case of Zimin, we are doomed to experience a dramatic disappointment. In Skrynnikov's understanding, it
turns out, "the Oprichnina terror, the limitation of the competence of
the boyar duma . . . unarguably promoted . . . the reinforcement of
the centralized monarchy, developing in the direction of absolutism."[71] The sacred invocation has been pronounced. Skrynnikov remains within the limits of the consensus. The "great purge" of Ivan
the Terrible, which Skrynnikov described with unexampled power,
nevertheless proves to be "historically inevitable and progressive."
The king is dead: long live the king! The Marxist-Platonovist hypostasis of the myth, once again advanced by Zimin, is once again
refuted—for the sake of a new triumph of its Marxist-Solov'evist
hypostasis.

On closer consideration of Skrynnikov's paradigm, we see clear
traces of the myth. Zimin had firmly denied "the notorious collision

68. Skrynnikov, *Oprichnyi terror*, p. 223.
69. Skrynnikov, *Ivan Groznyi*, p. 114.
70. Skrynnikov, *Oprichnyi terror*, pp. 247–48.
71. Skrynnikov, *Oprichnina Ivana Groznogo* (author's abstract of doctoral dissertation, Leningrad, 1967, p. 41).

of the boyardom with the service landholders" and rehabilitated the great oppositionists of the sixteenth century. In refuting him, Skrynnikov not only condemns "the treasonous relations of Kurbskii," but gives us to understand that the terror against the aristocracy, "which imprisoned the monarchy," was by no means such a bad thing. The outrageousness began when the terror spread to other social strata, who were objectively the allies of the monarchy in its struggle with the aristocracy. "The Oprichnina terror," he says, "weakened the boyar aristocracy, but it also did great damage to the service landholders, the church, the higher government bureaucracy—that is, to those social forces which served as the most reliable support of the monarchy. From a political point of view, the terror *against these strata and groups* was complete nonsense."[72]

Speaking in my terms, Skrynnikov sympathizes with the attempt of Ivan the Terrible to transform Russian absolutism into a despotic system by liberating it from the aristocracy. He rejects only the "political nonsense" and irrationality of despotism in destroying its own allies. As if, for Tsar Ivan, it was only the boyars, and not all his subjects, who were slaves—as Kliuchevskii already knew. In chapter two, by reference to the cases of Henry VIII and Louis XI, I have tried to explore the gulf between outbursts of ordinary tyranny (possible in any absolutist state) and despotism (which by distorting the sociopolitical process *makes tyranny permanent*). I am not the first to point out the distinction. Aristotle, Montesquieu, and Krizhanich did so centuries ago. But the logic of myth apparently precludes Russian historians, Marxist or not, from perceiving it.

Skrynnikov asserts that "meaningless and brutal beating of the entirely innocent population made the very concept of the Oprichnina a synonym for arbitrariness and lawlessness."[73] But in his analysis he almost unnoticeably shifts the stress from "arbitrariness and lawlessness" to natural catastrophe and increase in taxes:

> During the years of the boyar government [as Skrynnikov calls the Government of Compromise] the Novgorod peasants paid a small tribute in money . . . to the state. With the beginning of the Kazan' and particularly the Livonian wars, the state increased the money obligations for peasants manyfold. The increase in the tax burden and the exploitation by the landlords placed the small-scale peasant farms under extremely unfavorable conditions. But it was *not only the taxes* which were the cause

72. Skrynnikov, *Ivan Groznyi*, p. 121. Emphasis added.
73. Ibid., p. 152.

of the ruin which began in the country in the 1570s and 1580s. The catastrophe was provoked by *natural calamities* of enormous scale. . . . Unfavorable weather conditions ruined the harvest twice—in 1568 and 1569. As a result, the price of grain increased by factors of five and ten. Death by famine reduced the population of cities and villages. During the Oprichnina pogrom in Novgorod, starving citizens during the dark winter nights stole the bodies of the victims and ate them. . . . After the famine, a plague brought from the West began in the country. . . . The three-year famine and the epidemic brought death to hundreds of thousands of people. The calamities were completed by *the destructive incursion* of the Tatars.[74]

What with taxes, famine, the plague, the Tatars, the Oprichnina becomes almost invisible!

11. Grounds for Optimism

The evolution of Ivaniana during the 1960s nevertheless suggests hope. The foundations of the gray consensus are being irreversibly eroded. Admittedly, the radical revision proposed by Zimin did not bring results. But this in itself, after all, is an ill omen for the consensus. The contradiction between premises and conclusions in Skrynnikov's work is too obvious. How long can the consensus swing from Solov'ev to Platonov and back again, while continuing to pass itself off as Marxism? In essence it is clear that the consensus is in a cul-de-sac, from which it is impossible to escape without fundamentally new ideas. The following quotations—drawn from D. P. Makovskii (1960), S. M. Kashtanov (1963), S. O. Shmidt (1968), and N. E. Nosov (1969) respectively—suggest that these new ideas are beginning to show on the surface.

> In the middle of the sixteenth century in the Russian state, capitalist relationships came into being in both industry and agriculture, and the necessary economic conditions for their development were prepared. . . . But in 1570–90, an active intervention by the superstructure (the massive forces of the state) in economic relationships in the interest of the service landholders took place. . . . This intervention not only hindered the development of capitalist relationships and undermined the condition of the productive forces in the country but also called forth regressive phenomena in the economy.[75]
>
> Considering the Oprichnina in its social aspect, we can persuade ourselves that its main characteristic was its class tendency, which consisted

74. Ibid., pp. 144–45. Emphasis added.
75. Makovskii, *Razvitie* (1st ed.), p. 212.

in the introduction of measures which promoted the further enserfment of the peasantry. In this sense, the Oprichnina was certainly more
an *antipeasant* than an antiboyar policy.[76]

Today it is becoming ever more clear that the policy of the Chosen
Rada [the Government of Compromise] in much greater degree pro-
moted the further centralization of the state and its development in
the direction of absolutism of *European type* than did the policy of the
Oprichnina, which facilitated the triumph of absolutism, *saturated with
Asiatic barbarism.*[77]

It was precisely at this time that the question was decided about
which road Russia would travel—the road of renewal of feudalism
through the "new edition" of serfdom, or the road of bourgeois development. . . . Russia was *at the crossroads*. . . . And if in Russia as a result
of "Ivan's Oprichnina" and the "great ruination of the peasantry" at the
end of the sixteenth century, serfdom and the autocracy still won
out . . . this is by no means proof of their progressive nature.[78]

Of course, important unresolved questions remain. For example,
Makovskii is unable to explain *why* "active intervention by the superstructure," which called forth "regressive phenomena in the economy," suddenly took place in the 1570s. Furthermore, it is impossible
to explain this by the "development of commodity-and-money relationships in agriculture," as he tries to do. Kashtanov is unable to explain the *connection* between the antiboyar and the antipeasant policy
of the Oprichnina. It is impossible to do this while accepting the postulate of the myth as to the "reactionary nature of boyardom." Shmidt
is unable to explain what constitutes the political distinction between
"absolutism of European type" and "absolutism saturated with Asiatic
barbarism." And without this, the formulations he proposes remain
nonfunctional. Nosov is unable to explain what combination of forces
predetermined victory for the "renewal of feudalism" and the defeat
of "bourgeois development."

These lacunae are not accidental. Zimin, it will be remembered,
has called for "a radical reconsideration of the political history of
Russia in the sixteenth century." This radical reconsideration cannot
be expected (as Veselovskii anticipated in the 1940s) merely from
"new facts." New philosophical horizons must be opened up; new
means of political analysis must be devised; a new vision of history is
required. I have attempted here to make a start at the gigantic task of

76. Kashtanov, "K izucheniiu istorii oprichniny Ivana Groznogo," p. 108. Emphasis
added.
77. Shmidt, "K izucheniiu agrarnoi istorii Rossii XVI veka," p. 24.
78. Nosov, *Stanovlenie*, p. 9. Emphasis added.

constructing an alternative paradigm for Ivaniana—or at least breaking the vicious circle in which for decades we have been revolving like
squirrels in a wheel, endlessly and fruitlessly repeating ourselves and
our predecessors.

Are we still capable of breaking out of this circle of ancient stereotypes? I do not know. What I do know, however, is that we must try.
Otherwise, I am afraid, it could be too late; a new "historiographic
nightmare" may strike. After three of them, it is time, it seems, for
Russian historiography to come to its senses—to put an end to its
serflike dependence on Ivan the Terrible's "myth of the state" and the
obsolete classical "*vyskazyvaniia.*" It is time for Western historiography,
too, to help in the emancipation of its Russian colleagues. It can do so
by putting an end to its own dependence on the bipolar model of history, as well as to its archaic contempt for the "Tatar-Byzantine heritage" of Russia, borrowed from Miliukov, Chicherin, and other classics
of the "state school." It is time for the "absolutists" and the "despotists"
to end the civil war between them. For the inspiration and intuition of
both are needed for positive construction.

This may sound like a utopian dream—which it perhaps is to some
extent. What I am trying to stress, however, is that such construction
is necessary for both historiographic and historic reasons. Russia,
Nosov says, was at the crossroads in the middle of the sixteenth century. I am sincerely convinced that now, at the end of the twentieth
century, it is once again at the crossroads. Is Ivaniana destined to undergo a new "historiographic nightmare," or is the demiurge of all of
these nightmares—the "myth of the state"—finally expiring? What
awaits Russia: a new "absolutism saturated with Asiatic barbarism" (in
Shmidt's words) or, finally, after four centuries of delay, "absolutism
of European type"? This does not depend *only* on the historians. But
it does depend on the historians too.

APPENDIXES

APPENDIXES

APPENDIX I

Russia at the Crossroads:
Establishment Political Forces in the 1550s

Proto-Bourgeoisie	Non-Acquirers: reformist intelligentsia	Boyar Aristocracy	Tsar	Bureaucracy	Josephites: the Russian right	Service nobility: "the new class"

Political Left

Political Right

THE GOVERNMENT OF COMPROMISE

AUTOCRATIC (REVOLUTIONARY) COALITION

REFORMIST (ANTI-AUTOCRATIC) COALITION

APPENDIX II

The Cycles of Russian History

	CYCLE I (1564–1689)	CYCLE II (1689–1796)	CYCLE III (1796–1825)	CYCLE IV (1825–1881)	CYCLE V (1881–1917)	CYCLE VI (1917–1929)	CYCLE VII (1929–?)
Tyranny	1564–1584	1689–1725	1796–1801	1825–1855	1881–1894	1917–1921	1929–1953
Revolution of "de-Stalinization"	1584–1613	1725–1730	1801–1811	1855–1863	1894–1908	1921–1927	1953–1964
Attempts at reform, followed by political stagnation	1613–1689	1730–1796	1811–1825	1863–1881	1908–1917	1927–1929	1964–?

SELECTED BIBLIOGRAPHY

Aksakov, K. S. *Sochineniia istoricheskie* [Historical Works]. Moscow, 1889.

Alef, Gustav. "Aristocratic Politics and Royal Policy in the Late Fifteenth and Sixteenth Centuries." Unpublished paper presented for discussion, Berlin, 1978. Revised version in press, 1980: *Forschungen 3. Osteuropäische Geschichte* (Berlin).

Anderson, M. S. "English Views of Russia in the Age of Peter the Great." *American Slavic and East European Review* 17 (April 1954): 200–214.

Anderson, Perry. *Lineages of the Absolutist State*. London, 1964.

Andreev, N. "Mnimaiia tema" ["An Illusory Theme"]. *Novyi Zhurnal* [The New Review] 109 (1972): 258–72.

Andreski, S. *Elements of Comparative Sociology*. London, 1964.

Angliiskie puteshestvenniki v Moskovskom gosudarstve v XVI veke [English Travelers in the State of Muscovy in the Sixteenth Century]. Leningrad, 1937.

Aristotle. *Politika* [Politics]. Moscow, 1911.

Avrekh, A. Ia. "Russkii absoliutism: i ego rol' v utverzhdenii kapitalizma v Rossii" ["Russian Absolutism and Its Role in the Establishment of Capitalism in Russia"]. *Istoriia SSSR* [A History of the USSR], no. 2 (1968).

Backus, Oswald P., III. "The Problem of Unity in the Polish-Lithuanian State." In *The Development of the USSR: An Exchange of Views*, edited by Donald W. Treadgold, pp. 275–95. Seattle, 1964.

Bakhrushin, S. V. *Ivan Groznyi* [Ivan the Terrible]. Moscow, 1945.

———. "Izbrannaiia Rada Ivana Groznogo" ["The Chosen Council of Ivan the Terrible"]. In *Nauchnye Trudy* [Scholarly Papers], vol. 2. Moscow, 1954.

Balazs, E. *Chinese Civilization and Bureaucracy*. New Haven and London, 1964.

Bazilevich, K. V. *Vneshniaia politika russkogo tsentralizovannogo gosudarstva* [The Foreign Policy of the Russian Centralized State]. Moscow, 1952.

Begunov, Iu. K. "Sekuliarizatsiia v Evrope i Sobor 1503 v Rossii" [Secularization in Europe and the Assembly of 1503 in Russia"]. In *Feodal'naia Rossia vo vsemirno-istoricheskom protsesse* [Feudal Russia in the Process of World History]. Moscow, 1972.

———. "'Slovo inoe'—novonaidennoe proizvedenie russkoi publitsistiki XVI v. o bor'be Ivana III s zemlevladeniem tserkvi" ["'A Different Word'—A Newly Discovered Work of Russian Public-Affairs Writing of the Sixteenth Century on Ivan III's Struggle with Church Landholding"]. *Trudy otdela drevnerusskoi literatury* [Transactions of the Ancient Russian Literature Section], vol. 20. Moscow-Leningrad, 1964.

Belinskii, V. G. *Polnoe sobranie sochinenii* [Complete Works]. 13 vols. Moscow, 1953–59.

_____. *Sobranie sochinenii v trekh tomakh* [Collected Works in Three Volumes]. Moscow, 1948.

Belov, E. A. *Ob istoricheskom znachenii russkogo boiarstva* [On the Historical Significance of Russian Boyardom]. St. Petersburg, 1886.

Berdiaev, N. A. *Istoki i smysl russkogo kommunizma* [The Sources and Meaning of Russian Communism]. Paris, 1955.

Berezhkov, P. *Plan zavoevaniia Kryma* [The Plan of the Conquest of the Crimea]. St. Petersburg, 1891.

Biblioteka inostrannykh pisatelei o Rossii XV–XVI vekov [Library of Foreign Writers on Russia in the Fifteenth and Sixteenth Centuries]. St. Petersburg, 1836.

Blum, Jerome. *Lord and Peasant in Russia from the Ninth to the Nineteenth Century*. Princeton, 1961.

Budovnits, I. U. *Russkaia publitsistika XVI veka* [Russian Public-Affairs Writing of the Sixteenth Century]. Moscow-Leningrad, 1974.

Chaadaev, P. Ya. *Sochineniia i pis'ma P. Ya. Chaadaeva* [Works and Letters of P. Ya. Chaadaev]. 2 vols. Moscow, 1913–14.

Chargoff, Erwin. "Knowledge Without Wisdom." *Harper's,* May 1980.

Cherepnin, L. V. "K voprosu o skladyvanii absoliutnoi monarkhii v Rossii" ["On the Question of the Formation of the Absolute Monarchy in Russia"]. In *Dokumenty sovetsko-italianskoi konferentsii istorikov* [Documents of the Soviet-Italian Conference of Historians]. Moscow, 1968.

Cherkasov, N. *Zapiski sovetskogo aktera* [Notes of a Soviet Actor]. Moscow, 1953.

Chicherin, B. N. *O narodnom predstavitel'stve* [On Popular Representation]. Moscow, 1889.

Chistozvonov, A. N. "Nekotorye aspekty problemy genezisa absoliutizma" ["Some Aspects of the Problem of the Genesis of Absolutism"]. *Voprosy istorii* [The Problems of History], no. 5 (1968).

Christensen, A. *L'Iran sous les Sassanides*. Copenhagen, 1963.

Chukhontsev, Oleg. "Povestvovanie o Kurbskom" ["The Saga of Kurbskii"]. *Iunost'* [Youth], no. 1 (1968), p. 29.

Coulborn, Rushton, ed. *Feudalism in History*. Princeton, N.J., 1956.

Crummey, Robert O. "The Seventeenth-Century Moscow Service Elite in Comparative Perspective." Paper presented at the Ninety-third Annual Meeting of the American Historical Association. December 1978.

Custine, Astolphe Louis Léonard, Marquis de. *La Russie en 1839*. Paris, 1843.

D'akonov, I. M. *Obshchestvennyi i gosudarstvennyi stroi drevnego Dvurech'a: Shumer* [The Social and Political Structure of Ancient Mesopotamia: Sumer]. Moscow, 1959.

D'akonov, M. A. *Ocherki po istorii sel'skogo naseleniia v Moskovskom gosudarstve XVI–XVII vekov* [Outlines of the History of the Rural Population in the Muscovite State of the Sixteenth and Seventeenth Centuries]. St. Petersburg, 1898.

_____. *Vlast' moskovskikh gosudarei* [The Regime of the Muscovite Sovereigns]. St. Petersburg, 1889.

Davidovitch, A. I., and Pokrovskii, S. A. "O klassovoi sushchnosti i etapakh razvitiia russkogo absoliutizma" ["On the Class Essence and the Stages of Development of Russian Absolutism"]. *Istoriia SSSR* [A History of the USSR], no. 1 (1969).

Derzhavin, G. R. *Stikhotvorenia* [Verses]. Leningrad, 1957.

Dewey, Horace. "Immunities in Old Russia." *Slavic Review* 23 (December 1964): 644–59.

Dovnar-Zapol'skii, M. V. "Vremia tsaria Ivana Groznogo" ["The Time of Tsar Ivan the Terrible"]. In *Russkaia starina v ocherkakh i statiakh* [The Russian Past in Sketches and Essays], edited by M. V. Dovnar-Zapol'skii, vol. 2. Moscow, 1954.

Druzhinin, N. M. "O periodizatsii istorii kapitalisticheskikh otnoshenii v Rossii" ["On the Periodization of the History of Capitalist Relationships in Russia"]. *Voprosy istorii* [The Problems of History], no. 1 (1951).

Dubrovskii, S. "Protiv idealizatsii deiatel'nosti Ivana IV" ["Against Idealization of Ivan IV's Activities"]. *Voprosy istorii* [The Problems of History], no. 8 (1956): 121–28.

Eberhard, Wolfram. "Oriental Despotism: A Comparative Study of Total Power by Karl A. Wittfogel." *American Sociological Review* 23, no. 4 (1958): 446–49.

Egorov, D. "Ideia turetskoi reformatsii v XVI veke" ["The Idea of a Turkish Reformation in the Sixteenth Century"]. *Russkaia mysl'* [Russian Thought], no. 7 (1907).

Eisenstadt, S. N. "The Study of Oriental Despotisms as Systems of Total Power." *The Journal of Asian Studies* 17 (May 1958): 435–46.

Fennel, J. L. I. *Ivan the Great of Moscow*. London, 1961.

_____, ed. and trans. *The Correspondence Between Prince A. M. Kurbsky and Tsar Ivan IV of Russia, 1564–1579*. Cambridge, Engl., 1955.

_____, ed. and trans. *Prince A. M. Kurbsky's History of Ivan IV*. Cambridge, Engl., 1965.

Fletcher, G. *O gosudarstve russkom* [On the Russian State]. St. Petersburg, 1905.

_____. *Of the Russe Common Wealth*. Reprinted from the Hakluyt Society Publications. New York, n.d.

Gerberstein, S. *Zapiski o Moskovii* [Notes on Muscovy]. St. Petersburg, 1866.

_____. *Zapiski o moskovskikh delakh* [Notes about Muscovite Matters]. St. Petersburg, 1908.

Gershenkron, Alexander. *Continuity and Change in Russian and Soviet Thought*. Edited by E. J. Simmons. Cambridge, Mass., 1962.

_____. *Economic Backwardness in Historical Perspective*. Cambridge, Mass., 1962.

Gershenzon, M. *P. Ya. Chaadaev; Zhizn' i Myshlenie* [P. Ya. Chaadaev: Life and Thought]. St. Petersburg, 1908.

Gorskii, S. *Zhizn' i istoricheskoe znachenie kniazia A. M. Kurbskogo* [The Life and Historical Significance of Prince A. M. Kurbskii]. Kazan', 1856.

Grekov, B. D. *Krestiane na Rusi s drevneishikh vremen do XVII veka* [Peasants in Rus' from the Earliest Times to the Seventeenth Century]. Moscow-Leningrad, 1946.

Grobovsky, Anthony N. *The "Chosen Council" of Ivan IV: A Reinterpretation.* New York, 1969.

Heer, Nancy Whittier. "Political Leadership in Soviet Historiography." In *The Dynamics of Soviet Politics,* edited by Paul Cocks, Robert V. Daniels, and Nancy Whittier Heer. Cambridge, Mass., 1976.

Hegel, G. W. F. *Lectures on the Philosophy of History.* London, 1861.

Hellie, Richard. "In Search of Ivan the Terrible." Preface to S. F. Platonov, *Ivan the Terrible.* Gulf Breeze, Fla., 1974.

──────. "Ivan the Terrible: Paranoia, 'Evil Advisors,' Institutional Restraints and Social Control." Paper presented at the Thirteenth Annual Southern Conference on Slavic Studies, November 1978.

──────. "The Muscovite Provincial Service Elite in Comparative Perspective." Paper presented at the Ninety-third Annual Meeting of the American Historical Association, December 1978.

Herzen, A. I. *Kolokol; gazeta Gertsena. 1857–1867* [*The Bell*: Herzen's Newspaper, 1857–1867]. 6 vols. Moscow, 1962–64.

──────. *Sobranie sochinenii* [Collected Works]. Moscow, 1954.

Iarosh, K. *Psikhologicheskaia parallel'* [A Psychological Parallel]. Khar'kov, 1898.

Istoriia srednikh vekov [A History of the Middle Ages]. General editor: S. D. Skazkin. Vol. 2. Moscow, 1954.

Istoriia SSSR [A History of the USSR]. Moscow, 1966.

Ivan IV, Tsar. *Poslaniia Ivana Groznogo* [*Epistles of Ivan the Terrible*]. Prepared for publication by D. S. Likhachev and Ia. S. Lur'e. Moscow, 1951.

Karamzin, N. M. *Istoriia gosudarstva Rossiiskogo* [History of the Russian State]. St. Petersburg, 1821.

Kareev, N. N. *Zapadno-evropeiskaia absoliutnaia monarkhiia XVI, XVII i XVIII vekov* [Western European Absolutist Monarchy in the Sixteenth, Seventeenth, and Eighteenth Centuries]. St. Petersburg, 1908.

Kashtanov, S. M. "Ogranichenie feodal'nogo immuniteta pravitel'stvom russkogo tsentralizovannogo gosudarstva" ["The Limitation of Feudal Immunity by the Government of the Centralized Russian State"]. *Trudy Moskovskogo gosudarstvennogo istoriko-arkhivnogo instituta* [Transactions of the Moscow State Institute of Historical Archives], vol. 2. Moscow, 1958.

──────. *Sotsial'no-politicheskaia istoriia Rossii kontsa XV–pervoi poloviny XVI v.* [A Sociopolitical History of Russia in the Late Fifteenth and Early Sixteenth Centuries]. Moscow, 1967.

Kavelin, K. *Sochineniia* [Works]. Moscow, 1859.

Kazakova, N. A. *Vassian Patrikeev i ego sochineniia* [Vassian Patrikeev and His Works]. Moscow-Leningrad, 1969.

Kazakova, N. A., and Lur'e, Ia. S. *Antideodal'nye ereticheskie dvizheniia na Rusi XIV–nachala XVI veka* [Antifeudal Heretical Movements in Rus' from the Fourteenth to the Sixteenth Century]. Moscow-Leningrad, 1958.

Keenan, Edward L., Jr. *The Kurbskii-Groznyi Apocrypha.* Cambridge, Mass., 1971.

_____. "Vita: Ivan Vasil'evich, Terrible Tsar, 1530–1584." *Harvard Magazine*, January–February, 1978.

Kirchner, W. *The Rise of the Baltic Question.* Newark, Delaware, 1954.

Kliuchevskii, V. O. *Boiarskaia duma drevnei Rusi* [The Boyar Duma of Ancient Rus']. Moscow, 1909.

_____. *Sochineniia* [Collected Works]. 1st ed. Moscow, 1936–39.

_____. *Sochineniia* [Collected Works]. 2nd ed. Moscow, 1956–59.

Kopanev, A. I. *Istoriia zemlevladeniia Belozerskogo kraia v XV–XVI vekakh* [History of Land Tenure in Belozersk Krai in the Fifteenth and Sixteenth Centuries]. Moscow-Leningrad, 1951.

_____. "Ustavnaia Zemskaia Gramota trex volostei Dvinskogo uezda 25 fevralia 1552" ["A Regional Constitutive Decree for the 3 Volosts of Dvina Uezd, February 25, 1552"]. *Istoricheskii arkhiv* [Historical Archive] 8 (1952).

_____. "K voprosu o strukture zemlevladeniia na Dvine v XV–XVI vv" ["On the Question of the Structure of Land Tenure on the Dvina in the Fifteenth and Sixteenth Centuries"]. *Voprosy agrarnoi istorii: Materialy nauchnoi konferentsii po istorii sel'skogo khoziaistva i krestianstva Evropeiskogo Severa SSSR* [Problems of Agrarian History: Proceedings of a Scholarly Conference on the History of Agriculture and the Peasantry in the European North of the USSR]. Vologda, 1968.

Kostylev, V. I. *Ivan Groznyi* [Ivan the Terrible]. 3 vols. Moscow, 1944–47.

Kotoshikhin, Grigorii. *O Rossii v tsarstvovanie Alekseia Mikhailovicha, Sochinenie Grigoriia Kotoshikhina* [On Russia in the Reign of Alexei Mikhailovich, Written by Grigorii Kotoshikhin]. 4th ed. St. Petersburg, 1906.

Kritika burzhuaznykh kontseptsii istorii Rossii perioda feodalizma; Simpozium [Critique of Bourgeois Conceptions of the History of Russia in the Period of Feudalism: Symposium]. Moscow, 1962.

Krizhanich, Iurii. *Politika* [Politics]. Moscow, 1965.

Kurbskii, A. M. *Perepiska Ivana Groznogo s Andreem Kurbskim* [The Correspondence between Ivan the Terrible and Andrei Kurbskii]. Leningrad, 1972.

_____. *Skazaniia kniazia Kurbskogo* [Stories of Prince Kurbskii]. St. Petersburg, 1833.

Kurmacheva, M. D. "Ob otsenke deiatel'nosti Ivana Groznogo" ["On the Evaluation of the Activities of Ivan the Terrible"]. *Voprosy istorii* [The Problems of History], no. 9 (1956): 195–203.

Latkin, N. V. *Zemskie sobory drevnei Rusi* [The Assemblies of the Land in Ancient Rus']. St. Petersburg, 1885.

Lenin, V. I. *Polnoe sobranie sochinenii* [Complete Works]. 4th ed. 35 vols. Moscow, 1941–60.

Likhachev, D. S. "Ivan Peresvetov i ego literaturnaia sovremennost'" ["Ivan Peresvetov and the Literature of His Time"]. In *Sochineniia Ivana Peresvetova* [Ivan Peresvetov's Works]. Moscow-Leningrad, 1956.

Lomonosov, M. V. *Izbrannye proizvedeniia* [Collected Works]. Moscow-Leningrad, 1956.

Lunin, M. S. *Dekabrist Lunin, sochineniia i pis'ma* [Lunin the Decembrist, Writings and Letters]. Petrograd, 1923.

Lur'e, Ia. S. *Ideologicheskaia bor'ba v russkoi publitsistike kontsa XV–nachala XVI vv.* [The Ideological Struggle in Russian Public-Affairs Writing in the Late Fifteenth and Early Sixteenth Centuries]. Leningrad, 1960.

Makovskii, D. P. *Razvitie tovarno-denezhnykh otnishenii v sel'skom khoziaistve russkogo gosudarstva v XVI veke* [The Development of Goods and Monetary Relationships in the Agriculture of the Russian State in the Sixteenth Century]. Smolensk, 1960.

Maksim Grek. *Sochineniia prepodobnogo Maksima Greka v russkom perevode* [The Works of the Venerable Maxim the Greek in Russian Translation]. Part 1. Troitse-Sergievskaia Lavra, 1911.

Malinin, V. *Starets Eleazarova monastyria Filofei i ego poslanie* [Elder Filofei of the St. Eleazar Monastery and His Epistle]. Kiev, 1901.

Manglapus, Raul. "Asian Revolution and American Ideology." *Foreign Affairs* 45 (January 1967).

Marx, Karl. *Izbrannye proizvedeniia* [Selected Works]. Moscow, 1933.

———. *Secret Diplomatic History of the XVIII Century*. London, 1969.

———. *Sochineniia* [Works]. 2nd ed. 48 vols. Moscow, 1955–77.

———, and Engels, F. *Izbrannye pis'ma* [Selected Letters]. Moscow, 1948.

Mikhailovskii, N. K. "Ivan Groznyi v russkoi literature" ["Ivan the Terrible in Russian Literature"]. In *Sochineniia* [Works]. St. Petersburg, 1909.

Miliukov, P. N. *Ocherki po istorii russkoi kul'tury* [Outlines of the History of Russian Culture]. St. Petersburg, 1896.

———. *Ocherki po istorii russkoi kul'tury* [Outlines of the History of Russian Culture]. 3rd ed. St. Petersburg, 1909.

Miuller, R. B. *Ocherki po istorii Karelii XVI–XVII vekov* [Outlines of the History of Karelia in the Sixteenth and Seventeenth Centuries]. Petrozavodsk, 1947.

Moiseeva, G. I. *Valaamskaia beseda—pamiatnik russkoi publitsistiki XVI v.* [The Conversation of Valaam—A Document of Sixteenth-Century Russian Public-Affairs Writing]. Moscow-Leningrad, 1938.

Montesquieu, Charles de. *O dukhe zakonov* [L'esprit du loi]. St. Petersburg, 1900.

Nosov, N. E. *O dvukh tendentsiiakh razvitiia feodal'nogo zemlevladeniia v Severo-Vostochnoi Rusi v XV–XVI vekakh* [On the Two Tendencies in the Development of Feudal Land Tenure in Northeastern Rus' in the Fifteenth and Sixteenth Centuries]. Moscow, 1970.

———. *Stanovlenie soslovno-predstavitel'nykh uchrezhdenii v Rossii* [The Establishment of Institutions Representing Estates in Russia]. Leningrad, 1969.

Obolensky, Dimitri. "Russia's Byzantine Heritage." In *Readings in Russian History*, edited by Sidney Harcave. New York, 1962.

Pamiatniki russkogo prava [Sources of Russian Law], edited by L. V. Cherepnin, vols. 3–4. Moscow, 1955–56.

Pavlenko, N. I. "K voprosu o genezise absoliutizma v Rossii" ["On the Question of the Genesis of Absolutism in Russia"]. *Istoriia SSSR* [A History of the USSR], no. 4 (1970).

Pavlov, A. S. *Istoricheskii ocherk sekuliarizatsii tserkovnykh zemel' v Rossii* [A Historical Sketch of the Secularization of the Church Lands in Russia]. Odessa, 1871.

Pavlova-Sil'vanskaia, M. P. "K voprosu ob osobennostiakh absoliutizma v Rossii" ["On the Question of the Peculiar Features of Absolutism in Russia"]. *Istoriia SSSR* [A History of the USSR], no. 4 (1968).

Pavlov-Sil'vanskii, N. P. *Feodalism drevnei Rusi* [Feudalism in Ancient Rus']. Petrograd, 1924.

_____. *Gosudarevy sluzhylye liudi, liudi kabal'nye i zakladnye* [Service Landholders of the Sovereign, Debt Slaves, and Indentured People]. 2nd ed. St. Petersburg, 1909.

Perelomov, L. S. *Imperiia Tsin—pervoe tsentralizovannoe gosudarstvo Kitaia* [The Ch'in Empire—First Centralized State of China]. Moscow, 1962.

Pipes, Richard. *Russia under the Old Regime*. New York, 1974.

Platonov, S. F. *Ivan Groznyi* [Ivan the Terrible]. St. Petersburg, 1923.

_____. *Ocherki po istorii smuty v Moskovskom gosudarstve XVI–XVIII vekov* [Outlines of the History of the Rebellions in the Muscovite State in the Sixteenth–Eighteenth Centuries]. Moscow, 1937.

_____. "Problema russkogo Severa v noveishei istoriografii" ["The Problem of the Russian North in Current Historiography"]. *Letopis' zaniatii arkheografocheskoi komissii* [Chronicle of Studies by the Archeographic Commission], no. 35. Leningrad, 1929.

Plekhanov, G. V. *Sochineniia* [Works]. 24 vols. Moscow-Leningrad, 1923–27.

Pogodin, M. P. *Istoriko-kriticheskie otryvki* [Historical and Critical Fragments]. Moscow, 1846.

_____. *Sochineniia* [Works], vol. 4. Moscow [18–?].

Pokrovskii, M. N. *Izbrannye proizvedeniia* [Selected Works], book 3. Moscow, 1967.

_____. *Ocherkh istorii russkoi kul'tury* [Outline of the History of Russian Culture]. Moscow, n.d.

Polosin, I. I. *Sotsial'no-politicheskaia istoriia Rossii XVI–nachala XVII veka* [Sociopolitical History of Russia in the Sixteenth and Early Seventeenth Centuries]. Moscow, 1963.

Porshnev, B. F. *Feodalizm i narodyne massy* [Feudalism and the Popular Masses]. Moscow, 1964.

Pushkin, A. S. *Polnoe sobranie sochinenii* [Complete Works]. Leningrad, 1977.

Raev, M. "O knige Allena Bezansona" ["On Alain Besançon's Book"]. *Novyi Zhurnal*, no. 130 (1978).

Rannie slavianofily [The Early Slavophiles]. Moscow, 1910.

Riasanovsky, Nicholas V. *History of Russia*. New York, 1977.

_____. "'Oriental Despotism' and Russia." In *The Development of the USSR: An Exchange of Views*, edited by Donald W. Treadgold, pp. 340–45. Seattle, 1964.

Rubin, V. *Ideologiia i kul'tura drevnego Kitaia* [The Ideology and Culture of Ancient China]. Moscow, 1970.

Rubinshtein, N. L. *Russkaia istoriografiia* [Russian Historiography]. Moscow, 1941.

Russkoe proshloe. Istoricheskii sbornik [The Russian Past: A Historical Collection]. Petrograd-Moscow, 1923.

Ryleev, K. F. *Polnoe sobranie sochinenii* [Complete Works]. Moscow, 1934.

Rzhiga, V. "Maxim Grek kak publitsist" ["Maxim the Greek as a Publicist"]. In *Trudy otdela drevnerusskoi literatury* [Transactions of the Ancient Russian Literature Section], vol. 1. Moscow-Leningrad, 1934.

Sadikov, P. A. *Ocherki po istorii oprichniny* [Outlines of the History of the Oprichnina]. Moscow-Leningrad, 1950.

Sakharov, A. M. "Ob evoliutsii feodal'noi sobstvennosti na zemliu v Russkom gosudarstve XVI veka" ["On the Evolution of Feudal Land Ownership in the Russian State of the Sixteenth Century"]. *Istoriia SSSR* [A History of the USSR], no. 4 (July–August 1978).

Sakharov, A. N. "Istoricheskie faktory obrazovaniia russkogo absoliutizma" ["Historical Factors in the Formation of Russian Absolutism"]. *Istoriia SSSR* [A History of the USSR], no. 1 (1971).

Samarin, Iu. "O mneniiakh *Sovremennika* istoricheskikh i literaturnykh" ["On the Historical and Literary Opinions of the *Contemporary*"]. *Moskvitianin* [The Muscovite], no. 2 (1847).

Sergeevich, V. I. *Russkie iuridicheskie drevnosti* [Russian Juridical Antiquities], vol. 2. St. Petersburg, 1900.

Shapiro, A. L. "Ob absoliutizme v Rossii" ["On Absolutism in Russia"]. *Istoriia SSSR* [A History of the USSR], no. 5 (1968).

Shcherbatov, M. M. *Istoriia Rossiiskaia s drevneishikh vremen* [History of Russia from Ancient Times]. St. Petersburg, 1903.

Sheviakov, V. "K voprosu ob oprichnine Ivana Groznogo" ["On the Question of Ivan the Terrible's Oprichnina"]. *Voprosy istorii* [The Problems of History], no. 9 (1956): 121–28.

Shmidt, S. O. "K izucheniiu agrarnoi istorii Rossii XVI veka" ["Toward the Study of the Agrarian History of Sixteenth-Century Russia"]. *Voprosy istorii* [The Problems of History], no. 5 (1968).

———. *Stanovlenie Moskovskogo samoderzhavstva* [The Formation of the Muscovite Autocratic State]. Moscow, 1973.

Skazkin, S. D. "Osnovnye problemy tak nazyvaemogo 'vtorogo izdaniia' krepostnichestva v Srednei i Vostochnoi Evrope" ["Basic Problems of the So-called 'Second Edition' of Feudalism in Central and Eastern Europe"]. *Voprosy istorii* [The Problems of History], no. 2 (1958).

Skrynnikov, R. G. *Ivan Groznyi* [Ivan the Terrible]. Moscow, 1957.

———. *Oprichnyi terror* [Oprichnina Terror]. Leningrad, 1967.

———. *Perepiska Groznogo i Kurbskogo: Paradoksy Edwarda Kinnona* [The Correspondence of Ivan the Terrible and Kurbskii: The Paradoxes of Edward Keenan]. Leningrad, 1973.

Slovo kratko v zashchitu monastyrskikh imushchestv [A Brief Word in Defence of Monastic Properties]. Moscow, 1902.

Smirnov, I. I. *Ivan Groznyi* [Ivan the Terrible]. Leningrad, 1944.

————. *Ocherki politicheskoi istorii russkogo gosudarstva 30–50kh gg. XVI veka* [Outlines of the Political History of Russia from the 1530s to the 1550s]. Moscow-Leningrad, 1958.

Solov'ev, S. M. *Istorii otnoshenii mezhdu russkimi kniaz'ami Riurikiva doma* [History of the Relationships Between the Russian Princes of the House of Rurik]. Moscow, 1847.

————. *Istoriia Rossii* [History of Russia]. 3rd ed. 10 vols. St. Petersburg, n.d.

————. *Istoriia Rossii s drevneishikh vremen* [The History of Russia from Ancient Times]. 29 vols. (15 books). Moscow, 1959–66.

Spuler, Bertold. "Russia and Islam." In *The Development of the USSR: An Exchange of Views*, edited by Donald W. Treadgold, pp. 346–51. Seattle, 1964.

Staden, Heinrich. *O Moskve Ivana Groznogo* [On the Moscow of Ivan the Terrible]. Moscow, 1925.

Stalin, J. V. *Voprosy leninizma* [Problems of Leninism]. 9th ed. Moscow, 1931.

Strumilin, S. G. "O vnutrennem rynke Rosii XVI–XVIII vekov" ["On the Internal Market in Russia in the Sixteenth–Eighteenth Centuries"]. *Istoriia SSSR* [A History of the USSR], no. 4 (1959).

————. Preface to the 2nd edition D. P. Makovskii's *Razvitie tovarno-denezhnykh otnoshenii v sel'skom khoziaistve russkogo gosudarstva v XVI veke* [The Development of Goods and Monetary Relationships in the Agriculture of the Russian State in the Sixteenth Century]. Moscow, 1963.

Svirskii, Grigorii. *Na lobnom meste* [At the Place of Execution]. London, 1979.

Szamuely, Tibor. *The Russian Tradition*. London, 1976.

Tarle, E. V. *Padenie absoliutizma* [The Fall of Absolutism]. Petrograd, 1924.

Tatishchev, V. N. *Istoriia Rossiiskaia s samykh drevneishikh vremen* [History of Russia from the Very Earliest Times]. Moscow, 1768.

Teoriia gosudarstva u slavianofilov [The Theory of the State among the Slavophiles]. St. Petersburg, 1898.

Timofeev, Ivan. *Vremennik Ivana Timofeeva* [Chronicle of Ivan Timofeev]. Moscow-Leningrad, 1951.

Toynbee, Arnold. "'Oriental Despotism: A Comparative Study of Total Power' by Karl A. Wittfogel." *American Political Science Review* 52 (March 1958): 195–98.

————. "Russia's Byzantine Heritage." *Horizon* 16 (August 1947).

Treadgold, Donald W., ed. *The Development of the USSR: An Exchange of Views*. Seattle, 1964.

Troitskii, S. M. "O nekotorykh spornykh voprosakh istorii absoliutizma v Rossii" ["On Some Debatable Questions in the History of Absolutism in Russia"]. *Istoriia SSSR* [A History of the USSR], no. 3 (1969).

Twain, Mark. *A Connecticut Yankee in King Arthur's Court*. Edited by Bernard L. Stein. Berkeley and Los Angeles, 1979.

Ustrialov, N. T. *Russkaia istoriia* [Russian History]. St. Petersburg, 1845.

Vernadsky, George. *The Mongols and Russia*. New Haven, Conn., 1953.

Veselovskii, S. B. *Issledovaniia po istorii oprichniny* [Studies in the History of the Oprichnina]. Moscow, 1963.

_____. *K voprosu o proiskhozhdenii votchinnogo rezhima* [On the Question of the Origin of the Patrimonial Regime]. Moscow, 1926.

Vipper, R. Iu. *Ivan Groznyi* [Ivan the Terrible]. Tashkent, 1942.

Wallerstein, Immanuel. *The Modern World-System: Capitalist Agriculture and the Origin of the European World Economy in the Sixteenth Century*. New York, 1974.

Willan, T. S. "The Russia Company and Narva, 1558–81." *Slavonic and East European Review* 31 (June 1953): 405–19.

Wittfogel, Karl A. *Oriental Despotism*. New Haven, Conn., 1957.

_____. "Russia and the East: A Comparison and Contrast." In *The Development of the USSR: An Exchange of Views*, edited by Donald W. Treadgold, pp. 323–39. Seattle, 1964.

Yanov, Alexander. "Al'ternativa" ["The Alternative"]. *Molodoi kommunist* [The Young Communist], no. 2 (1974).

_____. *Détente After Brezhnev: The Domestic Roots of Soviet Foreign Policy*. Berkeley, 1977.

_____. "The Drama of the Time of Troubles." *Canadian-American Slavic Studies* 12 (Spring 1978).

_____. *The Russian New Right: Right-wing Ideologies in the Contemporary USSR*. Berkeley, 1978.

Zaozerskaiia, E. I. *U istokov krupnogo proizvodstva v russkoi promyshlennosti XVI–XVII vekov* [At the Sources of Large-Scale Production in Russian Industry in the Sixteenth and Seventeenth Centuries]. Moscow, 1970.

Zimin, A. A. *Oprichnina Ivana Groznogo* [The Oprichnina of Ivan the Terrible]. Moscow, 1964.

_____. "O politicheskoi doktrine Iosifa Volotskogo" ["On the Political Doctrine of Iosif of Volotsk"]. *Trudy otdela drevnerusskoi literatury* [Transactions of the Ancient Russian Literature Section], vol. 9. Moscow-Leningrad, 1952.

_____. *Reformy Ivana Groznogo* [The Reforms of Ivan the Terrible]. Moscow, 1960.

INDEX

Designer:	Eric Jungerman
Compositor:	G & S Typesetters
Printer:	Vail-Ballou
Binder:	Vail-Ballou
Text:	Baskerville
Display:	Perpetua